A Theory
of
Counterfactuals

*Publication of this work has been supported by
the National Endowment for the Humanities,
a federal agency which supports the study of such fields as
history, philosophy, literature, and languages.*

Winner of the 1981 Johnsonian Prize

A Theory
of
Counterfactuals

IGAL KVART

HACKETT PUBLISHING COMPANY
Indianapolis

Copyright © 1986 by Igal Kvart
Printed in the United States of America
Cover design by Jackie Lacy
Interior design by Jared Carter
For further information, please address
  Hackett Publishing Company, Inc.
  P.O. Box 44937
  Indianapolis, Indiana 46204

Library of Congress Cataloging in Publication Data

Kvart, Igal, 1948–
  A theory of counterfactuals.

  "Winner of the 1981 Johnsonian Prize."
  Revision of thesis (doctoral) — University of
Pittsburgh, 1975.
  Includes index.
  1. Counterfactuals (Logic)   I. Title.
BC199.C66K9   1985   160   84-22407
ISBN 0-915145-63-4
ISBN 0-915145-64-2 (pbk.)

To my parents

Contents

Foreword

How are we to analyze counterfactual statements? Suppose John had a fair amount of stock and, one day, after some deliberation, decided to sell it, and did so. Shortly afterward there was a huge rise in the stock market, and our poor John realized to his sorrow that

> Had he not sold his stock, he would have become rich a few weeks later.

Why is this counterfactual true? For it to be true the consequent must be inferable from the antecedent and some implicit premises. But which are those implicit premises? For this kind of counterfactual antecedent, which is compatible with the history of the world prior to it, this prior history should indeed be taken among them. But this is not enough. No adequate analysis will make this counterfactual come out true unless it has a legitimate premise to the effect that there was indeed a huge rise in the stock market shortly after his selling his stock. This statement, however, pertains to times after the time in which the antecedent event was supposed to have taken place, and thus will not be found in the above-mentioned history of the world prior to the antecedent event. The history prior to the antecedent event does not, then, exhaust the implicit premises.

In asking which are the implicit premises that are to be used in assessing counterfactuals such as the above, we ask, more generally, the following question: Which are the true statements, belonging to the actual history of the world, that should be taken as implicit premises so that the counterfactual will be true if its consequent is inferable from them taken together with the antecedent? Putting the matter differently, it is quite obvious that we cannot just take the actual history of the world among our implicit premises, on pain of inconsistency with the antecedent. So the question is: When countenancing a contrary-to-fact assumption, which *portions* of the actual history should we preserve for that assumption to be evaluated against them and which portions should we ignore?

Coming back to our example above, we now ask what is special about the actual event of the rise in the stock market vis-à-vis the antecedent event of John's holding on to his stock. I suggest that the occurrence of the antecedent event would not "endanger" the occurrence of the stock market rise, would not "put it at risk." And it is statements describing such events, whose occurrence is not "risked" by the antecedent event, that we should want to retain as implicit premises out of the history of the world from the time to which the antecedent pertains onwards. But what do these notions of "endangering the occurrence of" or "putting it at risk" amount to? They should amount to the antecedent event making some negative causal difference to the occurrence of those events. More precisely, they amount to the antecedent event bearing some *negative causal relevance* to such events. We thus want to preserve all true statements pertaining to times later than the antecedent event that describe events to which the antecedent event bears no negative causal relevance. Not to bear any negative causal relevance to an event is to be either causally irrelevant to it or to be purely positively causally relevant to it. We shall thus want among our implicit premises those true statements pertaining to times later than that of the antecedent event which describe actual events to the occurrence of which the antecedent event is either causally irrelevant or else is purely positively causally relevant. (And, of course, we shall want to preserve the laws of nature, too.)

This, in a nutshell, is what underlies the analysis that comprises the first portion of this book. It applies well to counterfactuals whose antecedents are compatible with the prior history of the world. Under a common-sense conception of a nondeterministic world this kind of counterfactual will cover the more useful of the counterfactuals we come upon, encompassing counterfactuals whose antecedents describe various human actions, decisions, etc. (when it is assumed that it was possible for the agent as of that time, to have acted otherwise). This kind of counterfactual will then be the kind with which we deal in cases of assigning responsibility — when we want to know whether a given action was the cause of some later damage or some other particular event for which the agent may then be held responsible. (It is thus counterfactuals of this kind that will be of primary interest in the analysis of legal discourse.) The notions of causal irrelevance and purely positive causal relevance should be unpacked, however. In this book I propose that this can be done via a probabilistic analysis, using a notion of objective conditional probability.

In Chapter 9 I extend this analysis further. There I consider those counterfactuals whose antecedents are not compatible with their prior history (relative to the laws, of course). For them, the above analysis is not directly applicable: the antecedent, the laws, and the prior history together will yield a contradiction. Yet the correct way (on my view) of analyzing such counterfactuals emerges as a natural extension of the above analysis. The key point is that, in order to assess such counterfactuals, we want to consider the variety of *processes that could have led* to the antecedent event and assess the consequent under various such processes separately. In order to assess the consequent under such a process, we will want to consider something like the schema presented above. That is, given such a process (which is to diverge from the actual-world description at some point), take that process description and the history prior to it; take also the antecedent and the laws; supplement these from the actual-world description in a way comparable to that of the previous account; and see whether the consequent follows. The supplementation from the actual-world description will be done by taking those true statements describing events to the occurrence of which the process (at its various stages) and the antecedent event are either causally irrelevant or else are purely positively causally relevant. So we no longer deal with one inferential schema, but rather with many such schemata, and the consequent must be inferable in them all.

Yet not all processes leading to the antecedent event will do. We do not want processes that are too esoteric. Consider the counterfactual:

> Had Reagan been the President on 1/22/77, an attempt would have been initiated in 1977 to expand the military budget.

Now a natural process leading to this antecedent event would be a process in which the Mississippi delegation voted for Reagan rather than for Ford, in the Republican National Convention in 1976, and in which Reagan then proceeded to win the general elections of that year. But another process one might consider as leading to this antecedent event would be one in which the Soviet Union occupied the United States and installed Reagan as puppet President of by then a satellite country. (Or, under an even more bizarre process that one might consider, an extraterrestrial culture would have occupied the United States and made Reagan President.) Now we shall not want processes of this kind to be taken into account in determining the truth value of a counterfactual such as the above. But how are we to set them aside and demarcate them from the processes we do want to consider in entertaining this counterfactual? My answer consists in excluding the *too esoteric* processes. A more precise rendering of this line would proceed again along probabilistic lines: We shall want to consider those processes which are *most likely to have led to the antecedent event*. Thus, we want to use a probabilistic selection on the variety of processes that could have led to the antecedent event and preserve those most likely to have done so. Then we should apply the above procedure and check whether the consequent is indeed inferable under each of them. Our previous account is thus a special case of this more general account: in our previous account the actual prior history is selected with no competing processes. This previous account will be applicable to cases in which the antecedent is compatible with the prior history of the world. It covers much of what we are interested in when we counterfactually assess human actions, which is perhaps the more useful and prevalent kind of counterfactuals. And still, it is just a special case of this more general account.

The distinctive features of the analysis proposed in this book are the following. First, a special emphasis is put on temporal features, in distinguishing statements pertaining to times prior to that of the antecedent event and statements pertaining to the interval between the antecedent event and the consequent event. Such notions will be clarified and introduced into a formal language. Second, a major tool of the analysis is the notion of objective conditional probability. The notions of causal irrelevance and of purely positive causal relevance used here are not primitive notions, but are mere intermediary notions to be analyzed in such probabilistic terms.

Further, the analysis attempts to provide truth conditions for counterfactuals, rather than conditions for justified assertability: the latter though, can be derived from the former. Still further, the analysis is not a possible-world analysis. Yet a formal semantics for counterfactuals (of the first sort) will still be provided. Nonetheless, the analysis can be formulated in terms of possible-world descriptions, for purposes of comparison with other approaches, which will be done below. More significantly, the analysis is not pursued in terms of notions of similarity between worlds nor in terms of minimal changes from the actual history (which are directions taken by Robert Stalnaker, David Lewis, and John Pollock), and is in fact clearly incongruent with such approaches. Finally, the analysis in its generality is not a species of metalinguistic theory in that it does not call for a single set of true implicit premises to be used in assessing a given counterfactual according to whether the consequent is inferable from them, as is clear from the leading-processes analysis sketched above.

In the chapters below I develop this approach to counterfactuals, and contrast it with alternative views. In chapters 2 and 9 the theory of counterfactuals that this book has to offer is presented, and in chapters 4 and 5 — the back-up probabilistic analyses of the notions of causal irrelevance and purely positive causal relevance. Chapter 6 offers a formal semantics. Chapter 1 and 3 contain a discussion of Chisholm, Goodman, and Stalnaker. In Chapter 3 it is shown how the theory presented in this book avoids Goodman's infinite-regress problem. Chapter 7 contains a discussion of minimal-change or maximal-intuitive-similarity approaches, and Chapter 8 contains a discussion of Lewis's more recent position. These discussions of other theories are largely conducted in the light of, and in comparison with, the theory offered in this book. Chapters 2, 4, 5, and 9, which contain the heart of the proposed theory, can be read independently of the other chapters.

The organization of this book requires some words of explanation, which in turn seem to require a few words concerning its writing history. Chapters 1-6 result from my Ph.D. dissertation with minor variations. The main elements of chapters 7 and 9 were originally written in 1974, but have been subsequently substantially expanded. Chapter 8 was added a few years later.

The reader will notice that in the formal apparatus of the latter part of chapter 6, section III, only natural-divergence type counterfactuals are accounted for. The reasons for that are that the account of leading-processes type counterfactuals was written only later and that the formal aspects of that account have been left somewhat tentative (in particular, the formal aspects of the manner of defining the most likely processes to have led to the antecedent, especially for continuous time). This account, therefore, did not seem ripe for incorporation into a formal system. Accordingly, no formal and systematic attempt has been made in this book to specify the logical truths (or valid inferences) concerning counterfactuals which this theory endorses. The validity of various inferences (with counterfactuals of the natural-divergence type) is informally discussed in the appendix. But again, I felt that a rigorous completion of this task may well await the satisfactory formal completion of the treatment of the leading-processes type counterfactuals as well. Yet the decision not to elaborate on the logic of natural-divergence type counterfactuals beyond the scope of chapter 6 and the appendix was indeed moot.

By the time I found it possible to prepare the manuscript for publication, an extensive literature on counterfactuals had appeared. I did not find it practical to try to trace points made in my earlier manuscript (my dissertation) to related or similar points that came out subsequently in the literature. My decision, therefore, was to leave the portion of the manuscript extracted from my dissertation pretty much as it was, but to amplify chapter 7, which contrasted my approach with what I considered to be the dominant trend in the literature — the maximal-similarity approach to counterfactuals, concentrating in particular on Lewis's *Counterfactuals* for purposes of comparison. I also decided to devote a chapter (chapter 8) to a close look at Lewis's subsequent view, which offered still more room for contrasting his approach and mine. I pursued this route at the expense of following the alternative (and perhaps equally useful) course of relating my approach more broadly to the contributions of various writers whose work had appeared in the meantime. Consequently, the book is lacking in comparative discussions of contributions that have appeared independently since the middle seventies. (A partial remedy is offered, however, in a few footnotes here and there.)

At two other points I have felt that better approximations could be achieved with further work. The first has to do with the logical-consequence character of the theory. It seems natural that in the next stage of the development of a theory of this sort, the replacement of the logical-consequence relation by probabilistic features should be explored. In addition to the logical consequence character of the theory, the accounts of causal irrelevance (and perhaps of purely positive causal relevance) in chapter 4 (and 5), despite being, I believe, basically on the right track, can be improved in certain specific ways, which will result in a more complicated theory.

The analysis proposed in this work is not a possible-worlds analysis, and my philosophical approach is quite inhospitable to realism about possible worlds. Yet it is analysis that provides truth conditions and is, as such, couched in a realist perspective concerning the actual world. I thus assume that sentences in the language (when freed of various context dependencies and vagueness) are true or false, and I allow myself to resort to laws of nature. I do not, however, attempt to analyze the notion of laws of nature; and this notion can be expected to prove dispensable in view of the notion of objective probability introduced in this book. Thus, as the theory in this book stands, the counterfactual construction is reduced to the notions of objective probability and the laws of nature. (The notions of casual irrelevance and purely positive causal relevance play only an intermediate, and *not* an irreducible, role, since they are in turn analyzed in terms of objective probability.) Dispensing with the notion of laws of nature will leave the account of counterfactuals based on the notion of objective probability alone, introduced in chapter 4 (sections I and IV).

I also do not take up the issue of the limits of the expressive capacity
of any particular language. This issue is of concern when attempts are made
to provide analyses via linguistic devices (rather than, say, propositions) in
a realist perspective. Yet even though the theory presented in this book will
be developed along lines of "actual realism", i.e., realism about the actual
world, my efforts in this book are directed not at defending such a realist
perspective, but rather at presenting a theory of counterfactuals while working *within* such a perspective. However, if a theory of this sort has merit,
it may well cast a favorable light on the perspective within which it is
formulated.

The development of detailed and articulate philosophical theories on
subjects as complex as counterfactuals is prone to be an ongoing process,
with further progress to be built upon earlier attempts, thus aiming at better and better approximations. Proposed accounts must therefore, it seems,
be judged not just as final and ultimate products, but also (and perhaps
primarily) in view of the extent to which they chart fruitful and interesting
courses and constitute advances and better approximations on which future
work can further improve. The theory proposed in this book, although (I
trust) novel in various respects, is put forward in this spirit. It is the best
picture I could offer by the time of its completion. Yet I am deeply aware
of various aspects in which it ought to be improved, and have given some
thought to various promising directions of improving it, which have not,
however, been incorporated into the present manuscript. Such a view of
one's philosophical work may suggest either of two courses: the single-
minded and continuous concentration on one's theory until one feels that
the theory is just right in every respect; or, otherwise, deciding that it is
nonetheless ripe for publication in the form reached at a given time. I found,
by experience, that the first course was not suitable (for me, at least) for
various reasons. First, I came to suspect that even after continuous and in-
tense efforts I will be likely to have some misgivings concerning some aspects
of the resulting theory. My experience has also been that improvements often
open the way to further articulations: at each new stage various promising
ways of improving the theory still further keep opening up. To aspire to
a complete theory on which one feels one doesn't know how to improve
may prove an unrealistic expectation (as long as one retains some critical
outlook and a modicum of ingenuity). Secondly, I have learned that I
couldn't expect to be able to work continuously on such a major project
over a very long period of time without interruptions. Life events take their
toll, and it seems too difficult, I find, to suppress interest in other philosophical questions for too long. I ended up concluding, therefore, that the
publication of a theory, once advanced enough, is preferable to the course
I had previously adopted — either complete to full satisfaction, or wait.

I have benefited from discussions concerning this manuscript with various people, to whom I am grateful. In particular, I wish to thank Allan
Gibbard, Hilary Putnam, Robert Stalnaker, Richard Jeffrey, Yael Cohen,

and Jonathan Malino. I also wish to thank Charles Parsons, Isaac Levy, Sidney Morgenbesser, and Bernard Berofsky for conversations pursuant to the announcement of the Johnsonian Prize. Special thanks are due to Nuel Belnap for helpful advice and counsel in early stages. Concerning some formal aspects of chapters 4, 7, and 8, I had the benefit of wise counsel from Jonathan Stavi, Menachem Magidor, Saharon Shelah, and Gideon Schechtman. I am greatly indebted for the encouragement I received from various people at times I needed it most, and particularly to Hilary Putnam, Wilfrid Sellars, and Avishai Margalit. I am grateful for the editorial help and suggestions I received from Nessa Ashtar, Sam Friedman, Yoram Gotgeld, Mark Moskowitz, and Dalia Dray. I also wish to thank the editorial board of the *Journal of Philosophy* and the Hackett Publishing Company for their award of the Johnsonian Prize for this manuscript, and for their assistance and patience in the preparation of the manuscript for the press. Finally I want to thank my wife Dianne. Had it not been for her support, endurance and wisdom, the ensuing account of counterfactuals might not have seen the light of day. It may be only appropriate to formulate the final acknowledgement for a treatise on hypothetical statements by using one.

Analytic Content

In the first chapter three works on counterfactuals will be critically discussed: the metalinguistic approaches of Roderick Chisholm and Nelson Goodman, who do not use possible worlds, and that of Robert Stalnaker, who does.[1] Both Chisholm and Goodman recognized major difficulties in their strategies. As will be shown, however, these strategies encounter serious difficulties (other than those considered by their authors), which not only leave them open to various counterexamples, but also expose them as outright trivializable. Those difficulties are shown to be sufficiently deeply rooted to make these strategies unlikely to have the potential to handle them without undergoing drastic fundamental changes. Stalnaker's account will be construed as offering a framework within which specific theories can be formulated, and as deliberately offering only very general guidelines for how they are to be fleshed out. (David Lewis's work will be discussed in chapters 7 and 8.)

In chapter 2 the proposed analysis for counterfactuals is developed. Section I prepares the ground by introducing the concept of "the time that a statement pertains to" and other related temporal distinctions, and the concept of "the history of the world up to a certain time." These concepts are treated more extensively in sections I and II of chapter 6. In section II counterfactuals are viewed as incomplete implications, and the basic scheme of the so-called "inferential model" is developed, according to which a counterfactual is true if and only if

$$A \cup \text{implicit premises} \rightarrow B$$

The major problem in this scheme is the functional determination of the so-called "implicit premises" of the inference. Also, the concept of possible-world descriptions and the basic scheme of the possible-world-description model are developed; the major question in this model is observed to be the functional determination of a set of possible-world descriptions to be associated with a given counterfactual. Some comparisons are made with Stalnaker's model. In section III the two major problems of the counterfactual analysis in the inferential model are distinguished; they concern the determination of two kinds of factual implicit premises — those which pertain to times later than the antecedent time and those which pertain to earlier times. It is argued that the answers to each of these two problems would in turn provide an analysis for a major group of counterfactuals:

an answer to the first problem would suffice for an analysis for those counterfactuals whose antecedents are compatible with the prior history of the world; an answer to the second problem would suffice for an analysis for those counterfactuals whose antecedents and consequents basically coincide temporally. All other counterfactuals embody either neither or both of these two problems. In chapter 2 only the first problem, and consequently the first type of counterfactual, the so-called counterfactuals of the *n-d type*, are discussed. However, in chapter 9 the treatment of the second problem is developed as an extension of that of the first problem. In section IV the methodological advantages of this way of recasting the problem are discussed, and the counterfactuals of the n-d type are shown to be an extensive and important set of counterfactuals. In section V various categories of factual statements are delineated, and examples are used to determine which of them should belong to the implicit premises for counterfactuals of the n-d type in the inferential model. In section VI counterexamples are employed in order to argue that no other statements belong to the implicit premises except those determined in section V. Related considerations are applied to the possible-world-descriptions model as well. It is concluded that the implicit premises for a counterfactual of the n-d type are the following: law statements, the history of the world prior to the antecedent time, and the set of statements that pertain to times between the antecedent time and the consequent time which describe events to which the antecedent event is either causally irrelevant or else is purely positively causally relevant. In section VII two types of semifactuals[2] are defined: *irrel-semifactuals* and *pp-semifactuals*. In irrel-semifactuals the antecedent event is causally irrelevant to the consequent event; in pp-semifactuals, the antecedent event is purely positively causally relevant to the consequent event. Next, a conjecture concerning the roles of various counterfactual constructions is entertained. According to this conjecture, the role of a contrary-to-fact assumption A is to call into consideration the effects that the change from $\sim A$ to A may have on the actual course of events. This conjecture in turn explains why the set of implicit premises found in the previous two sections is comprised as it is. Also, the role of irrel-semifactuals and pp-semifactuals is found to be that of preserving those portions of the actual course of events on the background of which considerations concerning such hypothetical effects are to be conducted, and the role of counterfactuals of the form $A > B$ is found to be that of predicting subsequent events in the case of a transition from $\sim A$ to A. In section VIII it is argued that all irrel-semifactuals and pp-semifactuals are in fact true; and indeed, this empirical generalization follows from the proposed scheme in the inferential model. Moreover, it is shown that this generalization is explained by the role theory, which is in turn empirically vindicated. Examples of both types of semifactuals are discussed. In section IX, the so-called *irrel-&-pp-semifactual analysis* of counterfactuals (according to inferential model) is presented, discussed, and illustrated. According to it, a counterfactual $A > B$ of the n-d type is true if and only if:

$$\{A\} \cup W_{t_A} \cup L \cup \left\{\begin{array}{l}\text{the set of consequents } C \text{ of irrel-}\\ \text{semifactuals and pp-semifactuals with}\\ \text{antecedent } A, \text{ for which } t_C \subseteq (t_A, t_B)\end{array}\right\} \to B$$

In section X an analysis within the possible-world descriptions model is developed, and proved equivalent to the irrel-&-pp-semifactual analysis. Some general equivalence results of schemata in the inferential model and the possible-world-descriptions model are proved as well.

In section XI a different perspective on the analysis of counterfactuals is taken. The resulting analysis amounts to having the factual implicit premises after the antecedent time be the consequents of true semifactuals with the same antecedents as the counterfactual in question. This analysis, however, called the *semifactual analysis*, seems *prima facie* to be at variance with the previous irrel-&-pp-semifactual analysis: In the semifactual analysis all consequents of the appropriate semifactuals are taken as implicit premises, whereas in the irrel-&-pp-semifactuals analysis — only the consequents of the appropriate irrel-semifactuals and pp-semifactuals are taken as implicit premises. The remaining group of semifactuals (the ones which are neither irrel-semifactuals nor pp-semifactuals), the so-called *con-type-semifactuals*, is investigated and illustrated, and some light is shed on its features by the role theory. Moreover, the semifactual analysis is then shown to involve a serious problem of infinite regress.

This double-edged problem of the semifactual analysis — the seeming infinite regress and the seeming conflict with the irrel-&-pp-semifactual analysis — is discussed in section XII, where it is resolved by a theorem showing a weak equivalence between the two analyses, which settles the conflict between them. This theorem reveals how the problem of infinite regress dissolves by virtue of the demonstrated logical superfluousness of the set of the true con-type-semifactuals within the semifactuals analysis. The set of true con-type-semifactuals is shown, as a corollary, to be expressible within the framework of the previous analysis, and further examples are discussed. In section XIII the first steps of the way in which irrel-semifactuals are to be analyzed probabilistically are sketched, the various functions discussed throughout the work are expressed in a complete form, and an explanation is provided, on the basis of the previous analysis, for how counterfactuals have empirical character.

Chapter 3 discusses Chisholm, Goodman, and Stalnaker again in view of the results of chapter 2. The strategies of Chisholm and Goodman are compared with the results of the inferential model reached in chapter 2. As semifactuals play a major role in the analysis of chapter 2, it is argued that all three authors have not accounted correctly for semifactuals. The strategies of Chisholm and Goodman are claimed to be ad hoc and thus unsuitable for a theoretical explanation in terms of a role theory. The development of Goodman's strategy is followed in detail, and it is shown that the difficulties it confronts along the way, which prompted certain crucial steps in Goodman's analysis, are adequately handled by the theory developed in chapter 2. The problem Goodman viewed as the most formidable obstacle — the infinite regress with which he ended up — is then considered, its roots are explored, and it is compared with the danger of infinite regress which besets the semifactual analysis. It is then shown how the theory developed in chapter 2 avoids this obstacle. Stalnaker's proposals are compared with the results of chapter 2, represented in the possible-worlds-descriptions model. It is shown where the theory of chapter 2 is fully specific whereas Stalnaker's proposal is only programmatic. The analysis according to the possible-world-descriptions model can thus be considered as offering a solution to the main problem which Stalnaker did not attempt to answer.[3] The difference between the theory developed in chapter 2 and Stalnaker's general guidelines is spelled out and defended.

The analysis of counterfactuals developed in chapter 2 reduces the counterfactual construction to the concepts of causal irrelevance and purely positive causal relevance. Chapter 4 motivates, presents, illustrates, and defends an analysis of causal irrelevance. Section I presents the so-called *equiprobability condition* '$P(C/A \& W) = P(C/\sim A \& W)$' as a candidate for an analysis of the causal irrelevance of the A-event (i.e., the event described by the statement A) to the (later) C-event. In section II it is shown that, although the equiprobability condition is a necessary condition for causal irrelevance, it is not sufficient. Section III locates the source of this insufficiency in the possibility that the occurrences of the A-event or the $\sim A$-event will differ in the extent to which they weaken or strengthen causal chains that lead to the C-event or the $\sim C$-event, although their probabilistic effects will nevertheless balance out. It proceeds to motivate a condition that will constitute a safeguard against this possibility. The condition is designed to block it by resorting to intermediate events between the A-event and the C-event. This condition requires that *all* events in this interval which affect the probability of C to occur in the A course of events or the $\sim A$ course of events will themselves be unaffected by the transition from $\sim A$ to A insofar as their own probability of occurring is concerned, and that their impact on C will be the same in the two courses. In section IV the above condition is formally presented and discussed. It reads as follows:

The A-event is causally *irrelevant* to the C-event[4] iff:
$\{W,A,L,C\}$ is consistent, and
For every actual event e between the A-event and the C-event, if it satisfies
either (7i) $\qquad P(C/e \& \sim A \& W) \neq P(C/\sim A \& W)$
or (7ii) $\qquad P(C/e \& A \& W) \quad \neq P(C/A \& W)$
then it satisfies both
(7iii) $\qquad P(e/A \& W) = P(e/\sim A \& W)$
and (7iv) $\qquad P(C/e \& \sim A \& W) = P(C/e \& A \& W)$.

(W is the history of the world up to the reference-time of A.[5]) This condition for causal irrelevance is called *the transmission condition* (on W,A,C). Notice that the transmission condition is expressed in terms of equalities between conditional probabilities only, and thus relies on no probabilistic metric. Section V illustrates the condition via some examples, and defends various features of it. Section VII raises concerns about the quantification over possible events in the transmission condition, especially in the context of an analysis of counterfactuals that steers away from a commitment to possible worlds. Section VIII leads to a resolution of this dilemma concerning the use of possible events in the transmission condition, a dilemma expressed in sections IV and VII, by proving *the possibility-elimination theorem*. According to this theorem, quantifying in the transmission condition over all events between the A-event and the C-event, possible as well as actual, on the one hand, and quantifying over such actual events *only*, on the other, yield logically equivalent formulations of the transmission condition. In section IX this theorem is further discussed. This theorem shows that no commitment to possibilia is required for the analysis of causal irrelevance presented in chapter 4. In section X the notion of objective probability used in this book (in particular in the analysis of causal irrelevance and purely positive causal relevance) is discussed. The notion utilized is that of probability as *degree of determination* (of some event — under a description — by an earlier history of the world and the laws). It is a notion of the probability, given the world history up to a certain time instant t, of a factual sentence p (pertaining to some time later than t). This notion of probability is thus taken to reflect the extent to which that earlier history of the world determines the occurrence of the p-event. In this section this notion is presented as a generalization of the notion of transitional probability (as in Markovian chains) — the probability of a transition from one state to another — applied to the world when construed as a state system (under discrete time), that is, the probability of the world moving from state Si at instant t to state Sj at the next instant.

Chapter 5 offers a probabilistic analysis for purely positive causal relevance. In section I the *probability-increase condition* '$P(C/A \ \& \ W) > P(C/{\sim}A \ \& \ W)$' is presented and discussed as a candidate for an account of purely positive causal relevance. It is shown that, although it is a necessary condition for purely positive causal relevance, it fails to be a sufficient condition. In section II the source of this failure is explored, and, in order to overcome it, an amendment is motivated and developed. As in chapter 4, the amendment makes use of intermediate events between the A-event and the C-event. It is thus the conjunction of the ammendment with the probability-increase condition which should be considered for the purpose of formulating a criterion of purely positive causal relevance. Roughly, the amendment is designed to require that the impact on C of causal chains leading to C in the ${\sim}A$ course of events is not weakened in the A course of events; that the impact on C of causal chains leading to ${\sim}C$ in the ${\sim}A$ course of events is not strengthened in the A course; and that causal chains leading to ${\sim}C$ in the A course would also do so in the ${\sim}A$ course. It thus roughly makes the following requirements: that if any intermediate event (between the A-event and the C-event) increases the probability of occurrence of C in the ${\sim}A$ course of events, then it does so also in the A course, and its own probability of occurring does not diminish in the transition from the ${\sim}A$ course to the A course; that, if it merely does not diminish the probability of occurrence of C in the $\sim A$ course, then it does not do so in the A course, and its positive impact on C in the A course is not diminished vis-à-vis the $\sim A$ course; that, if the effect of such an intermediate event on C in the $\sim A$ course is not positive, then its impact on C in the A course is not more negative than in the $\sim A$ course;[6] and that if its effect on C in the A-course is negative, then its probability of occurring is not greater in the A course than in the $\sim A$ course.

In section III the condition is expressed formally, explained, and further investigated. Formally, it looks as follows:

$P(C/A \ \& \ W) > P(C/\sim A \ \& \ W)$,
and $\{W,A,L,C\}$ is consistent, and
For every actual event e between the A-event and the C-event:
If $P(C/\sim A \ \& \ W) < P(C/e \ \& \ \sim A \ \& \ W)$
then
$P(C/A \ \& \ W) < P(C/e \ \& \ A \ \& \ W)$
and
$P(e/\sim A \ \& \ W) \leq P(e/A \ \& \ W)$.

If $P(C/\sim A \ \& \ W) \leq P(C/e \ \& \ \sim A \ \& \ W)$
then
$P(C/A \ \& \ W) \leq P(C/e \ \& \ A \ \& \ W)$
and
$P(C/e \ \& \ \sim A \ \& \ W) < P(C/e \ \& \ A \ \& \ W)$.

If $P(C/e \ \& \ \sim A \ \& \ W) < P(C/\sim A \ \& \ W)$, then
$P(C/e \ \& \ \sim A \ \& \ W) < P(C/e \ \& \ A \ \& \ W)$.

If $P(C/e \ \& \ A \ \& \ W) < P(C/A \ \& \ W)$
then $P(e/A \ \& \ W) \leq P(e/\sim A \ \& \ W)$.

Notice that only qualitative, not metric, features of probability are used here — only the predicates '$<$' and '$=$', applying to conditional probabilities, appear. In section IV the condition is illustrated and further discussed. It is shown, among others, to overcome the difficulties that the probability-increase condition encountered.

Chapter 6 provides analyses of the concept of "the history of the world up to a certain time" and of the concept of "the times statements pertain to" (both used in chapters 2, 4, and 5). It also provides a formal semantics for counterfactuals of the type analyzed so far, a semantics based on the analysis proposed in chapters 2, 4, and 5. Section I provides conditions for a set of statements to qualify as the "history of the world up to a certain time t" in terms of so-called "temporal testers." These are statements that describe features of the world at t, but have no (strictly) logical implications for times beyond t (t being a temporal instant). Section II further explains the notion of "the times statements pertain to," their so-called *reference times*, and proposes a regimentation of sentences that brings this reference time to the surface. Section III extends the formal languages of the propositional and first-order calculi so as to incorporate temporal features, mostly concerning reference times, and provides a semantics for them. These formal languages thus reflect the regimentation developed in section II. This temporal extension of the first-order language is then further extended to include a counterfactual symbol. A semantics for this language is then introduced, based on the analysis of counterfactuals developed in chapters 2, 4, and 5, on the one hand, and on the semantics for the base temporal first-order language developed in this section (section III, chapter 6) on the other.

Chapter 7 discusses the approach of analyzing counterfactuals via minimal changes, or the most similar possible worlds (where similarity is taken in an intuitive sense), and proceeds via comparisons with the view taken in the present book. [This approach covers Stalnaker (in his 1968 article), Lewis's book, Pollock's approach, and others.] In section I I present Lewis's basic approach (in his *Counterfactuals*) and discuss his notion of cotenability in contrast with Goodman's notion. In section II it is proved that the analysis I develop in this book is not an analysis of the most similar possible-worlds kind. In section III the contrast is further elaborated, and various of the theses of the preceding chapters are brought to bear against the intuitive similarity, or minimal-change, views. In particular it is proved that the analysis provided here cannot be made to conform to a closest-possible-worlds-descriptions analysis even if the retention of the kinds of statements argued for in the bulk of this book is adhered to. Section IV contains a discussion of some counterexamples to the closest-possible-worlds view (via intuitive similarity or minimal change), which help underscore the contrast between the latter view and the analysis proposed in this book. In section V a contrast between these two approaches concerning the context-dependence of counterfactuals is discussed. It is argued that on the analysis presented so far, the counterfactual construction is context-*in*dependent, in sharp contrast to Lewis's view. Section VI mentions briefly a few epistemic treatments of counterfactuals. (They are not discussed here since the approach in this book aims at the provision of truth-conditions rather than mere assertability conditions.)

In chapter 8 Lewis's recent view[7] is discussed. His approach there consists in taking a nonintuitive over-all similarity relation, comprising of respects and weights (or priorities) which need not be intuitive, with intuitive similarity relations coming only under such respects. Various problems in this approach are pointed out. In section II an exposition of some main elements in this approach is provided, and a problem of inconsistency in treating examples falling under the so-called *future-similarity objection* is pointed to. In sections III and IV counterexamples to this approach are provided under its weighted-similarity-respects version and its priority version respectively. In section V a general contrast is drawn between theories of counterfactuals that fall under the *selection-function theory* (such as the metalinguistic theories, Stalnaker's, and my own), on the one hand, and the *ordering theory* (such as Lewis's) on the other. The *independence characteristic*, which is possessed by the latter, is then discussed. The possession of the independence characteristic amounts to the ordering of worlds (or the selection function) being independent of any particular counterfactual. Arguments against the independence characteristic are then brought out. In section VI an argument against the ordering theory in its full generality is presented via the so-called Siamese-twins example. In section VII some aspects of context-dependence are further discussed.

So far in this book attention has mostly been limited to the case of counterfactuals whose antecedents are compatible with the prior history of the world. In chapter 9 (the Epilogue) I extend the approach taken in the previous chapters beyond this case. In section I the *1-p interpretation* ('1-p' — for leading-processes) is presented for counterfactuals with factual antecedents that are logically, law-wise, and metaphysically possible. This interpretation calls for a consideration of the variety of processes leading to the antecedent event and for the selection out of them of those most likely to have led to the antecedent. A natural extension of the inferential schema for counterfactuals of the type discussed in the bulk of this book is presented for each such selected process. Counterfactuals of the type discussed must fulfill these inferential schemata for each of the selected processes if they are to qualify as true. The notion of what it takes for a process to "lead to" the antecedent event is then clarified, and a proposal for the analysis of the notion of "the most probable processes to have led to the antecedent" is presented and discussed. In section II a variety of seemingly odd and unyielding sorts of counterfactuals is discussed. It is argued that proper names are sometimes not to be construed as giving rise to *de re* readings (i.e., are sometimes not to be construed as functioning in a capacity of rigid designators), but rather as functioning in a capacity of feature indicators. It is observed that this phenomenon (of proper names functioning as feature indicators) is frequent in various counterfactuals of the sort discussed, and that it allows for a natural interpretation of such counterfactuals along the lines of the 1-p interpretation via a *de dicto* reading (regarding those proper names, reflecting their role as feature indicators) rather than via a *de re* reading. In section III the respective domains of applicability of the natural-divergence interpretation, developed in the bulk of this book, and the 1-p interpretation, presented in section I of chapter 9, are contrasted. It is argued that both are applicable in a certain range of cases, for which a characterization is presented, thereby giving rise to an ambiguity between two readings that correspond to these two interpretations. Section IV contains a discussion of counterfactuals with reverse temporal order (i.e., counterfactuals whose antecedents pertain to times earlier than the times to which their consequents pertain to), of counterlegals, and of counterfactuals with impossible antecedents. It also contains further discussion of the objective character and of the lack of inherent context dependence of the counterfactual construction. In the discussion of counterlegals, an important distinction is introduced between counterfactuals which are world *de re* vs. counterfactuals which are world *de dicto*, and the relation of this distinction to the standard object *de re* — object *de dicto* distinction is discussed. [The new distinction roughly corresponds to the distinction between counterfactuals which are *about* the actual world (when evaluated there) and those which are not.] The discussion of counterfactuals with metaphysically impossible antecedents hinges upon a conception of *de re* modalities and necessity statements, which is briefly elaborated. It is contiguous with the theory of counterfactuals presented in this book, and involves the thesis that trans-world identity applies only to characters which belong to possible-world descriptions that diverge from each other during the lifetimes of the characters in question. Only such diverging possible-world descriptions allow for the trans-world identity of the characters in question to consist in their having a *common root.*[8] Essentialism of origins turns out to be a consequence of this theory of trans-world identification. Counterfactuals in which the strictures conferred by this conception are violated, are recognized as devoid of a literal *de re* interpretation. Lastly section V deals with the issue of counterfactuals in a deterministic world: in the bulk of the book counterfactuals were analyzed under indeterministic assumptions. The main thesis of this section is that counterfactuals in a deterministic world do not have a literal *de re* interpretation. It is argued that the historiophysical impossibility of the antecedent in such a world should be taken seriously, that this position is not counter-intuitive, and that it is called for by the conception of trans-world identification presented in section IV, 3. It is argued that this conclusion should be viewed as natural if the common-sense conceptual frame is a non-deterministic one. Yet, dispositional statements and various counterfactuals statements can obtain interpretation other than literal and *de re*: They can be taken to be elliptic to nomological statements and can be interpreted along world *de dicto* lines.

In the appendix the applicability of the theory of counterfactuals (of the n-d type) to issues of validity is illustrated via an informal discussion of the validity of several inferences concerning counterfactuals of this type.

Notes: Analytic Content

1. Stalnaker's work discussed here is his 1968 article "A Theory of Conditionals," in *Studies in Logical Theory*, Nicholas Rescher ed., A.P.Q. monograph no. 2. (Oxford, Blackwell, 1968).

2. Semifactuals are counterfactuals with true consequents.

3. Insofar as counterfactuals of the n-d type — the type discussed in this portion of the book — are concerned.

4. C is a true statement.

5. 'W' abbreviates '$W t_A$', where t_A is the reference–time of A. See chapter 2, section I, and Chapter 6, sections I, II.

6. This condition and the previous one are expressed in the formal presentation by somewhat weaker requirements.

7. In his article "Counterfactual Dependence and Time's Arrow," *Noûs* (1979).

8. The above formulation is not quite precise. The above conception of trans-world identification admits of some liberalization (e.g., roughly, in cases where the antecedent of an n-d type counterfactual is causally irrelevant to the circumstances of the individual in question coming into existence). I will not enter here into the precise formulation of this position.

A Theory
of
Counterfactuals

1 Chisholm, Goodman, Stalnaker

In this chapter the positions of Roderick Chisholm, Nelson Goodman, and Robert Stalnaker will be examined. The bulk of my own theory is developed in chapters 2, 4, 5, and 9. In chapter 3 I compare the positions of these philosophers with my own. The critical discussions of Chisholm in chapter 1 (I 2) and of Goodman (II 4) make for harder reading; skipping them will not affect comprehension of what follows.[1]

I Chisholm

1. Chisholm raised the problem of counterfactual conditionals in his paper, "The Contrary-to-fact Conditional"[2]:

> Like Russell in his theory of descriptions, we want to find a new way of saying something — in this case, in order to assure ourselves that we *can* restate what we ordinarily express in subjunctive conditionals (p. 486).

The problem then, is how to eliminate the contrary-to-fact conditional — that is to say, how to rephrase such conditionals in an acceptable way.

Obviously, a truth-functional analysis will not do. A counterfactual of the form 'If A then B' would normally have false antecedent and consequent, yet there are true as well as false counterfactuals of this kind.

Much of the inspiration for current treatments of counterfactuals derives from F. P. Ramsey's comments: "In general we can say with Mill that 'If p then q means that q is inferable from p, that is, of course, from p together with certain facts and laws not stated but in some way indicated by the context".[3] Chisholm, working with a counterfactual of the form 'if H were the case, W would be the case', proposes the following reformulation of Ramsey's suggestion: "we are saying that there is *some* true statement which, taken with H, entails W" (*op. cit.*, p. 490). Thus he reformulates the foregoing as "There is a statement p such that p and H entail W and p is true" (p. 491). This amounts to **Chisholms's Formula (CF)**[4]:

(CF) $(\exists p) [p$ is true & $(p \,\&\, H \to W)]$

Chisholm proceeds to consider two basic difficulties with his proposal. The first concerns possible trivializations of the formula using certain substituends for p. The second has to do with using accidental generalizations as parts of p.

Chisholm considers three cases of possible substituends for p that would trivialize his formula. The first case involves universal conditionals with antecedents, but not consequents, which include free variables that are also vacuous — that is, conditionals whose antecedents are not satisfied by any value of the variable. Consider the antecedent H of a counterfactual 'If H had been the case, W would have been the case'. Since H is false, it is possible in various cases to existentially generalize one of the singular terms in H so that the resulting statement would be false as well. Thus, if H is '. . . a . . .', assume that '$(\exists x)(. . . x . . .)$', which follows from H, is false too. Then the universal conditional '$(x)(. . . x . . . \supset W)$' is vacuous, and its antecedent (but not its consequent) includes free variables. However, since this universal conditional is logically equivalent to '$(\exists x)(. . . x . . .) \supset W$', it together with H imply W, since H implies the antecedent '$(\exists x)(. . . x . . .)$'. Moreover, the universal conditional is true, since the latter conditional is true, its antecedent being false. Thus the schema (CF) is satisfied [by p taken as the universal conditional '$(x)(. . . x . . . \supset W)$'], and the counterfactual 'If H had been the case, W would have been the case' comes out true. There were, however, no constraints placed on W in the above discussion; so, with the aid of such vacuous universal conditionals, many false counterfactuals could qualify as true according to Chisholm's formula. This can clearly be seen to be the case, since, if the above procedure can be carried out for the counterfactual 'If H, then W', it can also be carried out for the counterfactual 'If H, then not-W'. Thus, if the first comes out true under the above proposal, so does the second; but obviously both cannot be true.

Chisholm's remedy for that is to require that "Every universal conditional included in p must have 'existential import', that is, every universal conditional must have conjoined with it a statement asserting that there are members of the class determined by the antecedent" (p. 491).

Secondly, Chisholm notes that a similar threat of trivializing his proposal can be encountered even if we disallow vacuous universal conditionals as substituends for p. The problem can arise in the following way. Take a counterfactual of the form 'If Fa, then Ga', where 'a' denotes. (For example, consider the interpretation in which F is seeing the play and G is enjoying the play.) Now consider the following statement as a substituend for p: $(x)[x = a \supset (Fx \supset Gx)]$. Since '$a$' denotes, the problem is not immediately that of a vacuous universal conditional (viz., a universal conditional with an empty antecedent). But, since 'Fa' is false (inasmuch as it is the antecedent of a counterfactual), the proposed substituend for p is true, and, together with 'Fa', it clearly implies 'Ga', thus making the counterfactual come out true according to Chisholm's amended formula. But clearly many counterfactuals of this type are false.

To meet this difficulty, Chisholm suggests: "Let us say: p includes no universal conditional whose consequent includes any two functions which are logically equivalent to 'x sees the play' and to 'x does not enjoy the play'."[5]

Chisholm mentions a third case in which his formula can be trivialized — a case in which the consequent of the counterfactual is true. As a remedy he proposes a restriction: the indicative version of the consequent should not entail p. One way to show how the difficulty arises in this case is simply to choose for p the consequent of the counterfactual. This will normally make such a counterfactual come out true according to Chisholm's proposal. If his restriction that the consequent not entail p is imposed, this kind of trivialization is avoided.

Chisholm, however, does not consider these modifications to his formula sufficient to overcome these difficulties, and concludes: "In order to preclude such trivializations it is necessary to place exceedingly complex restrictions upon p" (p. 491).

The second type of basic difficulty that Chisholm considers (the first was possible trivializations by certain substituends for p) is that the use of accidental generalizations in p may warrant counterfactuals that are false. Here Chisholm touches upon a basic feature of counterfactuals: they may be warranted by genuine lawlike statements in a way in which they would not be warranted by mere (true) accidental generalizations. The problem here is, therefore, how to distinguish between lawlike statements and accidental generalizations.

Chisholm also mentions that counterfactuals of the form 'even if . . . , still ___' can be reduced to ordinary counterfactuals:

> And some types of subjunctive conditionals must be reformulated before the formula can be applied. E.g., "Even if you were to sleep all morning you would still be tired." This type of statement is what one gets by negating the consequent of an ordinary subjunctive conditional and then denying the whole thing: "It is false that if you were to sleep all morning you would not be tired." The "even if" conditionals must be reduced to this form (p. 492).

Thus, a counterfactual of the form 'Even if A were true, still B would be true' is reducible to ' $\sim$ (if A were true, then $\sim B$ would be true)'. We will return to Chisholm's treatment of this kind of counterfactual in chapter 3.

2. We shall not go into the problem of distinguishing lawlike from nonlawlike generalizations. But even so we can still see that Chisholm's proposal would not stand. Thus, one could take $A \supset B$ for p. Since A is false, $A \supset B$ is true, and $(A \,\&\, A \supset B) \to B$. So the original criterion is satisfied, and every counterfactual becomes true. No trivialization can be more troubling than one that shows that under the proposed criterion every counterfactual is true (or that every counterfactual is false). (Notice that this type of difficulty is related to the first case of possible trivialization — the case of choosing vacuous universal generalizations for p. This is so since these generalizations are true by virtue of the guaranteed vacuity of the antecedent, just as $A \supset B$ would be true by virtue of the guaranteed falsehood of A, and these generalizations would have B as their consequent as well.)

A natural move to overcome this difficulty would be to require that B not entail p, i.e., $B \not\rightarrow p$.[6] This move would, of course, do away with all the difficulties Chisholm specified: it would rule out taking p as '$(x) [x = a \supset (Fx \supset Gx)]$', in the second case[7]; in the same way it would rule out taking vacuous universal generalizations in the first case; and it would rule out taking p as B in the third case, which concerns counterfactuals with true consequents. However, this move is insufficient, since we can specify, for every counterfactual 'If A were true, B would be true', a statement M that does not follow from B, and take p as $A \supset (M \& B)$. In this case p is still true (since A is false), but in general $B \nrightarrow p$;[8] and, since $A \& [A \supset (M \& B)] \rightarrow B$, Chisholm's criterion is satisfied, and is thereby trivialized. Almost every counterfactual can be made to come out true in this way.

This move would clearly block the ways out that Chisholm mentioned for avoiding the three problems. First, since A need not be vacuous, such a choice of p will normally trivialize those cases which the requirement against vacuous universal generalizations would have prevented from being trivialized (in the absence of this move). Secondly, by using this substituend for p, we satisfy Chisholm's second emendation to his proposed formula—the consequent of p need not include both functions that appear in the antecedent and the consequent. Thirdly, by using this substituend for p, Chisholm's third emendation—that $B \nrightarrow p$—is normally satisfied, but counterfactuals with true consequents are still trivialized. Thus it can be shown that all Chisholm's emendations fail to overcome the difficulty they are designed to handle. The use of this type of substituend for p allows for across-the-board trivializations, not just counterexamples for particular cases.

The next move to save the proposal might be to put the blame on A, and to require that $\sim A \nrightarrow p$. In this case $A \supset (M \& B)$ would not be a suitable choice for p. But we can still trivialize the criterion, since we can select a true statement N such that $\sim A \nrightarrow N$ and $B \nrightarrow N$, and take p as: $N \& (A \supset B)$. In this case p is indeed true (since A is false and N is true); the restrictions are satisfied, since neither $\sim A \rightarrow N \& (A \supset B)$ nor $B \rightarrow N \& (A \supset B)$; and yet $A \& N \& (A \supset B) \rightarrow B$. Hence the criterion is satisfied, and arbitrary counterfactuals 'If A were true, B would be true' become true. Thus, the criterion is again trivialized.

In principle, of course, every trivialization procedure of the above kind may be avoided by an amendment to the criterion explicitly excluding it by stipulation. But it should be clear by now that the way is open for various modifications, which will differ both from this procedure and from its product, and still result in trivializations. Hence Chisholm's strategy of adding restrictions to his original proposal, let alone the original proposal itself, does not look promising.[9] Moreover, it is clear that any criterion that involves such complex and ad hoc stipulations against trivialization, let alone against counterexamples, cannot be a step in the right direction. Notice that the possibility of trivializing a criterion is fundamentally stronger than just falsifying it by producing a counterexample, since a trivialization provides for a whole family of counterexamples. In the absence of trivialization procedures, a criterion can fail by counterexamples; but trivialization procedures show that the trouble is pervasive and not limited to an isolated case. Chisholm's strategy, as we have seen, is open to repeated trivialization and thus is likely still to be similarly vulnerable once other ad hoc modifications are attempted.

II   Goodman

1. The analysis of counterfactuals, as Nelson Goodman sees it,[10] must conform to the following schema:

> A counterfactual is true if and only if the antecedent conjoined with relevant true statements about the attendant circumstances leads by way of true general principle to the consequent (p. 37).

Two major problems have to be dealt with if this analysis is to hold: "The first major problem is to define relevant conditions: to specify what sentences are meant to be taken in conjunction with an antecedent as a basis for inferring the consequent" (p. 8). The second problem is to characterize the laws. Since in this work I confine myself to the first problem, I shall not dwell on Goodman's discussion of laws.

Goodman limits his attention to counterfactuals with false consequents. He starts by considering a description of the actual state of the world as a candidate for the set of statements such that a counterfactual is true iff its antecedent, together with those statements, entails the consequent. At this point we are immediately confronted with one of the most persistent difficulties met in trying to specify the set of relevant conditions: the task of securing the compatibility of this set of statements with the antecedent. The immediate problem that arises when a description of the actual world is proposed as a candidate for this set is that the negation of the antecedent, which is a true statement, would belong to this set. However, simply excluding the negation of the antecedent from the description of the actual world will not do, as Goodman notes, since other statements in the set may still be individually incompatible with the antecedent through some general laws. Hence, Goodman proceeds to exclude from the set of all true statements which are to describe the relevant conditions all those which are individually incompatible with the antecedent and the laws. The resulting formulation is:

(0)   The set of statements describing the relevant conditions is "the set of all true statements each of which is both logically and non-logically compatible with A where non-logical incompatibility means violation of a non-logical law" (pp. 10/11).

However, the set of statements thus restricted may still include subsets that are incompatible with the antecedent and the laws. Goodman's example here (p. 11) concerns the antecedent:

(1)   If Jones were in Carolina, . . .

This antecedent is compatible with each of the statements:

(2)   Jones is not in South Carolina.
(3)   Jones is not in North Carolina.
(4)   North Carolina plus South Carolina is identical with Carolina.

(2)-(4) are not, taken together, consistent with the antecedent, though each statement taken separately is so consistent. Goodman's next move is to consider the following formulation:

(5)   A counterfactual is true if and only if "for *some* set S of true sentences, A·S be self-compatible and lead by law to the consequent" (p. 11).

(Compatibility is taken here as consistency via the laws.) However, this formulation is also unacceptable, Goodman argues, because, according to it, the counterfactuals

(6)   If Jones were in Carolina, he would be in South Carolina.

and

(6′)   If Jones were in Carolina, he would be in North Carolina.

would both be true — taking S to consist of (3) and (4) for (6), and to consist of (2) and (4) for (6′).

2. Notice that this last formulation (5) could have been motivated in a different and rather intuitive way, if one wished to avoid Goodman's process of elimination (from the set of all true statements). This would be a constructive approach leading to the same result as Goodman's eliminative strategy. Thus, under the general schema for counterfactuals according to which Goodman operates,[11] consider the following example: At time t I held a piece of chalk in my hand and did not drop it. Below my hand was a desk, and there was nothing in between. Now

(7)   If I had dropped the chalk from my hand at time t, it would have hit a desk.

is thus a true counterfactual. However, in order to establish its truth according to Goodman's general schema, we obviously need the relevant condition that below my hand was a desk and also a law concerning the free fall of unsupported bodies. Thus in order to substantiate it, according to this schema, we need both true sentences and laws. Moreover, the antecedent has to be compatible with the true sentences and the laws — otherwise the counterfactual obtained from (7) by negating its consequent would come out true as well. This result leads to formulation (5).

Notice that Goodman's last formulation of the truth conditions for counterfactuals is a variant of Chisholm's original formulation (CF), which was: $(\exists p)\,[p$ is true & $(p \,\&\, A \rightarrow B)]$. For Goodman, this formula is modified by the added requirements that p & A be self-compatible and that the entailment proceed via certain laws.

However, our line of argument against Chisholm's criterion applies equally well to Goodman's formulation. A choice of $A \supset B$ as p fulfills the requirements of leading to B by law (albeit vacuously) and of being compatible with A (except in the case in which A is incompatible with B, which is a relatively uninteresting and minor subcase). Thus, almost every counterfactual would qualify as true under formulation (5). Hence our criticism of Chisholm's formula and its prospects holds for this intermediate stage of Goodman's criterion as well. Our criticism indicates a systematic way of turning almost every false counterfactual into a counterexample for (5) and, thus, poses a considerably greater difficulty for formulation (5) than does Goodman's own single counterexample. Not only is (5) open to trivialization, but its prospects for escaping further trivializations by ad hoc measures are not promising.

3. Goodman's next move is to abandon the common form of the schemata he had been considering up to this point. These schemata amounted to having the consequent follow from the antecedent plus a certain set of statements on which certain restrictions are imposed. This form can be represented by

(8) $(\exists s)$ $[S$ & $(A$ & $S \overset{L}{\to} C)$ & $R(S,A)]$

where '$\overset{L}{\to}$' means inferability by law, and $R(S,A)$ is a constraint on S, which in (5) was the constraint that A & S be self-compatible.[12] Goodman now proposes the following criterion:

(9)   A counterfactual is true if and only if there is some set S of true statements such that $A \cdot S$ is self-compatible and leads by law to the consequent, while there is no such set S' such that $A \cdot S'$ is self-compatible and leads by law to the negate of the consequent (pp. 11/12).

Notice that this criterion has the following form (the consequent here being C):

(10) $(\exists S)$ $[S$ & $(A$ & $S \overset{L}{\to} C)$ & $R(S,A)]$
        & $\sim(\exists S')$ $[S'$ & $(A$ & $S' \overset{L}{\to} \sim C)$ & $R(S', A)]$

But this step, as Goodman notices, immediately confronts the problem that S' can be taken as $\{\sim C\}$, in case $\sim C$ is compatible with A. This would make the second conjunct false, thus trivializing the new addition to the criterion: (10) would always be false in this case, and consequently all counterfactuals would come out false as well. This problem is analogous to the problem that Chisholm's criterion came up against (see I above), that is, that p can be taken as B (the consequent in Chisholm's criterion) in the case of counterfactuals with true consequents (though there the trivialization amounted to all of them coming out true). So proposal (10), which differs from (5) by the addition of the second conjunct, is also vulnerable to trivialization.

Moreover, Goodman's criterion faces the same kind of difficulty that confronted Chisholm's criterion, a difficulty which proved resistant to ad hoc modification, as we saw at the end of I. We showed, in reference to Chisholm's criterion, that the choice of p (the analogue of Goodman's S) as $\{A \supset B\}$ trivializes the criterion by making all counterfactuals come out true. The same choice trivializes Goodman's first conjunct as well, since $A \supset C$ (C being the consequent in Goodman's case) is true (A being false), $A \supset C$ is compatible with A (except, again, in the small uninteresting set of cases where A and C are incompatible), and it leads (vacuously, by law) to C.

Goodman now modifies his criterion to read as follows:

(12)   . . . a counterfactual is true if and only if there is some set S of true sentences such that S is compatible with C and with $-C$, and such that $A \cdot S$ is self-compatible and leads by law to C; while there is no set S' compatible with C and with $-C$ and such that $A \cdot S'$ is self-compatible and leads by law to $-C$ (p. 13).

This (like the last criterion) also had the form of (10), except that here R_1 (S,A,C) replaces $R(S,A)$, where:

$R_1(S,A,C) = S$ is compatible with C and with $\sim C$ and A & S is self-compatible,

and $R_1(S',A,C)$ replaces $R(S',A)$, and so (12) yields (12'):

(12') ($\exists S$) $[S$ & (A & $S \overset{L}{\rightarrow} C$) & $R_1(S,A,C,)]$
          & $\sim (\exists S')$ $[S'$ & (A & $S' \overset{L}{\rightarrow} \sim C$) & $R_1(S',A,C)]$

Hence, (12') has the form of (10), with $R_1(S,A,C)$ and $R_1(S',A,C)$ replacing $R(S,A)$ and $R(S',A)$.

4. It is immediately evident, however, that this reformulation does not help avoid the trivialization we pointed to above. This is so because $A \supset C$ is always compatible with C (provided C is self-compatible), and $A \supset C$ is surely compatible with $\sim C$ in those cases in which A and C are both false, which are the cases under discussion, since Goodman discusses only counterfactuals with false antecedents and false consequents (see p. 4). Hence, the first half of Goodman's last formulation (12) applies to all the counterfactuals under consideration, except for a small set of uninteresting cases, and is thus trivialized again by the same choice of $\{A \supset C\}$ as S. Recall that in our discussion of Chisholm we examined the prospects of ad hoc conditions designed to eliminate such trivialization and found them unpromising.

Trivialization of formulation (9) via the second conjunct of (10) by choosing $\{\sim C\}$ there as S' has been avoided in (12) by the stipulation that S' be compatible with C and $\sim C$. However, this further restriction will still not suffice, since it allows other trivializations of the same kind. A choice of $\{A \supset \sim C\}$ as S' would trivialize the second conjunct in both (9) and (12'). Thus, $A \supset \sim C$ is true and compatible with A except in the uninteresting cases of true counterfactuals where A and $\sim C$ are incompatible, in which cases A alone leads to C by law. Except for such cases, then, the possible choice of S' as $\{A \supset \sim C\}$ always makes the second conjunct false, since with A it logically leads to $\sim C$ (again, vacuously, by law). Hence, except for those few cases in which the counterfactual is true in virtue of the incompatibility of A and $\sim C$, all counterfactuals become false according to Goodman's criterion (9).

Similarly, $A \supset \sim C$ is incompatible with C only when C and $\sim A$ are incompatible, and $A \supset \sim C$ is incompatible with $\sim C$ only if $\sim C$ is not self-compatible. Hence, except for this small set of relatively uninteresting cases, $A \supset \sim C$ fulfills the extra conditions of (12), and, since it trivializes the second conjunct of (9) [formalized as (10)], it trivializes the second conjunct of (12) [formalized as (12')] as well. Thus both (9) and (12) are open to trivialization of the first conjunct by the choice of S as $\{A \supset C\}$, and of the second by the choice of S' as $\{A \supset \sim C\}$.[13]

In the second edition of *Fact, Fiction, and Forecast* Goodman further modified his criterion by requiring that neither S nor S' follow by law from $\sim A$ (p. 13, fn 7). In our discussion of Chisholm above we showed that even with the requirement that S not follow by law from $\sim A$, the analogous proposal there can still be trivialized. The move there, adapted to our notation here, would be the choice of $\{N \mathrel{\&} (A \supset C)\}$ as S, for a true N such that $\sim A \overset{\text{L}}{\to} N$ and such that N is compatible with A and C conjointly. In this case, as before, $A \mathrel{\&} N \mathrel{\&} (A \supset C) \to C$, and $N \mathrel{\&} (A \supset C)$ is compatible with each of A, C, and $\sim C$ (the latter since $\sim A$, $\sim C$, and N are true), and $\sim A \overset{\text{L}}{\to} N \mathrel{\&} (A \supset C)$. The requirement that S' not follow by law from $\sim A$ still does not prevent the trivialization if the constraints on the trivialization of Chisholm's proposal presented above are appropriately modified. Choose $N \mathrel{\&} (A \supset \sim C)$ as S' and then $A \mathrel{\&} S' \overset{\text{L}}{\to} \sim C$; require that N be true, and S' will then be true (A is false). For S' not to follow by law from $\sim A$, require that $\sim A \overset{\text{L}}{\nrightarrow} N$. If we require that $N \overset{\text{L}}{\nrightarrow} (C \vee \sim A)$, we ensure that $\{N, \sim C, A\}$ is self-compatible and, hence, that S' is compatible with $\sim C$ and with A (separately); and if we require that $N \overset{\text{L}}{\nrightarrow} (A \vee \sim C)$, we ensure that $\{N, \sim A, C\}$ is self-compatible, and thus that S' is compatible with C, thus satisfying $R_1(S',A,C)$. Clearly (apart from relatively uninteresting cases) a statement N that satisfies these demands can be found, and hence in almost all cases there can be found a set S' that satisfies the requirements for the second conjunct of condition (12), with the additional requirement that S' not follow by law from $\sim A$. Hence, Goodman's corrections still allow for trivializations, and further such ad hoc corrections are not likely to do any better. We conclude that it is unlikely that these formulations can be saved from trivialization by anything less than very radical transformations.

Moreover, formulations (9) and (12) are quite cumbersome, and incorporate a variety of ad hoc conditions designed to handle the counterexamples that Goodman brought against their predecessors. Goodman also examines another major difficulty faced by formulation (12), different in kind from the trivializability problems we have examined so far. But even aside from the trivializability of Goodman's formulation and this further difficulty, one cannot but wonder, in view of its ad hoc character, whether it is on the right track to a solution of the problem of counterfactuals.

5. Goodman observed, as we just said, that formulation (12) poses a serious difficulty of a different sort. A further restriction is needed on the set S: it cannot include statements that, though true, would not be true if A were true. Goodman calls such statements *not cotenable* with A, and shows, using an example, that including such statements in S would result in affirming, via (12), false counterfactuals.

It is necessary, therefore, to eliminate such statements from S, in order to make S as a whole cotenable with A. But it will not do simply to exclude them from S by a direct restriction: cotenability was defined above in terms of the counterfactual construction, whereas the truth conditions for counterfactuals are now to depend on cotenability. Hence one is driven into an infinite regress. As Goodman puts it:

> . . . for such matters become rather unimportant beside the really serious difficulty that now confronts us. In order to determine the truth of a given counterfactual it seems that we have to determine, among other things, whether there is a suitable S that is cotenable with A and meets certain further requirements. But in order to determine whether or not a given S is cotenable with A, we have to determine whether or not the counterfactual "If A were true, then S would not be true" is itself true. But this means determining whether or not there is a suitable S_1, cotenable with A, that leads to -S and so on. Thus we find ourselves involved in an infinite regressus or a circle; for cotenability is defined in terms of counterfactuals, yet the meaning of counterfactuals is defined in terms of cotenability. In other words, to establish any counterfactual, it seems that we first have to determine the truth of another. If so, we can never explain a counterfactual except in terms of others, so that the problem of counterfactuals must remain unsolved.
>
> Though unwilling to accept this conclusion, I do not at present see any way of meeting the difficulty (pp. 16/17).

A resolution of the problem of how to exclude statements not cotenable with the antecedent is therefore required for any adequate analysis of counterfactuals. Goodman considers the issue of cotenability the crux of the problem. He sees the "problem of relevant conditions" as "most acutely felt as the problem of cotenability" (p. 37n). I will attempt to deal with this problem (among others) in chapter 2. In chapter 3 I will discuss whether my treatment resolves the problem that Goodman ends up with. I will claim that it does.

Finally, Goodman introduces the term **semifactual** for a counterfactual with a false antecedent and a true consequent (pp. 5, 36n). His analysis of semifactuals distinguishes their practical from their literal meaning. Their literal meaning, according to Goodman, makes them contraries but not contradictories of their corresponding counterfactuals (i.e., those counterfactuals resulting from them by negating their consequents). Thus he writes: "Literally, a semifactual and the corresponding counterfactual are not contradictories but contraries, and both may be false" (p. 6n). But the practical meaning of semifactuals, on the other hand, is that of *direct negation* of their corresponding counterfactuals. Thus he writes:

> Ordinarily a semifactual conditional has the force of denying what is affirmed by the opposite, fully counterfactual conditional. The sentence
>
> Even had that match been scratched, it still wouldn't have lighted.
>
> is normally meant as the direct negation of
>
> Had the match been scratched it would have lighted.
>
> That is to say, in practice full counterfactuals affirm, while semifactuals deny, that a certain connection obtains between antecedent and consequent (pp. 5/6).

A general indication, according to Goodman, of when the practical import is intended, is given by the idiomatic form 'even . . . , still ___'.[14]

Thus, according to Goodman, the meaning of the construction 'even if A, still B' (where A is false, B is true) is that of 'it is not the case that if A, then not-B', since in this form the practical meaning, i.e., that of direct negation of the corresponding counterfactual, is intended. Thus Goodman and Chisholm agree on the reduction of counterfactuals of the form 'even if A, still B' to regular counterfactuals. I will argue against this thesis in 3 II.

III Stalnaker

1. In his paper "A Theory of Conditionals," Robert Stalnaker[15] distinguishes three problems: the logical problem of "describing the formal properties of the conditional function" (p. 98); the epistemological problem: "How are conditions which are both empirical and contrary-to-fact possible at all?" (p. 99); and what he calls the *pragmatic problem* of counterfactuals:

> This problem derives from the belief, which I share with most philosophers writing about this topic, that the formal properties of the conditional function, together with all of the *facts*, may

not be sufficient for determining the truth-value of a counterfactual; that is, different truth valuations of conditional statements may be consistent with a single valuation of all nonconditional statements. The task set by the problem is to find and defend criteria for choosing among these different valuations (pp. 98/99).

That is to say, the state of the world at all times, the totality of facts, does not determine the truth value of a counterfactual. The question is, what other parameters should be specified so as to determine, together with the totality of facts, the truth value of the counterfactual, and how this truth value is determined by them. Thus, Stalnaker writes later: "the problem is . . . to find a set of truth conditions for statements having conditional form" (p. 102). The problem we shall deal with below will indeed be that of finding truth conditions for counterfactual statements.

Stalnaker's proposal is based on Ramsey's suggestion regarding how one is to decide whether or not to believe a conditional statement. According to Ramsey, if one has no opinion as to the truth of the antecedent, one should add it to one's stock of beliefs and check whether the consequent now follows from it. However, if the antecedent is believed to be false, the addition of the antecedent to one's stock of beliefs will result in a contradiction. Accordingly, Stalnaker suggests the following: "First, add the antecedent (hypothetically) to your stock of belief; second, make whatever adjustments are required to maintain consistency (without modifying the hypothetical belief in the antecedent); finally, consider whether or not the consequent is then true" (p. 102). Stalnaker then proceeds to tackle the problem of truth conditions along these lines. In his strategy he uses the concept of possible world as a basic concept, and his goal is to construct a possible-world semantics for conditional statements. Stalnaker's suggestion amounts to the following:

> . . . our semantical apparatus includes a *selection function, f,*
> which takes a proposition and a possible world as arguments and
> a possible world as its value. The *s*-function selects, for each
> antecedent *A,* a particular possible world in which *A* is true.
> The *assertion* which the conditional makes, then, is that the consequent is true in the world selected. A conditional is true in the
> actual world when its consequent is true in the selected world
> (p. 103).

The possible world that is taken as an argument of the selection function is called a *base world.* Thus, for a base world α, Stalnaker proposes the following condition:

(13) $A > B$ is true in α if B is true in $f(A,\alpha)$.
        $A > B$ is false in α if B is false in $f(A,\alpha)$ (p. 103).

We will be interested in the actual world as a base world, and thus we can reformulate Stalnaker's condition as follows:

(14) $A > B$ is true iff B is true in the world selected by the selection function.

The question then arises: What is the selection function (which Stalnaker also calls "s-function")? Stalnaker does not commit himself. He does, however, say that "the s-function establishes a total ordering of all selected worlds with respect to each possible world" (p. 105). The main requirement for the selection function is that the world selected, in which the antecedent A is to be true, be as close as possible (according to the ordering) to the base world. The ordering itself is to be based on similarity to the actual world.

The problem that remains, then, is the determination of the ordering of the possible worlds (relative to a given base world). Concerning this, Stalnaker says:

> . . . the world selected *differ*[s] *minimally* from the actual world. This implies, first, that there are no differences between the actual world and the selected world except those that are required, implicitly or explicitly, by the antecedent. Further, it means that among the alternative ways of making the required changes, one must choose one that does the least violence to the correct description and explanation of the actual world. These are vague conditions which are largely dependent on pragmatic considerations for their application (p. 104).

Moreover, Stalnaker recognizes that

> Those conditions on the selection function . . . are of course far from sufficient to determine the function uniquely. . . . The questions, "On what basis do we select a selection function from among the acceptable ones?" and "What are the criteria for ordering possible worlds?" are reformulations of the pragmatic problem of counterfactuals (p. 105).

And furthermore:

> This suggests that there are further rules beyond those set down in the semantics, governing the use of conditional sentences. Such rules are the subject matter of a *pragmatics* of conditionals. Very little can be said, at this point, about pragmatic rules for the use of conditionals (p. 110).

It is quite clear, then, that Stalnaker does not provide (or claim to provide) a complete specification of truth conditions for counterfactuals within his possible-worlds model. What remains to be specified is the selection function or the ordering relation on worlds. Stalnaker makes a few programmatic comments, quoted above, which he considers vague,

about this problem, but does not attempt to solve it. I will deal with the
problem in detail below.

A world selected by Stalnaker's selection function must be as close as
possible to the actual world (with A true in it). Thus Stalnaker's selection
function chooses one unique possible world even in cases where there may
be more than one "closest" possible world. This is unfortunate, since it may
sometimes make the truth value of the counterfactual depend arbitrarily
on the world chosen by the selection function. Consider, for example, the
following counterfactual:

> If the number of my hairs differed from what it is by just one, I
> would have one more hair.

This is, of course, false. But consider two types of possible worlds: in
worlds of the one type I do indeed have one more hair, and, in the worlds
of the other, one less. And suppose that, apart from this, these worlds differ minimally from the actual world. There seems to be no reason to believe that any world of the first type would be closer to the actual world
than every world of the second type, or vice versa. But the selection function will have to choose a world of either the first or the second type. If
a world of the first type is selected, the above counterfactual would come
out true, though it should not. And if a world of the second type is selected,
the counterfactual

> If the number of my hairs differed from what it is by just one, I
> would have one less hair.

would come out true. But this counterfactual is equally false. Thus, apart
from any considerations as to which the closest worlds are, in the selected
world either 'I have one less hair' or 'I have one more hair' will be true,
since in this world the antecedent is true. So, either way one of these
counterfactuals will come out true; but neither is true.[16]

Stalnaker's response to this sort of criticism, in a recent article,[17] is that
to rule out ties in similarity would indeed be highly implausible. Yet it
can be done if a structure of supervaluation is added to the semantics,
which feeds on selection functions that may differ in how they decide such
ties. Such supervaluations may then give a truth value to neither of the
above two counterfactuals, since they would be decided differently by different admissible selection functions. Yet, the principle of excluded middle, $A > B \lor A > {\sim}B$, would still be valid, even though in various cases
neither $A > B$ nor $A > {\sim}B$ would be true.

Notes: Chapter 1

1. Hereafter I will omit the words 'chapter' and section when the reference is clear: an arabic numeral preceding a roman numeral refers to a chapter; an arabic numeral following a roman number refers to a subsection; 1 II 4, for example, is chapter 1, section II, subsection 4.

2. *Mind*, LV, 220 (October 1946): 289-307; reprinted in Herbert Feigl and Wilfrid Sellars, *Readings in Philosophical Analysis* (New York: Appleton-Century-Croft, 1949), pp. 482-497; page references are to the reprinted version.

3. "General Propositions and Causality," in *The Foundations of Mathematics*, R. B. Braithwaite, ed. (London: Routledge & Kegan Paul, 1931; Paterson, N.J.: Littlefield, Adams, 1960), p. 247.

4. I shall use the arrow '→' for logical consequence.

5. Page 491. Chisholm there discusses this difficulty as instantiated in this example.

6. Chisholm made rather limited use of this requirement in order to avoid difficulties concerning counterfactuals with true consequents. In our present context this condition is used to block a sweeping trivialization that would apply to any counterfactual whatsoever.

7. Since $Ga \rightarrow Fa \supset Ga$.

8. Except for the uninteresting set of counterfactuals for which $B \rightarrow \sim A$, which are false because of the inconsistency of the antecedent and the consequent.

9. His own concern about the strategy is expressed on his p. 491, as quoted above.

10. *Fact, Fiction, and Forecast* (Indianapolis: Bobbs-Merrill, 1965, second edition); all page references will be to the second edition.

11. See the quotation from Goodman with which we opened this section.

12. In this section we shall follow Goodman in using 'C' for the consequent of an arbitrary counterfactual, though normally in what follows we will talk about an arbitrary counterfactual 'If A had been the case, then B would have been the case'.

13. As Goodman points out, W.T. Parry came out with the counterexample $A \supset C$ and $A \supset \sim C$. See Goodman, op. cit., p. 13, fn 7. See also Parry, "Reexamination of the Problem of Counterfactual Conditions," *Journal of Philosophy*, LIV (1957): 85-94.

14. Thus he writes, "The presence of the auxiliary terms 'even' and 'still', or either of them, is perhaps the idiomatic indication that a not quite literal meaning is intended."

15. In Nicholas Rescher, ed., *Studies in Logical Theory*, APQ Monograph No. 2 (Oxford: Blackwell, 1968).

16. See also related arguments presented by David Lewis in *Counterfactuals* (Cambridge, Mass.: Harvard University Press, 1973), pp. 79-82.

17. "A Defense of Conditional Excluded Middle," in William Harper, Robert Stalnaker, and Glenn Pearce, *Ifs* (Doudrecht: D. Reidel, 1981).

2 Counterfactuals

I Technical Preliminaries

1. In this section I briefly discuss certain technical notions concerning the temporal analysis of statements and some notation which I use below. Further discussion of the temporal analysis of statements will be deferred to chapter 6.

Temporal features play an important role in my analysis of counterfactuals. In particular, I use the notion of a sentence **pertaining to**, or **referring to**, a certain time. This notion seems to be clearer for syntactically simple sentences, that is, for sentences that do not contain subsentences. (We shall assume throughout that we are working within a given language, say English.) Complex sentences will be discussed in chapter 6. The times to which statements pertain are temporal intervals (including temporal instants, which are degenerate temporal intervals). Thus, for example, the sentence

(1)   J.F. Kennedy was president of the U.S. from January 20, 1961, to November 22, 1963.

pertains to the time interval between January 20, 1961, and November 22, 1963. Similarly, in the sentence

(2)   Stalin used to drink occasionally throughout his life.

the temporal interval to which the sentence pertains is that which covers Stalin's lifetime. The time to which a statement pertains may be specified explicitly, as in these examples, which will always be the case for context-independent sentences; in other cases, it may be signaled by the context. (We may occasionally refer to the time to which a statement pertains as the **time of reference** of the statement.)

In chapter 6 I will consider the time of reference of a statement from the perspective of its temporal quantificational structure. Syntactically simple sentences will be associated with temporal quantifiers; the time intervals to which they pertain will be their domains of temporal quantification. The temporal quantificational features of a sentence resemble in various ways those of ordinary quantification. Ordinary-language sentences that involve quantificational structure are normally represented symbolically by formulas whose interpretation in turn requires a domain of quantification. Quite often, the original ordinary-language sentence does not explicitly specify that domain. But generally if the sentence is unambigu-

19

ous in its context, the sentence and the context determine the domain; this is a normal phenomenon of context-dependence. Similarly, where the temporal quantificational structure of an ordinary-language sentence is concerned, the quantificational domain may not be specified explicitly by the sentence itself, but can be understood with the help of the contextual information.

2. Following a well-established usage, we shall take **statements** to be context-independent. This also applies to the time to which they pertain. In our examples, however, for the sake of convenience, we shall often allow context-dependence when there is no danger of confusion, even in cases where, strictly speaking, statements are called for. We shall also allow ourselves, where there seems to be no danger of confusion, to use 'sentence' in the above sense of 'statement'. But the analysis proposed below should be understood as dealing with statements in the strict sense, i.e., that of context-independence.

We shall represent the time to which a statement A refers as t_A (thus t_B, t_C, etc.). We shall say that one temporal interval is **earlier** (or **later**) than another if every temporal point in it is earlier (or later) than every point in the other. We shall say that a statement A pertains to a time **prior to** that of a statement B if t_A is earlier than t_B. One interval will be said to be **weakly earlier** (or **weakly later**) than another if its starting point is earlier (or later) than the starting point of the other. $\underline{t}$ will be the starting point of the interval t, and $\bar{t}$, its end point. If t', t'' are two temporal intervals such that $\underline{t}'$ is earlier than $\bar{t}''$, we shall use (t',t'') to designate the temporal interval whose starting point is $\underline{t}'$ and whose end point is $\bar{t}''$. A temporal interval t will be said to be *between* t' and t'', or alternatively, *within* the (t', t'') interval (when t' is weakly earlier than t'' and $\bar{t}''$ is later than $\bar{t}'$), if t is weakly later than t' but $\bar{t}$ is earlier than $\bar{t}''$.[1]

Proper substituends for the letters 'A', 'B', 'C', etc. will be names of statements. A counterfactual statement of the form 'If A had been true, B would have been true' will be symbolized as: $A > B$. (In order for a statement of the form 'If A had been true, B would have been true' to qualify as a *counterfactual* statement, as this term will be used in this book, its antecedent has to be false.[2]) Thus, '$>$' is taken as the counterfactual symbol. In the counterfactual statement $A > B$, A is called the **antecedent** and B the **consequent**. Logical symbols will signify themselves, and a juxtaposition of names of expressions will signify the concatenation of the expressions named by them. We shall use the expression '**the antecedent-time**' (or '**the consequent-time**') for a given counterfactual to mean: the time to which the antecedent (or the consequent) pertains.[3]

3. We will be referring to histories of the world which pertain to times prior to a particular point in time. We will assume, though not illuminate, a distinction between lawlike and nonlawlike statements. Let us designate as L the set of all true lawlike statements. The **history of the world** pertaining to times up to time t will be a set of nonlawlike, true factual statements

that describe the history of the world prior to t.[4] We shall designate it as W_t. If t is a temporal interval, the crucial temporal point concerning W_t is t's starting point $\underline{t}$. Thus, W_t is the same as $W_{\underline{t}}$. (In chapter 6 we go into the definition of W_t in greater detail.)

W_t should be consistent, since all its statements have to be true. Moreover, it should be the case that, if t is weakly earlier than t', then $W_t \subset W_{t'}$. When we want to refer to the history of the world which pertains to the time interval (t,t'), we shall designate it as $W_{t,t'}$; $W_{t,t'}$, then, is the set of members of $W_{t'}$ which pertain to times in (t,t').[5] In most cases, when we discuss a counterfactual with an antecedent A, the only use we will make of histories of the world will be in talking about W_{t_A}, the history of the world prior to the antecedent-time. Consequently, in such a context it will be convenient simply to talk about W. Thus, in contexts where only a counterfactual with antecedent A is discussed, W is W_{t_A}.

II The Inferential Model

1. The problem before us is to provide truth conditions for counterfactual statements: to specify the circumstances under which a statement of the form 'If A had been true, B would have been true' is true. For a counterfactual $A > B$, with the exception of a very special category of counterfactuals, t_A is weakly earlier than t_B. We shall henceforth confine our attention to such counterfactuals. We shall also consider only counterfactuals whose antecedents and consequents are factual statements.[6]

The problem of providing an analysis for counterfactual statements is intimately connected with another problem raised by counterfactual conditionals — the problem of how they can have empirical significance. Counterfactual statements do not in general express conceptual truths, yet they might not seem to be about the actual world, for they seem to concern, or be about, possible states of affairs other than the actual world. How can they, then, be empirically meaningful, if the evidence they require seems to be about nonactual states of affairs? Any adequate analysis of counterfactuals has to deal with this problem. Below we shall examine how it can be handled within the framework of our proposed analysis. Once truth conditions for counterfactuals are given, the problem of the empirical character of counterfactuals becomes reducible to the question of the empirical character of these truth conditions. An analysis of counterfactuals may therefore throw some light on this problem.

How, then, are we to analyze a statement of the form 'If A had been true, B would have been true'? The natural tendency is to take the 'If . . . then' construction seriously, i.e., as an implicational form of some kind. But what kind of implication is it? Clearly, the consequent of a counterfactual statement is not normally a logical consequence of the antecedent alone. To be interpreted as a statement of implicational form, it must be interpreted as an *incomplete implication*; that is, as a statement whose import is that the consequent follows logically from the antecedent taken together with other premises. These premises are not specified in the counterfactual statement itself; hence its character of an incomplete implication. Let us call these premises the **implicit premises** of the counterfactual statement. According to our interpretation, therefore, for every counterfactual there are certain implicit premises, collectively consistent with the antecedent A, such that the counterfactual statement is true if and only if they, together with A, entail the consequent. Thus our schema for analyzing counterfactuals holds that a counterfactual statement $A > B$ is true iff:

(3)   {implicit premises} $\cup$ $\{A\}$ $\rightarrow$ B

We shall call this schema of truth conditions for counterfactuals the **schema of the inferential model of counterfactuals.** The major problem, then, is to find out what the implicit premises are.

In practice, of course, we frequently evaluate counterfactual statements, and, if their interpretation as incomplete implications is representative of their mode of functioning in our conceptual framework, the implicit premises should play a role in such evaluations. But they are not specified either in the counterfactual statement itself or in its normal context of use. This gives rise to the problem of deciphering these implicit premises in particular cases, and also to the general problem of specifying the rule of their determination. The problem is to find a rule or a function that will determine the implicit premises for any given counterfactual (perhaps on the basis of some additional information that may be needed). This *functional* characterization of the implicit premises is an integral feature of the interpretation of the counterfactual schema under the inferential model, as I will use it. Under the inferential model, the implicit premises of a counterfactual are construed as a function of the counterfactual statement (though, perhaps, not of it alone) regardless of the truth value of the counterfactual. Thus, to provide an adequate account of the counterfactual schema, or an analysis of counterfactual statements, is in part to find this function. The counterfactual itself is surely one of its arguments, and the set of the implicit premises is its value. When such a function is incorporated into the schema of the inferential model to replace the as yet unanalyzed term 'implicit premises', the resulting schema of the inferential model yields the truth conditions for counterfactuals. Thus the task of finding the fuction is both to find the arguments and to find the function itself. This task lies at the core of the analysis of counterfactuals, and its accomplishment, in part, constitutes the goal of this book.

Because of its importance, this function deserves a name: in virtue of the products it is designed to deliver, we will call it the **implicit-premises function**, or, for short, the **i-p function**.

If we now represent the i-p function as $f(A > B, \ldots)$, we can represent the schema of the inferential model as:

(3') $f(A > B, \ldots)$ $\cup$ $\{A\}$ $\rightarrow$ B

Our task is to find out what $f(A > B, \ldots)$ actually is.

2. We have articulated the problem of counterfactuals within the framework of the inferential model. Another perspective from which it will be valuable to consider this problem utilizes the concept of a possible-world description. In this book I will present a framework of possible-world *descriptions*, rather than possible worlds, in which the truth conditions for counterfactuals will be formulated. This formulation will be shown (see X) to be equivalent to that developed within the inferential model. At this stage I will express the general schema of the inferential model in terms of possible-world descriptions, so that both models can be used for motivational purposes as we proceed.

A **possible-world description** is a set of factual (i.e., nonlawlike and nontautological) statements that is both consistent and complete (i.e., for every such statement either it is in it or else its negation is in it[7]) According to the inferential model, a counterfactual is true if its consequent follows from its antecedent together with the implicit premises. That a statement D implies a statement E can be expressed in the framework of possible-world descriptions by saying that E is true in all the possible-world descriptions in which D is true. Accordingly, the inferential schema can be mirrored in the possible-world-descriptions model as follows:

A counterfactual is true iff its consequent is true in all possible-world descriptions in which the antecedent and the implicit premises are true.[8]

If a possible-world description is consistent with a set of lawlike statements, that set will be considered true in that possible-world description.

The general question within the possible-world-descriptions model is: What is the set of all possible-world descriptions in which A is true, such that $A > B$ is true iff B is true in all of them? This set of possible-world descriptions will determine the truth value of the counterfactual. It will in general be a function of the counterfactual $A > B$ (since A has to be true in all of them). We shall represent this set as $M(A > B, \ldots)$. The schema of the possible-world descriptions model, then, is the following:

A counterfactual $A > B$ is true iff B is true in every member of $M(A > B, \ldots)$.

Let us call this formulation the **schema of the possible-world descriptions model for counterfactuals.**

The problem in this model is to find the functional characterizations of the set of possible-world descriptions $M(A > B, \ldots)$. Its determination will yield the truth conditions for counterfactuals within the schema of the possible-world-descriptions model. This question, in the model of possible-world descriptions, is analogous to the problem of the determination of the i-p function in the inferential model.

3. According to Stalnaker's analysis, we recall, a counterfactual is true iff its consequent is true in the world selected by the selection function whose arguments are the antecedent of the counterfactual and a world (as a rule we will assume that we evaluate counterfactuals in the actual world). The selection function selects the possible world most similar to the actual world from among those worlds in which the antecedent of the counterfactual is true. Let us assess the affinity of Stalnaker's strategy to our inferential model. We can show that a logical equivalent of Stalnaker's model fits the inferential model, on the assumption that there is a 1-1 correlation between possible worlds and their descriptions (which are, by our above definition, complete and consistent sets of statements). If $f(A > B, R)$ is Stalnaker's selection function (R being the actual world), choose an implicit-premises function $f'(A > B, R)$ as the function that yields the description of the world that $f(A > B, R)$ yields. Now consider the schema of the inferential model with f' as the implicit-premises function. We can show that it is logically equivalent to Stalnaker's truth conditions for counterfactuals:

> 1. If $A > B$ is true under Stalnaker's model, then B is true in $f(A > B, R)$. But then, $B \in f'(A > B, R)$, since $f'(A > B, R)$ is a complete description of $f(A > B, R)$. Hence: $f'(A > B, R) \cup \{A\} \rightarrow B$. [$f'(A > B, R) \cup \{A\}$ is consistent since $f'(A > B, R)$ is, and $A \in f'(A > B, R)$ since it is true in $f(A > B, R)$]. Hence $A > B$ is true according to the inferential model with f' as the i-p function.

> 2. Conversely, if $A > B$ is false under Stalnaker's model, then B is false in $f(A > B, R)$. Hence, by the same reasoning, since $\sim B$ is then true in $f(A > B, R)$, $\sim B \in f'(A > B, R)$. Hence $f'(A > B, R) \cup \{A\} \nrightarrow B$, and $A > B$ is false on the inferential model with f' as the i-p function. [Again, $f'(A > B, R) \cup \{A\}$ is consistent, since $f'(A > B, R)$ is, being a possible-world description, and $f'(A > B, R)$ includes A.]

This result, however, does not mitigate our previous criticism (in 1 III) of strategies such as Stalnaker's according to which a single possible world is chosen as the value of the selection function, selected with a view to minimizing departures from the actual world. The inferential model can cover a variety of particular schemata, since it leaves a substantial degree of freedom as to the choice of the implicit-premises function. Thus, many particular choices of this function can easily fail to be happy ones, that is, choices that render the inferential schema an extensionally adequate truth condition for counterfactuals.

The problem of characterizing the implicit-premises function is analogous to the problem of specifying the selection function in Stalnaker's model. Stalnaker acknowledges the centrality of this problem, as we have seen, but does not attempt to deal with it; he notes only that the selected world should be as close as possible to the actual world and indicates that pragmatic considerations should play a role in its determination. So the problem of specifying the implicit-premises function, which is our main concern, can be viewed as the analogue of his unresolved problem of specifying the selection function. We may note that the feature of Stalnaker's selection function criticized in 1 III — its selection of a single possible world — is analogous to requiring of an i-p function that the set of implicit premises be a complete (and consistent) set (a requirement which, of course, we did not make).

It is generally accepted that laws should play a role in the analysis of counterfactuals. We have seen that Goodman argued this point, and raised, along with the problem of the relevant conditions, the problem of distinguishing lawlike from nonlawlike statements. Though we shall (in V) incorporate the set of laws under the characterization of the implicit premises, we will not, in this book, go into the problem of analyzing lawlikeness. We will take the distinction for granted, and concentrate mainly on specifying the other implicit premises, i.e., the nonlawlike statements. I call these implicit premises the **legitimate premises** (of a counterfactual in the inferential model). The legitimate premises then, are the nonlawlike implicit premises. Once we take the implicit premises to cover the laws, the problem of the implicit-premises function is reduced to that of how to characterize the set of legitimate premises. The set of legitimate premises (for a given counterfactual) together with the true lawlike statements will constitute the range of the implicit-premises function for that counterfactual. It will be useful to look at the function derived from the i-p function $f(A > B, \ldots)$ which yields the legitimate premises, rather than the implicit premises, as its range — the **legitimate-premises function**, which will be represented as $f\text{-}(A > B, \ldots)$. We thus have:

(4) $f\text{-}(A > B, \ldots) = f(A > B, \ldots) - L$

in the sense that

$f\text{-}(A > B, \ldots) \cup L = f(A > B, \ldots)$

And thus the inferential schema of (3') can be represented as:

(4') $f\text{-}(A > B, \ldots) \cup L \cup \{A\} \rightarrow B$

Hence the choice of the symbol '$f\text{-}$' for representing the function f with L deleted from its values. As the set of laws is constant and does not vary with different counterfactuals,[9] clearly f and $f\text{-}$ will share the same arguments for a given counterfactual. Thus, to find the legitimate-premises function is to find the i-p function. We shall therefore concentrate on the former.

III   The Two Problems of the Legitimate Premises

1. It is convenient to approach the problem of the legitimate premises by contrasting them with the set of true nonlawlike statements (which constitute the description of the actual course of events). As will be shown below (in VII), we want the set of possible-world descriptions associated with the counterfactual to maintain a certain overlap with the actual-world description in very specific respects. It will prove instructive, though, to pursue the problem by examining both cases where an overlap with the actual-world description should be required, that is, where true statements qualify as legitimate premises, and cases where an overlap cannot be required, i.e., where true statements cannot qualify as legitimate premises.[10]

One source of the trouble lies, of course, in the antecedent A, with which our implicit premises have to be consistent. A is obviously not consistent with the description of the actual world, since that contains $\sim A$. But even if we delete $\sim A$ from that description, inconsistencies may still plague us. Since A is the root of this particular trouble[11] it is heuristically well advised, when we consider which particular statements should be among the legitimate premises, to divide our problem into two: the problem of the legitimate premises that pertain to times prior to t_A, and the problem of the legitimate premises pertaining to times weakly later than t_A.[12] The problems posed by these two groups are different, as we shall see, and call for different types of treatment. From the perspective of the possible-world-descriptions model, we are searching for the specification of the affinity to the actual-world description of the possible-world descriptions associated with a counterfactual [that is, those in $M(A > B, \ldots)$], i.e., we are searching for the invariant features they all share. The first problem, then, concerns the affinity of these worlds, insofar as their histories prior to t_A are concerned, to the actual-world description prior to t_A; the second problem concerns their affinity to the actual-world description insofar as their histories pertaining to times weakly later than t_A are concerned.

2. The first problem concerns statements that pertain to times prior to t_A. It arises when the antecedent A is *in*compatible with the prior history of the world (i.e., the history of the world prior to t_A, that is, W_{t_A}). In such a case, it is clear that this history, as a whole, cannot be retained among the legitimate premises. But in the other cases, when the antecedent *is* compatible with the prior history of the world, when it fits with the world's previous history (via its regularities and uniformities), when it is consistent with the world's prior history plus the laws of nature — in those cases that history can be retained among the legitimate premises. (Later I will argue that it *should* be retained in these cases — see V, VII, and XII.) These cases do not, then, pose a serious problem concerning the history of the world prior to t_A. If we consider such antecedents from the point of view of the possible-world-descriptions model, they will belong to a variety of possible-world descriptions that share their histories prior to t_A with

the actual-world description. [Again, I will later argue that it is possible-world descriptions of this sort which should be associated with the counterfactuals in such cases, i.e., as members of $M(A > B, \ldots)$.] We can say metaphorically that such possible-world descriptions "diverge" from the actual world at $\underline{t_A}$ (that is, at the starting point of t_A). Their affinity with the actual world will be complete for times prior to t_A. Antecedents of many counterfactuals fulfill this condition.[13] As an example, consider:

Example 1

> Ralph participated in a quiz show. There were two doors. Behind one of them was a brand new car. If Ralph picked the correct door, he would win the car. Not having the slightest idea which was the right door, he chose one randomly. (His choice was not necessitated, let us assume, psychologically or otherwise.) It turned out that the car was behind the other door.

Consider now the following counterfactual:

> If Ralph had chosen the other door, he would have won the car.

The antecedent in this case ('Ralph chose the other door')[14] is compatible with the prior history of the world (as our story indicates), and this counterfactual would therefore fall within the category under consideration.

However, in many other cases the situation is not so simple. In these cases the antecedent is incompatible with the previous history of the world (through the laws). In these cases, therefore, we do not have the option of choosing as possible-world descriptions associated with the counterfactual in question possible-world descriptions that diverge from the actual-world description at the beginning of the interval to which the antecedent pertains (and thus include the world's previous history among the legitimate premises). Such divergence times, if any, must be prior to the antecedent-time,[15] and in these cases we face the problem of specifying the affinity of courses of events associated with the counterfactual, with the actual course of events, insofar as times prior to t_A are concerned. As an illustration of such a case, consider:

Example 2

> A piece of butter lies in the middle of a cold, barren expanse, with no human beings around, at time t (the middle of winter).

and the associated counterfactual:

> If this piece of butter had been at a temperature of 175°F at t, it would have started to melt.

Given that the expanse is continuously cold at times close to t, the antecedent-event[16] could not have occurred naturally in accordance with the prior history of the world up to time t and the laws of nature. Some kind of process, which did not in fact occur and which is neither mentioned explicitly nor implied in the counterfactual or its context (partially provided by the description of the example), must have led up to it. The problem of specifying the legitimate premises in such a case is therefore quite serious. This is the first of the two problems mentioned above; and, since it concerns times prior to the antecedent-time, let us call it the **problem of the previous legitimate premises**, where by 'previous' we understand: pertaining to times prior to t_A. This problem will not be discussed until chapter 9 (the Epilogue).

3. The second problem concerns specification of those legitimate premises which pertain to the time interval between the antecedent-time and the consequent-time (for a counterfactual $A > B$), an interval which we will call (t_A, t_B) (this interval includes all temporal points later than t_A and earlier than $\bar{t}_B$).[17] The problem, then, is, the problem of the affinity to the actual-world description of the possible-world descriptions associated with the counterfactual, insofar as this time interval is concerned. Again, in some cases the problem need not arise; these are cases in which the **consequent-event** (that is, the event or state of affairs described by the consequent) is temporally sufficiently close to the **antecedent-event** (the event or state of affairs described by the antecedent). The butter example above (example 2) is a case in point, since the time of its starting to melt would be the time of its reaching 175 degrees. But usually this is not the case. Thus, consider the following:

Example 3

> Jones had owned some stock for a certain period of time. At one point he started to consider selling it, since he needed money, and one day he decided to sell and did so. A few weeks later there was a sharp rise in the stock market. Jones, in the meantime, continued to live his routine life without any significant changes in his economic situation, which was modest but stable.

Now consider the counterfactual:

(5)   If Jones had not sold his stock, he would have become rich a few weeks later.

This counterfactual is indeed true. However, the time interval between the antecedent-event and the consequent-event is significant — a few weeks. The question, then, arises, as to what the legitimate premises pertaining to this interval are.

Since this problem concerns the specification of the legitimate premises that pertain to the interval (t_A, t_B), let us call it the **problem of the subsequent legitimate premises**, where by 'subsequent' we mean: weakly later than t_A.

4. We have thus seen that the problem of the legitimate premises can be divided into two subproblems. Accordingly, a corresponding distinction is projected into the class of counterfactuals: we can specify two subgroups of counterfactuals, in the analysis of each of which only one of these two problems arises. One of these subgroups consists of those counterfactuals concerning which the reference times of the antecedent and the consequent would approximate two virtually coinciding temporal points; here it would hardly be significant to talk about the legitimate premises in the (t_A, t_B) interval. For such counterfactuals, the problem of the subsequent legitimate premises would hardly arise: there would be no legitimate premises in this time interval to speak of, hence there would be no problem concerning their specification. Therefore, the analysis of such counterfactuals confronts only the problem of the previous legitimate premises. Example 2 is a case in point: its counterfactual belongs to this group.

The second group of counterfactuals will display the characteristics we examined above: these are the counterfactuals whose antecedents are compatible (through the laws) with the previous history of the world. We shall later argue (in V) that for such counterfactuals we may take the whole prior history among the legitimate premises. The problem their analysis faces is the problem of the subsequent legitimate premises — the specification of the legitimate premises in the (t_A, t_B) interval. As we noted, the set of possible-world descriptions associated with such counterfactuals will diverge from the actual world at t_A (by which we shall henceforth understand: diverge at the starting point of t_A). The antecedent of such a counterfactual can serve as natural continuation[18] of the prior history of the world (by which we mean: prior to t_A)[19] since its truth value is undetermined by that history (through the laws). For that reason I shall call such counterfactuals **counterfactuals of the natural-divergence type** (or, for short, counterfactuals of the **n-d type**.

Since each of these two groups of counterfactuals raises only one of the two problems, a solution to either problem will in turn provide an analysis for the corresponding group of counterfactuals. Thus, determination of the previous legitimate premises is necessary in the case of counterfactuals whose antecedents are not compatible (through the laws) with the previous history of the world, and determination of the subsequent legitimate premises is necessary in the case of counterfactuals where t_A and t_B are not coinciding temporal points. A solution to our second problem, the problem of the subsequent legitimate premises, will provide us with an analysis of counterfactuals of the n-d type. It is with this problem, and thus with this type of counterfactuals, that we shall be primarily concerned in this book (until the Epilogue, where the other problem, and other types of counterfactuals, will be discussed).

There remains the major case of counterfactuals that fit neither of these two types. These are counterfactuals whose antecedent is not compatible with the prior history of the world and where t_A and t_B do not virtually coincide. In order to determine the legitimate premises for these counterfactuals, we must provide answers to both of the above problems. In cases where the antecedents are compatible with the prior history, and

t_A and t_B do virtually coincide, neither problem arises: these counterfactuals are true just in case their consequents follow (through the laws) from their antecedents together with the prior history. This kind of counterfactuals can therefore be set aside.

IV Methodology and the Scope
of the Natural-Divergence Type

1. It seems that up to this point our analysis has provided two distinct methodological advantages. First, we have been able to separate the problem of the legitimate-premises function [see II 3, especially (4)] into two distinct subproblems, which can be investigated independently of each other: the problem of the previous legitimate premises, which arises in full force when the antecedent is incompatible with the previous history, and the problem of the subsequent legitimate premises, the problem of determining which statements pertaining to the (t_A, t_B) interval should be retained as legitimate premises. We can thus separate the legitimate-premises function $f\text{-}(A > B, \ldots)$ into two functions, which reflect these two problems: a function $g(A > B, \ldots)$, which will yield the subsequent legitimate premises, and a function $h(A > B, \ldots)$, which will yield the previous legitimate premises. Thus: $g(A > B, \ldots) = f\text{-}(A > B, \ldots) \cap W(t_A, t_B)$; $h(A > B, \ldots) = f\text{-}(A > B, \ldots) - g(A > B, \ldots)$. As we shall see, $h(A > B, \ldots)$ can be determined independently of $g(A > B, \ldots)$.[20] That there are two distinct problems (which can be distinguished when the temporal aspects of the problem are taken into account), involving different types of difficulties, which can be handled in sequence rather than simultaneously, is heuristically important. One of the serious difficulties concerning multidimensional problems is the need to deal with interdependent variables simultaneously. To be able to isolate them and attack them separately is a promising step forward.

Secondly, the distinction between the two problems gave rise to two groups of counterfactuals, each of which exemplifies only one of the two problems, never both. Consequently, the features of each of the two difficulties can be examined in isolation. We can use case studies to test our theories about each problem separately, which enables us to locate the sources of any possible shortcomings more precisely. If a single, comprehensive solution to the problem had been proposed and then tested in case studies embodying all difficulties at once, a failure would be likely to pose the problem of locating the source of trouble. This difficulty, which heuristically is quite significant, is thus averted by our analysis. The boldness of a theory (to use Popperian terminology) increases with the separate falsifiability of its components. Such separate falsifiability diminishes the danger of a conventionalistic adherence to a repeatedly failing strategy by making ad hoc adjustments in various parts of the system. The above methodological advantages are valuable for scientific theories in general, and in particular, for our strategy in the analysis of the counterfactual construction.[21]

Furthermore: since answers to the two problems we have distinguished will provide the implicit premises for the two temporal segments, their conjunction will yield necessary and sufficient conditions for the truth of counterfactuals, which is what we are after. Moreover, because we are able to specify two groups of counterfactuals, each of which exemplifies only one of the difficulties, an answer to either of the two problems will immediately yield necessary and sufficient conditions for the truth of a subset of counterfactuals, independently specified, which is a substantial and important group. In this book (up to chapter 9) I shall offer an answer to the second problem, and therefore a necessary and sufficient condition for the truth of counterfactuals in the subgroup that corresponds to it — counterfactuals of the n-d type. In chapter 9 the theory will be extended, so as to cover other counterfactuals as well.[22]

2. So we now turn to the problem of the subsequent legitimate premises: the problem of specifying the legitimate premises that pertain to the (t_A, t_B) interval, that is, the problem of determining the i-p function when its range is restricted to that interval; in other words, the problem of determining $g(A > B, \ldots)$ (see the first paragraph of this section). Accordingly, we shall focus on counterfactuals of the n-d type. But first it is worth while to have a look at an important kind of counterfactuals that belong to this type and at some contexts of their customary use.

A major group of counterfactuals of the natural-divergence type have antecedents that describe human actions. In considering counterfactuals whose antecedents describe human actions, we contemplate what would have happened if a certain individual (or a group of individuals) had done something that in fact he (or they) did not do, or had not done something that in fact he (or they) did. Many such counterfactuals will be of the n-d type if a variety of human actions are not determined by the previous history, through physical or psychological determinism; that is, if it was possible, at the time, for the agents involved to do otherwise, in the sense that the antecedents of such counterfactuals are compatible with the previous history of the world. Whether human beings have such freedom is a question we shall not discuss here; but the applicability of our theory of counterfactuals of the n-d type to this group of counterfactuals hinges on the assumption that they do. It is furthermore arguable that this assumption (whether true or not) is prevalent in our common-sense frame-work. Since our analysis attempts to reflect correctly the rule of application of the construction in question (that is, the rule by which counter-factuals are evaluated in our conceptual framework as true or false), the external assumptions according to which our analysis is applied to particu-lar cases must match the assumptions operative in the processing of these cases in our common-sense framework if the analysis is to be extensionally adequate, that is, if the results of the analysis are to conform to common-sense intuitions concerning particular cases. We will therefore interpret the locution 'It was possible at that time for the agent to have done other-wise' in a sense in which the only constraint is that of logical consistency with the previous history of the world together with the laws; and we will assume in various particular cases that it was possible, in this sense, for the agent to have acted otherwise.[23]

We can point out three main areas where counterfactuals of the n-d type are extensively used. First, many such counterfactuals occur in common discourse. Their antecedents normally describe events, actions, situations, or states of affairs that are of interest in the common-sense conceptual framework (that is, outside any specialized conceptual framework, e.g., that of science). Often, counterfactuals of this kind are used when a person ponders alternative possibilities that could have materialized under certain contingencies, or just regrets his past actions. Their main use, though, is when normative evaluations of responsibility, blame, or praise for certain events or states of affairs, are ascribed to people for actions that they have or have not taken. Thus, typically, people will be held responsible, for better or for worse, for a certain event if (among other things) that event would not have taken place if they had taken certain actions they did not in fact take or if they had avoided taking certain actions they in fact took. Counterfactuals of this type are often used in hindsight when certain events are thought to throw light on past actions or hypothetical past actions which are being considered. That is, they are used for the purpose of drawing conclusions as to the effects or possible effects of such actions, thereby enabling us to learn from experience.

Another area where counterfactuals are often used is history. The evaluation of actual as well as hypothetical actions, events, and processes very frequently involves their analysis in the light of later developments. Actions are evaluated as to their wisdom or as to the extent to which they determined certain other events, states of affairs, or processes, and causal relations are investigated between various phenomena and processes. The determination by the historian of such relations and properties must involve hypothetical assumptions or judgments which take the form of counterfactual statements. What the consequences of an action are hinges on what actually happened in comparison with what could have happened if another action had been taken instead; and this is vital for the assessment of whether decisions or actions were right, successful, or fatal. Normally[24] one event cannot be the *cause* of another unless it is false that the second would still have occurred had the first failed to occur. And other types of reasoning that play a role in historical analyses have recourse to hypothetical assumptions in a similar manner.

Thirdly, many counterfactuals of the kind we are concerned with play important roles in legal contexts. Thus, the determination of an agent's guilt or responsibility for a certain event depends on an illegal action of his being some sort of a cause[25] of that event. The degree of involvement of various factors and agencies likewise depends on various counterfactual connections. The determination of such causal relations, which often play a key role in deciding questions of legal responsibility, hinges on such counterfactual connections.

V   Which the Subsequent Legitimate Premises Are

1. We now turn our attention to the problem of the subsequent legitimate premises and to the examination of counterfactuals of the n-d type. Our goal is to find the i-p function for such counterfactuals; here the task will

amount primarily (as we will shortly argue) to the problem of finding the function of the subsequent legitimate premises, of determining the function $g(A > B, \ldots)$. We shall pursue this goal by examining various groups of statements and by checking their fitness as subsequent legitimate premises by examples and counterexamples.

First, it should be noted that among the implicit premises for counterfactuals we must include statements that describe the laws of nature. Indeed, it is often quite obvious that true counterfactuals would not satisfy the inferential model unless these laws were accommodated in the implicit premises. Thus, consider the following:

Example 4

> I held a piece of chalk in my hand above the desk during a certain stretch of time which contained t. No special forces, except for gravitation, were operative.

The counterfactual 1 (7) of 1 II 2:

> If I had dropped the chalk from my hand at time t, it would have hit a desk.

is true under these circumstances. But if the consequent is to be derivable in the inferential schema, then among the implicit premises there must be information about the location of my hand and of the desk and about the operative gravitational forces. But there should also be a statement specifying Newton's law, determining that there will be free fall downward, or another law yielding the same effect. Without such a law the consequent will not follow, and the counterfactual will not satisfy the inferential model. Hence we have to count specifications of laws among the implicit premises.

We also see this from a more general perspective. Laws, and physical laws in particular, often have the following form: If conditions of type Q occur, then conditions of type R occur (where, of course, there is some functional relation between R and Q). Now some counterfactuals are "parasitic" on such laws; that is, they have the form: If condition Q had been satisfied in some particular situation, conditions R would have been satisfied in it. There are numerous true counterfactuals of this form. However, if we do not allow the specification of laws among the implicit premises, such counterfactuals will not in general satisfy the inferential model,[26] despite their being true. It is quite clear, though, that in such cases the circumstances are such that the consequent is inferable via the laws in question and a relatively unproblematic choice of legitimate premises (e.g., the prior history of the world)[27], and therefore that these counterfactuals would satisfy the inferential model if these laws were specified among the implicit premises. Hence, in general, laws should be specified among the implicit premises.

Many laws are irrelevant to the analysis of any particular counterfactual on the inferential model; in such cases, their specification in the implicit premises may be redundant. But in no case would it hamper the extensional adequacy of the inferential model; that is, their specification under the implicit premises would not result in true counterfactuals coming out false or false counterfactuals coming out true in the inferential schema. Thus we may take all laws to be expressed by the implicit premises. Let us denote the class of statements that express the laws by 'L'.

2. Next, we can see that, for a counterfactual $A>B$ of the n-d type, the prior history W (that is, W_{t_A}) is among the legitimate premises; i.e., $W_{t_A} \subseteq f(A>B, \ldots)$. As usual, in order to show that a set of statements should be included among the legitimate premises, we can argue that failure to include it would make true counterfactuals come out false on the inferential model. If, however, in addition, it were possible to show that its inclusion would be responsible for the failure of the model in a case where a false counterfactual comes out true, then we would have to conclude that our categorization does not hit the mark, that the set does not function as a unit in the inferential model, and that different categorizations of sets of statements should be sought to fit the picture. One could argue for and against this way by bringing examples or counterexamples. We shall call this the **pigeon-hole method**, because of its style of organization and categorizational character. At best, such a method establishes its thesis, but it hardly provides a motivation for it. For a motivational argument, we shall have to await the discussion of the roles of the various constructions under investigation (see VII and XI; see also XII).

In order to see that we have to retain W among the legitimate premises[28] of a counterfactual $A>B$, consider the following:

Example 5

> Harry was chronically and incurably suicidal. He got hold of a powerful bomb, and, one day, at time t, he blew it up without moving away and disintegrated completely.

Now consider:

(6)   If Harry had not blown up the bomb, he would have committed suicide at some later time.

Given Harry's chronic psychological condition, we can reasonably assume that this is true. But if we consider the facts only from t_A onwards, there is no Harry there—only miniscule parts of him, the remnants of his disintegrated body. We cannot, from this information and the laws, reconstruct Harry's previous psychological condition. But without it, we cannot substantiate the counterfactual. So since we need information about his psychological condition pertaining to times prior to the explosion, we need information in W among the legitimate premises.

As was the case with the laws, various (and even vast) portions of W may be redundant among the legitimate premises: the entailment relation that holds for true counterfactuals, according to the inferential schema, may require only a portion of W. However, those parts of W which are redundant are innocuous and do not, as legitimate premises, spoil the inferential model. Thus there is no reason to divide W up for particular cases, and we may retain W in its entirety among the legitimate premises.[29]

3. Now we can turn our attention to the subsequent legitimate premises $g(A > B, \ldots)$, i.e., those which pertain to the (t_A, t_B) interval. First, we should note, it is clear that not all true statements of this interval can belong to $g(A > B, \ldots)$ if it is to be consistent with A, L, and W. This consistency is essential for the inferential model in cases where $A > B$ is true but $A > {\sim}B$ is false, since, otherwise, both would pass the test of the inferential schema. And indeed, some statements of the (t_A, t_B) interval are plainly inconsistent with A, L, and W, and sometimes with A and L alone (whereas L and W have already qualified as sets of implicit premises, as we have argued above). The following example is a case in point:

Example 6

Consider a counterfactual with the antecedent:

(7)   George Wallace was killed in the assassination attempt of 1972

such as

(8)   If Wallace had been killed in the assassination attempt of 1972, the then Lt. Governor of Alabama would have been the Governor of Alabama in 1974.

However, among the true statements of (t_A, t_B) is

(9)   Wallace lived through 1973.

If we were to include (9) among the legitimate premises for (8), the result would be an inconsistency in the antecedent of the inferential schema.

Hence we are not free to include all the true statements of the (t_A, t_B) interval among the legitimate premises for the counterfactual $A > B$. Here we have seen how consistency considerations stand in the way. In the next section we will look at cases in which other considerations are involved. From Goodman's discussion it is quite clear that simply eliminating statements that are individually incompatible with A and W will not do, since there may be collective incompatibility as well. It might be suggested that we eliminate from the legitimate premises all statements belonging to a set that is incompatible with A and W and minimal as such; but this suggestion is too radical, since it would eliminate statements necessary for the validation of certain true counterfactuals. To see that, consider the following:

Example 7

An African dictator received an anonymous warning one morning that there would be an attempt to assassinate him. As a result he immediately started wearing his bulletproof vest. At midday his closest aide shot him in the chest.

The counterfactual:

Had the dictator not worn his bulletproof vest that morning he would have been injured.

is quite true. For the counterfactual to come out true under the inferential model, however, the statement:

(10)   The aide of the dictator shot him that day.

would clearly have to count among the legitimate premises. But the set of statements consisting of the true (10), the antecdent:

The dictator did not wear his vest.

and the true:

The dictator was unharmed that day.

is incompatible (with the laws). But to eliminate the members of this set (except for the antecedent) is to subvert the right outcome for the above counterfactual under the inferential model, for which (10) is crucial. Thus, eliminating from the legitimate premises all members of a set that is minimally incompatible with A and W will not do. What collective incompatibility calls for is a selection of those statements which are to be eliminated as opposed to those which are not.

The following question, then, arises: For a given counterfactual, what are the subsequent legitimate premises of its inferential schema? Which statements of those pertaining to the (t_A, t_B) interval qualify as legitimate premises, and which do not? And how are we to explain why, in our conceptual scheme, such a differentiation is made along the borderlines that indeed separate the two groups? To these questions we now turn.

4. It seems fruitful, at this stage, to present our problem from the perspective of the possible-world-descriptions model. As we saw (in II), the problem of the implicit premises is analogous to the question of which set of possible-world-descriptions is to be associated with a given counterfactual (in the framework of the model of possible-world descriptions). We have called such a set, in the context of the general problem of counterfactuals, which covers the problems of both the previous and the subsequent legitimate premises, $M(A > B, \ldots)$[30] (see III). A counterfactual $A > B$, then, is true iff B is true (i.e., is included) in all members of $M(A > B, \ldots)$.

The bulk of this book (up to chapter 2) is a study of the problem of the subsequent legitimate premises and is concerned with counterfactuals of the natural-divergence type. We are seeking the set of possible-world descriptions that fulfill the above condition for this kind of counterfactual (i.e., in which the antecedent is compatible with the prior history of the world). Thus, we are seeking a set of possible-world descriptions to be associated with a counterfactual of the n-d type: a set of possible-world descriptions such that the counterfactual is true iff its consequent is in each member of the set. Since counterfactuals of the n-d type are a subset of the class of counterfactuals, such a set would in principle be different from an acceptable candidate for $M(A > B, \ldots)$. We shall call such a set $V(A > B, \ldots)$, to be determined, for a given counterfactual $A > B$, by the function V. Our problem concerning counterfactuals of the n-d type in the possible-world-descriptions model, then, is to find out what $V(A > B, \ldots)$ is.

As we have already seen, W and L are among the implicit premises for a counterfactual of the n-d type. Therefore, we can already delimit $V(A > B, \ldots)$:[31] all members of $V(A > B, \ldots)$ are compatible (as sets of statements) with L, and each includes W. Thus all members of $V(A > B, \ldots)$ share their parts prior to t_A, i.e., W, though they may differ with respect to times weakly later than t_A.[32] Consequently, as we noted, they "diverge" from the actual-world description at t_A (since W belongs to it too). We can say that a possible-world description that shares that portion of itself which pertains to times prior to a certain time t with the actual-world description has t as its **divergence time**. So thus far in our search for $V(A > B, \ldots)$, we have delimited a set of possible-world descriptions (compatible with L) which have a common divergence time t_A. Let us call this set of possible-world descriptions **the world-range of A**. From now on we shall assume that the possible-world descriptions under discussion are compatible with L even when we do not say so explicitly.

We must now seek further constraints on our characterization of $V(A > B, \ldots)$. That is, we are looking for a subset of the world-range of A as a candidate for $V(A > B, \ldots)$. (More precise results pertaining to the relation between the inferential model and the possible-world-descriptions model will be given in sec. X.)

5. We now have to consider the true statements in the (t_A, t_B) interval and find out which of them should qualify as subsequent legitimate premises. We shall distinguish various subgroups of W_{t_A, t_B} (see I 3) according to a certain sort of *causal relations* that the antecedent-event bears to the events described by their members. As we shall see later (sections VII, XII), these sorts of causal relations are crucial for an adequate analysis of counterfactuals, though they themselves, of course, will not be left unanalyzed. Thus, it should be emphasized that ultimately counterfactuals are *not* about to be reduced in this book to causal relations. Rather, the pertinent causal relations will be analyzed probabilistically (cf. XIII below). The significance to counterfactuals of this sort of causal relation will come

out more clearly in our discussion of the roles of the various constructions under examination (see VII).

We shall first show that we should retain among the subsequent legitimate premises the set of all statements in the (t_A, t_B) interval which describe events to the occurrence of which the event described by the antecedent A, i.e., **the A-event**, is causally irrelevant. When we evaluate a counterfactual $A > B$, we consider whether B would be the case if the A-event were to occur, though in fact the $\sim A$-event actually took place. Thus, we consider the consequences of the *transition* of the course of events from the event described by $\sim A$, which in fact occurred, to the A-event, which did not. We shall refer to this transition as the $\sim A$-A **transition**. The causal irrelevance of the event described by A to a later event described by C would amount to the causal irrelevance to the C-event of the transition of the course of events from the $\sim A$-event to the A-event. That is, there would be causal relevance if this transition would make a difference to the occurrence of the event described by C. (We shall further discuss causal relevance in VIII of this chapter, and again, at greater length, in chapter 4, where its analysis will be attempted).

For the sake of fluency of exposition, I allow myself occasionally to ignore the distinction between the meta level and the object level insofar as statements and the events they describe are concerned. First, a statement may describe an event or a state of affairs. For convenience, we shall refer to both as *events*. Thus, we shall mean by 'the A-event' or 'the B-event' the event(s) or state(s) of affairs described by statements A and B, respectively. Secondly, when we want to talk about the relations of causal relevance, causal irrelevance, and the like between two events described by statements A and B, we may instead, for the sake of fluency, talk about the relations of causal relevance, causal irrelevance and the like between A and B or even, in a mixed manner, between an event and a statement.[33] There should not be any confusion here, once we agree that such locutions are mere place-holders for other locutions that do justice to the distinction between object and meta levels. We shall permit ourselves to interchange talk of the A-event with talk of A, to speak of the occurrences of A (rather than of the A-event), and to use expressions to the effect that a statement A makes a causal difference to a statement B, when we are really talking about the events they describe.

6. In order to see that in delimiting the legitimate premises for a counterfactual $A > B$ we have to retain the set of statements in the (t_A, t_B) interval to which A is causally irrelevant, recall example 3 of section III. The counterfactual in question was (5): If Jones had not sold his stock, he would have become rich a few weeks later. According to the example, the counterfactual is true, partly because in the meantime there was a sharp rise in the stock market. It is thus clear that in order for this counterfactual to pass the test of the inferential model, we need to include among the legitimate premises a statement describing this rise. However, since in the example Jones was not a major stockholder and since his action of selling was personally motivated (and thus did not reflect any general economic

trend), it is clear that his sale did not have any effect, either way, on the occurrence of the rise in the stock market: it was causally irrelevant to it. Thus, in order to make this true counterfactual pass the test of the inferential model, we have to retain as legitimate premises statements that describe events in the (t_A, t_B) interval to which the antecedent-event is causally irrelevant.

7. Statements of the (t_A, t_B) interval to which the antecedent is causally irrelevant are not, however, the only legitimate premises for the counterfactual in question which pertain to that interval. In addition to these, the legitimate premises include various statements to which the antecedent is causally relevant, but in a very special way. In general, as we shall see in the next section, statements to which the antecedent is causally relevant do not belong, as a group, to the set of legitimate premises. Even statements of that interval to which the antecedent is positively causally relevant do not belong, as such, to this privileged set. Positive causal relevance amounts to the antecedent's having an over-all positive effect on the occurrence of the event in question; it amounts to the $\sim A$–A transition's making an over-all positive causal difference to its occurrence. However, certain events, on the occurrence of which the antecedent-event has an over-all positive effect, *should* be retained as legitimate premises. These are the events on the occurrence of which the antecedent-event has a *purely positive causal effect*, that is, to which the antecedent-event is *purely positively causally relevant*. This relation of purely positive causal relevance holds between the antecedent-event and a later C-event in case the *only* effects of the $\sim A$–A transition on the occurrence of the C-event are positive. The causal effects of the transition on a later C-event can vary; some of them may be positive, others negative. The relation of purely positive causal relevance holds in case *all* the effects of the transition on the later C-event are positive. Statements that describe events to which the antecedent-event is purely positively causally relevant belong among our legitimate premises for the counterfactual $A > B$. We will further discuss the concept of purely positive causal relevance in VIII of this chapter, and in greater detail in chapter 5.

In section VI we bring an example of an A-event which, over all, is positively causally relevant to a C-event, but is not purely positively causally relevant to it, and show that, as a group, such events do not qualify as legitimate premises. In order to see, however, that we must retain as legitimate premises for a counterfactual $A > B$ statements pertaining to the (t_A, t_B) interval to which the antecedent is purely positively causally relevant, consider the following:

Example 8

> Tom is an architect who submitted a proposal to the board of directors of a bank that wanted to build a new branch. He requested x dollars for construction costs plus his commission. The board, being unanimously budget-minded, favored lower costs.

Tom got the contract and put up the building, but the construction costs turned out to be higher than he had estimated, and he did not make any profit.

He could then say:

(11) If I had asked for a thousand dollars less than I did, I would have lost money on this building.

and he would be right. However, for that counterfactual to pass the test of the inferential model, there should be, among the legitimate premises, a statement to the effect that he won the contract. The antecedent, indeed, is both causally relevant to such a statement, and positively so. But, more significantly, it is purely positively causally relevant to it. That is, the event of Tom asking for a thousand dollars less for his contract could affect his prospects of winning it only positively, and could in no way harm them. It could have no partial negative effect on his chances whatsoever — only a purely positive causal effect. Hence we have to retain, among our legitimate premises of the (t_A, t_B) interval, statements describing events to which the antecedent-event is purely positively causally relevant.

VI Which the Subsequent Legitimate Premises Are Not

1. Having established in the last section which categories of statements qualify as implicit premises, we now move to argue that this list is complete and that no other groups of statements qualify as subsequent legitimate premises, i.e., as belonging to $g(A > B, \ldots)$ (see IV 1).

As we saw in the last section, there are statements in the (t_A, t_B) interval which cannot be retained as legitimate premises. Some such statements are outright inconsistent with the antecedent and the laws. More commonly, however, such statements are inconsistent with the antecedent and the laws together with the legitimate premises we have already identified. These are statements which, though true, would nevertheless not have been true had the antecedent been true. Goodman called such statements *not cotenable* with the antecedent (see 1 II 5), and we adhere to this terminology. That there are such statements can be seen from the examination of a very extensive group of counterfactuals. Consider a true counterfactual $A > B$ whose consequent B is false and whose converse $A > \sim B$ is also false. If we were to retain $\sim B$ (which is true) as a legitimate premise for $A > B$, then either B could not be derived on the inferential schema, making the true $A > B$ come out false, or else the antecedent of the inferential schema would be inconsistent, in which case both $A > B$ and $A > \sim B$ would fulfill it. Hence the inferential schema would prove inadequate if $\sim B$ were retained as a legitimate premise. And indeed, when a counterfactual $A > B$ is true, $\sim B$ will sometimes be inconsistent with A and L (as we saw in the last section), sometimes with A, L, and W, and always with A, L, W, and $g(A > B, \ldots)$.

2. As can be expected, we cannot acknowledge as legitimate premises those events to which the antecedent-event is purely negatively causally relevant. To see this, consider the following:

Example 9

> John, an emotionally normal person, interviews Jane for a position in his department. He needs someone to work in the department, and he is looking for a person who is qualified and whom he feels he would like. He is authorized to make an offer. Jane is well qualified, John likes her, and consequently, he offers her the position at the end of the interview.

Now consider the following counterfactual:

(12)   Even if Jane, sadistically and for no reason, had slapped John across the face in the middle of the interview, he would still have offered her the position at the end of the interview.

This counterfactual is clearly false, given the situation alluded to. Now Jane's slapping John across the face is clearly purely negatively causally relevant to his liking her. But this antecedent-event is still causally irrelevant to the state of affairs at a time shortly after her slap, wherein John wanted to fill the position, his criterion of selection was to choose a well-qualified person he liked, and in which he was aware of Jane's professional qualifications. So such a description of this latter state of affairs qualifies as a legitimate premise for the counterfactual (12). Now if we were to recognize as legitimate premises descriptions of events to which the antecedent-event is purely negatively causally relevant, we would have to so recognize John's liking Jane after the slap as well. But if we were to do that, then the counterfactual (12) would fulfill the inferential model, the consequent would follow, and the counterfactual (12) would come out true — as it should not. Hence we cannot recognize as one of the legitimate premises a statement to the effect that John still likes Jane at times after the slap. Thus, we cannot include among the legitimate premises the set of statements to which the antecedent-event is purely negatively causally relevant.[34]

3. Lastly, we will show that the one remaining group of potential candidates cannot qualify, as a group, as a set of legitimate premises. These are statements in the (t_A, t_B) interval which describe events on which the antecedent-event has a mixed causal influence — partly positive, partly negative, to various degrees. To see this, consider the event described by the following contrary-to-fact assumption (which could serve as an antecedent for a counterfactual):

Example 10

(13) J.F. Kennedy chose Jackson (rather than Johnson) as his vice-presidential running mate in 1960.

This would clearly be causally relevant to the actual event described by

(14) Kennedy won the 1960 presidential election.

but in a nonuniform way. It would be negatively causally relevant in that Kennedy could very well have lost the South if he had picked Jackson; and (as the actual election results indicated), if the South had gone over to Nixon, Nixon might well have won. But (13) would have also had a positive effect on (14), since the state of Washington, which voted for Nixon, might well have voted for the Kennedy-Jackson ticket. Thus, (13) is causally relevant to (14) in a mixed way; it has both positive and negative effects. However, the counterfactual

(15) Even if Kennedy had chosen Jackson (rather than Johnson) as his vice-presidential running mate in 1960, Jacqueline Kennedy still would have been the first lady in 1961.

is clearly not true, since if the antecedent had been true, Kennedy might well have lost the election, and then Jacqueline would not have been first lady in 1961. However, if we retained (14) as a legitimate premise of (t_A,t_B) for the counterfactual (15), (15) would indeed come out true, since if Kennedy had chosen Jackson and we could rely on his winning the election, Jacqueline would have become first lady. Surely the choice of Jackson rather than Johnson is causally irrelevant to her and her husband's survival chances during the (t_A,t_B) interval, and thus their being alive in 1961 is, as such, a legitimate premise (see above, V 4). Hence, accepting (14) as a legitimate premise leads to evaluating a false counterfactual as true in the schema of the inferential model; so (14) has to be rejected. In general, statements of the (t_A,t_B) interval, to which the antecedent bears mixed causal relevance, partly positive, partly negative, do not qualify as such as legitimate premises for the inferential schema.[35]

More generally, inclusion of such statements as legitimate premises would give the possible-world descriptions that are members of $V(A>B, \ldots)$[36] an unwarranted tilt toward the actual-world description. This is especially clear in the case of those semifactuals (that is, following Goodman, counterfactuals with true consequents) whose antecedents are causally relevant to their consequents in a mixed way. If such statements are counted as legitimate premises, such semifactuals would come out true on the inferential model, since their consequents would be members of $g(A>B, \ldots)$,[37] but many of them are false. If we take (13) and (14) of example 9 above as the antecedent and the consequent, respectively, of a semifactual $A>C$, we have a case in point. This semifactual is not true, since, as we have seen, the choice of Jackson could very well have cost

Kennedy the presidency, and we have seen that A bears mixed causal relevance to C. But the inclusion of C [that is, (14)] among the legitimate premises would make $A > C$ true.

VII   Contrary-to-Fact Assumptions

1. We have examined the categories of events that should be described by the legitimate premises for a counterfactual of the n-d type and those which should not. We have accepted as legitimate premises the past history W and statements that describe events to the occurrence of which the antecedent-event is either causally irrelevant or purely positively causally relevant. We have excluded from among the legitimate premises statements describing events to the occurrence of which the antecedent-event is either purely negatively causally relevant, or even causally relevant in a mixed way—partly positive, partly negative. Thus, we have discovered that the subsequent legitimate premises, i.e., the members of $g(A > B, \ldots)$, describe events that are not adversely causally affected in any way by the occurrence of the A-event. In other words, we need to retain in $g(A > B, \ldots)$ those statements in W_{t_A, t_B} which describe events on the occurrence of which the transition from $\sim A$ to A does not have *any* negative causal effect: it does not cancel the effect of any previous positive causal antecedents of these events on them, nor does it lessen the effect of such causal antecedents on the events in question. Furthermore, we have seen that *only* statements describing these events should be taken as legitimate premises; that statements describing other events in the (t_A, t_B) interval do not qualify.

From the point of view of the model of possible-world descriptions, we have been concerned with the problem of finding the set of possible-world descriptions $V(A > B, \ldots)$ for a counterfactual $A > B$ (of the n-d type). In section II 2 we noted that a counterfactual is true iff its consequent is true in all possible-world descriptions in which the antecedent and the implicit premises are true. We can therefore apply our findings about the implicit premises to this problem, i.e., the problem of the determination of the possible-world descriptions to be associated with such a counterfactual. As we saw before (in V 4), only possible-world descriptions in the world range of A should be included, and now we can add that we should include only those which share with the actual-world description the subsequent legitimate premises. They need not share with it any other statements of the (t_A, t_B) interval. This determines the kind of affinity the possible-world descriptions in $V(A > B, \ldots)$ will have to the actual-world description: the affinity is complete, insofar as times prior to t_A are concerned, for counterfactuals of the n-d type, and it is determined by the above legitimate premises insofar as the (t_A, t_B) interval is concerned. We cannot retain *en bloc* all the statements from the actual-world description which describe events on the occurrence of which the transition from $\sim A$ to A has some negative effect. Figuratively speaking, we "trace" negative causal effects from A, and we retain events on which we find no such adverse effect. We thus want to delimit the possible-world descriptions that we allow in $V(A > B, \ldots)$, the class of possible-world descriptions to be associated with a counterfactual of the n-d type, by allowing variations from the actual-world descriptions in those event areas which are causally "infected" with some adverse effect by the antecedent-event. Statements describing the events that we are left with, i.e., those which are "clean" of such adverse causal relevance, are to be retained. They have to be shared by the other possible-world descriptions relevant to the determination of the truth value of the counterfactual. We will now turn our attention to those events, and examine them more closely.

It is instructive to view statements describing the subsequent legitimate premises $g(A > B, \ldots)$ in conjunction with the antecedent of the counterfactual in question, by considering counterfactuals with this antecedent and such a statement as a consequent. Since the legitimate premises are true statements, and since semifactuals are counterfactuals with true consequents,[38] these counterfactuals are semifactuals. A semifactual $A > C$ is typically expressed in the form: 'Even if A had been true, C would still have been the case'. We shall now turn to such semifactuals.

We can define two kinds of semifactuals; those in which the antecedent-event is causally irrelevant to the consequent-event, which we will call **irrel-semifactuals** (the 'irrel' stands for 'irrelevant'); and those in which the antecedent-event is purely positively causally relevant to the consequent-event, which we will call **pp-semifactuals** ('pp' for 'purely positive'). We can see that the statements in W_{t_A, t_B} which belong to the set of subsequent legitimate premises $g(A > B, \ldots)$, that is, those statements which describe events that are not in any way negatively causally affected by the antecedent-event of the counterfactual in question, are consequents of either irrel-semifactuals or pp-semifactuals which share their antecedents with the counterfactual in question.

2. We can now consider a general argument for the suitability as subsequent legitimate premises of the consequents of those irrel-semifactuals and pp-semifactuals which share antecedents with the counterfactual in question. This argument revolves around the role that contrary-to-fact assumptions play in our conceptual scheme.

In contemplating a counterfactual, we consider its antecedent, which, as a contrary-to-fact assumption, expresses a change from the actual course of events, which involves the $\sim A$-event, to an alternative course that involves the A-event. In considering the contrary-to-fact assumption, we consider this change, and only this change, and contemplate the possible effects *of this change* against the background of the actual course of events, and only these effects. Consequently, in considering this change, we are not prompted to question those actual events which have nothing to do with it, which would not be affected by it in any way, and whose occurrence is independent of it. So, if the role of a contrary-to-fact assumption is to draw attention to the possible effects of a change from the occurrence of the $\sim A$-event to the occurrence of the A-event against a background of the *actual* course of events, we would not, in considering it, unsettle those events that actually occurred which are unrelated to, or unaffected by, or independent of, this change. And events to which the antecedent is causally irrelevant belong to this category. We are thus to retain them in considering the effects of a contrary-to-fact assumption. Their retention preserves a part of the actual world *on the background of which* we want to evaluate the effects that the contrary-to-fact assumption might have. These events are described by the consequents of the irrel-semifactuals, with the contrary-to-fact assumption as antecedent.

The effect of this change from $\sim A$ to A, however, may not be adverse in any way with respect to certain kinds of actual events; the change may have only positive effects on their occurrence; it may only further enhance them.[39] In considering the effects that such a change may have, there is no reason to consider dropping these events: their being enhanced should not prompt us to consider their nonoccurrence in a course of events where A is the case, whereas they occurred in the actual course of events. The effects that the change to A might have are to be evaluated against a background of the actual course of events, and thus against the background of those events whose occurrence will not be affected by the change from $\sim A$ to A. Not being candidates for possible nonoccurrence as a result of this transition to A, they are to play a role in the evaluation of this transition. Occurring in fact, and being only further enhanced by A, their nonoccurrence is certainly *not* one of the *effects* that A might bring about. Thus, if, together with a contrary-to-fact assumption, we consider the effects that the change from $\sim A$ to A can have, and only these, those events which are only positively affected by the change are not among those whose occurrence is in danger as a result of the change from $\sim A$ to A. Those actual events whose occurrence is, in some way or other, negatively causally affected by this change are those whose occurrence comes into question — their nonoccurrence being a possible effect of the change — even if, in addition, this very change has various positive effects on them. Their occurrence will depend on the balance of the opposing effects. We retain the others without measuring such balances not because their occurrence has a higher probability in this case, but because their occurrence is not *called into question* by the contrary-to-fact assumption as a possible effect of the change, thus forming a part of the actual course of events on the background of which such a change is to be evaluated. To consider the effects of a change on the background of the actual course of events is to retain parts of it in the context of such evaluation; and the parts retained should include those events whose nonoccurrence is not a possible effect of this change.

The role of a contrary-to-fact assumption A, then, is to draw attention to the effects that the change from $\sim A$ to A might have, against a background of the actual course of events, and to call into question all those events upon the occurrence of which such a change has any negative effect. This role of contrary-to-fact assumptions, to draw attention to the effects of the transition on a background of the actual course of events, illuminates the role of regular counterfactuals: hypothetically to *predict* subsequent events in the case of the transition. We have seen that the consequents of irrel-semifactuals and pp-semifactuals should be retained when

a contrary-to-fact assumption is considered, so as to provide that portion
of the actual course of events on the background of which its effects are
to be evaluated. But the consequents of the rest of the true counterfactuals
with that contrary-to-fact assumption as antecedent function on a par
among themselves: they are true qua predictions on that background. In
this respect, counterfactuals that are not irrel-semifactuals or pp-semifactuals
play the same role irrespective of whether their consequents happen to be
true or false in the actual course of events. If the consequents of such counterfactuals are true, the transition has some negative effect on them, the
transition calls their occurrence into question, and thus they should be suspended from, rather than retained in, that portion of the actual course of
events on which the antecedent event has no negative effect, which is thus
not endangered by the antecedent, on the background of which the possible effects of the transition are to be determined. But such semifactuals
predict the occurrence of their consequent-events just as other counterfactuals, whose consequents are false, predict the occurrence of events that
did not in fact occur in the actual course of events. Thus, true semifactuals
of this sort are true qua predictions rather than in virtue of providing the
background upon which predictions are to be made. Hence the sameness of
role of all counterfactuals other than irrel-semifactuals and pp-semifactuals.

VIII   Irrel-semifactuals and pp-semifactuals

1. Irrel-semifactuals have, as semifactuals, the form 'even if A, still C',
and, moreover, their antecedents are causally irrelevant to their consequents. That is, the occurrence of the A-event rather than the $\sim A$-event
makes no causal difference to the occurrence of the consequent-event; the
C-event is an actual event whose occurrence is causally independent of
the occurrence of the A-event or the $\sim A$-event. In section V we saw that
in order to capture the true counterfactuals within the framework of the
inferential schema, statements which pertain to (t_A, t_B) and to which A
is causally irrelevant should belong in $g(A > B, \ldots)$. Thus, the subsequent legitimate premises $g(A > B, \ldots)$ include the consequents of irrel-
semifactuals with antecedents A.

   Notice that all irrel-semifactuals are true. Thus, the causal irrelevance
of the antecedent-event to the consequent-event in a semifactual (which
by definition makes it an irrel-semifactual) is a sufficient condition for its
truth [as well as for the membership of its consequent in $g(A > B, \ldots)$[40]].
A typical example of an irrel-semifactual is: 'Even if I had sneezed once
more (than I actually did) in 1969, the Vietnam war would have still gone
on in 1971'. There are thus no false irrel-semifactuals.

   That irrel-semifactuals are true is an obvious consequence of the inferential model: since the antecedent of an irrel-semifactual $A > B$ is causally irrelevant to its consequent, B is a member of the set of the legitimate premises of this counterfactual. Hence, on the inferential model, B
indeed follows from the implicit premises[41] for $A > B$, together with A, and
hence $A > B$ is true. Thus, in general, it is quite clear that any counterfactual whose consequent serves as a legitimate premise in its inferential

schema is true on the inferential model. Thus, members of the class of irrel-semifactuals are all true, and so are members of the class of pp-semifactuals. If $A > B$ is a pp-semifactual, B is a legitimate premise in its inferential schema, since A is purely positively causally relevant to it. Hence B follows from the implicit premises for this counterfactual together with A.

The main line of reasoning we have pursued in this chapter rests upon our working hypothesis: the inferential model. It was within its framework, and on the basis of our findings about $g(A > B, \ldots)$, that we discovered that all irrel-semifactuals are true. Leaving the inferential model for a moment, we now turn to our thesis, from the last section, about the role of contrary-to-fact assumptions, noting that the methodological status of the thesis that all irrel-semifactuals are true can be assimilated to that of an empirical generalization: it is confirmed by instances (some of which we have examined, or will later on) of irrel-semifactuals that are indeed true, coupled with failure to find a counterexample.[42] However, our thesis concerning the role of contrary-to-fact-assumptions gives motivational support to this empirical generalization. We have seen that the role of contrary-to-fact assumptions is to draw attention to the possible effects of the transition from $\sim A$ to A against a background of the actual course of events, and thus to draw attention to those actual events whose nonoccurrence is a possible effect of the transition, and only those actual events. We have seen that the events whose nonoccurrence is a possible effect of the transition are those which are adversely affected by it in some way. Since what has to be considered are the possible effects of the transition against a background of *the actual course of events*, those events whose occurrence is not called into question by the transition will therefore belong to that part of the actual course of events on the basis of which the possible effects of the transition are to be evaluated. Thus, these are to be retained in the context of evaluating such effects. To examine the effects of the transition against a background of the actual course of events is to examine them against a background of those events whose occurrence is not called into question by this transition. The most salient group of such events are those to which the antecedent-event is causally irrelevant. Hence, the truth of statements to which the contrary-to-fact assumption is causally irrelevant is to be preserved when the contrary-to-fact assumption is being considered; that is, these statements are to be considered true in this context, and hence the irrel-semifactuals they form are true.

Thus we see that the thesis concerning the truth of irrel-semifactuals is supported by our theory about the role of contrary-to-fact assumptions. Our theory of the roles of contrary-to-fact assumptions (and counterfactuals) is in turn further corroborated by true empirical generalizations that it yields, empirical generalizations which it thereby provides with theoretical support and explanation.

2. The other kind of statements that we decided to retain as legitimate premises are statements describing events that are only positively, that is, not in any way adversely, affected by the transition from $\sim A$ to A. We have called semifactuals with this relation between their antecedents and

consequents pp-semifactuals. For pp-semifactuals, the transition from $\sim A$ to A does not adversely affect any causal chain leading to their consequent-events or any positive impact of the causal background of the latter. But it does affect some such causal chains positively, since the antecedent-event is positively causally relevant to the consequent-event. The $\sim A$-A transition strengthens the impact of the causal background that leads to B without weakening it in any respect. This second kind of statements that qualify as legitimate premises consists, then, of consequents of pp-semifactuals with the same antecedent as the counterfactual in question. Such semifactuals are often expressed with the auxiliary locution 'a fortiori', e.g.: If the C-event had happened after the $\sim A$-event happened, a fortiori it would have happened had the A-event happened. We already saw (in V) that we have to retain the consequents of pp-semifactuals (which pertain to the appropriate time interval) among the legitimate premises of a counterfactual with the same antecedent [since statements in the (t_A, t_B) interval to which A is purely positively causally relevant are suitable members of $g(A > B, \ldots)$]. We will investigate purely positive causal relevance in greater detail in chapter 5.

We may notice here too that there are no false pp-semifactuals; if a semifactual fulfills the conditions for being a pp-semifactual, it is *ipso facto* true. If the transition to the A-event contributes *only* positive causal impact, the semifactual is both pp-semifactual and true in virtue of that.

That pp-semifactuals are true in the framework of the inferential model is quite obvious, as we mentioned in the discussion of irrel-semifactuals. Their consequents are among the legitimate premises for their own inferential schemata, and their truth is an immediate consequence of that.

3. That pp-semifactuals are all true constitutes, again, an empirical generalization. Our comments above about the methodological status of the truth of irrel-semifactuals apply, *mutatis mutandis*, to pp-semifactuals as well. Thus, this empirical generalization also follows from our thesis concerning the role of contrary-to-fact assumptions. Since their role is to draw attention to the possible effects of the $\sim A$-A transition against the background of the actual course of events, statements describing those events which are not candidates for change due to the transition, i.e., those events on which the transition has no negative effects whatever, are to be retained when the effects of the contrary-to-fact assumption are considered. Thus, statements describing those events to which the transition is purely positively causally relevant are to be retained through the transition and considered true in the context of the contrary-to-fact assumption; hence pp-semifactuals are true. That this empirically true generalization follows from our thesis about the role of contrary-to-fact assumptions provides further vindication of that thesis as well as theoretical support for the generalization itself.

We shall try to capture all this causal-relevance terminology in probabilistic conditions. Since the antecedent-event of a pp-semifactual is purely positively causally relevant to its consequent-event, the probability of the consequent-event of a pp-semifactual will be greater in the A-course than in the $\sim A$-course. (For further discussion of this point, see 5 I.) There are, however, statements other than consequents of pp-semifactuals with antecedent A, which describe actual events that have higher conditional probability in the A-course than in the $\sim A$-course. But, because they are not consequents of pp-semifactuals, the transition from the $\sim A$-course to the A-course will also have some negative effect on them, *even though* it may be compensated for by the transition in another way so as to result in a higher *net* probability in the A-course. We cannot admit these as legitimate premises, however, in spite of the increase in their conditional probability, since our requirement for admission is *not* high probability or probability higher than a given fixed limit, or even higher than in the $\sim A$-course. Our criterion consists in the requirement of pure *causal harmlessness* of the transition to the occurrence of those events — the absence of any negative causal effect resulting from the transition (and yet some positive effect). Only events to which the transition is *purely* positively causally relevant fulfill these requirements, and they are the consequents of pp-semifactuals.

We see that we cannot retain events on which the transition has a mixed impact, even though it results in a higher probability for their occurrence in the A-course, from the following:

Example 11

> Don participated in a lottery that had a thousand participants. Each participant had a card, and all the cards were put into a big basket from which the lottery manager was to draw one card. The person whose card was drawn would win the grand prize: a date with a girl and a salami. Now suppose it happened that Don won the lottery and thus won the date and the salami after having bribed an assistant to the lottery manager to do his best to put Don's card in a position where it was likely to be picked by the lottery manager. Now Don's chances of success, with the assistant's help, were limited by the conditions of the lottery — they were, say, 10% (compared to Don's 0.001% chances of winning otherwise). But consider the following possibility (which did not in fact materialize): suppose Don canceled his deal with the assistant manager and made another deal with the lottery manager himself, to the effect that the latter would help Don win, and get the salami in return. His chances of winning with the assistance of the lottery manager are higher, but are still limited by the conditions of the lottery: they are say, 30%.

Now consider the counterfactual $A > B$:

(16) If Don had opted out of his deal with the assistant manager in favor of a deal with the lottery manager, he would have won the date but not the salami.

This counterfactual is not true, since Don might very well have lost the lottery even in the case of a deal with the manager, his chance of success being only 30 %. This becomes clearer once we realize that the semifactual

(17) If Don had switched deals in the prescribed way, he would still have won.

is not true. We are not ready to retain a statement to the effect that he won under these circumstances, even though such an event occurred in fact, and its probability under these circumstances is considerably higher than in the ~A course of events. Now in this case, the antecedent-event has a mixed causal impact on the consequent-event, since on the one hand it generates a causal chain that leads to it, through the participation of the lottery manager, but on the other hand it spoils the effect of a previous causal chain which was positive vis-à-vis the consequent B — the one involving the intervention of the assistant manager.[43] Thus (17) is a semifactual whose antecedent bears mixed causal relevance to its consequent, even though its over-all effect is positive — Don's chances of winning are greater in the A-course than in the ~A-course. Nevertheless, its consequent does not qualify as a legitimate premise, since, if it did, counterfactual (16) would come out true [as well as semifactual (17)]. And, of course, in view of this mixed causal relevance, (17) is not a pp-semifactual, since its antecedent is not purely positively causally relevant to its consequent: there is some negative effect. Hence statements describing events on whose occurrence the antecedent has some negative effect should not, as such, be retained as legitimate premises in the inferential schema of the counterfactual in question even if the over-all effect of the transition is positive. Higher probability in the A-course is not a sufficient condition for being a legitimate premise.

Notice too that had we changed the probability of Don's winning in the hypothetical deal with the manager from 30 % to, say, 65 %, the falsehood of (16) and (17) would remain unchanged. Since the alternative outcome of his not winning is still a real possibility, we would not be prepared to predict his winning in such a hypothetical situation. Thus, we would not be entitled to retain the consequent of (17) among our legitimate premises if we are to avoid having these two false counterfactuals come out true on our inferential model. But since the consequent of (17) describes an actual event that would, in the new circumstances, have an over 50 % chance of occurring and yet does not qualify as a legitimate premise, we can rule out as a sufficient condition for legitimate premises not only being a true sentence describing an actual event whose probability increases as a result of the transition from ~A to A, but also being a true sentence describing an event whose probability surpasses 50 %, or both. Thus, high probability (over 50 %) of a statement describing an actual event in the A course of events is also insufficient to make this statement qualify as a legitimate premise.

IX   The Analysis of Counterfactuals

1. We can now present the resulting analysis of counterfactuals.[44] We started with the inferential model, i.e., with the schema of truth conditions for a counterfactual $A > B$, which was:[45]

(3′) $\{A\} \cup f(A > B, \ldots) \to B$

We saw that

$$f(A > B, \ldots) = L \cup W \cup g(A > B, \ldots)$$

and found out that $g(A > B, \ldots)$, the set of the subsequent legitimate premises, is the set of statements in (t_A, t_B) describing events that are not in any way adversely affected by the $\sim A$–A transition, and that this is the set of consequents of irrel-semifactuals and pp-semifactuals whose antecedents are A and whose consequents are in W_{t_A, t_B}. Thus, we are in a position to display the truth conditions for a counterfactual $A > B$ as follows:

Thesis 1.   A counterfactual $A > B$ of the n-d type is true iff[46]

(18) $\{A\} \cup W \cup L \cup \left\{ \begin{array}{l} \text{the set of consequents } C \text{ of irrel-} \\ \text{semifactuals and pp-semifactuals with} \\ \text{antecedent } A, \text{ for which } t_C \subseteq (t_A, t_B) \end{array} \right\} \to B$

We shall call this analysis the **irrel-&-pp-semifactual analysis of counterfactuals.**

In particular, we have seen that

(19) $g(A > B, \ldots) = \left\{ \begin{array}{l} \text{the set of consequents } C \text{ of irrel-} \\ \text{semifactuals and pp-semifactuals with} \\ \text{antecedent } A, \text{ for which } t_C \subseteq (t_A, t_B) \end{array} \right\}$

For convenience, let us call the antecedent of (18) $Q(A, W, L, t_B, \ldots)$, and the right-hand-side set in the union of the antecedent of (18) $\mathbf{CIP}(A > B, \ldots)$ (for consequents of irrel-semifactuals and pp-semifactuals). Thus:

(20) $Q(A, W, L, t_B, \ldots) = f(A > B, \ldots) \cup \{A\}$

We can therefore reformulate[48] (18) as:

(18′) $Q(A, W, L, t_B, \ldots) \to B$

and also as:

(18″) $\{A\} \cup W \cup L \cup \mathbf{CIP}(A > B, \ldots) \to B$

2. As we recall from the discussion of the goals of our analysis (at the beginning of this chapter), we wanted to determine the implicit premises function $f(A>B, \ldots)$ and, specifically, the subsequent legitimate premises function, i.e., $g(A>B, \ldots)$, for a given counterfactual $A>B$. We found that:

Thesis 2.   If $A>B$ is a counterfactual of the n-d type, then
$$g(A>B, \ldots) = \text{CIP}(A>B, \ldots).$$

and also that:

Thesis 3: $f(A>B, \ldots) = W \cup L \cup \text{CIP}(A>B, \ldots)$

We still have to determine the arguments of these functions, and will return to this question in section XIII, and later in chapters 4 and 5, where we shall deal with the analysis of $\text{CIP}(A>B, \ldots)$ in detail.[49]

3. Let us go back to example 3 about Jones and the stock market and see how schema (18) applies to it. As we saw in III 3, (5) was a true counterfactual. [(5) was "If Jones had not sold his stock, he would have become rich a few weeks later."] In our discussion in V 6 we saw that the sale of Jones's stock was causally irrelevant to the subsequent rise in the stock market. Hence the antecedent of

(5′)   Even if Jones had not sold his stock, there would still have been a rise in the stock market.

is causally irrelevant to its consequent, and thus (5′) is an irrel-semifactual. Now in order to substantiate (5), we do, of course, need information about W (e.g., that Jones was solvent, etc.). We also need the information conveyed by the consequent of (5′), as well as quite a lot of additional information about events and states of affairs that occurred in the (t_A, t_B) interval. We need to know that Jones did not have a financial disaster during that period (in which case a sudden profit could have saved him, but would not have made him rich); that the buying power of the dollar did not change extremely drastically during that interval; that he did not promise any sudden future wealth to his mother-in-law, etc. Now all these events and states of affairs we take to have actually occurred, according to our example. We can use them to substantiate the consequent along the lines of schema (18), since it is clear that they are events (or states of affairs) to which the $\sim A$–A transition (i.e., Jones's keeping his stock rather than selling it) is causally irrelevant, and so such statements describing these events are consequents of appropriate irrel-semifactuals with the same antecedent as (5). Hence they belong among the legitimate premises of (18) when applied to example 3. From these implicit premises, together with the antecedent A, the consequent B indeed follows, and thus (5) qualifies as a true counterfactual on our analysis — and indeed it is.

Notice that if some of the conditions that we have assumed to be operative in (t_A, t_B) are violated (e.g., if Jones went deeply into debt), schema (18) will come out false; but indeed it should — the counterfactual would then be false. Similarly, if his selling the stock was causally relevant to his financial solvency during (t_A, t_B) — for example, if his return on the stock saved him from financial calamity — then we cannot retain his satisfactory economic situation during (t_A, t_B) among the legitimate premises, and then (18) will not come out true. But this is as it should be: the counterfactual cannot be claimed true in such a case. This provides us with a perspective on the functional dependence of the truth value of a counterfactual on the actual course of events in the (t_A, t_B) interval and, thus, with some insight on how the truth value of a counterfactual depends on the actual world — which indeed is one of the things that makes it *about* the actual world in a strong sense, and highlights its empirical character.

X   The Equivalence of the Inferential-Model and the Possible-World-Descriptions Model Analyses

1. Having found the legitimate premises of the (t_A, t_B) interval and having formulated the schema of the inferential model explicitly, let us see how these results look in the possible-world-descriptions model. As we recall from V 4, the initial restriction of $V(A > B, \ldots)$ to the world-range[50] of A reflected a constraint resulting from the presence of L and W among the implicit premises of the inferential model. Now that we have found that the rest of the implicit premises are the members of $CIP(A > B, \ldots)$ — that is, the consequents of irrel-semifactuals and pp-semifactuals with antecedents A whose consequents belong to (t_A, t_B) — we can complete the specification of $V(A > B, \ldots)$ by taking into account the following constraint: All the members of $CIP(A > B, \ldots)$ should be true in all members of $V(A > B, \ldots)$.[51] If we now define the **cip world-range of A for t_B** as the subset of the world-range of A in all the members of which the members of $CIP(A > B, \ldots)$ are true, we can state the result as follows:

Thesis 4.   A counterfactual $A > B$ of the n-d type is true iff B is true in all the members of the cip world-range of A for t_B.

This, then, is the **analysis of counterfactuals in the possible-world-descriptions model.** Consequently, we have found out what an adequate $V(A > B, \ldots)$ would be:

Thesis 5.   In the possible-world-descriptions model, an adequate $V(A > B, \ldots)$ would be the cip world-range of A for t_B.

2. We have used the inferential model and the possible-world-descriptions model side by side throughout this chapter. We have also motivated and stated, explicitly and implicitly, arguments for the equivalence of the two models. Now that we have formulated our results within the frameworks of both models, we can prove this equivalence precisely.

Theorem 1.   The equivalence of the possible-world-descriptions-model
and the inferential-model analyses

Thesis 1, i.e.,

A counterfactual $A > B$ of the n-d type is true iff

(18″) $\{A\} \cup W \cup L \cup \text{CIP}(A > B, \ldots) \to B$

is logically equivalent to thesis 4, i.e.,

A counterfactual $A > B$ of the n-d type is true iff B is true in all
members of the cip world-range of A for t_B.

Proof. We shall prove that

(21) B is true in all members of the cip world-range of A for t_B.

is true iff

(18″) $\{A\} \cup W \cup L \cup \text{CIP}(A > B, \ldots) \to B$

Assume first that (18″) is true. If B were not true in all the possible-
world descriptions of the cip world-range of A for t_B, there would be a
possible-world description u in it in which $\sim B$ was true. Since u belongs
to the cip world-range of A for t_B:

$\{A\} \cup W \cup \text{CIP}(A > B, \ldots) \cup \{\sim B\} \subseteq u$

Hence:

$\{A\} \cup W \cup \text{CIP}(A > B, \ldots) \cup L \cup \{\sim B\}$

is consistent. But this contradicts (18″).

Now assume (21), i.e., that B is true in all the possible-world descriptions of the cip world-range of A for t_B. We shall show that (18″) is true.
If (18″) were not true,

$\{A\} \cup W \cup L \cup \text{CIP}(A > B, \ldots) \cup \{\sim B\}$

would be consistent. Hence there would be an extension u of

$\{A\} \cup W \cup \text{CIP}(A > B, \ldots) \cup \{\sim B\}$

into a set of nonlawlike statements consistent with L and complete.[52] u is
thus a possible-world description. Since W, A, and $\text{CIP}(A > B, \ldots)$ belong to it, u belongs to the cip world-range of A for t_B. Since $\sim B$ is true

in it, $\sim B$ is true in a possible-world description of the cip world-range of A for t_B, which contradicts our assumption. Therefore (18″) is true.

3. The theorem thus shows the equivalence of the results in the two models. Let us abbreviate 'a counterfactual $A > B$ is true' as $T(A > B)$. The criterion for the truth of $T(A > B)$ in the inferential model is (18) [which is tantamount to (18″)], in view of thesis 1 of section IX, to the effect that:

$$T(A > B) \leftrightarrow (18)$$

The criterion for $T(A > B)$ in the possible-world-descriptions model is (21), since thesis 4 was:

$$T(A > B) \leftrightarrow (21)$$

What have we proved above is that

$$(21) \leftrightarrow (18)$$

That is, the two criteria for the truth of such counterfactuals (i.e., the criteria in the two different models) are equivalent. Thus, the theorem shows that a counterfactual $A > B$ (of the n-d type) is true according to the inferential model iff it is true according to the possible-world-descriptions model.

We have seen that the possible-world-descriptions model was quite helpful for heuristic and motivational purposes. We saw that Stalnaker (among others) chose to base his analysis of counterfactuals on the notion of a possible world. Here we have used not possible worlds, but possible-world *descriptions*, and so we are not committed to possible worlds in any way. Heuristic purposes can, as we have seen, be well served by a model that uses possible-world descriptions rather than possible worlds. The former, which we defined explicitly, are ontologically fairly innocuous, in contrast to the latter. So no fundamental notion of possible world has been used in our analysis of counterfactuals. The ontological significance of this point is quite obvious, particularly to those who would not ontologically countenance possibilia.[53]

Since counterfactuals can be understood intuitively both via incomplete implications and via truth in various possible worlds, the possibility of generating two distinct analyses by means of these two rival strategies arises. We have, indeed, appealed to both strategies in our inquiry. However, insofar as the possible-world-descriptions model incorporates the heuristic and motivational advantages of working with possible worlds, our theorem is relevant to this issue, showing the equivalence of the results expressed in the two models. This equivalence enables us to use the two models interchangeably, so as to utilize whatever heuristic or motivational benefits they separately offer. Our policy of appealing to both models in the course of this inquiry has yielded two sets of conditions which, according to the theorem, are equivalent. Moreover, this equivalence should clear the use of the possible-world-descriptions framework of any suspicion of smuggling in possible worlds surreptitiously: the reduction clearly shows that its terminology is innocuous in this respect (relative to the inferential model), that no suspicious implicit ontological presuppositions were added through the back door.

4. More generally, we can show a relation between the schemata of the two models, rather than simply between two particular results in them. We can show that, without specifying what the implicit premises are, any result in the inferential model is expressible in the possible-world-descriptions model:

Theorem 2

> For a given counterfactual $A > B$, B follows from a set of non-lawlike statements (which we call "legitimate premises"), L and A iff B is true in all the possible-world descriptions in which the antecedent and this set of statements are true.[54]

This theorem vindicates our strategy of using the inferential model and the possible-world-descriptions model interchangeably: it guarantees that the solution to the problem of the implicit premises will pave the way for the formulation of the answer in the possible-world-descriptions model. The proof is similar in part to the proof of theorem 1:

Proof

> If a counterfactual $A > B$ fails to fulfill the second condition in the theorem, then B is not true in one of the possible-world descriptions in which the legitimate premises and A are true; hence $\sim B$ is true in it. Thus, $\sim B$ is consistent with the legitimate premises, L, and A; so B does not follow from them (and $A > B$ is thus not true on the inferential schema either).
>
> Conversely, if $A > B$ fails to fulfill the first condition in the theorem, then $\sim B$ is consistent with the legitimate premises, L, and A, and hence an extension of the nonlawlike statements among them into a complete and consistent set of nonlawlike statements (compatible with L) would yield a possible-world description in which B is false (hence $A > B$ would come out false on the schema of the possible-world-descriptions model).

Theorem 2 is larger in scope than theorem 1: whereas theorem 1 yields the equivalence of the specific results we arrived at concerning the truth conditions for counterfactuals, theorem 2 concerns the relations between the two models. That is, it provides a way of translating any results achieved in the first model into results in the second which are proved equivalent; that is, it ensures that any results in the schema of the inferential model can be expressed in a demonstrably equivalent way in the framework of the possible-world-descriptions model.

At the same time, it shows the limits of the affinity between the two models: a method of specifying a set of possible-world descriptions for the truth conditions of counterfactuals in the possible-world-descriptions model need not be expressible in the inferential model if this set of possible-world descriptions cannot be determined by a set of statements they all share; that is, if there is no set of statements such that the specified set of possible-world descriptions comprises all and only those possible-world descriptions which include those statements. Thus, the possible-world-descriptions model is richer, in principle, than the inferential model. We have seen that this extra power is not relevant to our analysis of counterfactuals. But it adds some extra weight to our policy of working with possible-world descriptions as well, without in any way compromising the absence of any implied commitment to possible worlds.

5. Let us define $Q'(A,W,L,t_B, \ldots)$ as the set of all statements shared by all the members of the cip world-range of A for t_B. Then (21) is equivalent to

$$(22) \quad Q'(A,W,L,t_B, \ldots) \rightarrow B$$

since, if B is true in all the members of the cip world-range of A for t_B, it belongs to $Q'(A,W,L,t_B, \ldots)$ and, hence, follows from it. And conversely, if B follows from $Q'(A,W,L,t_B, \ldots)$, then, because of the completeness of all possible-world descriptions, B belongs to and, hence, is true in, all the possible-world descriptions in which $Q'(A,W,L,t_B, \ldots)$ is true; that is, B is true in all the members of the cip world-range of A and t_B.

An interesting set of statements, for a given contrary-to-fact assumption A, is the set of consequents of counterfactuals that have A as their antecedent and have a fixed consequent-time t_B (though their consequents may vary). This set amounts to all the *counterfactual consequents* of A with time t_B; let us call it the **counterfactual span of A for t_B**. It yields the counterfactual force of A for t_B. Let us designate by $\overline{Z}$, for a given set of statements Z, the set of the factual logical consequences of Z, and, by Z^t, the subset of factual members of Z that pertain to time t. Z_T will be the subset of the true statements in Z. Recall that $Q(A,W,L,t_B, \ldots)$ was introduced as the antecedent of (18) of IX 1[55]. Notice that $\overline{Q(A,W,L,t_B, \ldots)}^{t_B}$ is the counterfactual span of A for t_B, according to the inferential model, and $Q'(A,W,L,t_B, \ldots)^{t_B}$ is the counterfactual span of A for t_B according to our results in the possible-world descriptions model [since obviously $\overline{Q'(A,W,L,t_B, \ldots)}^{t_B} = Q'(A,W,L,t_B, \ldots)^{t_B}$]. An interesting feature exhibited by the counterfactual span is that a condition for B's inclusion in it is B's being in the logical closure of a set that does not depend on B at all, but depends only on t_B. This is characteristic of our analysis of counterfactuals: it reflects the result that the implicit premises for the counterfactual $A > B$ do not depend on B, but depend only on t_B. It also reflects the fundamental difference in role between A and B in the truth conditions for the counterfactual $A > B$: B is a consequence of A together with a set of statements that depends not on B, but only on t_B, yet which critically depends on A.

Since (21) is equivalent to (18), (18′) is equivalent to (22), and so

(23) $\overline{Q(A,W,L,t_B, \ldots)}^{t_B} = Q'(A,W,L,t_B, \ldots)^{t_B}$

Hence, the counterfactual spans in the two models are the same. This yields another not surprising aspect of the equivalence between the two models: the counterfactual span of A for t_B is invariant in the two models.

Furthermore: from thesis 5 and the definition of $Q'(A,W,L,t_B, \ldots)$, it is quite clear that

(24) $Q'(A,W,L,t_B, \ldots)_T^{(t_A,t_B)}$

is precisely the set of consequents of true semifactuals with antecedent A and consequent in (t_A,t_B). Thus:

(25) $A > C$ is a true semifactual [where $t_C \subseteq (t_A,t_B)$]
      iff $C \in Q'(A,W,L,t_B, \ldots)_T^{(t_A,t_B)}$.

Or, more generally:

(26) $A > C$ is a true semifactual iff $C \in Q'(Q,W,L,t_B, \ldots)_T$

XI Semifactuals

1. Now, having formulated an answer to the problem of specifying the subsequent legitimate premises for a counterfactual $A > B$ (presented in III 3 and summarized in IX 1 above), let us take a fresh look at the problem. We have seen that a contrary-to-fact assumption has to be considered against a certain portion of the actual-world description of (t_A,t_B). But exactly which portion should this be? Against which partial background of the actual world in (t_A,t_B) is the contrary-to-fact assumption to be evaluated? Which portion of the actual world are we to retain when we evaluate a contrary-to-fact assumption? Which statements in the (t_A,t_B) interval should be considered together with the counterfactual? Interestingly, our conceptual apparatus contains the construction that enables us to answer this question directly. Intuitively it is clear that what we should retain as true when we make a contrary-to-fact assumption are precisely those true statements which would still have been true had the contrary-to-fact assumption been true. The affinity to the actual-world description in the (t_A,t_B) interval which we should preserve is specified precisely by all those statements which would still have been true even if A had been the case rather than $\sim A$. In other words, we should retain from the actual-world description all the statements C of that interval for which the semifactual 'Even if A had been the case, C would still have been the case' is true. Whatever the truth conditions for these semifactuals are, they form the conceptual signal that indicates what part of the actual-world descrip-

tion is to be retained, *by virtue of its still being true,* when a contrary-to-fact assumption is countenanced.

Let us now consider the situation from the perspective of the possible-world-descriptions model. What is common to the possible-world descriptions in $V(A>B, \ldots)$? They are descriptions of courses of events that diverge from the actual course of events by including A rather than $\sim A$, and what they share with each other and with the actual-world description after the divergence time is precisely what would still be true even if A were the case rather than $\sim A$. What should be retained from the actual-world description as a background against which the contrary-to-fact assumption will be evaluated are those statements which would still be true even if the contrary-to-fact assumption were true. They constitute those statements in the actual-world description whose truth value is *invariant* under the $\sim A$–A transition. It seems to me that the intuitive force of these semifactuals as indicators of retention is both compelling and deeply entrenched in our conceptual framework.

Notice that the set of consequents of the semifactuals in question together with W do not yield a complete possible-world description for the period up to (and including) t_B; they serve rather to define a *kind* of possible-world description, a set of possible-world descriptions which are in turn needed for the evaluation of the contrary-to-fact assumption in question and for testing of the counterfactual in question, attesting to its truth just in case its consequent is true in all of them. This is the *role,* the function, of semifactuals: to determine which statements in W_{t_A,t_B} remain true when a contrary-to-fact hypothesis is countenanced: which statements from W_{t_A,t_B} are to be retained in such a case in virtue of their remaining true in spite of the transition. Semifactuals *delimit* the set of possible-world descriptions that should be considered in conjunction with a given contrary-to-fact assumption; they determine the affinity of this set of possible-world descriptions to the actual-world description. Their function, then, is the *demarcation* of that portion of the actual-world description (in the (t_A,t_B) interval) which is *invariant* under the $\sim A$–A transition. As such, they also determine what information from W_{t_A,t_B} should not be retained in all the members of $V(A>B, \ldots)$: the information in those statements which are not consequents of true semifactuals.

We now understand the role of the semifactual construction and how that construction functions in the analysis of counterfactuals. What the members of $V(A>B, \ldots)$ share with the actual-world description in (t_A,t_B) is the set of consequents of true semifactuals with the same antecedent. Thus, we arrive at an analysis of counterfactuals along the following lines:

Thesis 6

> A counterfactual $A>B$ is true iff its consequent is true in all the members of the world-range of A which share with the actual-world description all consequents [belonging to (t_A,t_B)] of true semifactuals with the same antecedent.

This set of members of the world-range of A should, then, be $V(A > B, \ldots)$. Let us call this analysis: **the semifactual analysis of counterfactuals.**

2. It is not surprising that irrel-semifactuals and pp-semifactuals [the consequents of which are preserved among the members of $V(A > B, \ldots)$ in the context of the appropriate counterfactuals] are themselves true semifactuals. The remaining class of semifactuals, those which are neither irrel-semifactuals nor pp-semifactuals, can be characterized as those semifactuals whose antecedents have some negative causal effect on their consequents. In VIII we examined the lottery semifactual (16) and found it false. We also saw that its antecedent has some negative effect on its consequent. Hence it is neither an irrel-semifactual nor a pp-semifactual, but belongs rather to this third group of semifactuals. Hence some such semifactuals are false. Thus, in contrast to the other two groups of semifactuals that we have examined, semifactuals belonging to this third group are not true by virtue of their membership in it. (At the end of this section we will present an example of a true semifactual of this kind.) Such semifactuals, therefore, may be either true or false.

The important feature of these semifactuals (of this third group), however, is that they behave like regular counterfactuals, and have precisely the same analysis and logical structure. For that reason, let us call them **counterfactual-type semifactuals**, or, for short, **con-type semifactuals**. Consequently, their analysis will be the same as that of ordinary counterfactuals. They differ from ordinary counterfactuals only in that their consequents are true. But in contradistinction to the two other kinds of semifactuals, this feature does not differentiate their analysis from that of regular counterfactuals.

That con-type semifactuals fall under our analysis of regular counterfactuals is, again, an empirical hypothesis, which is, of course, open to refutation by counterexamples. But we can throw more light on this thesis and substantiate it in a theoretically more satisfying and, thus, more illuminating way, by examining once again the roles of contrary-to-fact assumptions and counterfactuals. As we saw above, when we evaluate a contrary-to-fact assumption, we consider the possible effects of the transition against a background of the actual course of events, i.e., against a background of those events which are not possible candidates for change as a result of the transition: those whose occurrence is not threatened by the transition, those on which the transition does not have any negative causal effect. As we saw, statements describing all other events are to be suspended.[56] All other statements concerning this new course will have the status of *predictions* in it. Now con-type semifactuals involve consequents on which the transition does have some negative causal effect. Hence their nonoccurrence may well be a possible effect of the transition, and so they are not to be retained in that part of the actual course of events on the background of which possible effects of the transition are to be determined. Thus, in light of the role of contrary-to-fact assumptions, con-type semifactuals are not to be true *as such*. (That this is empirically true — which, as we saw, it is, since there are false con-type semifactuals — reconfirms our thesis about the role of contrary-to-fact assumptions.) They thus have a different status, a different role: they *predict* the occurrence of their consequent-events in the A-course. Some hypothetical predictions yield statements that in actuality happen to be true, thus coinciding with some statements in the description of the actual course of events. Others yield statements that are actually false. But it is clear that con-type semifactuals do not play any privileged role, different from that of regular counterfactuals, because of the truth of their consequents, according to our thesis about the function of contrary-to-fact assumptions. Their role is the same as that of regular counterfactuals; therefore it should come as no surprise that their analysis is the same as that of regular counterfactuals.

3. Consider the following example of a con-type semifactual:

Example 12

> Smith was a security guard at a barn that belonged to a certain agricultural concern. At the time under consideration the barn was full of harvested produce. One hot day at 9:30 P.M. a passenger in a car passing the barn on a nearby road threw a lighted cigarette into the neighboring bushes; later that evening, at 11:00 P.M., a lighted match was thrown in a different place from another passing car. Both the cigarette and the match started small fires which remained small owing to the absence of wind. At 11:30 P.M. a breeze started, and drove both fires toward the barn. Each fire ignited the barn independently of the other. As a result, the harvest, which was stored in one big heap, was completely burned. Now Smith's responsibility included making occasional rounds of the barn area lasting about 20 minutes each. His evening rounds were to be made at 8:00 P.M., 10:00 P.M., and 1:30 A.M. That night he made his round at 8:00 P.M., but failed to make the 10:00 P.M. round. When he arrived at 1:30 A.M., he found the barn already burned to the ground. These facts came out in the investigation conducted by his company. The company's policy was to fire its employees in cases of negligence, but to retain them in one capacity or another if they performed their duties well. Smith's record, up to that time, had been satisfactory. But because he had failed to make his 10:00 P.M. round that night, he was fired.

Now consider the counterfactual

(27) Even if Smith had made his 10:00 P.M. round, the 11:00 P.M. fire would still have occurred.

This semifactual is clearly an irrel-semifactual, since the second cigarette's being tossed out of the car and causing a small fire was causally independent of Smith's making his 10:00 P.M. round. Similarly, the following semifactual is an irrel-semifactual too:

(28)   Even if Smith had made his 10:00 P.M. round, the breeze would still have started to blow at 11:30.

Surely his making or not making the round was entirely causally irrelevant to the occurrence of the breeze. Consequently, the following semifactual is true too:

(29)   Even if Smith had made his 10:00 P.M. round, the breeze would still have caused the 11:00 P.M. fire to ignite the harvested crops.

This is so since the process of the second fire's spreading and igniting the harvest occurred independently of both Smith's skipped round and the first fire. Smith's 10:00 P.M. round would normally take 20 minutes, and, if he had found the first fire, which was still small at that time, his trip would have taken no more than 5 minutes longer — the time required to extinguish the fire. That the second fire and the breeze would still have occurred is guaranteed by the truth of semifactuals (27) and (28). Consequently, (29) is an irrel-semifactual, and hence true. Hence, the following semifactual $A > C$ is true:

(30)   Even if Smith had made his 10:00 P.M. round, the barn would still have burned down.

This is so since, if the antecedent had been true, the second fire and the breeze would still have occurred, and the harvest still would have caught fire [as is guaranteed by irrel-semifactuals (27)–(29)] and would have been destroyed, since it was stored in a single heap. This process would clearly have taken place regardless of the occurrence or nonoccurrence of the 10:00 P.M. round. Hence (30) is a true semifactual by our irrel-&-pp-semifactual analysis (thesis 1 of IX 1) since its consequent follows from the antecedent, W (as outlined above), and the consequents of the appropriate irrel-semifactuals.

Notice, however, that the antecedent of (30) is negatively causally relevant to its consequent, since, if Smith had made his 10:00 P.M. round, he would have been likely to find the first fire and extinguish it. Since this fire did in fact eventually ignite the harvest, Smith's round might well have eliminated one of the causes of the barn's fire. Hence (30) is not an irrel-semifactual or a pp-semifactual, but rather a con-type semifactual. Thus, we see how a true con-type semifactual fits our analysis of counterfactuals according to the irrel-&-pp-semifactual analysis, as was required by our conclusion that con-type semifactuals have the same analysis as regular counterfactuals.

4. At this stage, the following two questions arise: first, in thesis 6 we analyzed counterfactuals in terms of semifactuals; but we had previously

(in thesis 1) given an account in terms of irrel-semifactuals and pp-semifactuals which was substantiated via the "pigeon-hole" argument-net of examples and counterexamples and the role of contrary-to-fact assumptions. What, then, is the relation between the two analyses? Are they compatible with each other? Do they entail each other?

Secondly, the semifactual analysis of counterfactuals raises a serious problem. On the semifactual analysis, the analysis of any counterfactual involves various semifactuals, among which, in general, there will be con-type semifactuals, since we included the consequents of true con-type semifactuals among the statements to be retained in all members of $V(A > B, \ldots)$. But con-type semifactuals themselves have the same analysis as regular counterfactuals. The analysis of counterfactuals, then, relies on the use of con-type semifactuals, which in turn require the same analysis. Thus, determination of the truth value of a counterfactual requires determination of the truth values of various con-type semifactuals, which in turn requires determination of the truth values of con-type semifactuals once again, and so on. Are we drawn into an infinite regress? Is this analysis defensible? Is it not circular? Is it not the same type of infinite regress that Goodman was drawn into? (See 1 II.)

These questions are interconnected, and we will turn to them now.

XII   The Semifactual Analysis versus the Irrel-&-pp-semifactual Analysis

1. As we have seen in the last section, con-type semifactuals have the same analysis as regular counterfactuals. Thus, their analysis according to the inferential model — the irrel-&-pp-semifactual analysis of thesis 1 [see (18′), section IX] — can be expressed as follows:

Thesis 7

(31)   A con-type semifactual $A > C$ is true iff $Q(A, W, L, t_C, \ldots) \to C$.

In thesis 6 we provided a semifactual analysis of counterfactuals according to which a counterfactual $A > B$ is true iff B is true in all members of the world-range of A in which the consequents of all true semifactuals with antecedent A, whose consequents are in (t_A, t_B), are true. By theorem 2, this is equivalent to:

Thesis 8.   A counterfactual $A > B$ is true iff

$$(32) \quad \{A\} \cup W \cup L \cup \left\{ \begin{array}{l} \text{the set of consequents } C \text{ of true} \\ \text{semifactuals of the form } A > C, \text{ with} \\ t_C \subseteq (t_A, t_B) \end{array} \right\} \to B$$

The irrel-&-pp-semifactual analysis of counterfactuals, however, of thesis 1, yielded that a counterfactual $A > B$ is true iff

(18) $\{A\}\ \cup\ W\ \cup\ L\ \cup\ \left\{\begin{array}{l}\text{the set of consequents } C \text{ of}\\ \text{irrel-semifactuals and pp-semifactuals}\\ \text{with antecedent } A, \text{ where } t_C \subseteq (t_A, t_B)\end{array}\right\} \to B$

We therefore have two distinct analyses for the analysand 'A counterfactual $A > B$ is true', which we abbreviated to '$T(A > B)$' in X 3. These are the irrel-&-pp-semifactual analysis of thesis 1, which criterion (18) provides, and the semifactual analysis of thesis 6, which criterion (32) provides. The question therefore arises: What is the relation between these two analyses, between these two criteria? We can present the following answer to this question:

Theorem 3. The semifactual weak equivalence theorem:

> The irrel-&-pp-semifactual analysis implies that the two criteria — those of (18) and (32) — are equivalent.

We will now prove this theorem. Then, in the following subsection, we will explain the proof informally and discuss the theorem.

Proof

> Notice that the set of true semifactuals with antecedent A is exhaustively and exclusively divided into irrel-semifactuals and pp-semifactuals on the one hand, and true con-type semifactuals on the other. Thus, the set of consequents of true semifactuals of the type mentioned in the right-hand part of the union in (32) can be exhaustively and exclusively divided into the set of consequents of the appropriate irrel-semifactuals and pp-semifactuals, and the set of consequents of the appropriate true con-type semifactuals. Hence, (32) is equivalent to

$$\{A\}\ \cup\ W\ \cup\ L\ \cup\ \left\{\begin{array}{l}\text{the set of conse-}\\ \text{quents } C \text{ of irrel-}\\ \text{semifactuals and}\\ \text{pp-semifactuals}\\ \text{of the form } A > C,\\ \text{where } t_C \subseteq (t_A, t_B)\end{array}\right\}\ \cup\ \left\{\begin{array}{l}\text{the set of con-}\\ \text{sequents of true}\\ \text{con-type}\\ \text{semifactuals of}\\ \text{the form } A > C\\ \text{where } t_C \subseteq (t_A, t_B)\end{array}\right\} \to B$$

Hence, according to the definition of $Q(A, W, L, t_B, \ldots)$ in section IX 1, (32) is also equivalent[57] to:

(33) $Q(A, W, L, t_B, \ldots)\ \cup\ \left\{\begin{array}{l}\text{the set of consequents of}\\ \text{true con-type semifactuals}\\ \text{of the form } A > C, \text{ where}\\ t_C \subseteq (t_A, t_B)\end{array}\right\} \to B$

For the sake of brevity, we will call the second part of the union in the antecedent of (33) **CCS**$(A > B, \ldots)$ (for Consequents of true Con-type Semifactuals, etc.).

We will get a formula equivalent to (33) if, instead of the left part of its antecedent, we take its logical closure.[58] Thus, (33) is equivalent to:

(34) $\overline{Q(A,W,L,t_B, \ldots)} \cup CCS(A>B, \ldots) \rightarrow B$

Because of thesis 7, the consequent of a true con-type semifactual $A>C$ belongs to the counterfactual span of A for t_C, which is $\overline{Q(A,W,L,t_B, \ldots)}\,{}^{t_C}$.[59] Hence:

(35) $CCS(A>B, \ldots) \subseteq \cup \; \overline{Q(A,W,L,t_x, \ldots)}^{t_x}$
$ t_x \subseteq (t_A, t_B)$

But clearly, if $t_x \subseteq (t_A, t_B)$, then:

$\overline{Q(A,W,L,t_x, \ldots)} \subseteq \overline{Q(A,W,L,t_B, \ldots)}$

and also

$\overline{Q(A,W,L,t_x, \ldots)}^{t_x} \subseteq \overline{Q(A,W,L,t_x, \ldots)}$

hence, for each $t_x \subseteq (t_A, t_B)$:

$\overline{Q(A,W,L,t_x, \ldots)}^{t_x} \subseteq \overline{Q(A,W,L,t_B, \ldots)}$

Hence:

(36) $\cup \; \overline{Q(A,W,L,t_x, \ldots)}^{t_x} \subseteq \overline{Q(A,W,L,t_B, \ldots)}$
$t_x \subseteq (t_A, t_B)$

By (35) and (36):

(36′) $CCS(A>B, \ldots) \subseteq \overline{Q(A,W,L,t_B, \ldots)}$

Hence (34), and consequently (32), are equivalent to[60]

$\overline{Q(A,W,L,t_B, \ldots)} \rightarrow B$

which is equivalent to

$Q(A,W,L,t_B, \ldots) \rightarrow B$

which is just (18′), which is equivalent to (18). Hence (32) is equivalent to (18). Q.E.D.

2. The semifactual weak equivalence theorem can be viewed in the following way: for $T(A>B)$ (which is our abbreviation for 'a counterfactual

$A > B$ is true') we had two analyses: the irrel-&-pp-semifactual analysis of thesis 1, which we have attempted to establish in several ways, which amounts to: $T(A > B) \leftrightarrow (18)$, and which thus yields (18) as a criterion for $T(A > B)$; and the semifactual analysis (theses 6, 8), according to which: $T(A > B) \leftrightarrow (32)$, thus yielding (32) as a criterion. The weak equivalence of theorem 3, which we have just proved, amounts to

(37) $\quad [T(A > B) \leftrightarrow (18)] \rightarrow [(18) \leftrightarrow (32)]$

That is, the first analysis guarantees that the two proposed criteria are equivalent. This is a *weak equivalence result*, which guarantees that the two proposed criteria, and thus the two analyses, are in accordance with each other.[61] Now the semifactual weak equivalence theorem together with the irrel-&-pp-semifactual analysis yield:

$\quad (18) \leftrightarrow (32)$

which expresses the equivalence of the criteria of the two analyses, and thereby the equivalence of the two analyses.

This result seems to allow us extra confidence in the viability of our approach: we proposed two different analyses of counterfactuals, stemming from two independent motivations. Each had strong independent arguments in its favor. We have now shown a weak equivalence result between them.

The explanation for the weak equivalence of the two criteria is that the consequents of true con-type semifactuals are none other than the logical consequences of the implicit premises plus A. In other words [see the definition of $CCS(A > B, \ldots)$ in (33)],[62]

$\quad CCS(A > B, \ldots) \subseteq \overline{Q(A, W, L, t_B, \ldots)}.$

This can readily be seen: in our first analysis (the irrel-&-pp-semifactual analysis of thesis 1), we gathered the consequents of the appropriate irrel-semifactuals and pp-semifactuals to serve as legitimate premises. As thesis 8, which is a reformulation of the semifactual analysis (of thesis 6), reveals, this latter analysis shares these legitimate premises, together with the other implicit premises W and L, with the first analysis; but, unlike the irrel-and-pp-semifactual analysis, it also includes the consequents of the appropriate true con-type semifactuals as additional legitimate premises. [This can be seen clearly by comparing (18') and (33).][63] These, however, being consequents of semifactuals that behave like regular counterfactuals (which con-type semifactuals are), are all (according to the irrel-&-pp-semifactual analysis) logical consequences of the rest of the implicit premises — those which the two analyses share. The difference in the two analyses lies, then, in that the implicit premises according to the semifactual analysis include, in addition to the implicit premises of the irrel-&-pp-semifactuals analysis, some of the logical consequences these premises yield when taken together with A. Thus, the logical closures of the antecedents of the inferential schema according to the two analyses are the same: so they share the set of consequents that pertain to time t_B (i.e., the counterfactual span of A and t_B which they both yield); therefore the two analyses also share the set of counterfactuals they determine as true.

The answers to the two questions we asked about the semifactual analysis of counterfactuals are now forthcoming. We saw that the two analyses of counterfactuals are compatible, in view of the weak equivalence result. We can now see how the semifactual analysis of counterfactuals fares vis-à-vis the danger of infinite regress. We did not have this problem with the irrel-&-pp-semifactual analysis, since we planned to provide independent analyses of these two kinds of semifactuals — irrel-semifactuals and pp-semifactuals. But since the semifactual analysis is weakly equivalent to the irrel-&-pp-semifactual analysis, the problem of infinite regress which the semifactual analysis faced can now be regarded as moot; for that analysis is (weakly) equivalent to an analysis that does *not* suffer from infinite regress. Thus, the semifactual analysis differs from the irrel-&-pp-semifactual analysis only in having the consequents of con-type semifactuals as *additional* implicit premises, and these statements, which posed the problem of infinite regress, are logical consequences of the *other* implicit premises, taken together with A [see (36')], and, thus, are *redundant* in the inferential schema and need not be provided with an independent analysis.

3. The difference between the irrel-&-pp-semifactual analysis and the semifactual analysis — best expressed in the contrast between formulations (18') and (33), and amounting to the occurrence of $CCS(A > B, \ldots)$ in (33) only — is illuminatingly related to the relation between the irrel-&-pp-semifactual analysis and the possible-world-descriptions analysis of thesis 4, which we proved equivalent in theorem 1. Above, the irrel-&-pp-semifactual analysis was expressed as

(18') $\quad Q(A, W, L, t_B, \ldots) \rightarrow B$

and the possible-world-descriptions analysis was expressed as

(22) $\quad Q'(A, W, L, t_B, \ldots) \rightarrow B$

where $Q'(A, W, L, t_B, \ldots)$ was the set of all statements shared by all the members of the set $V(A > B, \ldots)$ [that is, the cip world-range of A and t_B;[64] see above, X 1, particularly thesis 5, and section X 5, particularly (22)]. Since (following theorem 1) (18') is equivalent to (22),

(38) $\quad \overline{Q(A, W, L, t_B, \ldots)}^{-L} = \overline{Q'(A, W, L, t_B, \ldots)}$

where, if E is a set of statements, E^{-L} is E minus all the lawlike statements it includes. Since $Q(A, W, L, t_B, \ldots)$, and hence $\overline{Q(A, W, L, t_B, \ldots)}$, include L, but $Q'(A, W, L, t_B, \ldots)$, and hence $\overline{Q'(A, W, L, t_B, \ldots)}$, do not include any lawlike statements [since the members of $Q'(A, W, L, t_B, \ldots)$

are members of possible-world descriptions], we must strip $\overline{Q(A,W,L,t_B, \ldots)}$ of its lawlike statements to get $\overline{Q'(A,W,L,t_B, \ldots)}$; hence $Q(A,W,L,t_B, \ldots)^{-L}$ in (38). Notice, however, that $Q'(A,W,L,t_B, \ldots)$ is logically closed (for factual statements, in view of its definition and the completeness for factual statements of possible-world descriptions; see II 2), whereas $Q(A,W,L,t_B, \ldots)$ is not, in general, logically closed. Hence, in general,

(39) $Q'(A,W,L,t_B, \ldots) = Q(A,W,L,t_B, \ldots)^{-L}$

is false. Of course, $Q(A,W,L,t_B, \ldots)^{-L}$ minus A is nothing but the set of legitimate premises for $A > B$. Thus, the set of the legitimate premises for $A > B$ plus A is *not* in general the set of statements shared by all members of $V(A > B, \ldots)$. Rather, from (38):

(40) $Q'(A,W,L,t_B, \ldots) = \overline{Q(A,W,L,t_B, \ldots)}^{-L}$

and, thus, the set of statements shared by all members of $V(A > B, \ldots)$ is generally larger than the set of the legitimate premises for $A > B$ plus A. The set of the legitimate premises plus A, then, though shared by the members of $V(A > B, \ldots)$, does not include all the statements those members have in common. But statements shared by all members of $V(A > B, \ldots)$, which do not count among the legitimate premises plus A, are among the logical consequences of the union of the legitimate premises plus A with L.

Because of the equivalence of the irrel-&-pp-semifactual analysis and the semifactual analysis, which follows from thesis 1 and theorem 3, we have [see (18') and (33)]:

$$\overline{Q(A,W,L,t_B, \ldots)} = \overline{Q(A,W,L,t_B, \ldots) \cup CCS(A > B, \ldots)}$$

that is[65]:

(41) $CCS(A > B, \ldots) \subseteq \overline{Q(A,W,L,t_B, \ldots)}$

The source of the problematics of the equivalence of the irrel-&-pp-semifactual analysis and the semifactual analysis was that

(42) $CCS(A > B, \ldots) \not\subseteq Q(A,W,L,t_B, \ldots)$

in the strong sense that

(43) $CCS(A > B, \ldots) \cap Q(A,W,L,t_B, \ldots) = \phi$

since con-type semifactuals, irrel-semifactuals, and pp-semifactuals are mutually disjoint groups. What follows, then, from (41) and (43) is that

(44) $CCS(A > B, \ldots) \subseteq \overline{Q(A,W,L,t_B, \ldots)} - Q(A,W,L,t_B, \ldots)$

or [from (40), and since the members of CCS($A > B$, . . .) are nonlawlike statements]:

(45) CCS($A > B$, . . .) $\subseteq$ $Q'(A, W, L, t_B$, . . .) $-$ $Q(A, W, L, t_B$, . . .)

Thus, the consequents of the appropriate con-type semifactuals are logical consequents of $Q(A, W, L, t_B$, . . .) though they do not belong to it. The difference between the irrel-&-pp-semifactual analysis and the semifactual analysis [which is expressed in the difference between (18′) and (33)] is thus reflected in the relation between (18′) and (25), which express the criteria of the irrel-&-pp-semifactual analysis and the possible-world-descriptions analysis, respectively. According to (45), the set CCS($A > B$, . . .), which is what the difference between the irrel-&-pp-semifactuals analysis and the semifactual analysis amounts to, is included in the difference between the antecedents of the criteria of the possible-world-descriptions analysis and the irrel-&-pp-semifactual analysis, respectively, which were proved equivalent.

The set $Q'(A, W, L, t_B$, . . .) $- Q(A, W, L, t_B$, . . .) is quite interesting in that CCS($A > B$, . . .) is included in it. Notice that none of the members of this set is a consequent in (t_A, t_B) of an irrel-semifactual or a pp-semifactual with antecedent A, since these are all in $Q(A, W, L, t_B$, . . .). But since every true member C of this set which pertains to (t_A, t_B) immediately satisfies the condition on B in (22), $A > C$ is a true semifactual, and so a true con-type semifactual. Hence we reach the following result[66]:

The CCS($A > B$, . . .) analysis:

(46) CCS($A > B$, . . .) =
$(Q'(A, W, L, t_B$, . . .) $-$ $Q(A, W, L, t_B$, . . .$))_{T^{(t_A, t_B)}}$

or [by (40)],

(47) CCS($A > B$, . . .) =
$(\overline{Q(A, W, L, t_B, \ldots)} -$ $Q(A, W, L, t_B$, . . .$))_{T^{(t_A, t_B)}}$

Thus, the problematic set CCS($A > B$, . . .) is exactly the set of true non-lawlike logical consequences of $Q(A, W, L, t_B$, . . .) not themselves in $Q(A, W, L, t_B$, . . .) whose times are in (t_A, t_B).

4. We can now tie up some loose ends. On the one hand, we saw that semifactuals function in such a way as to demarcate exactly those statements in (t_A, t_B) which are common to the actual-world description and the members of $V(A > B$, . . .). We also saw that the set of semifactuals divides into three groups: irrel-semifactuals, pp-semifactuals, and con-type semifactuals, and we saw that, whereas all irrel-semifactuals and pp-semifactuals are true, con-type semifactuals may be true or false. On the other hand, we argued above (in VI and VIII 3) that true statements

in (t_A, t_B) which describe events in some way negatively causally affected by the antecedent, should not be retained *as such* (that is, on the basis of fitting this category) among the subsequent legitimate premises $g(A > B, \ldots)$, even if they are cotenable with the antecedent. Let us call this set of statements $\text{CNR}(A > B, \ldots)$ [for true statements in (t_A, t_B) that are Cotenable with A but with some Negative causal Relevance]. (Clearly, none of them can be a consequent of an irrel-semifactual or a pp-semifactual.) By comparing, then, the members of $\text{CNR}(A > B, \ldots)$ with the set of consequents of true con-type semifactuals [which is a subset of $\text{CNR}(A > B, \ldots)$], we see that our first result concerning the function of semifactuals vindicates the second [regarding the noninclusion of $\text{CNR}(A > B, \ldots)$ among the legitimate premises]: Our analysis of the role of semifactuals yields that the refusal to retain the members of $\text{CNR}(A > B, \ldots)$ *as a group* was necessary; only members that are consequents of *true* con-type semifactuals with the same antecedent should be shared by the actual-world description and the members of $V(A > B, \ldots)$, and only *some* of the members of $\text{CNR}(A > B, \ldots)$ are indeed consequents of true con-type semifactuals, whereas others are consequents of *false* con-type semifactuals. Those statements which are consequents of false con-type semifactuals (even if cotenable with A) should *not* be retained, on the semifactual analysis.

We can further clarify this point. A statement C is cotenable with the antecedent A provided C might still have been true had A been the case. In Goodman's words: "A is cotenable with S . . . if it is not the case that S would not be true if A were".[67] This amounts to:

$$C \text{ is cotenable with } A \text{ iff } A > \sim C \text{ is false.}$$

Now among the statements in (t_A, t_B) to which the A-event bears some negative causal relevance are some that are consequents of true con-type semifactuals and thus, of course, cotenable with the antecedent A. In (t_A, t_B) there are also true statements that are *not* consequents of true semifactuals with antecedent A, but are such that the counterfactual $A > \sim C$ is false too. They are therefore also cotenable with A. Of course, A bears some negative causal relevance to them as well. This latter group of statements C, then, fulfills the condition:

$$\sim(A > C) \ \& \ \sim(A > \sim C)$$

(We shall discuss an example of this sort in 3 I 2.) Not only are such statements not ruled out by our analysis, in either its irrel-&-pp-semifactual version or its semifactual version; that there are such statements is an obvious consequence of our analysis, if one does not assume the world to be overly deterministic.

According to the line of thought developed above, those statements in the (t_A, t_B) interval which are consequents of true con-type semifactuals (with antecedent A) are not among the subsequent legitimate premises for $A > B$. They are, however, shared by all members of $V(A > B, \ldots)$. This should not come as a surprise: we have seen that, when it comes to nonlawlike statements, the set of statements shared by the members of $V(A > B, \ldots)$, i.e., $Q'(A > B, \ldots)$, is larger than the set of legitimate premises plus A, i.e., $Q(A > B, \ldots)^{-L}$. This is because $Q'(A > B, \ldots) = \overline{Q(A > B, \ldots)}^{-L}$ [cf. (40), this section, 3, above], while $Q(A > B, \ldots)$ is not logically closed.[68] But, as shown by the weak equivalence theorem 3, the set of statements $Q'(A > B, \ldots) - Q(A > B, \ldots)^{-L}$ belongs to the logical closure of $Q(A > B, \ldots)$, and it is therefore *redundant* (though not mistaken) to include it among the legitimate premises. This point has crucial implications for the problem of infinite regress which threatens the viability of analyzing counterfactuals (see 3 II, below); for this set, $Q'(A > B, \ldots) - Q(A > B, \ldots)^{-L}$, resists independent analysis. Yet it is its *redundancy* relative to the rest of the set of implicit premises which makes it possible to extract an adequate analysis (the irrel-&-pp-semifactual analysis) from the semifactual analysis by deleting the members of this set from the legitimate premises, thereby avoiding infinite regress, as we saw above. It is thus instructive to notice that it is assured, for the set of true statements C in (t_A, t_B) to which A is in some way negatively causally relevant, that $A > C$ is a con-type semifactual, but it is *not* guaranteed that $A > C$ will be a *true* con-type semifactual *even if* C is cotenable with A.[69]

5. Example 13. We now return to example 12 of XI 3. Recall that we established [in (30)] that even if Smith had made his 10 P.M. trip, the barn would still have been gutted by fire. In this case nothing would have been left to guard, and Smith's job — guarding the barn — would have been eliminated. Smith, we recall, was fired because he failed to make his 10 P.M. round. The company's policy, however, was not to fire its employees unless they were negligent, and, when they were not negligent, to transfer them to other positions if they could not be kept in their old positions. Hence the following counterfactual $A > B$ is true:

(48) If Smith had made his 10 P.M. round (on that particular day), he would have been transferred to another job with the same company (after a certain time).

Thus, after being notified about the fire, the company would have realized that Smith no longer had a job to do and would have assigned him a new job some time thereafter.

We substantiated counterfactual $A > B$ of (48) by using (30): $A > C$ of (30), however, was a con-type semifactual, and thus our substantiation of (48) was along the lines of the semifactual analysis of counterfactuals, according to which the consequents of true con-type semifactuals [with consequents in (t_A, t_B)] belong among the legitimate premises. The semifactual weak equivalence theorem (theorem 3), however, proved that the two analyses — the semifactual analysis and the irrel-&-pp-semifactual analysis — were weakly equivalent. The point of the proof was that the inclusion of the consequents of true con-type semifactuals among the legitimate premises was redundant since they were consequents of the other implicit premises (plus the antecedent). Consequently, a counterfactual that is substantiated on one analysis ought to be capable of substantiation on the other.

In our example we used the consequent of (30) in order to substantiate the counterfactual (48). But the consequent of (30) followed (as we saw in example 12) from its own implicit premises (and A) and, since (30) and (48) share the same antecedent, they share (at least) the same implicit premises that are not subsequent legitimate premises. But since t_C is earlier than t_B,[70] and since $A > C$ and $A > B$ share the same antecedent, the statements in the (t_A, t_C) interval to which A is causally irrelevant or purely positively causally relevant qualify as legitimate premises in the inferential schema of $A > C$ just as much as in that of $A > B$. Hence the implicit premises (plus the antecedent) of $A > B$ will include those of $A > C$, and, since C followed from the former, it will follow from the latter as well. Hence we are allowed to use C in the irrel-&-pp-semifactual analysis of $A > B$ as a consequent of the implicit premises sanctioned by it (and A), and thus the above substantiation of C indicates that the irrel-&-pp-semifactual analysis of $A > B$ is satisfied as well. C is a consequence of the implicit premises (and A) in the irrel-&-pp-semifactual analysis of $A > B$, and thus need not occur among them, without any loss incurred thereby to the inferential schema of $A > B$. Thus we see that both the semifactual analysis and the irrel-&-pp-semifactual analysis are capable of substantiating $A > B$, which vindicates our semifactual weak-equivalence theorem. In particular, we have seen in example 13 a case of a consequent of an appropriate true con-type semifactual which is included in the logical closure of the implicit premises (and A) of the irrel-&-pp-semifactual analysis, which makes it redundant as an explicit premise thereof.

XIII   Toward a Probabilistic Analysis of Irrel-Semifactuals

1. In the foregoing account an attempt was made to resolve the problem of the subsequent legitimate premises of counterfactuals or, alternatively, to provide the truth conditions for counterfactuals of the n-d type. The upshot was, however, a reduction of these problems to an analysis, not yet provided, of irrel-semifactuals and pp-semifactuals. Even though, formally, these two kinds of counterfactuals fit our general schema, an independent characterization of which counterfactuals belong to these two groups is necessary in order to make our over-all effort amount to more than a reduction of a large group of counterfactuals to one that is smaller, yet still mysterious. Our previous analysis assures us that counterfactuals of these two kinds are true, but it does not tell us how to determine for any particular counterfactual whether it belongs to one of these two kinds, which is necessary for the assessment of counterfactuals *not* of these kinds (as well as for the assessments of counterfactuals of these two kinds). As we saw, if we were to proceed according to the semifactual analysis, without further ado about semifactuals, we would fall into an infinite regress,

a recurring threat on the road to providing an adequate analysis of counter-factuals. We avoided this regress by distinguishing the group of true con-type semifactuals from the group of irrel-semifactuals and pp-semifactuals (which cover the whole range of true semifactuals) and by claiming the redundancy of the first group. But such a move will be helpful in practice, when we want to use the analysis in assessing a particular counterfactual, only if there is a way to tell them apart — a way of independently charac-terizing the irrel-semifactuals and the pp-semifactuals. It is neccessary, therefore, that an independent analysis be provided for the concepts of causal irrelevance and of purely positive causal relevance, which charac-terize these two types of semifactuals.

We have seen that these two groups of semifactuals are fundamentally different from other counterfactuals in a variety of respects. First, their role is to provide the background on which the effects of the $\sim A$–A transi-tion (called for by the contrary-to-fact assumption A) are to be evaluated, whereas the role of the other counterfactuals is predictive in character. Furthermore, all irrel-semifactuals and pp-semifactuals are true, a feature which certainly does not characterize the group of all other counterfac-tuals, or any other category of counterfactuals that we have examined. And lastly, both irrel-semifactuals and pp-semifactuals are characterizable by variants of the relation of causal relevance between their antecedents and consequents — again, a feature that is not shared by any other category of counterfactuals we have examined. These features clearly set these counterfactuals apart. In chapters 4 and 5 we shall attempt an indepen-dent analysis of these counterfactuals in probabilistic terms. In the rest of this section we will comment on aspects of such an analysis, which will enable us to tie up some loose ends from our previous discussion. We shall thus put aside pp-semifactuals for a moment and make a first step toward the analysis of irrel-semifactuals, which will be continued in chapter 4.

2. Consider an irrel-semifactual $A > C$. We seek conditions under which the A-event is causally irrelevant to the C-event, and expect causal rele-vance to be mirrored by probabilistic characteristics. In cases of causal ir-relevance, we expect the probability of the occurrence of the C-event to be unaffected by the occurrence or nonoccurrence of the A-event. Whether the A-event or the $\sim A$-event occurred makes no difference to the occurrence of the C-event. This implies that the conditional probability of C, given the previous history W, is unaffected by information as to whether the A-event or the $\sim A$-event occurred.[71] We will therefore at-tempt to capture causal relevance by such a condition. Thus, the condi-tional probability of C on the basis of A and W is the same as the condi-tional probability of C on the basis of $\sim A$ and W. That is, the probability of C on the basis of W is unchanged if we add either A or $\sim A$ as additional evidence. Therefore, we can suggest the following: A semifactual $A > C$ is an irrel-semifactual iff

(52) $P(C/A \ \& \ W) = P(C/A \ \& \ W)$

Some comments are in order. We present this condition in terms of equiprobability. We do not commit ourselves to any particular metric, and can work with a qualitative interpretation of probability. Notice that a qualitative interpretation can involve the relation "greater than" between conditional probabilities, as well as that of equality. Although we do not need this relation in our explication of irrel-semifactuals, we will need it for the explication of pp-semifactuals.

Secondly, we did not specify the probability function. In chapter 4 we shall address the issue of analyzing the notion of causal irrelevance and also sketch the notion of probability suitable for such an analysis.

Thirdly, it should be noted that, although we motivated and informally defined irrel-semifactuals in causal terms, no causal terms occur in condition (52). So, strictly speaking, we reduce the counterfactual construction *not* to causal concepts, but rather to the concept of probability. Our probability conditions stand on their own, although they are designed to capture causality-related concepts and although their adequacy for our analysis of irrel-semifactuals will indeed be tested against the suitable conception of causal relevance. This applies to the probabilistic analysis of pp-semifactuals as well.

Finally, the above analysis of irrel-semifactuals is only a first approximation. In fact, the above condition is necessary, but not sufficient, for causal irrelevance. Before arriving at a complete analysis, further complications will have to be dealt with; they will be discussed in chapter 4.

3. At this stage it will be helpful to have another look at the problem we raised in II. We discussed the subsequent-legitimate-premises function $g(A > B, \ldots)$, which was $f\text{-}(A > B, \ldots)$, the legitimate-premises function, with range limited to (t_A, t_B). The value of the function $g(A > B, \ldots)$, the set of the legitimate premises pertaining to (t_A, t_B), turned out to be the set of statements to which the antecedent A is causally irrelevant or purely positively causally relevant. As we indicated in VIII and above, the analysis of these two relations is to be given in probabilistic terms (see chapters 4 and 5). The arguments and the form of the i-p function are thus determined by, among other things, the analysis of these two relations. Formula (52), which was a first approximation of a condition for causal irrelevance, yielded A, W, and C as the arguments of the conditional probability function. As we shall see below, these are indeed the arguments of the probability function to be used in the full-fledged conditions for causal irrelevance and purely positive causal relevance. These full-fledged conditions will, therefore, via this probability function, have the form of 3-place relations among C, A, and W, and will determine when A is causally irrelevant to C on the basis of W, or when A is purely positively causally relevant to C on the basis of W. Let us therefore symbolize these two relations as $R_{cir}(C, A, W)$ and $R_{ppcr}(C, A, W)$ and, for precision, replace 'W' with '$W_{\bar{t}C}$'. We can now, therefore, represent $g(A > B, \ldots)$ as:

(53) $g(A > B, \ldots) =$
$\{C \mid C \in W_{t_A, t_B} \ \& \ R_{cir}(C, A, W) \lor R_{ppcr}(C, A, W)\}$

This form of the function of the subsequent legitimate premises will become more explicit (see 5 V) once we plug in the probabilistic conditions that determine the relations R_{cir} and R_{ppcr}. It is now clear that we have discovered the arguments of this function: they are A and $W_{\bar{t}_B}$.[72] Hence:

(54) $g(A > B, \ldots) = g(A, W_{\bar{t}_B})$

From thesis 2, sec. IX, and (54) we also have:

(54') $CIP(A > B, \ldots) = CIP(A, W_{\bar{t}_B})$

In section IX (see theses 2 and 3) we expressed the i-p function $f(A > B, \ldots)$ in terms of $g(A > B, \ldots)$ as follows:

(55) $f(A > B, \ldots) = W \cup L \cup g(A > B, \ldots)$

Consequently, by (54), we now have

(56) $f(A > B, \ldots) = W \cup L \cup g(A, W_{\bar{t}_B})$

where $g(A, W_{\bar{t}_B})$ is given by (53). Hence it follows (taking L as a constant)[73] that

(57) $f(A > B, \ldots) = f(A, W_{\bar{t}_B})$

Moving to the legitimate-premises function $f\text{-}(A > B, \ldots)$, we recall (see II 3) that:

(4) $f\text{-}(A > B, \ldots) = f(A > B, \ldots) - L$

Hence [with (56)]:

(56') $f\text{-}(A > B, \ldots) = W \cup g(A, W_{\bar{t}_B})$

and therefore:

(57') $f\text{-}(A > B, \ldots) = f\text{-}(A, W_{\bar{t}_B})$

We have thus found the arguments of the i-p function for counterfactuals of the n-d type, as well as its form — up to the determination of the relations R_{cir} and R_{ppcr}. We can now, therefore, express the implicit-premises function in a more complete form [from (53), (56), (57)]:

(58) $f(A, W_{\bar{t}_B}) = W \cup L \cup \{C \mid C \in W_{t_A, t_B}$
         $\& \ [R_{cir}(C, A, W) \lor R_{ppcr}(C, A, W)]\}$

It is thus clear that we now have a solution to the problem of the i-p function for the (t_A, t_B) interval (provided we can unpack R_{cir} and R_{ppcr}), and that we have also found out what its arguments are, which were the problems we set for ourselves in section II.

As we recall from IX 1, $Q(A,W,L,t_B, \ldots)$ was defined as the antecedent of (18) or $\{A\} \cup W \cup L \cup g(A>B, \ldots)$. Thus:

(59) $Q(A,W,L,t_B, \ldots) = \{A\} \cup W \cup L \cup g(A,W_{\bar{t}_B})$

and so the only arguments of $Q(A,W,L,t_B, \ldots)$ are A and $W_{\bar{t}_B}$ (we are again taking L as a constant):

(60) $Q(A,W,L,t_B, \ldots) = Q(A,W_{\bar{t}_B})$

In XII 3 we found that

(40) $Q'(A,W,L,t_B, \ldots) = \overline{Q(A,W,L,t_B, \ldots)}^{-L}$

Hence the arguments of $Q'(A,W,L,t_B, \ldots)$ are the same as those of $Q(A,W,L,t_B, \ldots)$. Thus, by (60):

(61) $Q'(A,W,L,t_B, \ldots) = Q'(A,W_{\bar{t}_B})$

From thesis 5 of XI, the definition of $Q'(A,W,L,t_B, \ldots)$ in X 5, and (61) we get:[74]

(62) $V(A>B, \ldots) = \left\{ u \;\middle|\; \begin{array}{l} u \text{ is a possible-} \\ \text{world description} \end{array} \text{ and } Q'(A,W_{\bar{t}_B}) \subseteq u \right\}$

Hence:

(63) $V(A>B, \ldots) = V(A,W_{\bar{t}_B})$

Lastly, from (60) and (47) of XII 3, we have:

(64) $CCS(A>B, \ldots) = CCS(A,W_{\bar{t}_B})$

Thus, on the basis of the claim that the arguments of the probability function are as displayed in (52), and with the expectation of unpacking R_{cir} and R_{ppcr} in terms of such a probability function, we have provided the arguments as well as the form for all the functions that we have used in our discussion in this chapter.

4. We are now also in a position to provide a partial answer to the problem we posed in II 1, of how counterfactuals can have empirical significance (insofar as counterfactuals of the n-d type are concerned). An advantage of providing an explicit analysis is that such a question can be addressed to the analysans. According to the inferential model, the problem reduces to the empirical nature of the characterization of the implicit premises, i.e., the legitimate premises and the laws L. The legitimate

premises consisted of W and the subsequent legitimate premises $g(A,W_{\bar{t}_B})$. Clearly $W_{\bar{t}_B}$ is subject to empirical determination, as a portion of the actual world, and we shall expect that L is too (though we shall not discuss this question, since we do not pursue the analysis of lawlikeness here). The legitimate premises of the (t_A,t_B) interval are thus true factual statements that concern the actual world only and no possible worlds whatsoever. Their specification, as reflected in (53), is probabilistic in character, since R_{cir} and R_{ppcr} are to be expressed probabilistically. Even though we have delayed discussing the notion of probability suitable for analyzing these notions, it is clear that we expect one that will be empirically satisfactory. The probability function in question occurs only in R_{cir} and R_{ppcr}. On the assumption that the arguments of these two relations are W, A, and C, we can expect those two relations to be empirical in character (this will be further vindicated in 5 V). Therefore, on that assumption, the empirical character of n-d type counterfactuals, insofar as our present analysis is concerned, has been secured.[75] Incidentally, notice that if we do not consider the relations of causal irrelevance and purely positive causal relevance to be "facts" (which by no means implies that they are not empirical in character), we can concur with Stalnaker in

> . . . the belief, which I share with most philosophers writing about this topic, that the formal properties of the conditional function, together with all of the *facts*, may not be sufficient for determining the truth-value of a counterfactual (*op. cit.*, pp. 98/9).

since, as we saw, these two relations are indispensable for the truth conditions of counterfactuals developed above.

Notes: Chapter 2

1. This definition of 'within' raises no issues when open intervals are concerned. When an interval closed on one or both sides is involved, there are conflicting considerations as to the advisability of allowing another interval to be within it in case it includes one or both of its end points. The definition in the text reflects no conviction on my part that it is the better option, and I shall occasionally ignore issues concerning end points.

2. Here and in other places I will discuss only counterfactuals with false antecedents. But see footnote 32 in the epilogue for the general application of my analysis to the case of counterfactuals with true antecedents.

3. More precisely: to which its indicative version pertains in the context of the counterfactual to which it belongs.

4. And thus pertain to times earlier than t.

5. These features are brought out by my analysis of the notion of W_t in chapter 6, section I.

6. In requiring them to be factual we exclude lawlike statements and logical truths. See 9 IV 2 for a brief discussion of counterfactuals $A > B$ where t_A is not weakly earlier than t_B and for counterfactuals with lawlike antecedents (i.e., counterlegals). The limitation on the factual character of the consequent is made here for fluency of discussion only. Our conclusions will hold equally well for non-factual consequents, *mutatis mutandis*. Cf. fn 47 below.

7. Unless the statement or its negation have presuppositions not in the set.

8. The proof of this reformulation will be given in X, theorem 2.

9. Counter*factuals*, that is, not counterlegals. Obviously, my approach here does not resort to miracles of any sort. For comments on counterlegals, cf. 9 IV 2.

10. These questions will be discussed in detail in V and VI below. Cf. also 7 IV 1 for further discussion of this issue.

11. But also for other, more important reasons, as will become evident below.

12. See this chapter, section I, for the temporal terminology.

13. Cf. below, section IV, 2.

14. For brevity, I shall avoid differentiating explicitly between the antecedent of a counterfactual and its indicative version.

15. That is, the time to which the antecedent pertains; see I 2.

16. That is, the event type described by the antecedent.

17. See I 2 for this terminology; $\underline{t}_A$ and $\bar{t}_B$ are the lower and upper ends of t_A and t_B respectively.

18. That is, a continuation that does not violate the laws.

19. And the use of 'previous history' will be the same: the history pertaining to times earlier than the antecedent-time.

20. This holds both for counterfactuals of the n-d type, with which we shall deal up to chapter 9, and for counterfactuals *not* of the n-d type, with which we shall deal in chapter 9. For the latter, a generalization of the function $h(A > B, \ldots)$ will be required. Cf. also fn 22 below.

21. As a research program that attempts to provide the rule of application of a construction in a natural language, this strategy is indeed empirical.

22. We shall then also see that a generalization of the inferential schema (and thus of the notion of the previous legitimate premises) is necessary for dealing with the problem of the affinity with the actual history up to t_A of the set of possible-world descriptions to be associated with a counterfactual, when counterfactuals *not* of the n-d type are concerned. In the case of such counterfactuals, where the problem of the subsequent legitimate premises is *also* pertinent, the solution we have developed and defended here will turn out still to be essentially right, after an obvious modification designed to fit the generalized inferential schema is made.

23. Thus, in order to check the output of our analysis against the intuitions of speakers of the language, we must verify that they classify a given counterfactual in conformity with how we apply the analysis. My point is that, whether correctly or not, in the common-sense conceptual framework potential actions are arguably judged quite often to be compatible with the prior history, and the assumption that it was possible for the agents to have acted otherwise seems to be made in a large variety of cases. Given that, what intuitions of speakers concerning the truth values of such counterfactuals must match is the outcome of the analysis of those counterfactuals *as* n-d type counterfactuals in our model.

For those who hold that there is a "local determinism" of human actions, but not a global determinism, i.e., that particular actions are always necessitated by the prior history of the world immediately preceding them, but not necessarily by the history of the world up to a certain earlier point, the other kind of counterfac-tuals, discussed below in the Epilogue, will suit human actions better. But this will be a use of the counterfactual construction tailored to suit a particular philosophical position, and may well be incongruent with intuitions concerning the truth values of such counterfactuals judged common-sensically.

Our discussion in the rest of this book will largely proceed on the assumption of a nondeterministic universe. On my view, the rich semantical structure of the counterfactual construction is suitable only for a nondeterministic universe: in a deterministic universe it would be impoverished and would no longer possess the role and function it serves in a nondeterministic one. For further discussion of this issue, see 9 V.

24. Excluding, of course, cases of overdetermination.

25. Legalists distinguish, of course, among various types of causes.

26. Under any reasonable selection of legitimate premises, which are factual nonlawlike statements.

27. In many counterfactuals, t_B and t_A virtually coincide: they are so close that (t_A, t_B) plays no significant role in the determination of their truth value. Cf. above, III 4.

28. Recall that we use 'W' as an abbreviation for 'W_{t_A}'.

29. When arguing for the truth of a given counterfactual, however, only a relatively small portion of W will be used.

30. Strictly speaking, $M(A > B, \ldots)$ and $V(A > B, \ldots)$ (defined in the next paragraph below) are functions whose values are sets of possible-world descriptions. Thus, $V(A > B, \ldots)$ is a function variable that varies through the functions that fulfill the conditions specified below. When we talk of the set $V(A > B, \ldots)$ we mean a set type, or an arbitrary token of it, and we shall play on the usual ambiguity between a function f and its value for x in the notation '$f(x)$'.

31. See section II above for the relation between the inferential model and the possible-world-descriptions model.

32. See section I for the temporal terhminology.

33. My use of 'event' is semi-technical; thus, it covers states of affairs as well. Furthermore, as I use it here, the event described by a true context-independent sentence A is the (one or more) event-token(s) of the type specified in A which in fact occurred during the time interval to which A pertains. My use is therefore compatible with Donald Davidson's point in his "Reply to Martin" [pp. 129-137 of "Criticism, Comment and Defense," pp. 122-169 in his *Essays on Actions and Events* (New York: Oxford, 1980)], to the effect that a sentence may describe more than one event (as the term is *normally* used). That this may be the case is reflected, and indeed emphasized, in my treatment of the temporal quantificational structure of sentences (see 6 II). There a distinction between universal and existential temporal quantifiers is brought to the surface as elements in the canonical representation of the temporal structure of sentences, where the reference time of a sentence plays the role of the temporal quantificational domain. Of course, the introduction of temporal quantifiers would be utterly empty if the recurrence of the event-tokens of the type specified by the sentence in question during the temporal interval specified were not contemplated.

There have been notorious arguments to the effect that sentences cannot *refer* to events, states of affairs, etc. The point in these arguments has been that if sentences are to be considered semantic designators, their designata cannot be events, etc. I shall not engage this issue here. However, for my present purposes in this book my concern is *not* to propound a thesis about what the semantic reference of sentences ought to be, nor is it with the compositionality principle, which lurks behind much of this debate. Rather, my concern here is to point to events as *correlated* with, or *alluded* to by, sentences, as elaborated above. This is what I have in mind when I talk about the event described by a sentence. This sort of talk should *not*, therefore, be construed as a commentary on what the semantic reference of sentences ought to be under the compositionality principle (or whether there ought to be one at all).

The causal-relevance relation is a relation between actual events *under a description*. Thus, strictly speaking, I should talk of causal relevance (or purely positive causal relevance) between the events described by certain true sentences, *so described*. For brevity, I express myself *as if* it were a relation between the describing sentences, trusting that the reader will bear this qualification in mind. With this in mind, I allow myself occasionally to conflate the two levels to avoid cumbersome formulations.

34. Notice that I have treated the semifactual in (12) as though it followed the standard pattern for counterfactuals — the inferential model. This is a position I stand behind; but my claim that statements to which the antecedent is purely negatively causally relevant should be excluded is independent of that position. Consider the counterfactual (12') which is the converse of semifactual (12):

(12') Had Jane, sadistically and for no reason, slapped John across the face in the middle of the interview, then John would not have offered her the job.

Just as (12) was clearly false, (12') is clearly true. But we have shown that the consequent of (12) follows from the implicit premises taken together with the set under consideration (i.e., the set of statements describing events to the occurrence of which the antecedent-event is purely negatively causally relevant). Hence (12'), which shares its antecedent with (12), but has the negation of the consequent of (12) as its consequent, comes out false according to the inferential model under the above assumption. Thus, we can proceed to argue the same point, that the kind of statement under consideration here should be excluded from the implicit premises, but now without recourse to semifactuals. [Below, semifactuals such as (12) will be labeled "con-type semifactuals," and I shall argue that their analysis is the same as that of ordinary counterfactuals. See below, XI and XII.]

35. This is still the case even if the over-all effect of the antecedent, though mixed, is positive. See VIII 3.

36. The reader is reminded that $V(A > B, \ldots)$ is the set of possible-world descriptions to be associated with a counterfactual $A > B$ of the n-d type, as introduced in V 4, above.

37. $g(A > B, \ldots)$ is the subsequent-legitimate-premises function, introduced in IV 1.

38. Cf. chapter 1, section II, above.

39. Of course, such events need not be bound to occur, whether with this change or without it (actual though they are). The effect considered here is a strengthening of their causal roots and the degree to which they are affected by them.

40. When the consequent belongs to (t_A, t_B).

41. The notions of "implicit premises" and "legitimate premises" were introduced in II 3. Recall that the legitimate premises are the factual implicit premises (the laws excluded).

42. On this thesis implied by our analysis of counterfactuals, see thesis 1, section IX, below.

43. For a detailed discussion of such phenomena, see chapters 4 and 5.

44. We discuss only counterfactuals of the n-d type, here and in what follows (until chapter 9), even though we shall frequently omit this qualification.

45. A natural move would be to weaken the logical consequence relation in favor of high probability, so as to yield: $P(B/A, f(A > B, \ldots))$ is high. The impact of such a move would be to further emphasize the probabilistic character of the counterfactual construction and to eliminate the relation of logical consequence from the main schemata. This move will obviously cohere much better with an orientation toward counterfactuals (such as mine) which considers their role to be primarily couched in nondeterministic surroundings. I will not pursue this line here; but the modification of the theory presented here along such lines may well yield better approximations, improving upon the account offered in this book.

46. Recall that we use 'W' to abbreviate 'W_{t_A}'.

47. It may be better to talk about the consequent of the counterfactual's being inferable from, or being a logical consequence of, the implicit premises plus A instead of its being entailed by them. I shall, when I do, use the latter formulation for mere convenience.

Notice that even though our discussion is limited here to counterfactuals with factual antecedents and consequents, schema (18) would hold also for counterfactuals whose consequents are *not* factual, i.e., lawlike statements and tautologies (the latter if logical truths are considered logical consequences of any set of statements). According to this liberalization of scope, a counterfactual with an n-d type antecedent but with a consequent that is a tautology or a true lawlike statement, would count as a true counterfactual, as indeed it should.

48. When it comes to counterfactual statements with outside quantification, we will have a problem treating the indicative version of the antecedent as having a truth value. In such cases we will obviously have to deal with the antecedent prefixed by the appropriate quantifier. Some such cases may be handled by changing the above schema as follows:

Implicit premises $\rightarrow$ If A, then B

that is, omitting the counterfactual antecedent A from the antecedent of the logical consequence relation, and replacing the consequent B in that schema with the counterfactual statement itself reconstrued as a *material implication*. Another way which, perhaps, fits such cases better is to construe such counterfactual statements as conjunctions or disjunctions of the appropriate nonquantified statements, with the individual terms that replace the variable covering the quantificational domain of the variable (when it is finite). Since my main concern here is not quantified counterfactual statements, I shall not elaborate on this point.

49. In 9 III 1 we shall observe that, in certain cases, in addition to the analysis developed here, n-d counterfactuals also allow another reading, thereby giving rise to ambiguity.

50. In V 4 we defined the world-range of A as the set of possible-world descriptions in which A and W_{t_A} are true (and which are, of course, compatible with the laws).

51. See also theorem 2 below.

52. To show that there is such an extension, notice that we can arrange the set of well-formed nonlawlike statements in the language as a well-ordered set. Thus, for instance, first order them by number of letters. If A and B are two such statements with equal length, then A precedes B iff in the first place in them which is occupied by different letters, A's letter precedes B's alphabetically. Now we can specify the procedure for constructing such an extension: running through the above well-ordered set, add the nth sentence iff it is consistent with the set resulting from the $(n-1)$st stage together with L; otherwise, add its negation. [For the first stage consider the set $\{A\} \cup W \cup \text{CIP}(A > B, \ldots)$ itself as the result of

the previous stage.] It is clear that the set resulting from this procedure is a possible-world description, since it is a set of nonlawlike statements consistent with L and complete. [In the above procedure I ignore presuppositions: obviously, if at the nth stage, the nth sentence and its negation have a presupposition that is inconsistent with the result of the $(n\text{-}1)$st stage and the laws, skip them both and move to the $(n+1)$st stage. Such omissions obviously do not render the resulting set incomplete. Also, for the alphabetical ordering, take the alphabet enriched by punctuation signs plus a blank, ordered in some manner.]

53. Compare with 3 III 1, especially fn 17 (on the ontological status of sentences).

54. Recall that a possible-world description is assumed to be compatible with the laws. Also recall that L is the class of statements that express the laws (see V 1).

55. Accordingly, $Q(A,W,L,t_B, \ldots) = \{A\} \cup W \cup L \cup \mathrm{CIP}(A > B, \ldots)$.

56. That is, they are not to be retained as part of that background. This is not to rule out, of course, that some of them may logically follow from the antecedent of the inferential schema.

57. $Q(A,W,L,t_B, \ldots)$ is just the union of the first four sets in the antecedent of the previous formula.

58. This is so since if E and F are sets of statements, then $E \cup F \to B \leftrightarrow \overline{E} \cup F \to B$, that is, B is a consequence of E and F iff it is a consequence of F and all the logical consequences of E.

59. E^t, for a set of statements E, is the subset of E whose members pertain to t (see X 5 for notation). The counterfactual span of A for t_C is the set of consequents with reference times t_C of true counterfactuals with an antecedent A. The reliance on thesis 7 in subsuming con-type semifactuals under its schema $(18')$, which is a notational variant of (18), brings in reliance on the irrel-&–pp-semifactual analysis.

60. If $F \subseteq E$, then $E \cup F \to B$ iff $E \to B$.

61. The result, in fact, is stronger: we have not used the irrel-&–pp-semifactual analysis in its full scope: all we used was the requirement that con-type semifactuals fall under it, i.e., thesis 7. See also fn 65 below.

62. According to (33) (see previous subsection), $\mathrm{CCS}(A > B, \ldots)$ is the set of consequents C of true con-type semifactuals with antecedent A, such that $t_C \subseteq (t_A, t_B)$.

63. $(18')$ was: $Q(A,W,L,t_B, \ldots) \to B$ (cf. IX 1).

64. Recall that $Q'(A,W,L,t_B, \ldots)$ was the set of all statements true in all the members of the i-p world range of A and t_B.

65. (41) follows from the applicability of the irrel-&-pp-semifactual analysis to counterfactuals with true consequents, i.e., semifactuals. (41) is what we need for the equivalence of the irrel-&-pp-semifactuals analysis and the semifactual analysis. Theorem 3 can be restated as: If (41), then the two analyses are equivalent. In other words: if semifactuals (or more restrictively: con-type semifactuals) are governed by the irrel-&-pp-semifactual analysis, then the two analyses are equivalent. That semifactuals are governed by this analysis is of course part and parcel of its being an analysis of counterfactuals, of which semifactuals are a special subgroup. In particular, that con-type semifactuals are governed by the irrel-&-pp-semifactual analysis is expressed in (41).

66. For notation see the end of section X. Z_T is the subset of true statements of Z, and Z^t is the set of nonlawlike members of Z which pertain to time t. The addition of lawlike statements through the replacement of $Q'(A,W,L,t_B, \ldots)$ by $Q(A,W,L,t_B, \ldots)$ is canceled by the limitation to (t_A,t_B), signified by the superscript (t_A,t_B) in (47), which eliminates lawlike statements.

67. *Fact, Fiction, and Forecast*, p.15.

68. Thus, $Q'(A>B, \ldots)$ is logically closed under L. That is, if D is a (factual) consequence of $Q'(A>B, \ldots)$ plus L, then D is in $Q'(A>B, \ldots)$.

69. We shall discuss this point further in our discussion of Lewis in chapter 7.

70. Notice that we reserve 'C' for the consequent of (30), and 'B' — for the consequent of (48).

71. As usual, W is W_{t_A}.

72. t_A is a function of A, and, since t_A is weakly earlier than t_B, W_{t_A} is a function of $W_{\bar{t}_B}$ and t_A (see also 6 I). Thus W_{t_A,t_B} is a function of $W_{\bar{t}_B}$ and t_A. Recall that the upper limit of (t_A,t_B) is $\bar{t}_B$; see II above. Recall too that W is W_{t_A}, and that our discussion here is limited to counterfactuals of the n-d type.

73. Since the set of laws of nature is taken to be unique and unchanging, we do not take L as a variable in $f(A>B, \ldots)$.

74. If a world u contains $Q'(A,L,W,t_B, \ldots)$, it contains W and $g(A,W_{\bar{t}_B})$ and hence belongs to the i-p world-range of A and t_B, and thus, by thesis 5, belongs to $V(A>B)$.

75. That is, their empirical character is at least on a par with that of the laws of nature and of the notion of probability to be used.

3 Chisholm, Goodman, and Stalnaker Revisited

I Chisholm

1. Now that a specific proposal for the problem at hand has been made, it may be instructive to have another look at the three positions discussed in chapter 1. In 2 IX and 2 XIII we worked out the truth conditions of counterfactuals of the natural-divergence type on a schema that fits the inferential model. Formula 2 (56) [which henceforth will be our notation for formula (56) of chapter 2, and similarly for other formulas] amounted [together with 2(57)] to:

(1) $\quad f(A, W_{\bar{t}_B}) = W \cup L \cup g(A, W_{\bar{t}_B})$

Chisholm's criterion, on the other hand (as we saw in 1 II), had the form

(2) $\quad (\exists p)[p \ \& \ (p \ \& \ A \rightarrow B) \ \& \ C(p, A > B)]$

where $C(p, A > B)$ is a constraint on p (e.g.: $B \not\rightarrow p$; p is not a vacuous universal statement; etc.).

According to Chisholm's criterion, a counterfactual is true iff there is a true statement p which, together with A, entails B and which conforms to certain logical constraints. The role that p plays in Chisholm's schema is analogous to that of the implicit premises on our schema of the inferential model. The set of implicit premises yielded by our analysis consists of W, L, and the set of all true statements in the (t_A, t_B) interval to which A is not in any way negatively causally relevant. Thus the differences between the two approaches are considerable. On the one approach, there are constraints of logical character, which concern both the logical form of p by itself and p's relations to A and B, constraints that were designed to block trivializations and were thus doomed to be ad hoc. On the other approach, we have a characterization which emphasizes temporal features and various relations of causal relevance and which is supported by a theory concerning the role that contrary-to-fact assumptions play in our conceptual framework. These differences do not detract from the importance of Chisholm's paper, which, we should bear in mind, was written in 1946. But they do illustrate the difference in approach and in the type of considerations adduced, between the pioneering attempt of that time and the theory presented here.

85

2. As we saw in chapter 1, I, Chisholm offered an analysis of counterfactuals of the form 'even if A, still B', and his analysis was that such a counterfactual is true iff the counterfactual 'if A, then $\sim B$' is false. These counterfactuals, we have learned, are semifactuals; thus Chisholm's thesis amounts to the following:

(3)   If $A > B$ is a semifactual of the form 'even if A, still B',[1] then $A > B$ is true iff $\sim (A > \sim B)$ is true.

(Of course, if $A > B$ is a semifactual, $A > \sim B$ is not, and is thus a regular counterfactual.)

We have discussed semifactuals at some length in various places, particularly in 2 VIII, XI, and XII. We saw that there are three mutually exclusive and exhaustive groups of semifactuals, which differ in their analysis. Irrel-semifactuals and pp-semifactuals do conform to Chisholm's condition (3), thus:

(4)   If $A > C$ is an irrel-semifactual or a pp-semifactual, then:
        $A > C$ is true iff $A > \sim C$ is false.

But this is so only in the trivial sense that

(5)   If $A > C$ is an irrel-semifactual or a pp-semifactual, then $A > \sim C$ is false.

Since irrel-semifactuals and pp-semifactuals are all true, their corresponding counterfactuals (those which have the negations of their consequents as consequents) are all false: if $A > C$ is an irrel-semifactual or a pp-semifactual, then C belongs to the set of legitimate premises of $A > \sim C$, and C rather than $\sim C$ is inferable as a consequent on the inferential schema of $A > \sim C$. Thus, even though Chisholm's analysis (3) holds for some semifactuals of the form 'even . . . , still ____' (i.e., the irrel-semifactuals and pp-semifactuals of this form), it holds for them only trivially, and does not expose the source of this characteristic, which is the truth of all irrel-semifactuals and pp-semifactuals.

However, (3) fails to hold for con-type semifactuals. As we saw, con-type semifactuals have the same analysis as regular counterfactuals and are not all true. Thus a con-type semifactual $A > C$ will fail to be true if C belongs to some of the members of the cip world-range of A for t_C,[2] but not to all. In this case, however, the corresponding counterfactual $A > \sim C$ will also fail to be true. This is so since, for either $A > C$ or $A > \sim C$ to be true, its consequent has to be true in all the members of the very same set of possible-world descriptions $V(A, W_{\bar{t}_C})$. [This set is a function of A and $W_{\bar{t}_C}$, but not otherwise of C — see 2(63) of 2 XIII[3] — and is thus shared by a con-type semifactual $A > C$ and its corresponding counterfactual $A > \sim C$ as the set of possible-world descriptions in all of which the consequent of either one of these two counterfactuals has to be true for it to be true.] But in the case described, C is true in some of the members of $V(A, W_{\bar{t}_C})$ but false in others. Hence, a con-type semifactual $A > C$ and its corresponding counterfactual $A > {\sim} C$ can both fail to be true. So Chisholm's thesis (3) does not hold for con-type semifactuals. So it does not hold for semifactuals in general, and thus Chisholm's (3) is false.

We can also see that this is so by considering a variant of example 11 of 2 VIII:

Example 1

> The story is the same as that of example 11, except that Don did *not* win the lottery. That is, Don did bribe the assistant manager of the lottery, and the latter did his best to help, but the chances in this case being poor (only 10%), Don failed to win. As in the original example, consider the contrary-to-fact assumption of Don's switching deals: canceling his deal with the assistant manager and bribing the manager instead. His chances of winning in this case are, again, 30%. So consider the semifactual:

(6)   Even if Don had switched from a deal with the assistant manager to one with the manager, he would still have lost.

This semifactual is not true — in this case his chances of winning are much higher — 30%, and he might very well have won. The following counterfactual, however, is not true either:

(7)   If Don had switched from a deal with the assistant manager to one with the manager, he would have won.

This is so since, even though Don's chances increase substantially as a result of the switch, his chances are still low (even lower than 50%), and he might very well have lost in this case too.

As we can already see, however, (7) is the counterfactual corresponding to the semifactual (6), which has the form 'even . . . , still ___': they share the same antecedent and have contradictory consequents. But neither of them is true. Thus, clearly, neither one is equivalent to the negation of the other, as Chisholm's formula (3) states. We can see, however, that (6) is a con-type semifactual — for the same reason that 2(17) was[4] in example 11 above: the transition has some negative effect on its consequent-event. (Recall our discussion of this matter in 2 XII 4.)

II Goodman

1. Goodman's original conception of the general schema in which he wants to couch truth conditions for counterfactuals is in line with the inferential model. Thus, he writes:

(13)   A counterfactual is true if and only if the antecedent conjoined with relevant true statements about the attendant circumstances

lead, by way of a true general principle, to the consequent
(*Fact, Fiction, and Forecast*, p. 37).[5]

This, if the world 'relevant' is taken seriously as a place-holder for a specifying description (in need of unfolding), is in accordance with the schema
of the inferential model, according to which for every counterfactual $A > B$
there is a set of statements — the legitimate premises — such that the counterfactual is true iff they, together with the laws (thus comprising the implicit premises) and with A, imply B, which has the form of $2(4')$ (see 2
II):

$2(4')$ f-$(A > B, \ldots) \cup L \cup \{A\} \to B$

where f-$(A > B, \ldots)$ is the legitimate-premises function. In this formulation "the relevant true statements about the attendant circumstances" play
a role corresponding to that of the legitimate premises. Goodman's first
formulations[6] conform to the form of this general schema. Indeed, the last
of these [1(0) in 1 II) was:

1(0)   The set of relevant conditions is "the set of all true statements
        each of which is both logically and non-logically compatible
        with A where non-logical incompatibility means violation of a
        non-logical law" (Goodman, pp. 10/11).

This can be represented in the inferential schema by the following
legitimate-premises function f-$(A > B, \ldots)$:

(14) f-$(A, W_T) = \{p \mid (p \in W_T) \,\&\, \{p \,\&\, A\} \cup L$ is consistent$\}$

where W_T is the set of all true nonlawlike statements.[7] At that point,
however, in view of the difficulties encountered by this formulation,
Goodman considered another formulation [1(5) of 1 II]:

1(5)   A counterfactual is true iff "for *some* set S of true sentences, $A \cdot S$
        be self-compatible and lead by law to the consequent" (Good-
        man, p. 11).

In view of difficulties here as well, he moved to the next formulation [1(9)
of 1 II]:

1(9)   "A counterfactual is true if and only if there is some set S of true
        statements such that $A \cdot S$ is self-compatible and leads by law to
        the consequent, while there is no such set S', such that $A \cdot S'$ is
        self-compatible and leads by law to the negate of the conse-
        quent" (Goodman, pp. 11/12).

This formulation, however, *no longer* has the form of the general schema
(13), but has rather the form of 1(10):

1(10)   ($\exists S$) [S & (A & $S \xrightarrow{L} C$) & R (S,A)]
          & ~($\exists S'$) [S' & (A & S') $\xrightarrow{L}$ ~C) & R(S', A)]

This form, however, clearly deviates from that of Goodman's schema (13) above and also from the form 2(4′) of the schema of the inferential model. As we saw in chapter 1, sec. II, this new formulation still carries the same type of trivializability that plagued its predecessors, a problem not likely to be remedied by further ad hoc modifications. Thus, the drastic change in form does not go very far toward resolving this root problem. Formulation 1(9) and formulation 1(12), the last of Goodman's series of reformulations,[8] became, as we have noted, cumbersome and ad hoc, and thus unencouraging with regard to their prospects. Moreover, as we saw in chapter 2, an analysis of counterfactuals should account adequately for the role of contrary-to-fact assumptions as well as for the role of counterfactuals. We also saw the special relations that exist between the analysis of counterfactuals and the thesis concerning their role as presented in chapter 2: the thesis concerning their role illuminated, explained, supported, and was in turn confirmed by the account of their truth conditions.[9] Now a major disadvantage of ad hoc systematizations such as the above is that they are unlikely to shed light on the role of the concept they attempt to systematize, and are thus not likely to be provided with explanatory theoretical support. Such analyses, therefore, are unlikely to satisfy an important adequacy condition: adequately accounting for the role of the concept involved. These comments applied, as we recall, *mutatis mutandis*, to Chisholm's analysis as well. And, as we saw, reformulations of Chisholm's analysis, both his own and those we suggested, were found to be ad hoc as well.

2. Let us now consider the particular difficulties that prompted Goodman to make this transition. The difficulty with formulation 1(0) was that individual compatibility with the antecedent was not sufficient: collective compatibility of the set of statements describing relevant conditions with the antecedent was also necessary to preclude the inferability of both the consequent and its negation. But in any case of incompatibility of a set of statements, there is more than one way to eliminate some of its members so as to restore compatibility. This is why Goodman moved from formulation 1(0) to formulation 1(5), which requires only that there be *some* such set (that will be compatible with the antecedent and lead by law to the consequent). In 1 II 1 we cited the example Goodman used to motivate this move. It concerned the antecedent:

1(1)   If Jones were in Carolina, . . .

the indicative version of which was individually compatible with each of:

1(2)   Jones is not in South Carolina
1(3)   Jones is not in North Carolina
1(4)   North Carolina plus South Carolina is identical with Carolina.

though incompatible collectively with 1(2) - 1(4). In order to see how the treatment we proposed in chapter 2 deals with this case, let us somewhat modify Goodman's example, to ensure that the counterfactuals in question are of the n-d type, a feature which cannot be determined in his original example owing to lack of sufficient information. These modifications do not in any way change the logical characteristics under discussion. Let us consider

Example 2

Suppose Jones has never been to Carolina. At time t his plane was about to land in Carolina, but ultimately did not. The point where it was about to land was near the border between the two Carolinas, and there were adjacent airfields on both sides of the border.

Consider a counterfactual antecedent:

(15)   If Jones had landed[10] in Carolina at time t, . . .

Now the following statements are true:

(16)   Jones has never been to South Carolina.
(17)   Jones has never been to North Carolina.

In order to evaluate a counterfactual with the antecedent (15), we admit W_{t_A} into the implicit premises unselectively, since (15) is a counterfactual-antecedent of the n-d type; but we must not do the same with W_{t_A,t_B} (on our inferential model).[11] In W_{t_A}, we have

(16')   Jones has never been to South Carolina before time t.
(17')   Jones has never been to North Carolina before time t.

It is quite clear that the indicative version of (15) plus (16') and (17') are quite compatible. However, it is also clear that the event described in the indicative version of (15) is causally relevant to both

(16")   Jones has not been to South Carolina after time t.
(17")   Jones has not been to North Carolina after time t.

and not in a purely positive way. The indicative version of (15) is positively causally relevant to Jones's being in South Carolina as well as in North Carolina, and thus negatively causally relevant to his not being in either, which is what (16") and (17") state.[12] Hence neither of these qualify for membership among the legitimate premises in the analysis of a counterfactual with antecedent (15), since neither is a consequent of either an irrel-semifactual or a pp-semifactual with the same antecedent.

Therefore it is quite clear that the indicative version of (15) is collectively compatible with both (16′) and (17′); but, it is *not* collectively compatible with (16) and (17), and hence not with (16′), (17′), (16″), (17″) collectively. On Goodman's proposal 1(0), both (16) and (17) qualify as statements describing relevant conditions, and thus the incompatibility of the indicative version of (15) with them collectively would render *his* "legitimate premises" for 1(0) [i.e., f-(A, W_T) of (14)] plus the antecedent incompatible, thereby motivating him to abandon the inferential model in his transition from 1(0) to 1(5). But on the inferential model, (16) and (17) are *not* among the legitimate premises: only (16′) and (17′) are; and (16″) and (17″) are excluded as well. And there is no incompatibility between the indicative version of (15) and (16′) and (17′). Hence the trouble that Goodman encountered in this example was *needlessly* attributed by him to the *form* of 1(0), which was what motivated him to make the transition to 1(5) and subsequently to 1(9), thereby causing him to deviate from the inferential model. Closer attention to the exact specification of the legitimate premises would have resulted in eschewing the inconsistency while *remaining* within the framework of the inferential model, as the above application of our theory shows. Our treatment of counterfactuals was not motivated (or developed) for the purpose of salvaging this example: it is clearly *not* an ad hoc theory designed to resolve the difficulty that this example raises. Yet it is a vindication of the theory that it can adequately handle an example of this kind, which was crucial enough to have motivated Goodman to abandon the inferential model. This example falls squarely within the framework of our theory (which is an inferential-model theory) without any troubling inconsistency.

To recapitulate, it was due to proper *temporal* regimentation and correct *selection* of the legitimate premises in the (t_A, t_B) interval that no special difficulties confronted our treatment in this example. Goodman's move—the transition to 1(5) from 1(0), which was still in accordance with both Goodman's own schema (13) and our inferential-model schema 2(4′)—was, I believe, the first of Goodman's two major missteps. Thus, proper temporal regimentation and selection of the legitimate premises take much of the sting out of one crucial problem posed by counterfactuals: the problem of overcoming the incompatibility of the antecedent with the description of the actual world.

Again, the very same regimentation of the legitimate premises could have avoided the problem that forced Goodman to make the crucial move from 1(5) to 1(9), which is no longer in line with either his original schema or our inferential model. The problem, as he sees it, is that two opposing counterfactuals could come true under version 1(5), e.g., counterfactuals 1(6) and 1(6′) of 1 II. As we recall, these were:

1(6)   If Jones were in Carolina, he would be in South Carolina.
1(6′)   If Jones were in Carolina, he would be in North Carolina.

Under formulation 1(5), 1(6) would come true if S is taken to consist of 1(3) and 1(4); 1(6′) would come true if S is taken to consist of 1(2) and

1(4). In our presentation of the example, the counterfactuals corresponding to 1(6) and 1(6′) would be:

(6*)   If Jones had landed in Carolina at time t, he would have been
        in South Carolina (at some later time).
(6′*)   If Jones had landed in Carolina at time t, he would have been
        in North Carolina (at some later time).

However, insofar as our treatment of the variant of Goodman's example
is concerned, it is clear that there is no reason to hold either of these
counterfactuals to be true — a fortiori not both: the antecedent and the
legitimate premises, insofar as we have discussed them, are compatible
with (16″) and (17″) *separately*, and thus each of the negations of the
indicative versions of the consequents of counterfactuals (6*) and (6′*)
are compatible with the antecedent and the implicit premises mentioned
above, which are therefore not sufficient to support *either* of these two
counterfactuals. Thus, the problems that forced Goodman to move from
1(0) to 1(5) and then from 1(5) to 1(9), thereby deviating from his original general strategy (and from the schema of the inferential model), are
avoided by this way of handling the legitimate premises.

3. The difficulty that Goodman considered toughest with respect to the
problem of the relevant conditions, as we saw in 1 II, was how to exclude
statements that are not cotenable with the antecedent without falling into
an infinite regress. In sections 2 V and 2 VI we attempted to determine
what types of statements qualify as legitimate premises. Among those
which did not qualify were statements that were not cotenable with the
antecedent. These statements constituted a subgroup of those statements
pertaining to the (t_A, t_B) interval which did not belong to the set of
legitimate premises (as is clear from the diagram of the classification of
true statements in that interval; see 2 XII). The categories that we used
to delineate the various sets of statements in the (t_A, t_B) interval were
characterized by certain causal relevance relations that the antecedent
bore to these statements. Using this terminology we were able to characterize positively (i.e., noneliminatively) the statements that belonged to
the set of legitimate premises as those statements of that interval to which
the antecedent was either causally irrelevant or else purely positively causally relevant. The statements that were not cotenable with the antecedent
belonged to the complement of this set: the set of statements pertaining to
this interval to which the antecedent was, in one way or another, negatively causally relevant. Thus, we were not compelled to give an independent characterization of those statements not cotenable with the antecedent, since we instead characterized a larger set of statements containing
them: the set of statements that did not qualify as legitimate premises in
the (t_A, t_B) interval. Once this larger group was characterized, there was
no need to characterize independently any subgroup of it, in particular,
the group of statements not cotenable with the antecedent. This larger
group was characterized as the complement of the group of legitimate

premises belonging to this interval, the characterization of which has occupied a large part of this work. The task analogous to Goodman's task of determining the relevant conditions was that of determining the legitimate premises. This was accomplished without additional specification of subsets of the set of statements that failed to qualify as legitimate premises, such as the set of statements not cotenable with the antecedent.

A trap from which attempts to provide an analysis of counterfactuals must keep steering away is the menace of incompatibility of the antecedent and the implicit premises; such incompatibility yields outright inadequacy. There are, however, other traps which threaten various extensional inadequacies of analysis. Goodman first encountered the serious problem of the inconsistency of the antecedent and the implicit premises in his transition from 1(0) to 1(5) (in which the problem of statements not cotenable with the antecedent was not yet involved). However, instead of embarking on the task of sorting out the implicit premises, which is what is called for on the conception of the functional character of the implicit premises (cf. 2 II), Goodman retreated to a variant of Chisholm's formulation of existential quantification, and from there to 1(9) — thus making a radical departure from the form of the inferential model, as we saw above. We also saw that the way out of this difficulty consisted in adequate delineation of the legitimate premises, made possible by the temporal classification of candidates for such statements, the separation of the problem of the subsequent legitimate premises from that of the prior legitimate premises (see 2 III), and the use of various concepts of causal relevance. The resolution of the problem involving those statements not cotenable with the antecedent became possible in much the same way, by characterizing the implicit premises and excluding, within a single category, those statements which did not qualify as legitimate premises, a characterization which did not in turn rely on counterfactual statements. Thus we did not provide a characterization for statements not cotenable with the antecedent, a characterization which did not rely on counterfactuals again; but we found out that such a characterization is *unnecessary*, since the class of statements that do not qualify as legitimate premises is more comprehensive, and its delineation does not require counterfactual statements. The results of this account were expressed in the irrel-&-pp-semifactuals analysis in thesis 1 of 2 IX. In this way the infinite regress was avoided.

4. It is thus crucial to realize that the set of statements not cotenable with the antecedent is only *a part* of a larger set of statements that should be excluded from the legitimate premises. A failure to realize this will yield extensional inadequacy if it leads to the addition of *other cotenable statements* that do not belong there to the set of implicit premises. Moreover, it will also make it look necessary to provide an independent characterization of the group of statements not cotenable with the antecedent. But an attempt to provide such an independent characterization of cotenability will lead to an infinite regress. All of this is avoided when the set of statements not cotenable with the antecedent is taken for what it is — a mere part of the group of statements that do not qualify as legitimate premises

and, thus, are not in need of an independent characterization. So we see that the trap of infinite regress was grounded in a deeper misconception: the view that the main problem of the relevant conditions is to avoid incompatibility with the antecedent. For merely avoiding incompatibility with the antecedent does not require exclusion of all statements to which the antecedent is negatively causally relevant when these statements are cotenable with the antecedent. But their inclusion among the legitimate premises would result in the extensional inadequacy discussed in example 10 of 2 VI and in example 1 of this chapter. Below, we show how this deeper misconception also plagues other approaches to counterfactuals.

We can appreciate how serious Goodman's problem of the specification of the statements not cotenable with the antecedent was, if we consider the following point. Insofar as the analysis of counterfactuals of the n-d type is concerned, such statements pertain to times later than t_A.[13] However, true statements C that are not cotenable with the antecedent A are precisely those true statements which would not have been true had the antecedent A been the case; that is, those true statements C for which the counterfactual $A > \sim C$ is true. (Notice that this is not a semifactual.) Thus, *the set of true statements not cotenable with A coincides with the set of negations of consequents of true nonsemifactual counterfactuals with antecedent A:* for a true C, $A > \sim C$ is true iff A is not cotenable with C. Hence the problem of the determination of the class of statements not cotenable with A is precisely the problem of determining the false counterfactual consequents of A, which is *exactly* the problem of determining the true nonsemifactual counterfactuals with antecedent A. So the problem of specifying the statements not cotenable with the antecedent re-emerges as the very problem of specifying truth conditions for nonsemifactual counterfactuals, which is Goodman's original problem — a complete vicious circle.

In 2 XI, however, we used a different approach to the characterization of the legitimate premises, and characterized them as consequents of certain semifactuals.[14] In elaborating this analysis — the semifactual analysis — we recognized among them the con-type semifactuals, whose analysis was, in turn, the same as that of regular counterfactuals, and thus we faced the problem of infinite regress. The analogy between this quandary and Goodman's is quite clear: The set of true statements in the (t_A, t_B) interval can be divided into three exclusive and exhaustive sets: statements not cotenable with the antecedent; consequents of true semifactuals; and statements that do not belong to either of these sets, that is, statements that are not consequents of true semifactuals and whose negations are not consequents of true counterfactuals (all with antecedent A). Goodman believed he had ended up reducing the problem of counterfactuals to the problem of statements not cotenable with A; our semifactual analysis in turn involved a reduction to true semifactuals. That a (true) statement C is not cotenable with the antecedent A can be expressed as '(the true) C would not have been true had A been true', whereas a semifactual statement is of the form '(the true) C would still have been true had A been true'. Thus, true statements not cotenable with A and consequents of semifactual statements (which of course are also true) can be characterized, as above, in a clear-cut counterfactual form. Thus, both Goodman's analysis and our semifactual analysis yielded reductions to counterfactual forms, albeit different ones, and thus were threatened by infinite regress. However, if our results so far have been correct, the semifactual analysis was extensionally adequate and supported by the thesis concerning the role of contrary-to-fact assumptions, whereas Goodman's was not only extensionally inadequate but also, as we showed above, trivializable and ad hoc.

Yet, just as Goodman was unable to provide an independent analysis of statements not contenable with the antecedent, so we did not provide a complete and independent analysis of true semifactuals. We were, however, able to overcome the danger of infinite regress by discovering that there is a subset of the consequents of appropriate[15] true semifactuals which can be analyzed independently, i.e., in a way that does not necessitate recourse to counterfactuals — this subset consisted of the consequents of irrel-semifactuals and pp-semifactuals. Further, what was most important in the context of the semifactual analysis was the discovery that the set of consequents of all appropriate true semifactuals, including all those not in this subset, could be generated by this subset: this set of consequents belonged to the *logical closure* of the consequents of semifactuals in this subset taken together with the antecedent and the other implicit premises (i.e, W and L), and thus this set was readily characterizable by them. We expressed this characterization in formula 2(47),[16] in which $CCS(A, W_{\bar{t}_B})$ (that is, the set of consequents of appropriate con-type semifactuals) is expressed in terms of this subset, together with A and the other implicit premises. [$CCS(A, W_{\bar{t}_B})$ is the complement, in this set of consequents of all appropriate true semifactuals, of this subset which comprises the consequents of irrel-semifactuals and pp-semifactuals.] Thus, we found out that dependence on the counterfactual form plagued only *one* group of true semifactuals — the con-type semifactuals; and moreover, we were able to prove that their consequents were *redundant* in the analysis of counterfactuals, and thus did not require an independent analysis. This result was proved in theorem 3 of 2 XII — the semifactual weak equivalence theorem. But this result would not have been possible without an independent positive characterization of the legitimate premises, since otherwise it would not have been possible to prove the redundancy of the consequents of con-type semifactuals. This was why the semifactual analysis could not hold its own regarding the problem of possible infinite regress: the irrel-&-pp-semifactual analysis was still required. This is expressed by the semifactual weak equivalence theorem, in which the irrel-&-pp-semifactual analysis is shown to imply the equivalence of the two criteria, which in turn shows that the consequents of con-type semifactuals are redundant in the semifactual analysis. Thus, complete resolution of the problem of the infinite regress of the semifactual analysis required an independent analysis — the irrel-&-pp-semifactual analysis. Goodman, remaining within the limits of his own analysis, was understandably unable to untie the Gordian knot of the infinite regress created by the statements not cotenable with A.

4. Our analysis suggested an answer to the problem of the implicit premises (for counterfactuals of the n-d type), a problem which is a close counterpart of Goodman's problem of the relevant conditions. Our answer provided the functional characterization of the implicit premises on the basis of $A, W_{\bar{t}_B}$, and L, and was expressed by formula 2(58) of 2 XIII:

$$2(58) \quad f(A, W_{\bar{t}_B}) = W \cup L \cup \{A\} \cup \{C \mid C\epsilon W_{t_A, t_B} \\ \& \; [R_{\text{cir}}(C, A, W) \vee R_{\text{ppcr}}(C, A, W)]\}$$

Our proposed analysis empirically vindicates and is, in turn, supported by a thesis about the roles of contrary-to-fact assumptions, counterfactuals, and semifactuals. As we saw, the Chisholm and Goodman strategies were ad hoc and thus unlikely to accord with an adequate account of these roles. Provision of an account of the roles of the constructions which supports a proposed systematization is, I believe, a strong argument in favor of that systematization, and should be required as an adequacy condition for proposed systematizations. In view of the ad hoc character of the two strategies discussed above, it seems unlikely that they can be provided with a plausible account of the role of contrary-to-fact assumptions, semifactuals, and the counterfactual construction, and thus it is unlikely that they will be able to meet this criterion of adequacy.

5. In chapter 1, section II we surveyed Goodman's views about semifactuals. As we saw, according to Goodman, if $A > B$ is a semifactual, its practical import is given by: $A > B$ iff $\sim(A > \sim B)$. Thus Goodman's claim concerning the practical import of semifactuals is the same as Chisholm's claim about the meaning of semifactuals. We discussed Chisholm's view above (section I), arguing against it. This criticism therefore applies equally well to Goodman's thesis. We saw that con-type semifactuals, which are semifactuals and which can be (and very often are) represented by the form 'even if . . . , still ___', cannot be reduced to the form given above: they are not equivalent to the negations of their corresponding counterfactuals. Rather, con-type semifactuals of the form 'even if A, still B' have the *same* analysis *mutatis mutandis* as their corresponding semifactuals 'if A, then $\sim B$'. We saw that the Chisholm-Goodman analysis fails since con-type semifactuals and their corresponding counterfactuals can be both false (as, e.g., in example 1 in this chapter, section I).

The Chisholm-Goodman reduction of semifactuals of the form 'even . . . , still ___' holds, therefore, only for irrel-semifactuals and pp-semifactuals, and even for them only trivially (as we saw above, 3 I). Goodman sensed that the observation that semifactuals of the form 'even . . . , still ___' and their corresponding counterfactuals do not have the same nature, does not hold generally, and he distinguished between the literal and the practical imports of semifactuals, holding that the 'even . . . , still ___' form is indicative of the practical import. Yet his resorting to a distinction between these two imports in the case of semifactuals, although grounded in the correct observation that different semifactuals behave differently, results in a false thesis, as we saw, and does not reach the source of the problem. That different semifactuals behave differently results not from an ambiguity between two different senses, but rather from the division of semifactuals into distinct groups, each with its own distinct and unambiguous logical structure.

III   Stalnaker

1. As we saw in chapter 1, III, Stalnaker proposed the following formulation of the truth conditions for counterfactuals evaluated in the actual world:

(18)   A counterfactual $A > B$ is true iff B is true in $f(A)$.

where $f(A)$ is Stalnaker's selection function (with the second variable held constant as the actual world).

Insofar as our analysis is concerned, we have to compare Stalnaker's proposal with the formulation we provided in terms of possible-world descriptions. We found out from theses 4 and 5 of 2 X and 2(63) of 2 XIII that:

Thesis 1.   A counterfactual $A > B$ (of the n-d type) is true iff B is true in all the members of $V(A, W_{\bar{t}_B})$.

where $V(A, W_{\bar{t}_B})$ is the cip world-range of A and t_B (see 2 X 1).

Our analysis had the distinct advantage of offering equivalent formulations in terms of the inferential model and in terms of the possible-world descriptions analysis, which enables us to compare it with writers who worked in both directions. This was possible as a result of theorem 1 of 2 X — the theorem of the equivalence of the possible-world-descriptions model and the inferential model. Moreover, our analysis in the possible-world-descriptions model did not use a primitive, irreducible notion of possible world. Unlike Stalnaker, we used a notion of possible-world *descriptions*, rather than of possible worlds. Our notion thus involves a linguistic entity — a set of statements which fulfills certain conditions, which is therefore definable, and which we in fact defined (in 2 II 2). Thus, whereas Stalnaker's analysis is unacceptable to those who object to possible worlds on ontological or other grounds, our analysis can utilize the heuristic advantages that the notion of a possible world has to offer, which we did along the way, without being objectionable to those who balk at possible worlds.[17]

Unlike Stalnaker, we provided complete truth conditions for counterfactuals (of the n-d type): the above set $V(A, W_{\bar{t}_B})$ was completely specified.[18] As we noted in 1 III, Stalnaker does not provide a complete specification of truth conditions because his selection function f remains undetermined. It is quite clear that our function $V(A, W_{\bar{t}_B})$ is the analogue in our analysis of his selection function f. For Stalnaker, "These conditions [which he provides for his selection function] . . . are of course far from sufficient to determine the function uniquely" (*op. cit.*, p. 105). Our function $V(A, W_{\bar{t}_B})$, is, by contrast, completely determined. As noted above, Stalnaker stated that

> This suggests that there are further rules beyond those set down in the semantics, governing the use of conditional sentences.
> Such rules are the subject matter of a *pragmatics* of conditionals. Very little can be said, at this point, about pragmatic rules for the use of conditionals (p. 110).

Even though our approach differs from Stalnaker's in important respects, it can nevertheless be considered a proposed solution to the problem that he leaves open, insofar as counterfactuals of the n-d type are concerned.

In 1 III, we criticized Stalnaker for making his selection function choose a single possible world. In our treatment, the analogue of his selection function, the function $V(A, W_{\bar{t}_B})$, selects a set of possible-world descriptions, rather than a single one, and therefore is not open to that criticism.

2. Stalnaker did not completely specify his selection function, but he offered guidelines for the completion of the task. Those guidelines, however, are very different from the results we arrived at concerning the function $V(A, W_{\bar{t}_B})$. Stalnaker attempted to proceed by providing a total ordering relation, based on similarity, on the set of possible worlds, and to have the selection function choose a world as close as possible to the base world.[19] By contrast, we have not used any ordering relation between possible-world descriptions. Stalnaker's programmatic comments about this ordering relation specified that "the world selected *differ minimally* from the actual world" (p. 104). The set of possible-world descriptions selected by $V(A, W_{\bar{t}_B})$ fulfilled no such condition: its members clearly did not differ minimally from the actual-world description. This was so in the sense that an important portion of the set $V(A, W_{\bar{t}_B})$ consisted of possible-world descriptions distinctly less similar to the actual-world description than others in $V(A, W_{\bar{t}_B})$, possible-world descriptions which should have been dropped from $V(A, W_{\bar{t}_B})$ if "minimal difference" had been the guiding principle, thereby increasing the similarity between the actual-world description and the possible-world descriptions in $V(A, W_{\bar{t}_B})$. This is so since the set of statements that generates $V(A, W_{\bar{t}_B})$, the statements that are to be shared by all its members, could have been augmented by additional true statements without harm to consistency. The effect would have been the elimination of possible-world descriptions that belonged to the set before but did not include some of these statements, while preserving those which did, thereby making this set of possible-world descriptions closer and more similar to the actual-world description. Thus, in addition to having rejected the set of true statements in (t_A, t_B) which are not cotenable with A (see 2 VI) as belonging to all members of $V(A, W_{\bar{t}_B})$, since doing otherwise would result in an inconsistency, we have also rejected those true statements which, though cotenable with A, are still such that A is, in

some way, negatively causally relevant to them. We have argued (in 2 VI) that these should not belong to all members of $V(A, W_{\bar{t}_B})$. This allows a greater degree of freedom for members of $V(A, W_{\bar{t}_B})$ to differ from the actual-world description than would have been the case had we allowed various such statements to qualify as legitimate premises. Again, the rejection of such statements was *not* motivated by compatibility considerations: we could have retained such statements as legitimate premises with no risk of inconsistency. A case in point was example 10 in 2 VI, about Kennedy's election, which constituted a counterexample to the demand to limit the selected possible-world descriptions to those which share with the actual world statements to which the antecedent is negatively causally relevant (of course, when cotenable with the antecedent). These arguments thus constitute a case against Stalnaker's programmatic remark concerning the minimal-difference feature of the selection function, which is in turn substantiated by the extensional adequacy of our systematization (and its theoretical support by our theses concerning the roles of the constructions in question). Thus, we provided three arguments for this point: the (counter)examples 10 and 11 of chapter 2, sections VI and X; the semifactual analysis; and the role theory. [The semifactual analysis was weakly equivalent to our irrel-&-pp-semifactuals-analysis (through the weak equivalence theorem of 2 XII) which the role theory motivated.[20]]

Stalnaker concluded from his account that

> . . . the denial of a conditional is equivalent to a conditional with the same antecedent and opposite consequent (provided that the antecedent is not impossible). That is, $\Diamond A \supset \sim (A > B) \equiv (A > \sim B)$. This explains the fact, noted by both Goodman and Chisholm in their early papers on counterfactuals, that the normal way to contradict a counterfactual is to contradict the consequent, keeping the same antecedent (p. 107).[21]

This conclusion is inconsistent with our account and, as we argued in the discussion of Chisholm and Goodman, false: we argued that both $A > B$ and $A > \sim B$ may be false when $\Diamond A$ is true, and brought counterexamples against the cited thesis, which was shared by Chisholm, Goodman, and Stalnaker (cf. sections I, II, this chapter).

We have argued against Stalnaker's requirement of taking as the value of the selection function (from among those worlds in which A is true) a world as close as possible to the base world. As a natural modification of this position, one can take not a closest world, but the set of all closest worlds from this set, and require that the consequent be true in all of them for the counterfactual to be true.[22] Inasmuch as it may seem that there need be no such single closest possible world, not only in that there might be more than one, but also in that there might be none,[23] it is also the case that there might be *no set* of closest (and equally close) possible worlds in which A is true. Even if one modifies this position again, and interprets the set of such closest worlds as those in some ϵ-vicinity of the actual world (in the sense of being "sufficiently close"), one is still in trouble. The reason is that the aspiration to stay with worlds as close as possible to the actual world, allowing only necessary modifications required by the introduction of the antecedent in question for the purpose of maintaining consistency and compatibility with the laws, is misguided.[24] This aspiration seemed to have originated with Goodman, who started his journey in the inferential model with all true statements that maintain individual compatibility with the antecedent,[35] and then struggled with problems resulting from the collective incompatibility of the antecedent and these relevant conditions, finally excluding specifically all statements not cotenable with the antecedent. We have argued against this orientation by showing that we do not wish to retain certain statements even though they are cotenable with the antecedent. This claim applies, *mutatis mutandis*, to the suggested modification of Stalnaker's position, as well as to his original pre-analytic motivation. A true statement in the (t_A, t_B) interval for which it is not true that it would still be the case if the antecedent holds, should not be retained, as we have argued at length. But as long as it is not the case that it would be false were the antecedent true, such a statement *can* be retained without inconsistency, and the above approach of picking out an ϵ-vicinity of the actual world (as well as Stalnaker's original motivation of staying as close as possible to the actual world in all respects except for what is essential for the consistent accommodation of the antecedent), would retain such statements, in a way that will indeed do "least violence to the correct description and explanation of the actual world" (p. 104). In contrast with Stalnaker's desideratum of remaining as close as possible to the actual world when a counterfactual is being evaluated, we remained close to the actual-world description only in what we claimed to be the requisite respects, which are described by the legitimate premises.

Notes: Chapter 3

1. Since all counterfactuals of the form 'even . . . , still____' are semifactuals and since every semifactual can be expressed in this form, thesis (3) does not impose any further restriction by specifying this form, and this specification is therefore redundant.

2. See 2 X 1 for the definition of the cip world-range of A for t_C.

3. Note that t_C is the same as $t_{\sim C}$. See also 6 II.

4. 2(17) was: If Don had switched deals in the prescribed way, he would still have won.

5. In numbering formulas in this chapter, I have skipped numbers 8 - 12 in order to avoid confusion with cited formulas of chapter 1.

6. See 1 II; see also Goodman, *op. cit.*, pp. 9, 10.

7. We have been using '*W*' for W_{t_A}. Here I use 'W_T' for the actual-world description, to avoid confusion.

8. 1(12) improved over 1(9) [and thus over 1(10)] by further modifying $R(S,A)$. See 1 II.

9. See in particular 2 VII 2 and 2 VIII 1.

10. Landing is taken here as the process of making the final descent and re-maining on the ground for a while.

11. If one wishes, the story can be augmented to clarify this point. Suppose the plane was not scheduled to land in either Carolina, but was hovering around the border, about to land, due to mechanical failure, the pilot leaving it to the last moment, as a matter of a purely arbitrary decision, which of the two airports to land in. At the last moment, however, while in the air, he decided that the mechanical difficulty in the plane was not serious enough, and the plane continued on its way. Moreover, assume that John was strongly inclined to tour the areas adjacent to where he was about to land.

12. See thesis 1 of 2 IX.

13. For counterfactuals of the n-d type surely W_{t_A} is cotenable with A. ($\underline{t}_A$ is the greatest lower bound of t_A).

14. Cf. thesis 8, 2(32), of 2 XII.

15. By "appropriate" we mean of the form $A > C$, where t_C belongs to (t_A, t_B).

16. 2(47) (of 2 XII) was (with the arguments fixed according to 2 XIII):

$$CCS(A, W_{\bar{t}B}) = \overline{(Q(A, W_{\bar{t}B})} - Q(A, W_{\bar{t}B})_T^{(\underline{t}_A, t}{}_B)}$$

which can be expressed as:

$$CCS(A, W_{\bar{t}B}) = \overline{Q(A, W_{\bar{t}B})}_T^{(\underline{t}_A, t_B)} - Q(A, W_{\bar{t}B}))_T^{(\underline{t}_A, t_B)}$$

17. Some philosophers, though, may be unhappy with quantification over sentences. I will not pursue this ontological issue, except for the following comment. If one allows for functions, then, for a given alphabet (of some language), the sentences in the language are included among the finite strings of elements from the alphabet (enriched by punctuation signs and the blank). Those strings can be regarded as functions from the natural numbers to the alphabet (so enriched). If the legitimacy of those functions (hence those strings) is recognized, then the problem of specifying which strings are well-formed in the language, though formidable, is no longer of *ontological* significance. (Cf. Chisholm, "The Contrary-to-Fact Conditional," pp. 496/7, where the problem is raised.)

18. Except for specification of the concepts of causal irrelevance and purely positive causal relevance, which will be analyzed in chapters 4 and 5 below.

19. As we noted in chapter 1, he later allowed for various acceptable total orderings, subject to a supervaluation device.

20. For further discussion of this point, see the discussion of Lewis in chapters 7 and 8 below.

21. I have taken the liberty of inserting the horseshoe (in place of '-') in the quoted formula, correcting what appears to have been a typographical error.

22. This point was made in my dissertation, on which this book is based, which was written before Lewis's *Counterfactuals* came out. For further discussion see chapter 7, on Lewis, below.

23. That is, there may be a series of worlds converging to the actual world. Lewis called the claim that there is no such series *the limit assumption*. See the previous note for the origins of this observation.

24. For more on this issue, see below, 7 IV 1.

25. Cf. formulation 1(0) in 1 II, and also in this chapter, section II.

4 Causal Irrelevance

I The Equiprobability Condition

1. In section XIII of chapter 2 I presented, by way of a first approximation, a condition for when a semifactual is to count as an irrel-semifactual.
The condition was probabilistic in character, and I made there some comments about my use of probabilistic concepts in the attempt to provide
irrel-semifactuals and pp-semifactuals with an analysis independent of the
analysis of regular counterfactuals. The condition[1] presented there was

2(52) $P(C/A \ \& \ W) \ = \ P(C/\sim A \ \& \ W)$

Let us call this condition the **equi-probability condition** (for irrel-
semifactuals). (Again, 'W' abbreviates 'W_{t_A}'.)

Taking the discussion in that section as our starting point, we will now
proceed to work our way toward a more complete analysis of irrel-
semifactuals [to be presented in (7) of sec. IV]. In chapter 5 we will proceed toward an analysis of pp-semifactuals.

In sec. VII I will comment on the sort of objective interpretation for
the probability concept that should be used in analyzing counterfactuals.
In essence the concept I have in mind is that of a *partial degree of determination*, on the basis of the actual history of the world up to a certain
time and of the laws, of a later event (under a description). If you will,
this is an extension of the notion of a chance setup, when the whole world
up to a certain time is taken as a setup. The probability on the basis of W_t
(and L) of a later event (i.e., $t_C > t$) described as C would provide the
degree to which the world history up to t and the laws determine the occurrence of C.

This notion of probability, of course, comes to supplement, not to
replace, some other notions of probability, especially the frequentist and
degree-of-belief interpretations. Obviously, many probability judgments
do not fit various constraints of the framework required above, e.g., that
the sentence C be assessed from a temporal point earlier than t_C, i.e., that
only information pertaining to times earlier than that temporal point be
taken as a basis. Yet I hold that this use of probability is prevalent. In cases
in which this notion is used, our judgments are made as *estimates* of this
realistic notion. That is, estimations of conditional probabilities of the sort
used in this book [as in 2(52) above] can be assimilated to the assessment
made at a given time t of the probability of a future event C, on the basis
of past information (i.e., concerning the previous history of the world)

available at t, conjoined with either A or $\sim A$.[2] Such qualitative assessments (if not quantitative ones) appear in various areas of discourse as a matter of course. Most decision-making, when an action is being contemplated, involves such assessments of probabilities: past information is taken into account, and the conditional probabilities of future contingencies are assessed on the basis of this or that possible action. Thus assume, for instance, to take the simplest sort of case, that a country has to decide whether to modernize its armed forces or not, in connection with the possibility of a breakout of warfare, and that this issue is discussed at time t, say 1/1/72. Viewed in a somewhat simplified way, a decision of this kind would have to rely (among other things) on the assessment of the probability of warfare made on the basis of all the relevant information available at t, on the assumption that the armed forces are modernized, compared with the corresponding assessment of the probability of warfare on the assumption that they are not, made again on the basis of all the relevant information available at t. Thus, the decision will involve an estimation of

$$P(C/A \ \& \ W_t)$$

as compared with an estimation of

$$P(C/\sim A \ \& \ W_t)$$

where C is 'Warfare breaks out within a reasonable time after t', and A is 'The armed forces are modernized shortly after t'. The available information relevant for the purpose of evaluating these probabilities will be the relevant known portion of W_t.

This notion of probability that I propose will be further discussed in sec. VI. I hope, however, that within the scope of its legitimate use (i.e., when the probability of an event later than t is estimated on the basis of information available at t), this notion can be recognized as intuitive and prevalent. (Of course, the probability notion needed for our purposes of analyzing causal relevance and purely positive causal relevance falls within this scope.) In the analysis of causal relevance and purely positive causal relevance below (in this and the next chapter) I will thus rely on what, I would argue, are intuitive probability judgments of this sort, which I will attempt to motivate, and, of course, I will rely on the probability calculus.

2. It was argued above that 2(52) constitutes a necessary condition for a semifactual $A > B$ to be an irrel-semifactual (see 2 XII). The reasoning was as follows: irrel-semifactuals are semifactuals whose antecedents are causally irrelevant to their consequents. So, in looking for an analysis for irrel-semifactuals, we in fact look for a suitable analysis of causal irrelevance. To say that A is causally irrelevant[3] to C, in the sense that we are after, is to say that whether the A-event or the $\sim A$-event occurred makes no difference to the occurrence of the C-event; that is, the transition from the A course of events to the $\sim A$ course of events would have no effect on

the occurrence of the C-event — would make no causal difference regarding its occurrence. That is, the past history of the world has the same effect on C with A as with $\sim A$. The occurrence of the A-event, rather than the $\sim A$-event, would not, on the basis of the past history, affect the occurrence of the C-event. In other words, whatever effect a causal background pertaining to times prior to t_A has on the occurrence of C, the transition from $\sim A$ to A would not alter its effect on C. I shall try to capture such alterations of causal effects on C and the making of such causal differences, with probabilistic conditions. Thus, in attempting to assess the causal effects on C of the transition from the $\sim A$ course to the A course, we shall look for possible differences in the conditional probabilities of C that such a change would bring about, differences in the probability of C in the A course of events as compared with its probability in the $\sim A$ course. Differences in those conditional probabilities of C will reflect causal differences that the transition brings about with respect to C, or alterations in the impact that the causal background of C (prior to t_A) has on C as a result of this transition. Thus, we compare the conditional probabilities of C on the basis of W with A on the one hand, and on the basis of W with $\sim A$ on the other. This comparison is represented in 2(52). If there is a probabilistic difference, i.e., if 2(52) is false for some specified W, A, and C, i.e., if the transition from $\sim A$ to A changes the conditional probability of C, then the transition makes a causal difference with respect to C. (Remember that the A-event is temporally prior to the C-event). Thus, changes in this conditional probability and changes in such causal effects are tightly connected: a difference in the conditional probability between the two courses of events is indicative of a change in the causal status of C due to the transition from one course of events to another. If there are no such causal changes, if the transition from the $\sim A$ course to the A course is causally immaterial to C, there will be no change in the conditional probability of C: the two conditional probabilities (corresponding to the two courses — the A course and the $\sim A$-course) will be the same, and condition 2(52) will be true. Thus our claim that 2(52) is a necessary condition for the causal irrelevance of the A-event to the C-event is substantiated.

We can formulate this claim as:

Thesis 1.   If $A > C$ is an irrel-semifactual, then:

2(52) $P(C/A \ \& \ W) = P(C/\sim A \ \& \ W)$

3. Moreover, if A is causally irrelevant to C, that is, if the impact of the causal background of C (prior to t_A) is equally preserved in the A course and in the $\sim A$ course, if it is preserved irrespective of whether the A-event or the $\sim A$-event occurs, if the probability of C in both courses is equal — then the addition of either A or $\sim A$ to the conditional probability of C on the basis of W should not result in a different value for the conditional probability. That is, the conditional probability of C based on W should be the same as the conditional probability of C based on either $W \ \& \ A$ or

A Theory of Counterfactuals

W & $\sim A$: the addition of A or $\sim A$ should not change the value of the conditional probability if A makes no causal difference to C. Thus, if A is causally irrelevant to C:

(1) $P(C/A$ & $W) = P(C/W)$

and similarly:

(2) $P(C/\sim A$ & $W) = P(C/W)$

We have thus motivated different necessary conditions for A's being causally irrelevant to C. Before I proceed to give examples and discuss the conditions, I shall first clarify the relation between them in the following obvious theorem:

Theorem 1

Conditions 2(52), (1), and (2) are logically equivalent.

Proof

Lemma: For $0 < \alpha < 1$ and any x, y, the three numbers x, y, $\alpha x + (1-\alpha)y$ are either all different or all equal. *Proof*: If $x = y$, also $\alpha x + (1-\alpha)y = x = y$. If $x \neq y$, let $x < y$. Then $x < \alpha x + (1-\alpha)y < y$ (so x and y are on *different* sides of $\alpha x + (1-\alpha)y$).[5] Q.E.D.
   Let: $\alpha = P(A/W)$
        $x = P(C/A$ & $W)$
        $y = P(C/\sim A$ & $W)$
Then $P(C/W) = \alpha x + (1-\alpha)y$ (since $P(C/W = P(A/W)\cdot P(C/A\&W) + P(\sim A/W)\cdot P(C/\sim A\&W))$. Hence equality of any two among $P(C/W)$, $P(C/A$ & $W)$, and $P(C/\sim A$ & $W)$ is equivalent to equality of any other two. If equality does not obtain, $P(C/W)$ is between the two other. Q.E.D.

From the theorem it follows that: 2(52) $\leftrightarrow$ (2) $\leftrightarrow$ (1). Thus, the various formulations we have produced as probabilistic conditions that should hold if A is causally irrelevant to C are all equivalent.

4. Example 1. Consider example 3 of 2 III, concerning Jones and the stock market. We saw already that the counterfactual $A > C$:

2(22) Even if Jones had not sold his stock, there would still have been a sharp rise in the stock market.

which we discussed in example 11 of 2 IX, is an irrel-semifactual, its antecedent being causally irrelevant to its consequent. Let us examine conditions 2(52), (1), and (2) when applied to this example. Condition (2) would state that the conditional probability of a sharp rise in the stock market (given the previous history W) would not change if we added, as an additional datum, the item $\sim A$, i.e., that Jones sold his stock. And indeed, assuming (as we did) that Jones owned little stock and that his act of selling was motivated by personal considerations and was unrelated to any general trend, his selling the stock would have had practically no effect on the condition of the stock market. Thus, as an item added to the previous history, it would not have affected either way the possibility of a future rise in the stock market. Hence the probability of the occurrence of such a rise on the basis of the previous history of the world W, i.e., $P(C/W)$, would not change if we added the information that Jones sold his stock, that is, $P(C/\sim A \ \& \ W)$. Since A is irrelevant to C, adding $\sim A$ to W in the conditional probability of C would not change the value of that probability: the information that Jones sold his stock would neither increase the probability of a rise in the stock market, based on the previous history W, nor decrease it. Hence:

$$P(C/W) \ = \ P(C/\sim A \ \& \ W)$$

which is (2).

Similarly, had the event of Jones retaining his stock occurred, this again would not affect the stock market in the situation under consideration, and information to this effect would not change the probability of a rise based on the previous history W. Hence:

$$P(C/W) \ = \ P(C/A \ \& \ W)$$

which is (1). Hence (1) and (2) hold in this case.

2(52) follows from either (1) or (2), by theorem 1, and therefore holds in this example as well. Thus, the conditional probability of the rise, based on the previous history W, will have the same value when based, in addition, on the information that Jones sold his stock and when based, instead, on the information that he did not. It should indeed be intuitively clear that in our example 2(52) holds: it expresses the lack of effect on the conditional probability of a rise in the stock market, given the previous history, either of adding the information that Jones sold his stock or of adding the information that he did not. Thus we see that (1), (2) and 2(52) hold in this example. And indeed, the semifactual $A > C$:

2(22)   Even if Jones had not sold his stock, there would still have been a sharp rise in the stock market.

is intuitively true. Since A is causally irrelevant to C, this is, then, an irrel-semifactual which is, as such, true.

II   The Insufficiency of the Equi-probability Condition

1. We have argued that 2(52), the equi-probability condition, is a necessary condition for the causal irrelevance of A to C. Is it a sufficient condi-

tion as well? Is the satisfaction of the equiprobability of 2(52) an unfailing indication of the causal irrelevance of A to C? Unfortunately not. It may happen that A is causally relevant to C and the equiprobability condition 2(52) still holds.

To see this, consider a causal chain pertaining to times prior to t_A and leading to C. By a "causal chain" I mean a sequence of events, each of which "leads" to the next, i.e., is positively causally relevant to the next (its occurrence increases the probability of the chain's next link). Similarly, by the "causal background" of C I mean the variety of causal chains leading to C (or to $\sim C$) in W (together with other events or states of affairs in W relevant to their being such causal chains). Now it may well happen that the occurrence of the $\sim A$-event, rather than the A-event, would interfere with the transmission to C of the effect of this causal chain (which leads to C), diminish it, or even block it (whereas the occurrence of A would instead strengthen the causal effect of this chain on C). The occurrence of A, rather than $\sim A$, or vice-versa, would thus make a difference to the transmission to C of the effect of this causal chain. But it may well happen that prior to t_A there are two such causal chains, each leading to C, such that the occurrence of A or $\sim A$ would filter their effects on C differently. Thus it may well happen that the occurrence of A, rather than $\sim A$, would favorably filter the effect on C of the first causal chain, but interfere with that of the other (whereas the occurrence of $\sim A$, rather than A, would do the opposite). Thus, the effect of the $\sim A$–A transition on C would be mixed: the transmission of the effect of one causal chain leading to C would be strengthened, that of another weakened. And it might accidentally happen that the products of these weakenings and strengthenings balance out. Furthermore: coincidental probabilistic equality may occur not just with two causal chains, but with many, and not just with causal chains leading to C, but also with causal chains leading to $\sim C$. In such cases, when the impact on C of each such causal chain, which is differentially affected by the transition, is accidentally counterbalanced by another, the condition $P(C/A \ \& \ W) = P(C/\sim A \ \& \ W)$ will still hold. Obviously, however, in such cases the transition from A to $\sim A$ is causally relevant to C, since it affects the relation between C and its causal background. In extreme cases, such a transition may wipe out the impact of one causal chain while, at the same time, sufficiently increasing that of another so as to compensate for it probabilistically. But changes of this type would modify the various effects on C of its causal background and thus would obviously indicate that the transition is causally relevant to C. A semifactual whose antecedent is so related to its consequent cannot be retained on the basis of inertia, that is, on the basis of C's being unaffected by the transition. Such events would be among those affected by transition, just like those events D for which the $\sim A$–A transition would bring about the sort of change in their causal backgrounds that would increase their conditional probability [so that $P(D/A \ \& \ W) > P(D/\sim A \ \& \ W)$]. As we noted in 2 VI, a mere increase in the probability of events as a result of the $\sim A$–A transition does not automatically make the statements describing them retainable as legitimate premises for a counterfactual with antecedent A; in such cases only purely positive causal relevance would make them retainable. Likewise, it is causal irrelevance, and not (mere) equiprobability or probabilistic invariance, that licenses retainability as a legitimate premise. A lack of causal relevance is not compensated for by probabilistic equality that results from shifts within the over-all balance of the effects on C among the various antecedent causal chains, shifts which the $\sim A$–A transition yields (even though the over-all balance of effects does not change). So there may be causal relevance while the equi-probability condition 2(52) obtains, and 2(52) is not a sufficient condition for causal irrelevance. Hence, to get a necessary and sufficient condition for causal irrelevance, and thus for irrel-semifactuals, we need to modify 2(52).

2. Example 2. Consider the counterfactual $A > C$, where:

A = 'China intervened in the Vietnam war in 1968'
C = 'The U.S. did not use atomic weapons in the Vietnam war (between 1968 and 1973)'

Now $A > C$ is the semifactual:

(3)   Even if China had intervened in the Vietnam war in 1968, the U.S. would still not have used atomic weapons (between 1968 and 1973).[6]

I claim that $A > C$ is not an irrel-semifactual: the antecedent A is not causally irrelevant to the consequent C. This is because it is not true that China's intervention would have made no difference to the use of atomic weapons by the U.S. A Chinese intervention would have changed substantially the ways that the causal background of a potential use of U.S. atomic power bears on such a use, and it would make a causal difference to the occurrence of such a use.

Thus, consider the prominence of the different causal antecedents of C in the A course and in the $\sim A$ course. In the $\sim A$ course, in which China does not intervene, the causal background of the use of atomic weapons includes the following elements: there is a strong inclination to avoid a use of atomic weapons, as long as victory, or at least a settlement, achieved through the use of conventional forces, seems feasible, does not take a very long time, and does not require a substantial increase of American man-power. There is also, on the other hand, an increasing tendency to resort to atomic power in proportion to the anticipation of the danger of defeat, or indefinite stalemate, and in proportion to a decrease in domestic pro-tests against the use of such weapons. The chances of the use of atomic weapons in this course are determined by the impact of such considera-tions and perceptions on key decision-makers, political circles, power blocs, and public opinion.

Consequently, a causal chain leading to C would involve the processes through which the superpower balance, which created a deterrent to the use of atomic weapons, was reached: processes through which American public opinion against the use of atomic weapons in Vietnam evolved; the progress of the negotiations with North Vietnam; and so forth. A causal chain leading to ∼ C would involve processes such as increasing sensitivity to American involvement and loss of life in Vietnam; a growing conviction that the U.S. could not afford to lose a war against a smaller nation; rising sentiments to terminate the war no matter what; gloomy evaluations as to the efficacy of the ongoing military efforts and as to the eventual outcome of the war, if limited to conventional weapons, and so forth.

The combined effect of such causal antecedents determines the probability of C in the ∼ A course: some (those factors which are elements of causal chains leading to C) will increase it, others will decrease it. Let us designate the probability of atomic weapons not being so used in the ∼ A course by 'p' (whatever it may be here). Thus: $P(C/\sim A \ \& \ W) = p$.

Consider, on the other hand, the profile of the causal background for the use of U.S. atomic power in case China intervenes in the war. A causal chain leading to a use of U.S. atomic power would then prominently involve factors such as: political pressures motivating the U.S. not to lose a "head-on" confrontation among the superpowers for fear of losing a deterrent capacity; gloomy evaluations of the chances of winning a conventional war against the Chinese; the projected cost of such a conventional war; etc. These factors will weigh against others, such as the estimated risks inherent in an atomic war, apprehensions as to the danger of creating a precedent for initiating the use of atomic weapons, and so forth. Factors such as the latter will play a role in a causal chain leading to a decision not to use atomic weapons. Notice that the effect on C of causal factors that are weighty in the ∼ A course diminishes substantially in the A course, and that factors that are crucial in the A course do not play much of a role in the ∼ A course. For instance, factors bearing on the motivations for winning the war that are effective in the ∼ A course become negligible in the A course, in view of global considerations which make it imperative not to lose a superpower confrontation. Thus, we see how the transition from the ∼ A course to the A course can change the prominence and the effects on C of certain causal chains, and thereby alter the relation of C to its causal background. These changes, due to the transition, determine its causal relevance to C.

Let us designate the probability of the U.S. not using atomic weapons in the A course by 'q'. Thus $P(C/A \ \& \ W) = q$. We did not elaborate on considerations concerning the quantitative determination of p and q. But it is clear from our discussion that the prominent causal antecedents of C in the two courses, and thus the values of the respective probabilities $P(C/A \ \& \ \sim W)$ and $P(C/A \ \& \ W)$ are, to a large extent, independent. Thus, it may well be the case that the values of these two probabilities, p and q, happen to coincide — that the chance of the U.S. not using atomic power in case China intervenes (say, just to give it a figure, 60%) turns out to equal the chance of the U.S. not using atomic power in case China does not intervene, even though the causal backgrounds that prominently determine these probabilities are quite different. In this case the condition:

$P(C/A \ \& \ W) = P(C/\sim A \ \& \ W)$ would be satisfied, and thus 2(52) would come out true, *even though* $A > C$ is *not* an irrel-semifactual. Thus, even though the ways the causal background of C bears on it in the two courses may vary, the probabilities may *accidentally* come out the same. The equiprobability condition is *not* a sufficient condition for the causal irrelevance of A to C.

3. The misguided acceptance of the equiprobability condition as a necessary and sufficient condition for causal irrelevance and its use for the characterization of irrel-semifactuals as they function in the theory presented in chapter 2, would render that theory inadequate. This can be seen via the example above. Assume that there has been a firm Chinese policy not to be the *first* to use atomic weapons under any circumstances, including a war in Vietnam with the U.S. Now consider the counterfactual $A > B$, where:

> $B =$ 'China does not use its atomic weapons in the Vietnam war (until 1973)'.

I claim that this counterfactual $A > B$: If China had intervened in the Vietnam war in 1968, it would not have used its atomic weapons during that war (before 1973). is false: For all we know, if China had entered the war, the U.S. might have used its atomic weapons in Vietnam (we have considered above the causal antecedents for such a use), in which case China might have retaliated with atomic power, which would not be incompatible with its policy as described above.

However, if we accept the equiprobability condition as necessary and sufficient for irrel-semifactuals, then $A > C$ qualifies as an irrel-semifactual, and hence is true. Thus, in this example, under the hypothesis that A is true, the U.S. would not introduce atomic power in Vietnam, China would not be the first to use its own, and hence China would not use atomic power in Vietnam at all, which makes our counterfactual $A > B$ true. We therefore see that the equiprobability condition does not adequately characterize irrel-semifactuals and that if it were nevertheless accepted as characterizing them in the framework of our general analysis of counterfactuals, it would make false counterfactuals (such as $A > B$) come out true.

III   *Toward a Criterion of Causal Irrelevance*

1. Realizing that the equiprobability condition, though necessary for a counterfactual to be an irrel-semifactual, is not sufficient, we will attempt to find a necessary and sufficient condition by modifying it. In order to find such a condition, we have to ask ourselves how to block a situation of the type described in the previous section, where the equiprobability condition failed to screen out causal relevance between A and C. In this type of situation there is (prior to t_A) more than one causal chain relevant to the occurrence of C: one such chain is blocked (or interfered with) in

the A course and another in the $\sim A$ course, even though the conditional probability of C happens (accidentally) to be the same in the two courses. The causal relevance in this case amounts to the transition from $\sim A$ to A modifying the impact on C of causal chains prior to t_A that lead to the occurrence of C or $\sim C$. Thus, A is causally irrelevant to C if the occurrence of A rather than $\sim A$ (or conversely) leaves the relation between C and its causal background intact; if, as judged on the basis of the previous history (prior to t_A), causal chains (prior to t_A) that lead to C or to $\sim C$ would still do so regardless of whether A or $\sim A$ took place, and have the same effect on C in both courses; if the transition from one course of events to another does not screen out, or filter, the impact on C of its causal background in any significant way; if neither A nor $\sim A$ plays a role in transmitting to C effects from its causal background; if C would occur or fail to occur irrespective of whether the A course or the $\sim A$ course took place. Where A is causally irrelevant to C, the transition from one course to another has no effect on the impact of causal chains prior to t_A, so far as C is concerned: the subsequent development of the paths of such chains in the (t_A, t_C) interval and the way their effects on C would be transmitted in it are not dependent on which course materializes. Since the effects of such causal chains on C have to be transmitted through intermediate events, the occurrence of events in the (t_A, t_C) interval which would be significant for the transmission to C of effects of such causal chains prior to t_A would not itself be affected by the transition. That is, the transition would not affect events in the (t_A, t_C) interval in such a way as to affect the transmission to C of effects of previous causal chains. The transition would not interfere with the effects of previous causal chains on C by not interfering with their transmission to C through intermediate events in the (t_A, t_C) interval. Thus, with no screening effect upon the impact of previous causal chains on C, the transition would not affect either the *occurrence* of events in the (t_A, t_C) interval that are material to the transmission of the effect of previous causal chains to C, or the *effect* on C to be transmitted through these events.

Thus, causal relevance of A to C is reflected in the effects that the transition has on events in the (t_A, t_C) interval which are important for the transmission of the effects of previous causal chains on C. Since the causal chains prior to t_A would have to be connected to C by intermediate events in order to discharge their effect on C, the causal irrelevance of the transition should be detectable by its effects (or lack of effects) on such intermediate events. Events in the (t_A, t_C) interval which are significant for the transmission of the causal effect of such a previous causal chain to C should not, if the transition is causally irrelevant, be affected by it insofar as their occurrence is concerned, nor should their role in transmitting, strengthening, or weakening these causal effects be affected by the transition. Such an effect of the transition from $\sim A$ to A on these events would amount to "filtering" the effects of previous causal chains. If the transition affects positively the occurrence of events in this interval whose occurrence makes (in both courses) a positive contribution to the transmission of the effect of a previous causal chain leading to C, then the transition thereby serves to enhance or secure the effectiveness of the causal chain by increasing the chances of its proper transmission. Similarly, a negative effect on the occurrence of such events would decrease the effectiveness of the chain. Alternatively, if the transition minimizes the effects on C of such an event which, without the transition, would serve to amplify the transmitted effects on C of a previous causal chain, the transition thereby diminishes the effects on C of that causal chain, and thus diminishes the chain's effectiveness. Likewise, by maximizing the effect of such an event, the transition would amplify the effect of the causal chain on C.

In other words, the effect of the transition on the relations between C and its previous causal chains can be traced by its effect on the way causal effects are to be *transmitted* from these causal chains to C in the (t_A,t_C) interval. That is, the relevance of the transition can be traced by its effect on significant events in the (t_A,t_C) interval: events whose occurrence is significant for the transmission to C of the causal effects of previous causal chains in one of the courses; events whose occurrence would provide for their participation in the transfer of these effects of such causal chains or which would themselves be relevant to it, if they occurred, in one of the courses; events whose occurrence makes a difference for the transmitted effect on C in such a course; events whose occurrence would change the effectiveness of such a causal chain on C in such a course; events whose occurrence either strengthens or weakens the transfer of the effect of some such causal chain to C in such a course. The effect of the transition on such events can take the form of affecting the probability of their occurrence, as well as of affecting their transmitting capacity: the transition may minimize or maximize the role they would have (if they occurred) in transmitting the causal effect on C from previous causal chains, thereby altering the amplifying or restraining effect they would have as transmitters of these causal chains. This may happen if the transition affects the chances of occurrence of events that are important for the transmission of the effect of previous causal chains, or if the role, or effectiveness, they would have in transmitting this effect becomes differentiated between the two courses. In such a case of causal relevance, for some events in the (t_A,t_C) interval which are significant for the transmission of the effect of a previous causal chain to C in one of the courses, there would be either a difference in the probability of their occurrence or a difference in the effect they would transmit to C between the two courses. Conversely, events in the (t_A,t_C) interval, which are significant for the transmission of the effects of previous causal chains to C and which are affected by the transition as to their own occurrence or their role in transmitting those effects, should be indicative of the causal relevance of the transition to C.

This is, then, the condition for causal relevance that can compensate for the inadequacy of 2(52). In section IV we will reformulate this condition with greater formal precision. If indeed there are such effects of the transition on some events in the (t_A,t_C) interval, these events are indeed *indicators* of the causal relevance of A to C; and if A is causally relevant to C, then this causal relevance should manifest itself in such intermediate indicative events. We have, therefore, established a necessary and sufficient condition for causal irrelevance, with the aid of intermediate events in the (t_A, t_C) interval, which can now replace condition 2(52).

IV The Transmission Condition for Causal Irrelevance

1. When the occurrence of an event in (t_A, t_C) is material to the transmission of the effect of a previous causal chain to C in a given course, its occurrence (contrasted with its nonoccurrence there) makes a difference to the occurrence of C in that course; this difference is reflected in a change in the probability of the occurrence of C. In view of the analysis we reached at the end of section III, we arrive at the following formulation:

(4) A is causally relevant to C iff, for some actual event in (t_A, t_C), whose occurrence affects the probability of the occurrence of C in the A course or the $\sim A$ course, the $\sim A$–A transition would change either the probability of its own occurrence or its effect on C.

As I have argued, this is a necessary and sufficient condition for the causal relevance of A to C. As such, it also takes care of the failure of the equiprobability condition 2(52) to capture causal relevance in the case of two previous mutually neutralizing causal chains. Therefore (when expressed as a condition for causal irrelevance), it also replaces the equiprobability condition as a necessary and sufficient condition for a counterfactual's being an irrel-semifactual. This, then, is the condition we have been seeking.

2. Let us express condition (4) in equiprobability terms, thus reducing irrel-semifactuals and, in turn, counterfactuals, to probabilistic terms, as intended.

A is causally relevant to C iff:

(5)   Either $\{A, W, L, C\}$ is inconsistent[7]
          or there is an actual event e in the (t_A, t_C) interval, which satisfies:
          either   (i) $P(C/e \ \& \ \sim A \ \& \ W) \ \neq \ P(C/\sim A \ \& \ W)$
          or   (ii) $P(C/e \ \& \ A \ \& \ W) \ \neq \ P(C/A \ \& \ W)$
          and which also satisfies:
          either   (iii) $P(e/A \ \& \ W) \ \neq \ P(e/\sim A \ \& \ W)$
          or   (iv) $P(C/e \ \& \ \sim A \ \& \ W) \ \neq \ P(C/e \ \& \ A \ \& \ W)$.

(5i) requires that the event e make a difference for the occurrence of C in the $\sim A$ course, and (5ii) requires that it make such a difference in the A course. It does so by specifying that e changes the probability of the occurrence of C in the respective courses. In other words, to require that (5i) or that (5ii) is to require that the probability of C in one course (at least) will vary with the added assumption that e happens, and similarly for $\sim e$. [Remember that (5i) is equivalent to:

$$P(C/e \ \& \ \sim A \ \& \ W) \ \neq \ P(C/ \sim e \ \& \ \sim A \ \& \ W)$$

as well as to
$$P(C/ \sim A \ \& \ W) \ \neq \ P(C/ \sim e \ \& \ \sim A \ \& \ W)$$

by theorem 1, and that, similarly, (5ii) is equivalent to:
$$P(C/e \ \& \ A \ \& \ W) \ \neq \ P(C/ \sim e \ \& \ A \ \& \ W)$$

as well as to
$$P(C/A \ \& \ W) \ \neq \ P \ (C/ \sim e \ \& \ A \ \& \ W).]$$

(5iii) requires that the $\sim A$–A transition make a difference to the occurrence of e, by requiring that the transition affect the probability of occurrence of e. We will see below what (5iv) expresses.

It would be helpful to formulate explicitly the necessary and sufficient condition for causal *ir*relevance, which is the condition for irrel-semifactuals. Since (5) expresses a necessary and sufficient condition for causal relevance, we obtain it by taking the negation of (5).

The transmission condition (on W, A, and C) (for the causal irrelevance of A to C) is:

(7) $\{W,A,L,C\}$ is consistent, and:
        For every actual event e in the (t_A, t_C) interval, if it satisfies
        either   (i) $P(C/e \ \& \ \sim A \ \& \ W)$ $\neq$ $P(C/ \sim A \ \& \ W)$
        or   (ii) $P(C/e \ \& \ A \ \& \ W)$ $\neq$ $P(C/A \ \& \ W)$
        then it satisfies *both*:
                (iii) $P(e/A \ \& \ W)$ $=$ $P(e/ \sim A \ \& \ W)$
        and   (iv) $P(C/e \ \& \ \sim A \ \& \ W)$ $=$ $P(C/e \ \& \ A \ \& \ W)$.

Since the analysis in (7), as in (5), is based on the idea that causal relevance is reflected by differential transmission between the two courses to C of effects of previous causal chains via intermediate events, we call (7) **the transmission condition** (for causal irrelevance).

3. I added the condition that W, A, L, and C be consistent, since otherwise $A \ \& \ W \overset{\text{1}}{\nrightarrow} \sim C$, but $\{A,W,L\}$ is consistent (since we deal here with n-d counterfactuals). Obviously, the $\sim A$–A transition is causally relevant to C, since $W \overset{\text{1}}{\nrightarrow} \sim C$, since $\{W,L,C\}$ is consistent (they are all true), and $A > C$ cannot be an irrel-semifactual (we do not have to worry about $\{W, \sim A, L, C\}$: it is consistent since they are all true).

I have explained conditions (5i), (5ii), and (5iii); through them the import of conditions (7i), (7ii), and (7iii) becomes clear too. Now what condition (7iv) expresses is that the $\sim A$–A transition does not make a difference to the effect that e would transmit to C. It expresses the claim that the effect of e on C in the two courses is the same. To see this, note that a literal formulation of the claim that the transition does not change the effect that e has on C, i.e., the claim that e has the same effect on C in both courses, is:

(6) $P(C/e \ \& \ A \ \& \ W) - P(C/A \ \& \ W) =$
     $P(C/e \ \& \ {\sim}A \ \& \ W) - P(C/{\sim}A \ \& \ W)$

But on the basis of 2(52), (6) reduces to (7iv), i.e.: $P(C/e \ \& \ {\sim}A \ \& \ W) = P(C/e \ \& \ A \ \& \ W)$.

Now, in order to explain this import of (7iv), we needed the equiprobability condition 2(52). But notice that 2(52) is, as we have seen in section I, a necessary condition for causal irrelevance. Since the transmission condition (7) is to be a necessary and sufficient condition for causal irrelevance, 2(52) ought to follow from (7). If it does, we would be justified in using it for the explanation of the import of (7iv). That 2(52) follows from (7) is thus clearly an adequacy condition for our analysis. And indeed:

Theorem 2

The transmission condition implies the equiprobability condition.
Proof

> Suppose (7) obtains. Of course, $P(C/C \ \& \ {\sim}A \ \& \ W) = 1$.
> (Notice that the conjunction $C \ \& \ {\sim}A \ \& \ W$ is consistent, since all the conjuncts are true.) Hence, except for the case when $P(C/{\sim}A \ \& \ W) = 1$:
> $P(C/C \ \& \ {\sim}A \ \& \ W) \neq P(C/{\sim}A \ \& \ W)$, and C satisfies (7i).
> Now if $P(C/{\sim}A \ \& \ W) = 1$, then either $P(C/A \ \& \ W) = 1$ or not. If $P(C/A \ \& \ W) = 1$, then obviously
> $P(C/{\sim}A \ \& \ W) = P(C/A \ \& \ W)$, which is 2(52). Otherwise, if $P(C/A \ \& \ W) \neq 1$, then
> $P(C/C \ \& \ A \ \& \ W) \neq P(C/A \ \& \ W)$, since
> $P(C/C \ \& \ A \ \& \ W) = 1$ as well (recall that $\{W, A, L, C\}$ is consistent), and C satisfies (7ii). Thus, C satisfies either (7i) or (7ii) (or else, as we already saw, 2(52) obtains). But then, by (7), C also satisfies (7iii), i.e.:
> $P(C/A \ \& \ W) = P(C/{\sim}A \ \& \ W)$, which is, again, 2(52), the equiprobability condition. Therefore, on the assumption that (7), the transmission condition, obtains, 2(52), the equiprobability condition, obtains too.   Q.E.D.

4. We have, accordingly, seen that the equiprobability condition is implied by the transmission condition, as we would have expected. I prefer the use of (7iv) to (6) in (7), since it is simpler and contains only equiprobability conditions. We have just seen how to interpret (7iv); the interpretation of (5iv) (which we delayed discussing) is, of course, analogous. If the equiprobability condition obtains, (5iv) expresses the condition that the transition changes the effect of e on C, since ${\sim}(6)$, which expresses precisely that, follows from 2(52) and (5iv).[8]

To sum up, the upshot of this section[9] is as follows:

Thesis 2: A semifactual $A > C$ is an irrel-semifactual iff: A is causally irrelevant to C iff the transmission condition (7) holds.

1. Example 3. To illustrate the transmission condition for causal irrelevance, consider the following case:

> Once upon a time there was a king in a country named Kingdom. Kingdom was on bad terms with its neighbor, Republic. There were two influential factions in Kingdom: the nationalists, who felt that a war should be waged against Republic to restore the honor of Kingdom, and the military industrialists, who were interested in war even more than the nationalists in order to conquer some rich neighboring part of Republic for economic advantage. There were also those who did not want war at all. The king had a weak personality, and his political decisions were completely dominated by the woman who happened to be his mistress at the time. The king maintained, by disposition, a very deep, though fixed, degree of monogamous attachment with each of his successive mistresses. His mistress at the beginning of that period was a strong nationalist, and consequently so were the king's policies. It happened that one day, for some reason, Republic arrested Kingdom's ambassador. The nationalists in Kingdom demanded war against Republic to avenge this affront, and their enthusiasm for war reached the level of the military industrialists'. During the war debate, the King accidentally met another woman, Berta, at a party in his palace. Berta's convictions were typical military industrialist — as much as the king's former mistress's convictions were typical nationalist.

So far we have supplied, for the analysis to follow, information to be included in the previous history of the world W.

> The king, however, became infatuated with Berta upon their meeting at the party, and consequently abandoned his former mistress. True to his character, he became infatuated with Berta to the same extent he had been with his former mistress.
>
> Republic, however, wanted to avoid war at that time. It released the captured ambassador and offered compensation (and thereby cooled down the temper of the nationalists and their desire to wage war). The king, however, under the influence of the military industrialists, refused to acknowledge this conciliatory gesture, and launched a war.

Consider now the following statements:

> A = 'The king did not become infatuated with Berta (at the party)'
>
> C = 'Kingdom waged war against Republic'
>
> e = 'Republic released the captured ambassador and offered compensation'

2. Consider the counterfactual $A > C$:

> Even if the king had not met Berta, Kingdom would still have waged war against Republic.

Its consequent is true, and hence it is a semifactual; but it is *not* an irrel-semifactual. The reason is that A is crucially causally relevant to C, since the king waged war in response to the urgings of the military industrialists, whose influence he was under at the time, thanks to Berta. Had the king not met Berta, he would have waged war only at the urging of the nationalists, under whose influence he would have been at the time through his former mistress. We can therefore safely assume, given the story of our example, that since the enthusiasm of both groups for war (prior to the release of the ambassador) was equal, and since the commitments of his two mistresses to their respective camps were also the same, and so were the king's characteristic attachments to his mistresses, the pressures on the king through his respective mistresses were equal. Hence the probability of the king waging war on the assumption that he fell in love with Berta and the probability of his waging war on the assumption that he did not, when both probabilities are based on W, i.e., the course of events prior to the romantic turnabout, are the same. Therefore:

(8) $P(C/A \ \& \ W) = P(C/{\sim}A \ \& \ W)$

which is our equiprobability condition 2(52). Since $A > C$ is not an irrel-semifactual, this is another example illustrating why 2(52) is not a sufficient condition for a semifactual to be an irrel-semifactual.

However, had the king not fallen in love with Berta, the release of the ambassador would have cooled his then dominant nationalist motivations for war and the probability of war would have diminished. Hence,

(8′) $P(C/e \ \& \ A \ \& \ W) < P(C/A \ \& \ W)$

But in the actual case, the release did not affect his motivations at all, since they were military-industrialist in character. Thus:

(8″) $P(C/e \ \& \ {\sim}A \ \& \ W) = P(C/{\sim}A \ \& \ W)$

By (8), (8′), and (8″) we get:

(9) $P(C/e \ \& \ A \ \& \ W) < P(C/e \ \& \ {\sim}A \ \& \ W)$

hence:

(10) $P(C/e \ \& \ A \ \& \ W) \neq P(C/e \ \& \ {\sim}A \ \& \ W)$

and from (8′) we get:

(11) $P(C/e \ \& \ A \ \& \ W) \neq P(C/A \ \& \ W)$

(11) is just condition (7ii), but (10) is just condition $\sim$(7iv). Hence e satisfies (7ii) and $\sim$(7iv), the transmission condition is violated, and, by thesis 2, A is judged causally relevant to C; hence $A > C$ does *not* come out as an irrel-semifactual, which indeed it is not.[10]

It seems that this example illustrates how there can be two different causal backgrounds to C, prior to t_A, and how the $\sim A$–A transition can amplify the impact of one and weaken that of the other, and thereby become causally relevant to C. In such a case $A > C$ is not, of course, an irrel-semifactual. In our case, one causal background pertains to the pressures toward war from the nationalists, whereas the other pertains to the pressures from the military industrialists. Here, the two causal backgrounds are respectively screened out in each branch of the transition: the first causal background is neutralized by $\sim A$, the second by A. However, it turns out accidentally that the equiprobability condition 2(52) holds, in spite of the filtering effect that the transition has on the previous causal background. This is accordingly a case of two causal backgrounds each of which is neutralized in one branch of the transition.

3. We can also apply our transmission criterion to example 2, discussed in section II. Recall that we examined the semifactual $A > C$ ['Even if China had intervened in the Vietnam war in 1968, the U.S. would still not have used atomic weapons (between 1968 and 1973)'], and concluded that it was not an irrel-semifactual, even though the equiprobability condition obtained.

To apply criterion (7), consider:

e = 'The U.S. was not winning a conventional war in Vietnam (in 1969)'

Given the way we specified W in our discussion of this example in section II and our comments there, the danger of the U.S. using its atomic weapons first, if China had intervened, would have been greater had the U.S. faced an impasse or even a defeat in a conventional war: such a prospect would have strengthened earlier convictions that the U.S. cannot afford not to win a war to another power, and this would have increased the willingness to use atomic weapons. This strengthened motivation in favor of atomic power would in turn raise the probability of its use. Hence:

$P(C/e \ \& \ A \ \& \ W) < P(C/\sim e \ \& \ A \ \& \ W)$

and thus

$P(C/e \ \& \ A \ \& \ W) \neq P(C/A \ \& \ W)$

(by theorem 1), and therefore *e* fulfills condition (7ii).

Moreover, it is quite clear that Chinese intervention in the war would considerably change the ratio of enemy/U.S. power, decreasing the chances of the U.S. winning a conventional war. Therefore:

$$P(e/A \ \& \ W) > P(e/\sim A \ \& \ W)$$

Hence

$$P(e/A \ \& \ W) \neq P(e/\sim A \ \& \ W)$$

and so *e* violates condition (7iii).

Hence *e* violates (7), the transmission condition; by thesis 2, *A* is causally relevant to *C*; and $A > C$ comes out as a *non*-irrel-semifactual. Thus, our criteria and analysis are upheld, and the case study is explained.[11]

4. It may be useful to examine how condition (7), in particular the provision (7iii), propelled us beyond the problems of 2(52). The problem with 2(52) was, as we recall, the possibility of two (or more) causal chains, which are differentially affected by the $\sim A$–A transition insofar as their effects on *C* are concerned, thereby being indicative of causal relevance, which yet accidentally yield equiprobabilistic balance. But (7) is formulated in equiprobability terms as well, and it might be asked whether the previous problems with 2(52) may not therefore recur with (7).

For the sake of clarity, we can present the transmission condition in the following ways:

A is causally irrelevant to C iff (7); i.e., iff[12]

(e) {e is actual ⊃ {[(7i)∨(7ii)] ⊃ [(7iii)&(7iv)]}}
(e) {e is actual ⊃ { ∼[(7i)∨(7ii)]∨[(7iii)&(7iv)]}}
(e) {e is actual ⊃ {[∼(7i)& ∼(7ii)]∨[(7iii)&(7iv)]}}

Notice that all four conditions ∼(7i), ∼(7ii), (7iii), and (7iv) are equiprobability conditions [of the form $P(\_\_) = P(\ . \ . \ . \ )$]. Let us ignore (7iv) for a moment. An event *e*, then, would satisfy the condition in case it satisfies ∼(7i) and ∼(7ii), which are equiprobability conditions akin in form to 2(52) with $\sim A \ \& \ W$ and with $A \ \& \ W$ replacing *W*, respectively (recall theorem 1)[13]; or else, it satisfies (7iii), which is also of the form of 2(52) (for *e* instead of *C*). Have we not, it may be asked, replaced the equiprobability condition 2(52) for *C* by breaking it into, on the one hand, equiprobability conditions for *C* in the two courses (*W* being supplemented once by *A* and once by $\sim A$), and, on the other, an equiprobability condition for *e*? Could (7) not be interpreted as requiring causal irrelevance of the $\sim A$–A transition to *e*, or causal irrelevance to *C* by *e* in each course, so that if the transition proves causally irrelevant to *e* or if *e* proves causally irrelevant to *C* in both courses (for every appropriate *e*), we establish that the transition is causally irrelevant to *C*? But wouldn't the problem of the inadequacy of the equiprobability condition as an indicator of causal irrelevance plague us here again in either of the two stages, since we are using equiprobability again? Couldn't it happen, even if one of these equiprobability conditions obtained, that there would still be a corresponding causal relevance due to interference by the transition with the impact of two prior causal chains, whose effects accidentally balance out in the two courses? Wouldn't there then indeed be causal relevance of A to C (by transitivity), even though our condition will yield otherwise? Have we not simply pushed the problem with 2(52) that plagued us before, back to conditions that involve e (instead of C or A, respectively) without really solving it or showing how to avoid it?

5. The answer, I believe, is *no*. True, any equiprobability in one of these three conditions, for a given event e, will be insufficient for the corresponding causal irrelevance, for the same reason that 2(52) is insufficient. But the point ignored in the above argument is that in (7) we do not deal with a *particular* event e; instead we quantify over events that satisfy its provisions. The condition states that there is causal irrelevance if *all* events e between t_A and t_C satisfy those conditions. It may well happen that this or that particular event may be indicative of causal relevance, while suffering from the phenomenon of such an *accidental* equiprobability yielded by the impact of two such causal chains being affected yet balanced out by the transition. But the import of the condition is that if A is causally relevant to C, this would not happen to *all* such events e: not all those events e which are significant for the transmission of the effects of any of the causal chains that together yield the equiprobability in 2(52) would in turn accidentally be the victims of the same phenomenon. In case of causal relevance, an event could be found whose significance for the transmission would manifest itself in lack of equiprobability in the appropriate conditions. In (7) we add to the probabilistic manifestations of A expressed in 2(52) the probabilistic manifestations of a *large variety* of events that are significant for the transmission of the effects of prior causal chains, all of which would not be subject to such an accident in a case of genuine causal relevance, thought some might be. But in 2(52) the probabilistic manifestations of A *alone* were displayed, and, being a single event, such an exceptional phenomenon as the accidental balancing out by the transition of the effects of two prior causal chains whose impacts are differentially affected by it, could indeed take place.[14]

6. Moreover, in our discussion above we ignored (7iv) for the sake of argument. But even if the indicativeness of causal relevance of an event e is undermined by the vulnerability of the equiprobability form of condition (7iii), condition (7iv) can still make e yield the desired result, thus saving its indicative character and restoring the adequacy of condition (7) even before we resort to *other* events in the interval that the transmission condition avails itself of. As is clear from (7), condition (7iv), just like condition (7iii), *must* be satisfied by any event that maintains (7i) or (7ii) if the transmission condition is to hold and thus for causal irrelevance to be established by it. But (7iv) is not of the same form as 2(52)[15], and the above

argument, which derives its force from the problematics of 2(52), does not therefore, as is, apply to (7iv). Even if accidental equiprobability were to plague (7iii) for a given event, in spite of causal relevance, the event in question would still have to satisfy (7iv), which is not vulnerable to the same kind of difficulty and which could thus reveal the causal relevance even when (7iii) is so impaired.

VI   Probability

1. So far I have commented only briefly on the notion of probability which I have been using (cf. 4 I 1). Surely what is required for the purpose of an objective analysis of counterfactuals is an objective notion of probability. Such a notion, however, it seems, might constitute a significant ingredient in various realist perspectives, regardless of whether or not counterfactuals are discussed. In this section I shall elaborate further on how such a notion may be fleshed out.

To begin with, consider, as an approximation, the world under discrete (and well-ordered) time. That is, every temporal point has a successor, and in the passage of time the world moves from one state to another. What will govern the transitions from one state to another will be **transitional probabilities**. Thus, there will be a certain probability of the world's moving from an arbitrary state S_j to some state S_i as its consecutive state. Now I shall assume that the world is a Markovian system, in that the transitional probabilities of moving directly from state S_j to state S_i depend solely on these two states. In particular, the transitional probabilities do not depend on the history of the world prior to the state S_j. Thus, the transitional probabilities will have the form:

(12) $P(S_i/S_j) = q$

What (12) therefore expresses is that the probability of the world moving from state S_j directly to state S_i is q. (Of course, certain constraints must be imposed to ensure a proper probability function.)[16]

2. What has been said so far sets the stage for presenting a more general notion of transitional probabilities. So far we have considered the probabilities of direct, unmediated transitions from a given state to another, which we may call **consecutive transitional probabilities**. But we need not restrict ourselves to these: we may consider in general the probability of moving from state S_j to state S_i after n transitions (rather than just one). Such probabilities of moving from one state to another after a specified number of stages (i.e., of units of time) can be called **generalized transitional probabilities**. Generalized transitional probabilities can be specified on the basis of consecutive transitional probabilities. Thus, suppose we are interested in the probabilities of transitions from a given state S after n units of time. Consider then the space consisting of n-tuples of states. The probability of each such n-tuple $\langle S_1, \ldots, S_n \rangle$ can be specified in terms of consecutive transitional probabilities as:

(13) $P(\langle S_1, \ldots, S_n \rangle / S) = P(S_1/S) \cdot \prod_{i=1}^{n-1} P(S_{i+1}/S_i)$

Thus, the probability of moving from state S to state S' after n stages would then be (where $s_i = \langle S_{i_1}, \ldots, S_{i_n} \rangle$):

(14) $\sum_i P(s_i/S)$ $S_{i_n} = S'$

We can designate this probability as $P_n(S'/S)$.

3. Now let us focus again just on consecutive transitional probabilities and consider the probability of a given sentence being true at the next stage, given state S.[17] For a given state S and a sentence r, consider first the variety of states in which r is true.[18] The probability of r being true at the next stage, given S, is clearly the sum of the consecutive transitional probabilities of transitions to states in which r is true, given S. Thus, suppose $\delta_r(S_i)$ is a characteristic function which yields 1 or 0 according to whether r is true or false at S_i. Then the probability of r being true at the next stage, given S, is:

(15) $\sum_i P(S_i/S) \cdot \delta_r(S_i)$

with i varying over the indices of all the different states. We can mark this probability as $P(r/S)$.

Clearly this notion of the probability of a sentence r being true at the next stage, given S, can be generalized to the notion of the probability of a sentence r being true at the nth stage, given S. Thus, using the notion $P_n(S'/S)$ of the generalized transitional probability of moving to state S' from state S after n stages, the probability of a sentence r being true after n stages, given S, would be:

(16) $\sum_i P_n(S_i/S) \cdot \delta_r(S_i)$

We can mark this probability as $P_n(r/S)$.

4. The account presented above needs to be generalized and elaborated in a number of directions. At this point I would only mention a couple of such directions.

First, the treatment of time as discrete has to be abstracted from in favor of continuous time. This will lead to the generalization of the notion of $P_n(r/S)$, the probability of sentence r after n stages, given stage S, in favor of the notion of $P_t(r/S)$, the probability of r after an interval of length t, given stage S (t being any positive real number).[19] Secondly, one would want to generalize this notion so as to allow for the notion of the probability of a sentence r being true *at a time interval T after time t*, given stage S, that is, $P_t(r_T/S)$. Thus, we may want to consider the probability of r being true not just at a temporal point, but at an interval of length T stretching after the passage of a time-interval t. For that purpose our discussion in 6 I, II below concerning temporal regimentation of sentences would be useful, since it provides for the decomposition of a sentence into its temporally quantified temporally pure projection and its reference time. Usually, of course, we would be concerned with sentences whose reference times are intervals rather than temporal points. This notion, then, of the probability of a sentence being true at a time interval T after time t, given stage S, would then be a basic notion to be used in the probabilistic analysis of counterfactuals. In addition, when an infinite, and perhaps a nondenumerable, number of different states are considered, the probability function will have to be defined over some Borel-field of sets of them, and not necessarily for individual states.

The above comments, and even the preceding discrete-time discussion, call for further elaboration, mostly formal. (For instance, one has to ensure that the notions developed fulfill the probability axioms.) The account provided in this section is of course a mere sketch of a notion of objective probability.[20] Yet I hope that this discussion, cut short at this point, will still give a reasonably clear idea of the notion of probability I have in mind and of the direction in which it ought to be developed.[21]

Notes: Chapter 4

1. References to conditions in other chapters are, as usual, made by putting the number of the chapter before the number of the condition. Thus, 2(52) is condition (52) in chapter 2. When the reference is to a condition in the same chapter, this chapter number is omitted; e.g., '(7)' refers to a condition in the chapter in which the reference is made.

2. This notion of *conditional* probability here is strictly literal: when we consider $P(N/M)$, we evaluate the probability of N on the basis of M *only* with no other factual information. The sign '&' in the conditional probabilities is to be interpreted either as the union of the sets involved (with sentences that occur separately, e.g., A, viewed as their corresponding singletons, i.e., $\{A\}$) or as the conjunction of their members, if they are finite.

3. Causal relevance applies primarily to actual events and states of affairs under descriptions. We shall allow ourselves, for convenience, to talk about causal relevance between sentences in a derivative sense, which will amount to causal relevance between the events described by them (so described). In the same sense we shall allow ourselves to talk about causal relevance between sentences and events (with the events in question specified by sentences that constitute the relevant descriptions). By 'events' we will mean events, processes, states of affairs, etc. Such sacrifice of precision, when no confusion is likely to result, will spare us cumbersome and unduly long formulations. See also chapter 2, fn 33. Talk of the A-event (when A is a false counterfactual antecedent) being causally irrelevant to the C-event (for a true C) should be understood as tantamount to talk about the causal irrelevance of the $\sim A$-event to the C-event. (This is reflected in the symmetry of A and $\sim A$ in the conditions presented below.) Talk of the occurrence (or

nonoccurrence) of the A-event (or the $\sim C$-event) is obviously elliptic for talk of the nonoccurrence (occurrence) of the $\sim A$-event (or the C-event).

4. Recall that all that is required of the A course is that W_{t_A} obtain, plus Ax and, of the $\sim A$ course, that W_{t_A} plus $\sim A$ obtain (plus adherence to the laws).

5. This is so since if $x < y$, $\alpha(x-y)+y < y$ and $(1-\alpha)x < (1-\alpha)y$.

6. Stalnaker uses a somewhat similar example in his "A Theory of Conditionals."

7. I assume all along that C is true. I exclude from our discussion cases in which $P(\pm C / \pm A \ \& W) = 1$; these cases deserve special treatment. (To exclude cases in which the condition . . . $\pm A$ . . . obtains is to exclude cases where . . . A . . . or . . . $\sim A$ . . . obtains.)

8. Admittedly, this interpretation need not hold once the equiprobability condition 2(52) is not true [this is clear, since $\sim (6)$ does not follow from (5iv) and $\sim 2(52)$]. But in this case, there is causal relevance [since 2(52) is a necessary condition for causal irrelevance], and (5) must obtain as well, and so we need not care about the precise import of (5iv) for this case. [(5) would obtain in this case, since, according to Theorem 2, $(7) \rightarrow 2(52)$; but $(7) \leftrightarrow \sim (5)$, hence $\sim 2(52) \rightarrow (5)$.]

9. As indicated in fn 7, we should exclude from thesis 2 the cases where any of the probabilities involved in (7) are 1 or 0. These require special treatment.

10. More explicitly: since, by (7), every event that satisfies (7ii) must satisfy (7iv), e is an event that violates the conditions that, according to (7) (which is a necessary and sufficient condition for causal irrelevance), every event should satisfy. Since (7) is violated, A is causally relevant to C.

11. Notice that e rather amplifies, or strengthens, the impact of causal chains (consisting, e.g., of the prevalent conviction that the U.S. must win a war in which it is already engaged) that lead to $\sim C$ (the use of atomic power by the U.S.) rather than to C, in both the A course and the $\sim A$ course.

12. Assuming that $\{W,A,L,C\}$ is consistent, and limiting our discussion to events e which belong to the (t_A, t_C) interval.

13. But this is so only if $t_e > t_A$; otherwise our notion of a transition on the basis of an *earlier* prior history does not apply. So the problem under discussion would arise at most only when $t_e > t_A$.

14. One may worry whether *all* intermediate events can indeed be plagued with accidental equiprobability in cases of causal relevance; but recall that condition (7i) [or (7ii)] and (7iii) are quite independent. Yet cases of accidental equiprobability are cases of fragile equilibrium; cases where there is no accidental equiprobability are not. Thus, if (7iii) is plagued by accidental equiprobability in a case of causal relevance, one may expect that some e', which is a small variation of e, would upset this equilibrium in (7iii) without yielding equiprobability in (7i) [or (7ii)] and would thus indicate causal relevance in accordance with (7). [A similar consideration applies to accidental equiprobability that may affect (7i) or (7ii)].

15. Unless $t_e < t_A$, we cannot talk of a $\sim A$-A transition on the background of $W \ \& \ e$. But $t_e \not< t_A$, since e belongs to the (t_A, t_C) interval.

16. Such limitations may impose a finite number of states or nonzero values for only a finite or a countable number of states. Such limitation would have to be imposed to ensure, for instance, that the sum of these consecutive transitional probabilities for any fixed S_j be 1. I shall not attempt any further scrutiny here.

17. This will be applicable to sentences for which it is determined whether they are true or false at any particular state. I shall not elaborate on this point here.

18. This will presumably require sentences whose reference times are not specified, and which can be applied to a temporal instant. The temporally pure

projections discussed in chapter 6, sections I, II would be of this sort. Cf. also below, subsection 4.

19. The extension to the case of continuous time may also require taking more than one instantaneous stage as a base.

20. I hope to expand on this account of objective probability in the near future, emphasize its empirical characteristics, and elucidate it further by comparing it with the prevailing conceptions of chance setup, long-run relative frequencies, degrees of belief, degrees of entailment, and with various epistemic accounts.

21. Although I will not pursue it further here, one may attempt to consider the notion of objective probability as degree of determination, presented here as making the notion of laws of nature otiose: The transitional probabilities may, on this line, be regarded as embodying the nomological information to an extent that would make a further resort to laws of nature unnecessary. If such a line is successfully pursued, the notion of laws of nature may be entirely omitted from the above analysis. (Cf. also chapter 2, fn 45, for a more specific motivation of where this notion of objective probability is to replace the relation of logical consequence, and thus, if this line is correct, the relation of nomological consequence — i.e., logical consequence via the laws — in the main counterfactual schemata.)

5 Purely Positive
Causal Relevance

I   The Condition of Probability Increase

1. In chapter 2 we established that, for counterfactuals of the n-d type, on the inferential model, two types of statements have to be retained as legitimate premises: consequents of irrel-semifactuals and consequents of pp-semifactuals of the appropriate sorts. In chapter 4 we provided an analysis of irrel-semifactuals. Now to complete our analysis of n-d type counterfactuals, we shall provide an analysis for pp-semifactuals as well.

A pp-semifactual $A > C$ is a semifactual whose antecedent, unlike that of an irrel-semifactual, is causally relevant to its consequent — but only positively so. The transition from the $\sim A$ course of events to the A course affects C *purely positively*: no negative effects on C result from the transition. As in the analysis of irrel-semifactuals, such effects on C are to be understood in terms of causal chains belonging to the causal background of C prior to t_A. For $A > C$ to be a pp-semifactual, no causal chain prior to t_A which leads to C in the $\sim A$-course should be negatively affected, insofar as its effect on C is concerned, by the transition from $\sim A$ to A. Similarly, for $A > C$ to be a pp-semifactual, the transition from $\sim A$ to A should not strengthen the impact of any causal chain prior to t_A which leads to $\sim C$. Of course, the $\sim A$–A transition must have some positive effect on C (so as not to be simply causally irrelevant to C), and thus must constitute a filter of the effects of the causal background of C: it must filter in the positive effects on C, and, in addition, either amplify them or block or diminish negative effects, or both. Thus it must strengthen the impact of causal chains leading to C or weaken the impact of causal chains leading to $\sim C$. In other words, the transition must have a positive effect on C, while at the same time neither increasing negative effects nor decreasing positive effects on C of such previous causal chains.

2. Now, if the transition from $\sim A$ to A indeed strengthens the impact of that part of the causal background of C which is conducive to C in a purely positive way, i.e., without weakening the impact of any causal chain leading to C or strengthening the impact of any causal chain leading to $\sim C$, then this must be reflected in the conditional probability of C in the two courses: the conditional probability of C in the A course should be greater than the conditional probability of C in the $\sim A$ course, since the strengthening of causal chains leading to C in the A course or the weakening of causal chains leading to $\sim C$, in the absence of any increase of effects

adverse to C, will increase the probability of C in that course. Consequently we can conclude that if $A > C$ is a pp-semifactual, then:

(1) $P(C/A \ \& \ W) > P(C/\sim A \ \& \ W)$

We call this the **probability-increase condition** for pp-semifactuals.

3. (1), then, is a necessary condition for a semifactual $A > C$ being a pp-semifactual. The question arises whether (1) is also a sufficient condition. We encountered a similar question in 2 VIII: there we inquired whether the probability-increase condition [(1) here] is a sufficient condition for the inclusion of C (which pertains to the appropriate time interval) among the legitimate premises of the inferential model for a counterfactual with antecedent A. Using a counterexample (example 11), we showed there that it is not. We also brought a number of arguments to the effect that the consequents of appropriate pp-semifactuals should be retained as legitimate premises. These considerations thus yield that the answer to whether (1) is a sufficient condition for a semifactual being a pp-semifactual is negative. This is so since if (1) were a sufficient condition for a semifactual being a pp-semifactual, then it would also be a sufficient condition for the appropriate retention as legitimate premises of statements C that satisfy it; but the latter was shown (by example 11 of 2 VIII) not to be the case.

4. Before we proceed, let us look at two cases in point. First, recall example 8 of 2 V 7, about the architect's contract. We considered there the true counterfactual 2(11) (put here in the third person): If the architect had asked for a thousand dollars less than he did, he would have lost money on the building. Now consider the following semifactual $A > C$ with the same antecedent: If the architect had asked for a thousand dollars less than he did, a fortiori he would still have been awarded the contract. This semifactual surely constitutes a genuine pp-semifactual. If the architect had asked a thousand dollars less, the attractiveness of his bid would have been enhanced without any adverse side-effect, and thus the probability of his getting the contract would have risen. Thus, in this case,

$P(C/A \ \& \ W) > P(C/\sim A \ \& \ W)$

and (1) indeed obtains as it should, being a necessary condition for pp-semifactuals.

Secondly, consider a variant of example 3 of 4 V, concerning the war between Kingdom and Republic:

Example 1

> Assume that after the king met (the military-industrialist) Berta, the prestige of Kingdom in the world declined somewhat owing to the provocation by Republic, which resulted in some worsening of its economic position in a way that hurt to a certain ex-

tent the typical military-industrialist but not at all the typical nationalist. Let us also assume (as a modification in W, thus prior to t_A) that Republic, which followed developments in Kingdom closely, was not interested in war with Kingdom and intended to defuse the tension between the two countries in order to limit the risk of war. (We shall not make use of this information now, but it will be useful toward the end of this chapter.) Let us also assume, as a further modification in W, that the nationalists and the military-industrialists differed considerably in their zeal for war after the ambassador's arrest: the nationalists were then much more eager for war than were the military-industrialists. Thus, assume that the probability that the king would go to war under the influence of his previous mistress (after the ambassador's arrest) was 0.4, whereas the probability of his going to war under the influence of Berta was 0.2.

Let us use the same notation we used in example 3 of 4 V: there A was 'The king did not meet Berta (at the party)', and C was 'Kingdom started a war'. We thus have:

$$P(C/A \ \& \ W) = 0.4 \qquad P(C/\sim A \ \& \ W) = 0.2$$

Hence:

$$P(C/\sim A \ \& \ W) < P(C/A \ \& \ W)$$

and (1) holds.

Notice, however, that here $A > C$ is *not* a pp-semifactual. The reason is that the causal chain that in fact led to C, i.e., Berta's influence on the king in the $\sim A$ course, is ineffective in the A course, in which he did not meet Berta. In other words, even though in the A course there is a causal chain leading to C — that is, the influence on the king of the nationalists through his previous mistress — the causal chain that was dominant in the $\sim A$ course is inoperative in the A course. Thus, the effects on C of the $\sim A$–A transition are *not* purely positive: they adversely affect a causal chain that leads to C in the $\sim A$ course. Hence $A > C$ is not a pp-semifactual. And indeed, the fact that we would not be ready to affirm $A > C$ categorically is indicative of the fact that $A > C$ is not a pp-semifactual, since pp-semifactuals are *all* true. Thus, (1) holds, but $A > C$ is not a pp-semifactual. Hence (1) is not a sufficient condition for a semifactual's being a pp-semifactual.

We see that, in our quest for necessary and sufficient conditions for pp-semifactuals, (1) will have to be supplemented. We need a condition that in conjunction with (1) will yield a necessary and sufficient condition. Our strategy will be to ask what could go wrong in cases where (1) obtains which would prevent $A > C$ from being a pp-semifactual. How can A fail to be purely positively causally relevant to C if the probability of C is greater in the A course than in the $\sim A$ course?

II   Toward a Condition
for Purely Positive Causal Relevance

1. The answer to the last question seems clear: $A > C$ will fail to be a pp-semifactual if the effectiveness of some causal chain leading to C is adversely affected by the $\sim A$–A transition, or if the effectiveness of some causal chain leading to $\sim C$ is enhanced by the transition. In such a case, the transition will not have a purely positive effect on C, since a weakening of the positive effect on C, or the strengthening of the negative effect on C, of a previous causal chain, would constitute a negative effect. As we saw in example 1, the probability of C in the A course may nonetheless on the whole increase in case such a negative effect of the transition is more than balanced by a strengthening of the positive effect on C of some other causal chain. An over-all increase in total probability, in such a case, though, will involve some negative effect on the transmission of a positive impact on C by its causal background, or some positive effect on the transmission of a negative impact on C by its causal background, whereas for $A > C$ to be a pp-semifactual the effect of the transition must be purely positive. Our task is to find out how to supplement condition (1) by a condition that will exclude the cases in which the effectiveness of some causal chain leading to C is weakened by the transition and cases in which the effectiveness of some causal chain to $\sim C$ is strengthened by the transition, despite net probabilistic gain. Since the line of reasoning here is quite similar to that of section III of the last chapter, we shall proceed more quickly.

As we observed in that section, the effects of causal chains leading to C must be transmitted to C through intermediate events. The impact of the $\sim A$–A transition on the effectiveness of previous causal chains leading to C (or to $\sim C$) can be detected through the impact of the transition on intermediate events that are important for the transmission of the effects of these causal chains. Thus, a weakening of the effectiveness of a previous causal chain leading to C would be manifested in the weakening in the A course (as compared to the $\sim A$ course) of its transmitted positive effect to C through some intermediate events. The strengthening of a causal chain leading to $\sim C$ would likewise manifest itself in an increase in the negative causal effect transmitted to C through intermediate events in the A course (as compared with the $\sim A$ course). Similarly, the probability of events whose occurrence is conducive to the transmission of a positive causal effect to C (in both courses) may decrease as a result of a transition that does not have a purely positive effect on C, thus lowering the chances of that positive causal effect being transmitted through them to C. Likewise, the probability of events whose occurrence would enhance the transmission of a negative effect to C (in both courses) may increase owing to a transition that does not have a purely positive effect on C, thus increasing the chances of that negative causal effect on C being transmitted through them. And similarly, an intermediate event whose occurrence in the $\sim A$ course is conducive (or harmless) to the transmission of a positive effect on C may become detrimental to it in the A course. The appearance of such symptoms in intermediate events would thus be indicative of a negative causal effect on C due to the transition. A weakening of some positive impact on C of its causal background, or a strengthening of some negative impact on C of its causal background, as a result of the $\sim A$–A transition, would thus be manifested by any of the following: a decrease in the positive causal effect to be transmitted through some events (were they to occur); an increase in the negative causal effect to be transmitted by others; a decline in the probability of events whose occurrence in both courses is conducive to the transmission of a positive impact on C: an increase in the probability of events whose occurrence (in the A course) is conducive to the transmission of a negative impact on C; or, finally, by an event whose occurrence in the $\sim A$ course is conducive to C but whose occurrence in the A course is conducive to $\sim C$ (or at least not conducive to C).

Otherwise, if indeed the transition is purely positively causally relevant to C, no negative effect on C of the transition could be traced through intermediate events material to the transmission to C of the effects of its causal background. Thus, if the occurrence of some event would enhance the transmission to C of the positive effect of a previous causal chain in the $\sim A$ course, its occurrence would continue to enhance it in the A course, and the effect transmitted via such an event (were it to occur) in the A course would not decrease in comparison with the $\sim A$ course, nor would the probability of such an event decrease. And if the occurrence of a certain event would enhance the transmission of some negative causal effect to C in the $\sim A$ course, the negative effect it would transmit (were it to occur) in the A course would not increase, nor would its own probability increase (as long as its occurrence would still enhance the transmission of some negative effect to C in the A course as well), and thus the transition would not result in the amplification of negative causal effects transmitted to C in the A course of events as compared with the $\sim A$ course. Nor would events whose occurrence would not enhance the transmission of negative causal effects to C in the $\sim A$ course be any different in the A course insofar as amplifying negative transmitted effects to C is concerned; for this would be indicative of an amplification, generated by the transition, of negative causal effects on C. (A local amplification could, of course, be outweighed over all.) Indeed, if all these features obtain: if, as a result of the transition, there is no increase in negative causal effect nor any decrease in positive causal effect that would be transmitted to C via intermediate events (were they to occur), and if the probability of events conducive to the transmission of positive (negative) causal effects to C does not decrease (increase) as a result of the transition, then indeed the transition from $\sim A$ to A has no negative effect on C. Moreover, if an increase in the over-all positive causal effect transmitted to C does take place, then the transition has a purely positive causal effect on C.

In other words, *a necessary and sufficient condition for purely positive causal relevance* can be obtained if the probability-increase condition is augmented by the following requirement: If the occurrence of an actual event e would enhance the transmission of positive effects to C in the $\sim A$ course, it should continue to do so in the A course: its combined effect in the A course (i.e., when taken together with A) should increase (as compared with its combined effect in the $\sim A$ course),[1] and its probability in the A course should be no less than in the $\sim A$ course. If the occurrence of e is immaterial to the transmission of causal effect in the $\sim A$ course, then its occurrence should not enhance the transmission of any negative effects in the A course.

But if the occurrence of e advances the transmission of negative effects to C in the $\sim A$ course, then its combined effect on C in the A course should be lower than in the $\sim A$ course.[2] And if the occurrence of e enhances the transmission of negative effects in both courses, its probability in the A course should be no greater than it is in the $\sim A$ course. We will now express this requirement in probabilistic terms.

III The Condition of Purely Positive Causal Relevance

1. **The filtering transmission condition** (on W, A, and C):

(2) $\{W, A, L, C\}$ is consistent, and:
Every actual event e in the (t_A, t_C) interval
fulfills the following conditions A and B:

  A. 0. If $P(C/e\ \&\ \sim A\ \&\ W) \geq P(C/\sim A\ \&\ W)$,
  then the following three conditions obtain:
  1. $P(C/e\ \&\ A\ \&\ W) \qquad \geq P(C/A\ \&\ W)$,
  (with strict inequality in case of strict inequality in A.0)
  2. $P(C/e\ \&\ A\ \&\ W) \qquad > P(C/e\ \&\ \sim A\ \&\ W)$
  In case of strict inequality in A.0:
  3. $P(e/A\ \&\ W) \qquad\qquad \geq P(e/\sim A\ \&\ W)$.

  B. 1(1) If $P(C/e\ \&\ \sim A\ \&\ W) < P(C/\sim A\ \&\ W)$, then:
  1(1*) $P(C/e\ \&\ \sim A\ \&\ W) < P(C/e\ \&\ A\ \&\ W)$
  and
  2(1) If $P(C/e\ \&\ A\ \&\ W) \quad < P(C/A\ \&\ W)$, then:
  2(1*) $P(e/A\ \&\ W) \qquad\qquad \leq P(e/\sim A\ \&\ W)$.

As distinct from the transmission condition for causal irrelevance [4(7)], which was designed to ensure that the transmission of previous causal effects to C be undisturbed by the $\sim A$–A transition, the filtering transmission condition for purely positive causal relevance (2) is designed to ensure, in combination with the probability-increase condition (1), a filtering effect on the transmission to C (of previous causal effects on C) that would be purely positive for the occurrence of C. Having found the condition needed to supplement the probability-increase condition (1), we can now state the truth conditions for pp-semifactuals as follows:

Thesis 3. If $A > C(t_A < t_C)$ is a semifactual, then:

$A > C$ is a pp-semifactual iff
A is purely positively causally relevant to C iff
the probability-increase condition (1) and the filtering
transmission condition (2) obtain.

Some commentary on this condition is in order.[3]

2. A.0 focuses on events whose occurrence is either positively significant
or at least not negatively significant, for the transmission of causal impact
on C in the $\sim A$ course. A.1 expresses the requirement that such an event
function in the same way in the A course as well. [That is, an event whose
occurrence provides for the transmission of an over-all positive (or at least
not negative) impact on C of the causal background of C in the $\sim A$ course,
would do the same in the A course as well.] If the occurrence of such an
event results in the transmission of an over-all positive causal impact in the
$\sim A$ course, it should do so in the A course too (hence the qualification concerning strict inequality in A.1).

Condition A.2 ensures that the probability increase effected by the
transition would still hold, given the occurrence of an event e (of the sort
required in A.0) in both courses; i.e., that the occurrence of such an e
would preserve the enhancement of C via the transition. Condition A.3
ensures that the probability of events that enhance the occurrence of C in
the $\sim A$ course, would not be decreased by the transition. (Of course, this
requirement has been duly restricted to events whose occurrence enhances
the transmission of positive effect to C in the $\sim A$ course; hence the limitation in A.3 to cases of strict inequality in A.0.) Thus, part A deals with intermediate events whose occurrence in the $\sim A$ course does not have a
negative over-all effect on the occurrence of C. Other events are dealt with
in part B.

Now in B.1(1) we are concerned with events whose occurrence enhances a negative effect on C in the $\sim A$ course. We want to ensure that
the negative effect does not upset the positive impact on C of the transition. We also want to require that the transition not be conducive to the
occurrence of events that enhance a negative effect on the occurrence of
C in the A course. B.1 takes care of the first concern, and B.2 of the
second.

Notice that the filtering transmission condition assures us that events
e that fulfill B.2(1) — i.e., enhance the occurrence of $\sim C$ in the A course
— must violate A.0 (since they violate A.1, which must obtain if A.0 does);
therefore such events e must enhance the occurrence of $\sim C$ in the $\sim A$
course as well and, therefore, also fulfill B.1(1) (which is the negation of
A.0). And this is as it should be: events that are counterproductive to C
in the A course must also be so in the $\sim A$ course if the transition is to be
purely positively causally relevant to C.

We can also notice that part B of the filtering transmission condition
can be reformulated, given part A [and the probability-increase condition
(1)], in such a way that B.1(1*) and B.2(1*) appear as consequences of
B.2(1) (with B.1(1) omitted altogether). This reformulation will yield **B**':

(B′)   0. If $P(C/e \,\&\, A \,\&\, W) < P(C/A \,\&\, W)$, then
      1′. $P(C/e \,\&\, {\sim}A \,\&\, W) < P(C/e \,\&\, A \,\&\, W)$ and
      2′. $P(e/A \,\&\, W) \leq P(e/{\sim}A \,\&\, W)$

If we replace B by B′ in (2) we get an equivalence condition. B′ conveys the information that if the occurrence of e in the A-course makes an overall negative contribution to the occurrence of C, then the contribution of the transition to the occurrence of C, given e, if still positive, and the occurrence of e is not enhanced by the transition. In our treatment of examples in the next section we shall use this version of B in thesis 4, since it is easier to apply.

3. Proof of the equivalence of B and B′. We shall show that, given (1), every event fulfills A and B in (2) iff it fulfills A and B′.

> Suppose e fulfills A and B. If it fulfills B′.0, then, by B.2, it fulfills B′.2′. If it fulfills B.1(1), then it fulfills B′.1′, since it is B.1(1*). If it does not fulfill B.1(1), then it fulfills A.0, and thus fulfills A.2, which is B′.1′.
>   *Conversely*, suppose e fulfills (1), A, and B′. Then obviously (by B′.0 and B′.2′) it fulfills B.2. Now suppose e fulfills B.1(1). If e fulfills A.1, then, by transitivity of inequality, B.1(1*) follows from the conditions B.1(1), A.1, and (1). Otherwise, if e does not fulfill A.1, then it fulfills B′.0, and thus, by B′, it fulfills B′1′, which is B.1.(1*).

Notice, also, that we can make (2) more compact, by canceling B.1, while moving A.2 from its position, which is conditional on A.0, to an unconditional position. If we present (2) (ignoring the condition concerning the consistency of $\{W, A, L, C\}$) as:

$$(2) \leftrightarrow (e) \left\{ \begin{array}{l} [e \text{ is an actual} \\ \text{event in } (t_A, t_C)] \end{array} \supset \begin{array}{l} \{[A.0 \supset (A.1 \& A.2)] \\ \& \, (A.0^* \supset A.1^* \& A.3) \& (B.1 \& B.2)\} \end{array} \right\}$$

where 'X^*' is 'X' with the strict inequality '$<$' rather than '$\leq$', then we can see that we can present (2) also in a new form as (2′):

$$(2') \leftrightarrow (e) \left\{ \begin{array}{l} [e \text{ is an actual} \\ \text{event in } (t_A, t_C)] \end{array} \supset \begin{array}{l} [A.2 \& (A.0 \supset A.1) \\ \& \, [(A.0^* \supset (A.1^* \& A.3)] \& B.2]\} \end{array} \right\}$$

$(2') \leftrightarrow (2)$, since A.2 = B.1(1*), whereas A.0 and the condition B.1(1) on which B.1(1*) is predicated, are complementary. Hence, according to (2), A.2 holds unconditionally. Yet form (2) has certain advantages over (2′) for purposes of motivation and presentation.

IV   Example and Discussion

1. Recall example 1 in section I of this chapter, concerning Republic and Kingdom, where A was 'The king did not meet Berta (at the party)'

and C was 'Kingdom started a war'. We saw that $A > C$ was *not* a pp-semifactual, but that it nevertheless fulfilled (1). Let us now see whether it fulfills (2) and thesis (3). Let e describe the event mentioned in the example, namely, that in the meantime the economic situation of Kingdom somewhat declined (via loss of prestige) owing to Republic's arrest of the ambassador, in a way that hurt the typical military-industrialist but not the typical nationalist; so $t_C > t_e > t_A$. Hence

(3) $P(C/e \ \& \ {\sim}A \ \& \ W) > P(C/{\sim}A \ \& \ W)$

obtains, since e would strengthen the demand of the military-industrialists for war, and so the king, who was (in the ${\sim}A$ course) influenced by them through Berta, would be under heavier pressure to declare war. However, we can nevertheless assume that

(4) $P(C/e \ \& \ A \ \& \ W) = P(C/A \ \& \ W)$

obtains, since e would have no impact on the nationalists — they were not really hurt economically. Hence, if the king was influenced by the nationalists through his previous mistress, e would have no real impact on his decision whether to start a war. But (3) and (4) are contrary to provision A in (2) which requires strict inequality in A.1 in case there is strict inequality in A.0. We have in this example strict inequality in (3), which corresponds to A.0, but we do not have it in (4), which corresponds to A.1. Hence the provisions of our criterion are not satisfied, and $A > C$ *does not* qualify as a pp-semifactual, which, in fact, it is not.

2. We can also see in another way that $A > C$ does not qualify as a pp-semifactual if we consider part B of (2). Take e' to be 'Republic released the ambassador' (again $t_C > t_{e'} > t_A$). Then

(5) $P(C/e' \ \& \ A \ \& \ W) < P(C/A \ \& \ W)$

obtains, since, as we noted in our discussion in chapter 4, this release would weaken the nationalists' motivation to go to war, and in the A course the king is under the influence of his former mistress, who is a nationalist. But

(6) $P(e'/A \ \& \ W) > P(e'/{\sim}A \ \& \ W)$

obtains as well, because Republic was interested in avoiding war and, thus, would be more inclined to release the ambassador if that act helped prevent war, i.e., if it were likely to so affect the king's decision. The release of the ambassador would have an impact on the king's decision when he is under the nationalist influence via his former mistress, but not so great an impact when he is under Berta's military-industrialist influence. Thus, for this variant of the example, part B does not hold, since (5) is B.2(1), the condition of B.2, and (6) is the negation of its consequent

B.2(1*); thus provision B.2, and hence condition (2), do not hold. So $A > C$ once again fails to qualify as a pp-semifactual under thesis 3.

3. Recall example 8 of 2 V which we have discussed further in I 4 of this chapter — the case of the architect. $A > C$ was 'If the architect had asked for a thousand dollars less than he did, a fortiori he would still have been awarded the contract'. We saw that $A > C$ is a pp-semifactual, and that it fulfills condition (1). Now in order to show that $A > C$ fulfills the other condition of thesis 4, i.e., the filtering transmission condition (2), and thus meets our standard for a pp-semifactual, we must produce a plausibility argument, since condition (2) involves a universal quantification, which is easier to refute than to substantiate. Consider the type of event e that will satisfy

$$P(C/e \ \& \ \sim A \ \& \ W) > P(C/\sim A \ \& \ W)$$

Notice that events in (t_A, t_C) of this type, events whose occurrence would enhance the transmission of positive effects on C of the previous causal background, will be events such as the committee members' appreciation for our architect's proposal, or the submission of recommendations concerning his proficiency, or the decision of some potentially dangerous rival not to participate in the tender. Take a typical event e of this kind. There is no reason to believe that the occurrence of such an event would not be conducive as well to our architect's getting the job (the C-event in this example) in case he lowered his bid by $1000; that is,

$$P(C/e \ \& \ A \ \& \ W) > P(C/A \ \& \ W)$$

We can defend the strict inequality here, since it seems that every such event that increases the architect's chances of getting the job at the original rate would also increase his chances at the lower rate. Furthermore,

$$P(C/e \ \& \ A \ \& \ W) > P(C/e \ \& \ \sim A \ \& \ W)$$

since there is every reason to believe that, for any such event, its combined positive effect on C with $\sim A$, i.e., in the case of the original offer, would be higher than its combined positive effect with A, i.e., in the case of the lower offer. Notice that the lowering of the fee would undoubtedly be conducive to his chances of getting the contract; that is, (1) obtains:

$$P(C/A \ \& \ W) > P(C/\sim A \ \& \ W)$$

Similarly, it is plausible that, for the sort of events we have considered,

$$P(e/\sim A \ \& \ W) = P(e/A \ \& \ W)$$

because the probability of such events would not depend on the amount he asked for (other applicants do not know what he asked for anyway,

since tenders are confidential). And finally, events in (t_A, t_C) whose occurrences do not affect the probability of C in the $\sim A$ course would not
seem to affect it adversely in the A course. Thus, part A of the filtering-
transmission condition (2) obtains.

Now we shall see why part B′ [which we proved equivalent to B in
the context of conditions (1) and (2)] obtains. A type of event that would
satisfy

$$P(C/e \ \& \ A \ \& \ W) \ < \ P(C/A \ \& \ W)$$

i.e., that would lower the architect's chances of getting the contract with
the lower bid, would be the kind of event that would also lower his
chances when combined with his actual bid, e.g., an attractive bid by
some other architect.[4] [Yet the kind of event that would lower his chances
of getting the job when combined with his actual (higher) bid need not
necessarily lower his chances when combined with his revised (lower) bid.
An example of such an event would be a bid from some other, equally
good, architect which was less than our architect's actual bid but more
than his revised bid.] But then

$$P(C/e \ \& \ \sim A \ \& \ W) \ < \ P(C/e \ \& \ A \ \& \ W)$$

since such an event would certainly not do him more harm when combined with his lower bid than it would when combined with his higher
bid, and thus his chances to win the contract with such an event would
still be higher in the case of his lower bid than in the case of his higher
bid [remember that (1) holds]. Also,

$$P(e/A \ \& \ W) \ = \ P(e/\sim A \ \& \ W)$$

since the probability of such an event (e.g., a competing bid) seems to be
independent of our architect's bid. Since condition (2) is satisfied by the
type of events we considered representative in this case, (2) seems to hold
in this case. Hence our pp-semifactual $A > C$ satisfies the conditions of
thesis 3.

4. The role that our filtering-transmission condition (2) plays in comple-
menting the probability-increase condition (1) can be viewed as not unlike
the role of its analogue in the causal-irrelevance case. First of all, the
filtering-transmission condition (2) overcomes the difficulty that (1) still
fell short of handling (i.e., the problem of excluding cases with over-all
probability increase despite some local negative effect) by no longer having
the form of the probability-increase condition, thereby not allowing the
kind of peculiarity that the probability-increase condition allows. This
peculiarity (namely the mixed filtering effect that is not purely positive
though positive over-all) is manifested via transmitting events in the
(t_A, t_B) interval whose occurrence is important for the transmission of effects of the previous causal background, and would be ruled out by condi-

tion (2) (which deals with such events in this interval). Furthermore, condition (2) improves upon condition (1) by shifting the weight from the single event C to a large spectrum of events in the (t_A, t_C) interval; this way, in certain cases that fall short of purely positive causal relevance, peculiarities or accidents that may afflict a single event e would not be fatal, since they would not afflict all the events in the interval (even if they afflict some). [Thus, if some events were to transmit to C negative causal effects of the transition, while still fulfilling (1) and (2), other events that do the same would violate (1) and (2), and thus serve as indicators of a failure of purely positive causal relevance.]

V   Counterfactuals Again

1. On the basis of the discussion in chapter 4 and in the present chapter we can shed more light on the analysis of counterfactuals presented in chapter 2. We can express thesis 2 of 4 IV as follows[5]:

Thesis 4. A semifactual $A > C$ is an irrel-semifactual iff

(8) $\{W, A, L, C\}$ is consistent, and

$(e) \left\{ \begin{matrix} [e \text{ is an actual} \\ \text{event in } (t_A, t_C)] \end{matrix} \right. \supset \{[(7i) \lor (7ii)] \supset [(7iii) \& (7iv)]\}\}$

It is clear from conditions (7i) − (7iv) that these conditions depend on the parameters W, A, and C only (L is held constant).

We can similarly express thesis 3 of section III of the present chapter as follows:

Thesis 5. A semifactual $A > C$ is a pp-semifactual iff

(9)   (1) obtains, $\{W, A, L, C\}$ is consistent, and (e) [e is an actual event in (t_A, t_C) ⊃ (2A) & (2B)]

[(2A) and (2B) are parts A and B in (2).] It is clear from conditions (1), (2A), and (2B) that these conditions depend on W, A, and C only (W here is W_{t_C}).

Consequently, using theses 4 and 5, we can now express the relations $R_{cir}(C, A, W)$ and $R_{ppcr}(C, A, W)$ of 2 XIII, that is, the relations of causal irrelevance and purely positive causal relevance, as follows:

(10) $R_{cir}(C, A, W,) \leftrightarrow \{W, A, L, C\}$ is consistent, and

$(e) \left\{ \begin{matrix} e \text{ is an actual} \\ \text{event in } (t_A, t_C) \end{matrix} \right. \supset \{[(7i) \lor (7ii)] \supset [(7iii) \& (7iv)]\}\}$

where (7i) − (7iv) are the conditions of thesis 4, specified in chapter 4.

(11) $R_{ppcr}(C,A,W)$ ↔ (1), and $\{W,A,L,C\}$ is consistent, and
       (e) $\{e$ is an actual event in $(t_A,t_C) \supset [(2A)$ & $(2B)]\}$

where (1), (2A), and (2B) are the conditions of thesis 5, specified in III.

Given the empirical character of the probability function (see 4 VI), the character of these two relations is clearly empirical as well. Thus we can now present the function of the subsequent legitimate premises $g(A,W_{\bar{t}_B})$ on the basis of 2(53) and (10) and (11) of this chapter as follows:

(12) $g(A,W_{\bar{t}_B}) = \{C \,|\, C \in W_{t_A,t_B}$ & $\{W,A,L,C\}$ is consistent, and

$\{(e) \begin{Bmatrix} e \text{ is an actual} \\ \text{event in } (t_A,t_C) \end{Bmatrix} \supset [((7i)\vee(7ii)) \supset ((7iii)\&(7iv))]\}\}$

$\vee\{(1)$ & $(e) \begin{Bmatrix} e \text{ is an actual} \\ \text{event in } (t_A,t_C) \end{Bmatrix} \supset \{(2A)$ & $(2B)]\}\}\}$

As we recall from 2 XIII [see 2(56) and 2(57)],

(13) $f(A,W_{\bar{t}_B}) = W \cup L \cup \{A\} \cup g(A,W_{\bar{t}_B})$

Thus, we have provided the full form of the i-p function, our task for counterfactuals of the n-d type.

Notes: Chapter 5

1. A seemingly more adequate formulation of this last consequent (after the colon) would be: its positive contribution in the A course (i.e., when taken together with A) should not decrease (as compared with its positive contribution in the $\sim A$ course).

2. A seemingly more adequate formulation of this consequent would be: then its negative contribution in the A course should not be higher than in the $\sim A$ course.

3. The filtering transmission condition constitutes an attempt to capture the notion of purely positive causal relevance as elaborated above via the use of the equality and "higher than" relations between probabilities alone. However, in fns 1 and 2 above, alternative and seemingly more adequate formulations have been offered as improvements on those in the text. In order to reflect them correctly, we would need to resort to differences in probabilistic values as well, and thus go beyond the merely qualitative use of the above two probabilistic relations. Once we allow that, we would be able to capture the notion that the contribution to the transmission of a positive effect to C by an intermediate event e is not harmed by the transition, using a condition such as A*, replacing A.1 and A.2:

A*. $P(C/e \ \& \ A \ \& \ W) - P(C/A \ \& \ W) \geq P(C/e \ \& \ {\sim}A \ \& \ W) - P(C/{\sim}A \ \& \ W)$

(with a strict inequality in case of a strict inequality in A.0).

If we replace A.1 and A.2 in A by A*, obviously A.1 and A.2 follow.

Thus, on this suggestion, condition A would be replaced by: If A.O, then A* and A.3.

Similarly, we could then replace condition B by the following condition B^*, which expresses more succinctly the idea that the contribution of an event e to the transmission of a negative causal effect to C must not increase via the transition:

B*. If $P(C/e \ \& \ {\sim}A \ \& \ W) < P(C/{\sim}A \ \& \ W)$, then:
if $P(C/e \ \& \ A \ \& \ W) < P(C/A \ \& \ W)$, then:$P(C/A \ \& \ W) - P(C/e \ \& \ A \ \& \ W) \leq P(C/{\sim}A \ \& \ W) - P(C/e \ \& \ {\sim}A \ \& \ W)$, and $P(e/A \ \& \ W) \leq P(e/{\sim}A \ \& \ W)$.

Clearly B.1 and B.2 follow from B*.

I will not, however, pursue these suggested improvements here.

4. This is so since we have seen that part A of (2) obtains, and, because of A.0 and A.1, every appropriate event that satisfies B'.0 would also violate A.0.

5. Thesis 2 of IV was:

A semifactual $A > C$ is an irrel-semifactual iff:
A is causally irrelevant to C iff the transmission condition (7) holds.

Condition (7) of chapter 4 was:

$\{W,A,L,C\}$ is consistent, and:

(e) $\left\{ \begin{array}{l} \geq e \text{ is an actual} \\ \text{event in } (t_A, t_C) \end{array} \right\} \supset \{[\,(7i) \vee (7ii)\,] \supset [\,(7iii) \& (7iv)\,]\} \Big\}$

Note also that theses 1,2 of chapter 4 and theses 3,4,5 of chapter 5 constitute one sequence; there is, e.g., no thesis 1 of this chapter.

6 World Histories, Reference Times, and Formal Semantics

I World Histories

1. In this chapter I first provide an account of the notions "the history of the world up to a certain time," and "the time a statement pertains to." I then develop formal temporal languages and semantics suitable for accommodating these notions and extend them into a formal system for counterfactuals.

The problems associated with providing an account of "the history of the world up to t" arise from the convoluted way that temporal features appear in sentences of natural languages such as English. Not only may a sentence be syntactically complex, in which case various subsentences or subclauses may make their own contributions to the temporal character of the sentence as a whole, but even syntactically simple sentences, that is, sentences that contain no subsentences,[1] may contain locutions that allude to times other than the time of purported occurrence of the main event (or state of affairs) described. Such complications raise the serious difficulty of ascertaining that all parts of a complex sentence point only to times earlier than t, since sentences that do not cannot qualify as members of W_t.[2]

An obvious desideratum for an account of the history of the world up to t is that that history be informationally complete concerning times up to t. An obvious tool to use for this purpose is the reference time of sentences: we want to include in that history only true factual[3] sentences which pertain only to times earlier than t and which yet suffice for factual informational completeness. If we were to include *every* true factual sentence that genuinely pertains only to times earlier than t, we would have to undertake the task of characterizing the reference time of complex sentences as well. In the next section an attempt will be made to provide a characterization of reference time for syntactically simple sentences and to extend that characterization to propositional-attitude sentences. But in this book I will not discuss in detail its extension to other complex (English) sentences.

The problem that will concern us here, therefore, is how to overcome the allusion by locutions in syntactically simple sentences to times beyond (in our case, later than) the reference times of the sentences that contain them. Such sentences would have to be excluded from W_t if such allusions concern times later than t. An example of such a sentence would be:

141

The 37th president of the U.S. ate breakfast on 1/1/1940.

Clearly, the reference time of this sentence is 1/1/1940, yet this sentence should not qualify in $W_{1/1/1950}$, since it alludes to later events (the 37th presidency). (Such a sentence, though pertaining to 1/1/1940, does not *genuinely* pertain to that time, because of the allusion of a locution in it to a time outside that reference-time interval.)

In order to overcome this difficulty, we shall define a set of sentences that will serve as **testers** for the specification of world histories. These will be sentences which purport to describe events or states of affairs that occur at a certain time *instant* and which do not logically imply any events at *other* temporal instants. Thus, whereas the event purportedly described by the sentence 'John slept through the afternoon of 1/1/74' did not occur within a single time instant, the event purportedly described by the sentence 'John was asleep at 3 P.M. on 1/1/74' did. Similarly, whereas the sentence 'The second human landing on the moon occurred at t' logically implies the occurrence of another event at another time,[4] namely, the first landing on the moon, the sentence 'Human beings landed on the moon at t' does not.

Consider, then, syntactically simple English sentences.[5] They may include temporal locutions of various kinds. First, there may be locutions specifying time delimitations within which the event purportedly described by the sentence took place (e.g., 'On 3/7/74', tenses of verbs). Second, there may be locutions that temporally characterize the purported occurrence of the event described *within* such temporal delimitations (e.g.: 'frequently', 'occasionally', 'during . . .', 'all through . . .'). Third, there may be locutions with temporal implications which appear in descriptions used in the sentence in question ('a *future* president of the U.S.', 'the *second* atomic war in history', etc.). In order to transform such sentences into temporal testers which purport to describe events or states of affairs at a certain temporal instant without any logical temporal implications beyond it, we shall first require that all such locutions be deleted and that the tenses of the verbs in the sentences be changed to the present tense, which we shall construe as tenseless. The result of such an operation need not be a well-formed sentence. If it is not, the original English sentence will not serve as a temporal tester. In many cases, however, the result will be an English sentence. In other cases, the result can be transformed into an English sentence by making minor grammatical adjustments that are insignificant from a temporal point of view. (The end product, in such cases, may coincide with the result of putting some *other* English sentences through the above procedure.) The resulting sentences would normally serve functions similar to those served by what Nicholas Rescher and Alasdair Urquhart called "chronologically pure" sentences or "purely phenomenological" characterizations.[6] We shall call such sentences **temporally pure**. A temporally pure sentence produced from a statement p along the lines described above will be called a **temporally pure projection of** p, and we will symbolize it by '$\underline{p}$'. Such a sentence will describe an event-type of which the event purportedly described by p is an event-token. Hence, a temporally pure projection of a statement p will describe an event-type abstracted from the event-token described by p along the lines of complete temporal abstraction, and along those lines only.

Temporally pure sentences have two features that are important to us here: First, they are indeterminate with respect to the time of occurrence of the events they purport to describe. Secondly, they lack any strictly logical implications concerning events at other times.[7]

Example 1. Consider the following syntactically simple sentence:

(1)   J.F. Kennedy was occasionally sick during his adult life.

The locution 'during his adult life' belongs to the first type of locution mentioned above: locutions that temporally delimit the occurrence-time of the events purportedly described. The locution 'occasionally' belongs to the second type, characterizing the temporal position of the event(s) described within the temporal limits set by the first locution. Omitting these two locutions and changing the tense of the sentence, we obtain:

(1′)   J.F. Kennedy is sick.

which is a temporally pure sentence.

We have thus far considered as temporally pure only syntactically simple sentences. We will now extend this consideration to a category of sentences that are not syntactically simple. These are sentences of the form 'John believes that . . .', 'Tom hopes that . . .', etc., that is, sentences that express propositional attitudes (taken *de dicto*). We shall not impose any condition on the embedded sentences, but the embedding sentences must themselves be temporally pure, according to the above characterization. (The embedding sentences will also be restricted to the syntactically simple.) Thus, for a sentence like 'John believes that p' to be temporally pure, no constraints are to be put on p, but the embedding sentence, 'John believes' must fulfill the requirements of temporal purity (as indeed it does).

The purported occurrence time of the event-type described by such a propositional-attitude sentence depends on the temporal features of the embedding sentence. The embedded sentence of a propositional-attitude sentence may pertain to any time; but it puts no purely logical constraints upon the time of occurrence of the event consisting of an individual's having the described propositional attitude. This latter time is determined when a specification of the reference time of the embedding sentence is provided. Thus, sentences of this kind, whose embedding sentences qualify as temporally pure, will also be considered temporally pure. (This kind of embedding sentence would not include sentences with propositional verbs known as "factives," such as 'know', 'realize', etc., which involve an implication concerning the truth of the embedded sentence.)

2. We can now consider prefixing temporally pure sentences with the operator 'It is true at time t that' (the 'is' may be considered tenseless). A

similar operator, R_t, called 'the temporal realization operator', was introduced by Rescher and Urquhart (*op. cit.*, p. 31), where $R_t p$ is to read: *p* is realized at time *t*. We shall adopt their notation and use the symbol 'R_t' as well. Henceforth we will be interested in temporally pure sentences preceded by 'R_t', for some temporal *instant* *t*, which we will call **temporal testers**. Thus, (1') prefixed by '$R_{(3:00\ P.M.,\ 3/1/60)}$' yields:

(1″) $R_{(3:00\ P.M.,\ 3/1/60)}$ J.F. Kennedy is sick.

which is a temporal tester, to be read as: It is true at 3:00 P.M., 3/1/60, that J.F. Kennedy is sick.[8] Thus, a temporal tester of the form $R_t p$, where *t* is a temporal instant, asserts that the world at *t* is in accordance with what is described by *p*.

3. We shall now present an account of the notion *the history of the world up to time t*, which we symbolized (in 2 I) as W_t. Such a world history is a set of sentences of a particular language, say English, which is *informationally complete* (relative to it, and concerning times prior to *t*). (One may also require that the set be *syntactically complete*, in the sense of requiring that *every* true sentence that genuinely describes events as occurring exclusively prior to *t* belong to this set, and only such sentences.) All the sentences in this set are thus true factual sentences (lawlike sentences and logical truths are excluded). Now the leading idea is that the history of the world prior to time *t* (taking *t* as a temporal *instant*) is logically compatible with any possible history of the world after *t*.[9] Here the emphasis is on *logical* compatibility, regardless of the laws of nature. Given an instant *t* and the history of the world prior to *t*, there are no *purely logical* constraints on the world's future history (that is, after *t*). Thus, if a sentence describes events only as genuinely prior to *t*, it cannot be inconsistent with any sentence, true or false, which just describes events as genuinely after *t*. If a sentence is found to be involved in an inconsistency with a sentence that describes events as genuinely after *t*, it does not belong to the history of the world prior to *t*. Such a test, then, requires an examination of the logical consistency of the candidate sentence with sentences that describe events as genuinely after *t*. A *temporal tester* $R_t p$ is a sentence that describes an event as occurring at the temporal instant *t*, and the temporal purity of *p* guarantees that it has no logical implications concerning occurrences at times other than *t*. Thus, our temporal testers constitute a suitable device for checking whether a sentence indeed belongs to the history of the world up to time *t*:

(2') For a true sentence to belong to W_t, it must be logically consistent with any consistent set of temporal testers whose times are later than *t*.

This condition, however, though necessary, is not sufficient. Thus, consider the sentence:

A future president of the U.S. was born in 1917.

This is a true factual sentence, but it should not belong to W_t for $t = 1/1/1930$, since it alludes to Kennedy's presidency, which occurred only after 1930. However, this sentence is logically consistent with $\{R_{t'}q \mid t' \geq 1/1/1930\}$, where q is: 'No person born in 1917 is president of the U.S.'. The missing piece of information, whose absence makes this consistency possible, is the correct information concerning W_t, that no person born in 1917 was president *prior* to 1930. Thus clearly, logical consistency of a candidate for W_t with temporal testers later than t is not sufficient; we also have to include true temporal testers prior to t. A true factual sentence will thus belong to W_t iff it is logically consistent with the set of true testers prior to t, together with any set of testers later than t. Thus, we arrive at the following definition of W_t:

$$(2'') \quad W_t = \left\{ p \ \left| \ \begin{array}{l} p \text{ is a true, factual sentence, logically consis-} \\ \text{tent with any consistent set of sentences of} \\ \text{the form } R_{t'}q, \text{ such that if } t' < t, R_{t'}q \text{ is true} \end{array} \right. \right\}$$

However, even this condition is not strong enough. Problems arise with respect to true sentences that pertain to intervals that *include* t and times later as well as earlier than t (or complex sentences that contain such sentences as subsentences). These sentences should not belong to W_t, since the time to which they pertain is not prior to t. Now if the event purportedly described by such a sentence indeed occurred only later than t, such a sentence would indeed be ruled out by our condition $(2'')$. But if the occurrence time of the actual event described was earlier than t, condition $(2'')$ will fail to exclude it. The reason is that excluding such a sentence under $(2'')$, via inconsistency, requires testers that deny the occurrence of the event described at the time interval to which the sentence in question pertains, which includes a portion of time earlier than t as well. But since the event described indeed occurred before t and since the testers concerning times prior to t must be true, such a selection of testers necessary to rule out the sentence in question will not qualify under $(2'')$.

The way to remedy the situation, then, is to exclude from W_t sentences whose reference times are not prior to t. Limiting our discussion to syntactically simple sentences (in which we shall include, for our purposes here, propositional-attitude sentences, whose reference time will also be analyzed in the next section), this can be done explicitly, thus yielding:

$$(2^*) \quad W_t = \left\{ p \ \left| \ \begin{array}{l} p \text{ is a true, syntactically simple factual sen-} \\ \text{tence with reference time prior to } t \text{ which} \\ \text{is logically consistent with any consistent} \\ \text{set of sentences of the form } R_{t'}q, \text{ such that} \\ \text{if } t' < t, R_{t'}q \text{ is true} \end{array} \right. \right\}$$

However, even (2^*) needs some further adjustments. For the requirement of consistency in (2^*) may not do the work it was designed to do, since reference times may be specified via the mediation of factual information rather than by explicit (numeric) temporal specification (e.g., via 'during J.F.K.'s lifetime' rather than via 'between 5/29/1917 and 11/22/1963'), which is the way the times of the temporal testers are to be specified.[10]

This problem can be remedied by introducing a function that maps reference-time phrases into explicit (numeric) temporal specifications. (The function will therefore be dependent on factual information. Of course, if a reference-time phrase fails to pick up an interval owing to factual misfit, the sentence will not qualify in W_t.) Let us call the function that yields an explicit (numeric) specification of the reference time of p, $f(p)$, and let us have p' result from p by replacing the phrase specifying its reference time by '$f(p)$'. We can now reformulate (2*) as follows:

$$(2) \quad W_t = \left\{ p \; \left| \; \begin{array}{l} p \text{ is a true, syntactically simple factual sentence} \\ \text{such that } f(p) < t \text{ and such that } p' \text{ is logically} \\ \text{consistent with any consistent set of sentences} \\ \text{of the form } R_{t'}q, \text{ such that if } t' < t, R_{t'}q \text{ is true} \end{array} \right. \right\}$$

As we noticed in the beginning of this section, the mere specification of reference times will not do to determine inclusion in W_t. We still needed the mechanism presented above, in order to rule out allusions to later times that come in cryptic ways, as in singular terms, e.g., in the sentence: The 37th president of the U.S. ate breakfast on 1/1/1930, the truth of which requires the occurrence of a later event—the 37th presidency, and does not therefore belong to $W_{1/1/1940}$.

The above proposal yields the notion of W_t for syntactically simple sentences (among which we include here propositional-attitude sentences). One may expect that this notion of W_t would yield informational completeness as well, which is of course an important adequacy requirement for this notion. This limitation to syntactically simple sentences is natural here, since I will not go into a discussion of reference times for complex sentences, in line with our general limitation of the discussion in this book to syntactically simple sentences. But if we assume that, for a complex sentence to belong to W_t, the "stretched interval" of the reference times of its components (i.e., the minimal interval that includes them all) must be prior to t, then one may proceed along such lines to extend (2) beyond the limitation to syntactically simple sentences, and obtain thereby syntactical completeness as well in the analysis of W_t.

W_t is to be defined in the same way for noninstantaneous times t (with the sign '$<$' read as 'earlier than'). We can now also define $W_{t,t'}$ more precisely. In analogy with our definition of W_t, the history of the world up to t, we can define $W_t\#$, the history of the world *from t* on. $W_t\#$ is symmetric to W_t along the temporal line (on the "other side" of t, temporally speaking): it includes all and only true (syntactically simple) factual sentences which pertain to times weakly later than t. The definition of $W_{t\#}$ is exactly like that of W_t, except that the "earlier than" relation is to be replaced by the "weakly later" relation.

$W_{t,t'}$, which describes the history of the world between t and t', must therefore belong both to $W_{\bar{t}}{}'$ and to $W_{t\#}$. We can thus provide an adequate definition for $W_{t,t'}$ as follows:

$$W_{t,t'} = W_{\bar{t}}{}' \cap W_{t\#}$$

II   Canonical Representations

1. We now move to a more detailed analysis of the time of reference of sentences. We shall limit our discussion to syntactically simple sentences that are context-independent in every respect (unless we specify otherwise).[11]

In 2 I we considered a few examples of the time intervals to which sentences pertain. We now notice that a syntactically simple sentence typically involves a temporal quantifier associated with that time interval. Consider, for instance, Example 2:

(4)   It rained all day on 1/20/74.

The time interval to which this sentence pertains is the duration of the day indicated. However, with respect to this particular day, one could assert that it rained continuously throughout the day, as in sentence (4), or only at certain times during the day. The feasibility of making this distinction suggests a structure analogous to that of quantification over a domain of individuals. Here, temporal points constitute the domain.[12] We can therefore interpret the above sentence as involving universal quantification. Similarly, a sentence like

(5)   Exchanges of fire occurred in the Mideast intermittently through-
        out 1969.

pertains to the time interval indicated, viz., the year 1969. This sentence should be interpreted as involving an existential temporal quantifier, since the event type it purports to describe, exchanges of fire, is not said to have occurred at every moment of this interval — only at some of them. The temporal quantification thus covers the time interval to which the sentence pertains.

The failure of the distinction between universal and existential quantifiers to do justice to the variety of quantifying expressions in natural languages (like 'most', 'a few', 'many', etc.) is notorious. The same can be said about temporal quantification; therefore, since this failure is not unique to temporal quantification, we need not dwell on this issue in the context of temporal analysis.

2. Consider the time of occurrence of the event (or state of affairs) purportedly described by p. The information that the sentence p may provide

concerning this time of occurrence may vary in its degree of specificity. The sentence may specify a time interval during every instant of which the event described is alleged to take place, or the sentence may specify a time interval *within* which the event described is said to occur. This time interval T, specified by the sentence p, may thus *coincide* with the time of alleged occurrence of the event described by the sentence or may *contain* it. In the first case, the event is said to take place at *every* instant of T, in the second only at *some* instants of T. In the first case, when p specifies that the time of occurrence of the event it describes is T, p can be represented, following the convention discussed at the beginning of this chapter, as: $R_T p$, where the import of $R_T p$ is that $R_T p$ is true for *every* t in T.[13] In the other case, when what is specified is only an interval T *within* which the event purportedly described by p is said to occur, the import of p is that $R_t p$ holds for *some* t in T.

This indicates a logical structure of temporal-quantificational character, involving a temporal quantifier 'every' or 'some', which covers the temporal interval T. Let us, then, represent p in the first case as $((t)p, T)$, that is, as an ordered pair whose last element specifies the temporal interval T, and whose first element is the concatenation of a universal quantifier symbol and the temporally pure sentence p. In the second case, we will, analogously, symbolize p as $((\exists t)p, T)$. We will call T **the time of reference** of the sentence p. In the first case, the event purportedly described by p is said to occur at every instant of T; in the second case, at some instant of T. T thus functions as a domain of temporal quantification: for a universal temporal quantifier in the first case and for an existential quantifier in the second. The *time to which a sentence pertains*, then, is its *domain of temporal quantification*.[14]

Thus, we have arrived at a regimentation of a syntactically simple context-independent sentence. Such a sentence p is represented by an ordered pair, the first element of which is a concatenation of a quantifier symbol and a sentence which is a temporally pure projection of the original sentence p, and the second element of which is a phrase specifying the time of reference of the original sentence p, which is its domain of temporal quantification. Thus, in general, we may represent such a sentence p as:

$$(6) \quad \left(\left\{ \begin{array}{c} (t) \\ (\exists t) \end{array} \right\} \begin{array}{c} \text{a temporally pure} \\ \text{projection of } p \end{array} , \quad \begin{array}{c} \text{a specification of the} \\ \text{reference time of } p \end{array} \right)$$

We shall refer to this regimentation as the **canonical representational of** p.

A translation into English of a canonical representation '$((t)p, T)$' (where p is a temporally pure sentence and T is a temporal domain) will thus be: 'Throughout the period T, p' (with tense adjustments in p according to the relation between T and the utterance time). Similarly, '$((\exists t)p, T)$' would be translated (likewise, with tense adjustments) as: 'At some times within the period of T, p.'

3. Example 3. In 2 I we considered the sentence [2(1)]

(7)   J.F. Kennedy was president of the U.S. from January 20, 1961,
       to November 22, 1963.

We noted there that the time of reference of this sentence was the time interval specified in it. Eliminating this temporal specification and adjusting the tense yields a sentence that is a temporally pure projection of (7):

(7̲)   J.F.K. is the president of the U.S.

which specifies an event-type of which (7) is an event-token. The event purportedly described by (7̲) — J.F.K.'s being president — is said there to have taken place throughout the interval specified, which is (1/20/61, 11/22/63). Thus the quantification here is universal, the time of reference serving as the quantificational domain. Hence the canonical representation of (7) would be:

(8) $((t)(7̲),\ (1/20/61,\ 11/22/63))$

Example 4: At the beginning of this chapter we looked at the sentence

(5)   Exchanges of fire occurred in the Mideast intermittently
       throughout 1969.

and observed that the reference-time of (5) was the year 1969. Abstracting from the temporal information in (5) (and adjusting the tense), we obtain (5̲), a temporally pure projection of (5):

(5̲)   Exchanges of fire occur in the Mideast.

which specifies an event-type of which the events purportedly described in (5) are event-tokens. Clearly, the event-type of (5̲) is not said in (5) to have taken place continuously through the time of reference of (5), but rather at some times within it. Thus, the temporal quantificational character of (5) is existential, the time of reference being, as usual, the quantificational domain. Hence the canonical representation of (5) is:

(9) $((\exists t)(5̲),\ \text{the year 1969})$

4. A few comments are in order. First we note that the temporal quantificational structure of sentences yields two components normally associated with quantificational structures: a quantifier and a domain of quantification. However, in the regimentation proposed above (which will soon be further developed in our formulation of a formal language) there are two distinctive features that are *uncommon* in standard symbolizations of quantificational structures. One is that the domain of quan-

tification is represented by a component in the regimentation (and later, by a variable in the object language), rather than kept behind the scenes in the semantics. The second distinctive feature is that the quantifier symbols, though clearly in accordance with the *import* of standard quantifiers, do not behave *syntactically* as quantifiers: they do not bind any variables, since we do not have bindable temporal variables. In these two respects the temporal quantificational structure presented differs from the standard regimentation of quantificational structures.

Secondly, in section I 1, we extended the concept of a temporally pure projection of a sentence to context-independent sentences describing propositional attitudes the embedding sentences of which are syntactically simple. The concept of canonical representation described above applies to such sentences as well, *mutatis mutandis*, that is, when the transformations are applied to the embedding sentence only, leaving the embedded sentence intact. (However, this extension will not be pertinent to our present project—the development of a formal semantics for the counterfactual construction, as will be made clear later.)[15]

Thirdly, we restricted the application of the canonical representation to sentences that are context-independent. This requirement can also be relaxed. Thus, for instance, if a sentence is context-independent except for the specification of individuals referred to in it, its canonical representation is well defined according to our guidelines; but its temporally pure projection, which will be a component in its canonical representation, will also be context-dependent in this particular respect. A case in point is that of complex English sentences whose structure involves individual-quantifiers (as distinct from temporal-quantifiers) whose scopes cover more than one syntactically simple subsentence. If each subsentence is syntactically simple and context-independent except for reference to individuals, it can be provided with canonical representation. (When we move to the formal languages, this will allow extra formalizational capacity in various cases.[16])

Finally, insofar as the times of reference of the antecedents and consequents (of counterfactuals) which are themselves complex sentences are concerned, it seems that they should be taken as the "stretched" unions of the reference times of their syntactically simple components—that is, as the intervals whose lowest (highest) point is the lowest (highest) point of any of the intervals corresponding to the component sentences. This remark, however, goes beyond the analysis of counterfactuals whose components are syntactically simple, which is the chief concern of this book, and thus we shall not dwell on this point in greater detail here.[17]

III Formal Semantics

1. In this section a formal semantics for counterfactuals is developed. The idea is to extend a first-order language by the addition of a counterfactual connective and to provide the extended language with a semantics that will reflect the truth conditions for counterfactual statements developed in

chapters 2, 4, and 5. As we saw in chapter 2, however, our analysis of counterfactuals required use of the concepts of world history and of the reference-time of sentences, which we have explicated in this chapter (sections I, II), ending up with the temporal canonical representation of sentences. In order for our formal semantics to reflect the above analysis, the formal language for which it is to be provided must possess the requisite temporal characteristics. Thus the language to which we shall add the counterfactual connective will be a first-order language that reflects the regimentation of sentences along the lines of the temporal canonical representation. Accordingly, the language will differ from a standard first-order language, and its semantics will have to interpret its special temporal characteristics.

For the sake of clarity, we shall first present a propositional language that incorporates the temporal analysis of sentences we have been discussing, and provide a semantics for it. The structure of its sentences will thus reflect the temporal canonical representation discussed above. We will then proceed to present its first-order analogue (language and semantics), extend this analogue by adding a counterfactual connective, and provide a semantics for this counterfactual-connective-enriched system. We shall thus discuss three formal systems. The three languages, respectively, will be **PTL**, propositional temporal language; **QTL**, quantificational temporal language; and **CQTL**, counterfactually enriched QTL.

The temporal characteristics of the first two languages will be introduced at the level of atomic formulas. Now the development below of the propositional language will serve primarily as a preamble for the first-order language to follow. Therefore, and since the atomic formulas of a first-order language represent syntactically simple English sentences, it will be sufficient, for the purpose of representing temporal features at the level of the propositional language to be constructed, to allow the propositional variables to correspond only to syntactically simple English sentences as well. Thus, the structure of atomic sentences of the propositional language will be designed to reflect the temporal canonical representation discussed above. (The temporal canonical representation presented above was primarily, but not exclusively, designed to fit syntactically simple sentences. It also applied, as noted in section II above, to sentences describing propositional attitudes whose embedding sentences are syntactically simple. The atomic formulas of the propositional language to be developed below can thus be viewed as formal representations of both types of sentences. This extension of the domain of representable sentences, though, will of course not be reflected in the first-order formal language.) From the viewpoint of providing a formal analysis of temporal structures, the propositional language will provide for the representation of only these two categories of English sentences, together with the modes of sentence composition representable in a standard propositional language. Since the main purpose of developing the propositional language is to facilitate the introduction of the first-order language to follow, this limitation of scope will not be harmful to our present concerns.

2. The temporal canonical representation discussed above had the form $\left(\left\{ \begin{matrix} (t) \\ (\exists t) \end{matrix} \right\} \underline{p}, T \right)$, where $\underline{p}$ was a temporally pure sentence, and T a temporal domain. Accordingly, we shall use, in symbolizing temporally pure sentences, two types of variables, which will be called **propositional component variables** and **temporal component variables**, respectively.

The Language PTL

Primitive symbols

1. An indenumerable number of **propositional-component variables**, over which the syntactical p^1, p^2, . . . vary.
2. An unlimited number of **temporal-component variables**, over which the syntactical variables t_1, t_2, . . . vary.
3. Two-place predicates symbols: $\subseteq$, $<$, $\leq$, $\widetilde{<}$
4. A two-place function-symbol: $\cup$
5. The following symbols: (,), , , $\sim$, &, (t)

DEF.: $t_1 \cup t_2 \cup \ldots \cup t_n$ $(n > 0)$ is a **temporal term**.

We shall allow the syntactical variables t^1, t^2, . . . to vary over temporal terms.

Formation Rules

1. $((t)p^1, t^1)$, $((t) \sim p^1, t^1)$, $(\sim (t)p^1, t^1)$, $(\sim (t) \sim p^1, t^1)$ are wffs of PTL, called **atomic propositional wffs.**
2. $t^1 \subseteq t^2$, $t^1 < t^2$, $t^1 \leq t^2$, and $t^1 \widetilde{<} t^2$ are wffs of PTL, called **atomic temporal wffs.**
3. If α, β are wffs of PTL, so are $\sim \alpha$, α & β. (If α, β are propositional wffs (temporal wffs), so are $\sim \alpha$, α & β).

Semantics for PTL

A **PTL-model** is an ordered pair $\langle Q, V \rangle$ such that: Q is a function from propositional-component variables into $\text{ß}R$ (R is the set of real numbers; $\text{ß}R$ is the power set of R; see commentary below), and V is a function that maps all the temporal-component variables into $\text{ß}R$ and[18] all the wffs of PTL into $\{0,1\}$, and fulfills the following conditions:

1. $V(t^1 \cup \ldots \cup t^n) = V(t^1) \cup \ldots \cup V(t^n)$.
2. $V((t)p^1, t^1) = 1$ iff $V(t^1) \subseteq Q(p^1)$.
   $V((t) \sim p^1, t^1) = 1$ iff $V(t^1) \cap Q(p^1) = \phi$.
3. If $(\sim \alpha, t^1)$ is a wff, then $V(\sim \alpha, t^1) = 1$ iff $V(\alpha, t^1) = 0$.
4. $V(t^1 \subseteq t^2) = 1$ iff $V(t^1) \subseteq V(t^2)$.
5. $V(t^1 < t^2) = 1$ iff for every τ^1 and τ^2, if $\tau^1 \in V(t^1)$ and $\tau^2 \in V(t^2)$, then $\tau^1 < \tau^2$.
6. $V(t^1 \leq t^2) = 1$ iff for every $\tau^2 \in V(t^2)$ there is $\tau^1 \in V(t^1)$ such that $\tau^1 \leq \tau^2$.

7. $V(t^1 \widetilde{<} t^2) = 1$ iff for every $\tau^1 \in V(t^1)$ there is $\tau^2 \in V(t^2)$ such that $\tau^1 \leq \tau^2$.
8. If α is a wff of PTL, then
$$V(\sim\alpha) = 1 \text{ iff } V(\alpha) = 0.$$
9. If α, β are wffs of PTL, then:
$$V(\alpha\&\beta) = 1$$
$$\text{iff } V(\alpha) = V(\beta) = 1.$$

DEF.: $(\exists t) = \sim (t) \sim$

Thus, it follows that:

$$V((\exists t)p^1, t^1) = 1 \text{ iff } V(t^1) \cap Q(p^1) \neq \phi.$$

The role of the function Q, when applied to a propositional-component variable p^1, is analogous to that of assigning to a temporally pure sentence $\underline{p}$ the set of time instants in which event-tokens of the type specified by $\underline{p}$ occur; this, indeed, is the set $\{t \mid R_t \underline{p}\}$. The valuation function assigns 0 or 1 to atomic propositional wffs in accordance with whether the time assigned by Q to the propositional component variable intersects or includes the time assigned by V to the temporal term in that wff. This is analogous, in the case of sentences in canonical representation, to basing a decision as to the truth value of the sentence on whether the set of occurrence-times of event-tokens of the type described by $\underline{p}$ includes or intersects with the time to which the sentence pertains (subject to the temporal quantifiers and negation symbols involved). The temporal relations 'earlier' and 'weakly earlier', defined in 2 I, are the analogues of the predicate-symbols '$<$' and '$\leq$', respectively, under the above interpretation.

3. The second language we will discuss, **QTL**, differs from PTL in one respect: whereas PTL symbolized temporally pure projections propositionally as propositional component variables, QTL will symbolize them in a first-order form. Thus, the temporally pure sentences in the temporal canonical representations will be symbolized along the lines of standard quantificational theory. Symbolic representability in QTL is thus in a certain respect more limited than that of PTL: sentences whose temporally pure projections in their canonical representations do not have a structure that can be formalized by standard quantificational theory cannot be formalized in QTL, but they may be formalizable in PTL. (Example: sentences describing propositional attitudes whose embedding sentences are syntactically simple.) The deficiency in "formalizational force" is of course compensated for by the added richness of the logical structure formalized. This relation between QTL and PTL is thus quite analogous to that between a standard first-order language and a standard propositional language, and is reflected in the relation between the propositional-component variables of PTL and the first-order wffs that replace them in QTL.

The Language QTL

Primitive symbols

1. An unlimited number of individual variables. The syntactical variables x, y, z, . . . vary over them.
2. Predicate symbols of various degrees (an unlimited number). The syntactical variables P_1, Q_1, R_1, . . . (for the first degree), P_n, Q_n, R_n, . . . (for the nth degree, $n > 0$) vary over them.
3. An unlimited number of individual constants: their syntactical variables are e_1, e_2, . . .
4. An unlimited number of temporal-component variables with the syntactical variables t_1, t_2, . . .
5. Two-place predicate symbols: $=, \subseteq, <, \leq, \overline{<}$
6. A two-place function symbol: $\cup$
7. The following symbols:), (,,, $\sim$, &, (t)

DEF.: As in PTL: $t_1 \cup t_2 \cup \ldots \cup t_n$ $(n > 0)$ is a **temporal term**. The syntactical variables t^1, t^2, . . . vary over temporal terms.

DEF.: x, y, z, . . . e_1, e_2, . . . are **individual terms**. The syntactical variables a_1, a_2, . . . b_1, b_2, . . . vary over individual terms.

Formation Rules

I. Preliminary definitions

A. 1. $\pm a = b$ and $\pm P_n a_1$, . . . , a_n are **atomic quasi formulas** ('. . . $\pm \alpha$ . . .' is tantamount to 'both . . . α . . . and . . . $\sim \alpha$ . . .').
2. If α is an atomic quasi-formula, so are $\pm (x)\alpha$.
3. If α is an atomic quasi-formula, then $(\pm (t)\alpha, t^1)$ are **temporal atomic quasi formulas**.
4. If α is a temporal quasi-formula, then α is a **temporal quasi formula**.
5. If α, β are temporal quasi formulas, then $\pm \alpha$, $\alpha \& \beta$ and $\pm (x)\alpha$ are also temporal quasi formulas.

B. 1. $t^1 \subseteq t^2$, $t^1 < t^2$, $t^1 \leq t^2$, and $t^1 \overline{<} t^2$ are **temporal wffs**.
2. If α, β are temporal wffs, then so are $\sim \alpha$, $\alpha \ \& \ \beta$.

II. Main Definition

1. If α is a temporal quasi formula in which no individual variable is free or if α is a temporal wff, then α is a **wff of QTL**.
2. If α, β are wffs of QTL, so is $\alpha \ \& \ \beta$.

Semantics for QTL

A **QTL-model** is an ordered pair $\langle D, V \rangle$, where D is a set and V is a function such that V maps all the individual terms into D; it maps all the temporal-component variables into $ßR$; it maps all the predicates into $ß(D^n \times R)$ (so that, for every predicate P_n, $V(P_n) \subseteq D^n \times R$); it maps all temporal quasi formulas and wffs of QTL into $\{0,1\}$, and it fulfills the following conditions:

1. $V(t^1 \cup \ldots \cup t^n) = V(t^1) \cup \ldots \cup V(t^n)$
2. $V((t)a_1 = a_2, t^1) = 1$ iff $V(a_1) = V(a_2)$.
3. $V((t)P_na_1, \ldots, a_n, t^1) = 1$ iff for every $\tau \in V(t^1)$, $< V(a_1), \ldots, V(a_n), \tau > \in V(P_n)$.
4. $V(t) \sim P_na_1, \ldots, a_n, t^1) = 1$ iff, for every $\tau \in V(t^1)$, $< V((a_1), \ldots, V(a_n), \tau > \notin V(P_n)$.
5. If $\alpha = ((t)(x)\beta, t^1)$ is a temporal atomic quasi formula, then $V(\alpha) = 1$ iff, for every value-assignment function V', differing from V at most at x: $V'((t)\beta, t^1) = 1$.
6. If $((t)\alpha, t^1)$ is a temporal atomic quasi-formula, then: $V((t) \sim \alpha, t^1) = 1$ iff, for every value-assignment function V' that differs from V at most at t_1, and such that $V'(t_1) \subseteq V'(t^1)$: $V'((t)\alpha, t_1) = 0$; and $V(\sim (t)\alpha, t^1) = 1$ iff $V((t)\alpha, t^1) = 0$.
7. If $(x)\alpha$ is a temporal quasi formula, then $V((x)\alpha) = 1$ iff, for every value-assignment function V', differing from V at most at x, $V'(\alpha) = 1$.
8. If α is a temporal quasi formula of QTL, then $V(\sim \alpha) = 1$ iff $V(\alpha) = 0$.
9. If α, β are temporal quasi formulas of QTL, then $V(\alpha \& \beta) = 1$ iff $V(\alpha) = V(\beta) = 1$.

10-15. These rules are the same as conditions 4-9 in the semantics for PTL (changing 'PTL' to 'QTL' in rules 8, 9). (The role that Q fulfilled in PTL is here fulfilled by V when applied to predicate symbols.)

DEF.: A set of wffs of QTL is **QTL-consistent** iff there is a QTL-model $\langle D, V \rangle$ such that, for every wff α in the set, $V(\alpha) = 1$.

4. We will now present a formal language for counterfactuals — **CQTL** — and its semantics. The language will consist of QTL, enriched by a counterfactual connective '$>$'. In constructing the semantics, we will adopt the main features of the analysis of counterfactuals developed in chapters 2, 4, and 5, and will attempt to express them with our formal machinery.

The analysis provided in chapter 2 had prominent temporal features. Thus, the classification there of the two types of counterfactuals utilized the concept of "the history of the world prior to a certain time," and the proposed truth conditions themselves involved this notion and a derivative of it ("the history of the world between t and t'"). The temporal limits of histories of this sort as used there were determined by the times of reference of the antecedent and consequent of the counterfactual under examination. In section II of this chapter we provided an account of the time of reference of sentences, concentrating on two types (syntactically simple sentences and propositional-attitude sentences with syntactically simple embedding sentences). This account was formally mirrored by the two languages we developed above, PTL and QTL, which formalized the temporal structure of statements as elaborated by the previous account, the first for a propositional language, and the second for a quantificational one.

Since the quantificational language QTL is the richer in terms of logical structure, we shall introduce the counterfactual connective into QTL. Thus, the components of a counterfactual statement will be formulas of QTL, and other auxiliary formulas of the object language will be used to express the desired truth conditions. The resulting language will thus be a counterfactually enriched temporal first-order language. Moreover, since the truth conditions for counterfactuals involve the notion of logical implication, in our formal account we will use the best approximation to logical implication available in the language we are using: that of QTL-consistency. If we wish to have a stronger account of consistency, we will have to find a richer underlying formal language. However, to the extent that a first-order language reflects certain structural aspects of sentences of natural language and ignores others, the projection of the notion of consistency definable for such a language back to the natural-language sentences that were formalized in that first-order language will do only limited justice to these sentences. This introduces an element of approximation into our formal account: the notion of logical consistency (and thus of logical implication) is that capturable by the base language, which is a first-order language.

The account of counterfactuals which we shall attempt to capture in our formal semantics is that of 2(21), following theses 1 and 2 of 2 IX, which, together with 2(52) of 2 XIII, yield the result that

A counterfactual $A > B$ of the n-d type is true iff

(10)　$W \cup L \cup \{A\} \cup \{C \mid C \in W_{t_A, t_B}$ &
　　　　$[R_{cir}(C, A, W) \lor R_{ppcr}(C, A, W)]\} \to B$

Throughout the previous discussion we have concentrated on counterfactuals of the n-d type only, ignoring non-n-d type counterfactuals. Accordingly, the counterfactual connective '>' which appears in the formal language CQTL will be used in symbolizing counterfactuals of the n-d type only.

We provided an account of the concept of the history of the world up to time $t - W_t -$ in the first section of this chapter, which dealt with natural rather than formal languages. However, once we are working with a formal language that is temporally adequate, i.e, in which simple formulas display their reference times, another way of expressing this concept is readily available. Clearly, a simple sentence will not belong to W_t unless its reference time is strictly prior to t. As for complex sentences, the most natural move is to say that such a sentence will not belong to W_t

unless the reference time of each of its subsentences is strictly prior to t. In a formal language such as QTL, the reference times of all syntactically simple sentences, whether components of other sentences or not, are displayed via temporal terms. Thus, this condition of strict priority to time t is readily expressible by means of the temporal terms that appear in the candidates for membership in W_t. For the purpose of stating this condition, we shall define a temporal function that will, for a given sentence, yield the "stretched" interval of the temporal intervals that constitute the reference times of its simple constituents (that is, the smallest interval that includes them all). Obviously, in addition to meeting the condition of priority to time t, in order to qualify for membership in W_t a sentence will have to be nonlawlike, nontautological (in QTL) and true.[19] This line of thinking will naturally be extended for the definition of $W_{t,t'}$, the world history between t and t'.

Throughout this book we have presupposed, rather than analyzed, the notion of lawlikeness; this will be reflected in our formal treatment. In our semantics we shall take as the set of laws simply a set L of true wffs of QTL. The approximation reached thereby can be improved, once an account of lawlikeness is available, by further conditions to be superimposed on the set L.

As for the last component in (10) above, we shall use the analysis of irrel-semifactuals and pp-semifactuals developed in 4 V, thesis 2, and in 5 III, thesis 4, since '$R_{cir}(C,A,W)$' and '$R_{ppcr}(C,A,W)$' in (10) are to be replaced by conditions for the causal irrelevance and purely positive causal relevance of A to C (on the basis of W), respectively. These analyses of irrel-semifactuals and of pp-semifactuals were given in qualitative probabilistic terms which involved only the relations of "less than" and "equal to" between two conditional probabilities, and did not require any probabilistic metric. Analogously, in our formal semantics we introduce two probabilistic relations, that of equiprobability and that of "less than" between probabilities. Since conditional probability has two arguments, the relations of "equal to" and "less than" between conditional probabilities are 4-place relations. Thus, if $P_=$ is to symbolize the relation of equiprobability, then '$P(A/\alpha) = P(C/\gamma)$', where A and C are statements and α and γ are sets of statements (or conjunctions thereof), will be expressed as: $P_=(A,\alpha,C,\gamma)$; and similarly for the "less than" relation, $P_<$. The probabilistic conditions of the analyses of irrel-semifactuals and pp-semifactuals in chapters 4 and 5 will thus be expressed in terms of these two 4-place probabilistic relations.

5. The Language CQTL. We shall define CQTL as an extension of QTL.

Primitive symbols: Those of QTL, plus the symbol '$>$'.

Formation Rules

　　1. If α is a wff of QTL, it is a wff of CQTL.
　　2. If α,β are wffs of QTL, then $\alpha > \beta$ is a wff of CQTL.
　　DEF.: If α is a wff of QTL, then $T(\alpha)$ is the term $t^1 \cup t^2 \cup$

. . . $\cup$ t^n, where t^1, . . . ,t^n are all the second (temporal) components in the temporal atomic quasi formulas in α in their order of appearance in α.

Semantics for CQTL.

A **CQTL-model** is an ordered quintuple $\langle D,V,L,P_=,P_< \rangle$, which fulfills the following conditions:

1. D is a set.
2. V is a value-assignment function that fulfills, with respect to the symbols and wffs of QTL in CQTL, the conditions for V in a QTL model. [$V(\alpha > \beta)$ will be defined later.]
3. L is a set of CQTL wffs which are also QTL wffs, which are QTL-consistent, such that if $\alpha \epsilon L$, $V(\alpha) = 1$.
4. $P_=(\alpha,U,\beta,V)$ and $P_<(\alpha,U,\beta,V)$ are 4-place relations, where α and β are wffs of QTL, and U, V are set of wffs of QTL, such that, for every wffs α, β and sets of wffs U, V of QTL, exactly one of the following holds:[20] $P_<(\alpha,U,\beta,V)$; $P_<(\beta,V,\alpha,U)$, $P_=(\alpha,U,\beta,V)$.

Before we move on to $V(\alpha > \beta)$, we shall define W_{t^1}, W_{t^1,t^2} and $CIP(\alpha,T(\beta))$.

DEF. 1:
$W_{t^1} = \{\alpha \mid \alpha$ is a wff of QTL; α is not QTL-valid; $V(\alpha) = 1$; $\alpha \notin L$; $V(T(\alpha) < t^1) = 1\}$

DEF. 2: If $V(t^1 \leq t^2) = 1$, then:
$W_{t^1,t^2} = \{\alpha \mid \alpha$ is a non-QTL-valid wff of QTL; $V(\alpha) = 1$; $\alpha \notin L$; $V(T(\alpha) \overline{<} t^2) = 1$; $V(t^1 \leq T(\alpha)) = 1\}$.
(It is easy to see that W_{t^1,t^2} is
$\{\gamma \mid$ for every t^3, if $V(t^2 < t^3) = 1$, then $\gamma \in W_{t^3}$; and $t^1 \leq T(\gamma)\}$.

DEF. 3: $P_\leq(\alpha,U,\beta,V) = P_=(\alpha,U,\beta,V)$ or $P_<(\alpha,U,\beta,V)$

DEF. 4: If α,β are wffs of QTL, and $V(T(\alpha) \leq T(\beta)) = 1$, and $\{W_{T(\alpha)},L,\alpha\}$ is QTL-consistent, then:

$CIP(\alpha,T(\beta))$ is the set of QTL-wffs γ, such that $\gamma \in W_{T(\alpha),T(\beta)}$; $\{W_{T(\alpha)},L,\alpha,\gamma\}$ is QTL-consistent; and either of the following conditions I or II obtain:

I. For every wff ζ of QTL;
If $\zeta \in W_{T(\alpha),T(\gamma)}$ and if:
    either not $P_=(\gamma,\{\zeta,\sim\alpha,W_{T(\alpha)}\},\gamma,\{\sim\alpha,W_{T(\alpha)}\})$
    or not $P_=(\gamma,\{\zeta,\alpha,W_{T(\alpha)}\},\gamma,\{\alpha,W_{T(\alpha)}\})$,
    then:
    $P_=(\zeta,\{\alpha,W_{T(\alpha)}\},\zeta,\{\sim\alpha,W_{T(\alpha)}\})$
    and $P_=(\gamma,\{\zeta,\sim\alpha,W_{T(\alpha)}\},\gamma,\{\zeta,\alpha,W_{T(\alpha)}\})$.

II.
1. $P_<(\gamma,\{\sim\alpha,W_{T(\alpha)}\},\gamma,\{\alpha,W_{T(\alpha)}\})$
2. For every wff ζ of QTL, if $\zeta \in W_{T(\alpha),T(\gamma)}$, then:
2.1 If $P_<(\gamma,\{\sim\alpha,W_{T(\alpha)}\},\gamma,\{\zeta,\sim\alpha,W_{T(\alpha)}\})$, then
    $P_<(\gamma,\{\alpha,W_{T(\alpha)}\},\gamma,\{\zeta,\alpha,W_{T(\alpha)}\})$; and
    $P_\le(\zeta,\{\sim\alpha,W_{T(\alpha)}\},\zeta,\{\alpha,W_{T(\alpha)}\})$;
2.2 If $P_\le(\gamma,\{\sim\alpha,W_{T(\alpha)}\},\gamma,\{\zeta,\sim\alpha,W_{T(\alpha)}\})$, then,
    $P_\le(\gamma,\{\alpha,W_{T(\alpha)}\},\gamma,\{\zeta,\alpha,W_{T(\alpha)}\})$, and
    $P_\le(\gamma,\{\zeta,\sim\alpha,W_{T(\alpha)}\},\gamma,\{\zeta,\alpha,W_{T(\alpha)}\})$.
2.3 If $P_<(\gamma,\{\sim\alpha,W_{T(\alpha)}\},\gamma,\{\zeta,\sim\alpha,W_{T(\alpha)}\})$, then:
    $P_<(\gamma,\{\zeta,\sim\alpha,W_{T(\alpha)}\},\gamma,\{\zeta,\alpha,W_{T(\alpha)}\})$.
2.4 If $P_<(\gamma,\{\zeta,\alpha,W_{T(\alpha)}\},\gamma,\{\alpha,W_{T(\alpha)}\})$, then:
    $P_\le(\zeta,\{\alpha,W_{T(\alpha)}\},\zeta,\{\sim\alpha,W_{T(\alpha)}\})$.

Now, as to $V(\alpha>\beta)$, we require the following:
1. $V(\alpha>\beta)$ is defined iff:
    $\alpha>\beta$ is a wff of QTL; $V(\alpha)=0$;
    $V(T(\alpha)\le T(\beta))=1$; $\{L,\alpha,W_{T(\alpha)}\}$
    is QTL consistent; $\alpha,\beta \notin L$.
2. If $V(\alpha>\beta)$ is defined, then:
    $V(\alpha>\beta)=1$ iff
    $\{\alpha,\ W_{T(\alpha)},L,\ CIP(\alpha,T(\beta)),\sim\beta\}$
    is QTL-*inconsistent*.

Notice that a feature of this semantics for counterfactuals of the n-d type is that $V(\alpha>\beta)$ is not always defined even when $\alpha>\beta$ is a wff. The reason is that many of the requisite restrictions that should be imposed on the sort of formulas $\alpha>\beta$ for which we want $V(\alpha>\beta)$ to be defined are semantic in nature.

Notes: Chapter 6

1. From the point of view of generative grammar, a sentence may be considered syntactically simple if its tree contains one S only.

2. t is *earlier* than t' (or: *prior* to t') iff every point in t is earlier than every point in t'. For the temporal terminology, see 2 I. W_t, the history of the world up to t, covers only sentences pertaining to times earlier than t.

3. That is, nonlawlike and nontautological.

4. Even if t is a temporal instant.

5. By 'sentences' I mean factual, indicative context-independent sentences (unless explicity specified otherwise).

6. *Temporal Logic* (New York: Springer-Verlag, 1971), pp. 144-151.

7. That is, if a sentence of this sort is conjoined with a specification of a time-instant so that the resulting sentence expresses that the event-type described in this original sentence occurs at that time instant there are no strictly logical implications to regarding the occurrence of other events at any other time.

8. Time readings are taken as relative to some fixed point of reference, e.g., Eastern Standard Time.

9. For a somewhat related idea, see Rescher & Urquhart, *op. cit.*, p. 147. Taking t in W_t as a temporal instant is done for mere convenience here. Obviously, if t' is an interval and t is the greatest lower bound of t', $W_{t'} = W_t$.

10. Notice that reference-time phrases can be determined via temporal testers as well; e.g.: L.B. Johnson's lifetime can be determined by $\{t \mid {}'R_t{}'\text{L.B.J. is alive'}$ is true$\}$.

11. We will not be concerned with tense considerations at all; once the time of reference is given, tense-indicators are reducible to it and the time of utterance. We are not concerned here with the pragmatic analysis of sentences, and, dealing with context-independent sentences, we can afford to abstract from the time of utterance.

12. An equally attractive interpretation is to choose not temporal points but rather temporal intervals.

13. t is to be substitutible for temporal instants here; and T for temporal intervals.

14. When the determination of the temporal interval to which a sentence pertains is context-dependent, we are faced with the familiar pragmatic problem of how to functionally determine the contextual information. It requires the elaboration of pragmatic bridge rules which connect the specification of the temporal interval to the overt features (linguistic or nonlinguistic) of the context, bridge rules whose nature is still obscure. This, however, is not a problem unique to temporal features, but common to all context-dependent characteristics (compare the analogous case of the context-dependence of the ordinary domains of quantification).

15. The reason is that we will couch the counterfactual connective in a first-order language not rich enough to formalize propositional-attitude sentences.

16. Thus, if the propositional connections between these subsentences are representable in a standard propositional language, then the whole sentence can be symbolized in, say, an extended first-order language (see language QTL below, this chapter), when the temporally pure projections of its subsentences can be symbolized in it (since in that case, as we shall see in section III, these subsentences can be so symbolized as well).

17. Antecedents with the temporal character of existential quantification may call for special consideration in our treatment. Suppose we take the antecedent 'Had there been a war in the Mideast during 1970. . . .'. Its indicative version has an existential temporal structure: some time during 1970 there was a war in the Mideast. Now the evaluation of a counterfactual with this antecedent on the inferential schema requires that the role of this counterfactual antecedent in the antecedent of the inferential schema be filled by an *open sentence* describing an event-type (i.e.: a war erupts in the Mideast) as occurring at t, where 't' is a variable ranging over time intervals within the reference time of the counterfactual antecedent (i.e., 1970). The counterfactual schema for such an n-d type counterfactual will then have the following form:

$$(\exists t \in T)[\,(W_t \ \& \ A(t) \ \& \ \mathrm{CIP}(A(t), W_{\bar{t}B})) \overset{\mathrm{L}}{\to} B\,]$$

Thus, what $A(t)$ expresses is that the event-type described in the antecedent occurred at time t, which is some interval within T, the reference time of the antecedent (1970 in the above example). I shall not, however, incorporate this modification in the formal treatment below.

18.   In order to be more faithful to our informal analysis, we could have V map the temporal-component variables into segments of R, to reflect intervals rather than any subsets of R. Such a requirement is not incorporated here.

19.   The account of a world-history in the first section of this chapter can be readily formalized for the semantics of CQTL using the notion of QTL-consistency. Because of the availability of the temporal machinery of QTL, however, the account proposed here seems more natural. Alternatively, the applicability of the account proposed here to statements of natural language will require an extension of the concept of reference time to all statements of that language. We have, however, provided such an account for certain categories only, and not for every variety of compound sentences. Such an extension is beyond the scope of this book. These two strategies can be expected to yield equivalent results; but further discussion of this claim will not be pursued here.

20.   Keeping these constraints on the relations as they are obviously leaves a lot to be desired. A refined treatment will have to reflect their probabilistic characters by introducing further constraints.

7 Intuitive Similarity
And Minimal Change

In this chapter I contrast my approach with the closest-possible-worlds approach, paying special attention to David Lewis's theory of counterfactuals as put forward in his book *Counterfactuals*.[1] (In the next chapter I will discuss a new version of this theory which Lewis proposed in a recent article.[2]) Sections I, II, and the second part of III of this chapter are relatively technical in nature. Section I involves exposition and relatively minor critical notes; II and III contrast the two approaches under examination. Sections IV and V focus on further differences between Lewis's account and mine; section V is *not* technical and can read independently.[3]

I *Lewis's Account*

1. In his book Lewis proposes a theory of counterfactuals formulated in terms of possible worlds, using a notion of similarity between them. Lewis works with spheres of worlds around a world i, which are sets of worlds such that each world in a given sphere is more similar to i than any world outside that sphere and such that all worlds at least as similar to i as some world in the sphere are in it (pp. 9, 14). He then assigns to each world i a system $\$_i$ of spheres around i (p. 13). Lewis defines truth conditions for counterfactuals (using the notation '$\Box\!\!\rightarrow$' instead of our notation '$>$') as follows:

> $\phi\Box\!\!\rightarrow\psi$ is true at a world i (according to a system of spheres $\$$) iff either (1) no ϕ-world belongs to any sphere S in $\$_i$, or (2) some sphere S in $\$_i$ does contain at least one ϕ-world, and $\phi\supset\psi$ holds at every world in S (p. 16).

where a ϕ-world is a world in which ϕ is true.

Lewis's condition amounts to the following: first, it relativizes the truth of a counterfactual to a system of spheres; secondly, if for the antecedent to hold in a world requires that world to be too dissimilar to i for it to be in $\cup\$_i$, the counterfactual is (vacuously) true in i (according to $\$$); thirdly, if this is not the case and there is a world in some sphere in $\$_i$ in which ϕ is true, then for the counterfactual to be true there must be a sphere in $\$_i$ in all of whose members in which ϕ is true, ψ is true as well.

2. Lewis defines his notion of a system of spheres as follows:

> Let $\$$ be an assignment to each possible world i of the set $\$_i$ of sets of possible worlds. Then $\$$ is called a (*centered*) *system of*

spheres, and the members of each $\$_i$ are called *spheres* around *i*,
if and only if, for each world *i*, the following conditions hold.
(C) $\$_i$ is *centered on i*; . . .
(1) $\$_i$ is *nested*; . . .
(2) $\$_i$ is *closed under unions*; . . .
(3) $\$_i$ is *closed under (nonempty) intersections* (p. 13/4).

Now Lewis's relativization to a system of spheres is designed primarily
to reflect a relativization to the relevant similarity relations. But beyond
this, it is also designed to yield, as far as his truth conditions for counterfactuals are concerned, the result that beyond a certain degree of similarity
to the center world *i*, worlds don't count [in the way reflected in (1) of his
truth conditions]. But for Lewis it should also be the case that, for any
degree of similarity (exemplified by a possible world similar to *i* to that
degree), there will be a sphere of worlds around *i* which contains all and
only those worlds which are similar to *i* to at least that degree. For, if this
requirement is not met, two systems of spheres $\$_i{}^1$ and $\$_i{}^2$ could contain
exactly the same worlds even though $S_i{}^1$ would contain fewer spheres than
$\$_i{}^2$. This could make a difference for the truth value of counterfactuals as
interpreted in $\$_i{}^1$ and $\$_i{}^2$.[4]
When this requirement is met by all systems of spheres \$, the only
relativization that counts (in Lewis's relativization to the system \$, once
the similarity relation has been fixed), is to $\cup\$_i$ — the set of all worlds in
spheres in $\$_i$. But this requirement does not follow from Lewis's formal
definition of systems of spheres quoted above, which is expressed in set-
theoretical terminology expressing topological notions, rather than in
terms of degrees of similarity. It makes little sense to relativize the truth
value of counterfactuals to how rich a system of spheres is (i.e., to how
many spheres it contains for a given set of worlds and a given similarity
relation): this feature seems to reflect nothing of value in the ordinary-
language use of counterfactuals, and would only be an additional source
of ambiguity. The discrepancy here, it seems, is due to the difficulty of expressing this requirement in set-theoretical or topological terminology
without introducing a measure of similarity or at least a 3-place relation
of similarity (*j* is at least as similar to *i* as *k* is) into the above definition
of a system of spheres.
Similarly, one should assume that every sphere in every $\$_i$ includes, for
every world in that sphere, all the worlds more similar to *i* than to that
world. If this condition were not fulfilled, this would also affect the truth
values of counterfactuals, which would then vary relative to systems of
spheres that differ in this respect. [If $\phi > \psi$ is made false by $\$_i{}^1$, I could
construct $\$_i{}^2$ from $\$_i{}^1$ by omitting all the ϕ-worlds that are not ψ-worlds
in some suitable (small enough) sphere in $\$_i{}^1$.] Again, such a relativization
would seem very odd, and would reflect nothing. It seems fairly clear,
though, that this condition is presupposed by Lewis, though not explicitly
required in his formal definition.

3. For purposes of comparison with my proposed analysis, let us concentrate on the actual world W_0 as the world in which the truth values of counterfactuals are to be evaluated. Thus far we have dealt with counterfactuals of the n-d type, and I shall restrict myself to these here too. The antecedents of such counterfactuals are compatible with the prior history of the world, and thus we can reasonably assume that there will be worlds "close enough" to the actual world in which the antecedent is true. Now Lewis's analysis is relativized to a system of spheres $\$_i$, whereas my proposed analysis involves no such relativization.[5] For the sake of comparing our analysis with Lewis's, let us examine systems of spheres $\$_i$ sufficiently far from the actual world to allow the requisite variation from it for antecedents of n-d type counterfactuals not to fall under clause (1) of Lewis's condition. This allows us temporarily to ignore clause (1), which deals with cases where the antecedent is true only in worlds beyond the set of spheres $\$_i$. With this understood, a counterfactual $\phi > \psi$ is true according to Lewis iff there is in $\$_i$ a sphere of worlds around the actual world which contains some ϕ-worlds, in all the ϕ-worlds of which ψ is true. However, since spheres are determined by similarity of worlds, this amounts to allowing that a counterfactual $\phi > \psi$ is true iff there is some ϵ-vicinity of worlds around the actual world which includes a ϕ-world, in all of the ϕ-worlds of which ψ is true (where ϵ could represent a degree of similarity between worlds). This is the very modification of Stalnaker's position that we discussed above (3 III). Thus, insofar as the scope of our inquiry is concerned, Lewis's proposal coincides with the modification of Stalnaker's position considered above, and our arguments against that position can be equally well directed against Lewis's.

Notice that if Lewis had characterized sets T_i as sets of worlds such that p is possible in i (for any p) iff p is true in some world in T_i, he could have availed himself of references to such T_i's (for each world i) and thus could have avoided a separate *relativization* to $\cup \$_i$ (so long as the similarity relation has been fixed): disagreement as to which the T_i's are would not then be expressed via a relativization. We might therefore take Lewis's relativization as implying that in some sense he does not consider such a delineation "objective", and wishes to let it vary from speaker to speaker and from context to context (see V below). However, this is not explicitly reflected in his discussion of the modal operators. The way he puts things has the following unwelcome result: suppose you and I agree on our notion of similarity and agree that ϕ is possible, yet disagree on the limit of the possibility sphere: for you it is $\cup \$_i{}^1$, for me it is $\cup \$_i{}^2$. Now it seems to me that when we discuss the counterfactual $\phi > \psi$, we can nevertheless mean by it exactly the same thing. Yet, according to Lewis's analysis, I read it relative to $\cup \$_i{}^2$, you read it relative to $\cup \$_i{}^1$, and we do not discuss the same *statement* (even if our judgments as to its truth value have to agree).[5]

In his book Lewis has a relation of over-all similarity between worlds determine their ordering into spheres. The general thrust of his discussion is that it is the *intuitive* over-all similarity that he is interested in for the purpose of analyzing counterfactuals. He recognizes that the notion of over-all similarity involves respects and weights, but in his book this seems to be part and parcel of the intuitive notion of over-all similarity. In particular, the notion of over-all similarity is context-dependent, and thus the weights and respects might change from context to context. But this, again, is part of what is involved in our intuitive notion of over-all similarity.[6] Lewis thus says:

> Somehow we *do* have a familiar notion of comparative overall similarity, even of comparative similarity of big, complicated, variegated things like whole people, whole cities, or even — I think — whole possible worlds. However mysterious that notion may be, if we can analyze counterfactuals by means of it we will be left with one mystery in place of two (p. 92).

Thus the notion of over-all similarity to which Lewis seems committed here is presented as an intuitive notion of over-all similarity (though context-dependent, and though we are not in a position to provide a specific analysis of it). This is how Lewis has been generally understood.[7]

4. Lewis defines cotenability as follows:

Quote A

> Let us say that χ is *cotenable* with ϕ at a world i (according to a system of spheres \$) if and only if either (1) χ holds throughout $\cup\$_i$, or (2) χ holds throughout some ϕ-permitting sphere in $\$_i$ (p.57).

Together with this definition, he offers an account of counterfactuals along metalinguistic lines which is equivalent to his own, as follows:

Quote B

> A counterfactual $\phi\,\square\!\!\rightarrow\psi$ is true at i (according to my truth conditions) if and only if the premise ϕ and some auxiliary premise χ, cotenable with ϕ at i, logically imply ψ (p.57).

Apart from his main definition of cotenability given above, Lewis is willing to accept others. Thus:

Quote C

> Other definitions of cotenability also would yield metalinguistic theories equivalent to my theory. We might simply say that χ is cotenable with ϕ if and only if χ is true at i and $\phi\,\square\!\!\rightarrow\chi$ is true (according to my theory) at i (p.70).

I shall refer to this definition as **Lewis's alternative cotenability definition**.

The notion of cotenability was coined by Nelson Goodman, who defined it (see 1 II; 3 II) as follows (for a true χ):

χ is not cotenable with ϕ iff $\phi > \sim\chi$.

that is:

χ is cotenable with ϕ iff $\sim(\phi > \sim\chi)$.

Now $\phi > \chi \equiv \sim(\phi > \sim\chi)$ is invalid for Lewis[8] (and for me; see 3 III). Of course, $\phi > \chi \supset \sim(\phi > \sim\chi)$ is valid for both of us; but $\sim(\phi > \sim\chi) \supset \phi > \chi$ is not. But Lewis's main definition of cotenability (in quote A) — and obviously his second definition (in quote C) — yield that $\phi > \chi$ is true if χ is cotenable with ϕ. But Goodman's aforementioned notion of cotenability, to which I have adhered in this book, does not yield that result under my account or even under Lewis's, as we have just noted. Hence, as Jonathan Bennett has pointed out,[9] Lewis's notion of cotenability is not Goodman's notion, which has been the standard notion in the literature (at least until Lewis's book), and Lewis therefore does not seem to be right in believing that his "definition of cotenability . . . captures the intentions of metalinguistic theorists."

Of course, Goodman's notion of cotenability can be defined in terms of Lewis's second notion. For Goodman, χ is cotenable with ϕ in case $\sim(\phi > \sim\chi)$, and on Lewis's second definition of this notion (quote C), χ is cotenable with ϕ in case $\phi > \chi$. χ is cotenable with ϕ in Goodman's sense, then, just in case $\sim\chi$ is not cotenable with ϕ in Lewis's second sense. This is not surprising, since both notions of cotenability are defined in terms of counterfactuals.

The way Lewis's own notion of χ being cotenable with ϕ functions in the above (quote B) account of counterfactuals in terms of cotenability, is indeed akin to our notion of χ qualifying as a conjunction of implicit premises for the antecedent ϕ. In that respect (disregarding, again, what I take to be an unfortunate choice of the notion of cotenability), this account is similar to our preliminary unpacked inferential analysis (using an unpacked notion of implicit premises).[10]

5. Consider now the following inference, call it **inference I**:

$$\phi > \chi$$
$$\underline{\phi\&\chi \to \psi}$$
$$\phi > \psi$$

Inference I is valid for Lewis and (with a certain restriction) is valid on my account as well.[11] Also, both for Lewis and (with a certain restriction) for me:

(1) $[\phi > (\phi \supset \psi)] \equiv (\phi > \psi)$

is logically true.[12] It is easy to see that Lewis's metalinguistic account
(quote B) of counterfactuals (for counterfactuals with false antecedents,
considered in the actual world), interpreted under his second cotenability
definition (of quote C), is provable, given the validity of inference I and
the logical truth of formula (1) (when, of course, both the account of
counterfactuals and the definition of cotenability are stripped of the
clauses that relativize them to Lewis's truth conditions). This metalinguistic account, with Lewis's second definition of cotenability plugged
in, would read as follows (for a false ϕ, at the actual world):

(2)   A counterfactual $\phi > \psi$ is true iff ϕ and some true χ such that
       $\phi > \chi$, logically imply ψ.

[The proof, given inference I and formula (1), is immediate: in one direction, via inference I; in the other, via formula (1), taking $\phi \supset \psi$ as χ.]
    Thus, the truth of this combined account (2), i.e., the above meta-
linguistic account of counterfactuals (quote B) combined with Lewis's second definition of cotenability (quote C), is acceptable to *every* analysis
that recognizes the validity of the above inference and the logical truth of
the above formula. (For me, this account would hold under certain restrictions.)[13] But the degree of agreement between Lewis's analysis and mine
on the truth of the above account of counterfactuals (quote B) with his second notion of cotenability plugged in, should *not* be interpreted as implying that our respective analyses are extensionally equivalent. Since this
combined account (2) relies on the notion of counterfactuals (via Lewis's
second definition of cotenability), it is circular (as an account of counterfactuals) and, thus, need ·not distinguish between *extensionally different*
analyses of counterfactuals, which nevertheless make this account true.
The circularity of this account renders it useless as an analyses of counterfactuals; yet *different* analyses of counterfactuals which agree on the validity of inference I and the logical truth of formula (1) would still make
this account (2) true, however extensionally different they might be.
Recall that my notion of cotenability is Goodman's notion, which, we
have noted above, is extensionally different from Lewis's. It is therefore
important to guard against mistakenly concluding (via quote B) any extensional equivalence between Lewis's analysis and my own, by keeping it in
mind that the notion of cotenability Lewis uses is his own and different
from that used by Goodman and by me, and, moreover, is in turn defined
in terms of counterfactuals, which constitutes a crucial point.[14]

II $\in$-A-*Vicinities*

1. Let us now elaborate on the contrast between the $\in$-vicinity-of-possible-
worlds approach to counterfactuals (cf. I 3 above) and my approach.
Much of our discussion of Stalnaker's position (in 3 III) applies equally to
Lewis, and need not be repeated. Consider again, for a counterfactual

$A > B$ of the n-d type, the set $g(A, W_{\bar{t}B})$ of the legitimate premises in (t_A, t_B), which is, as I proposed and argued for at length, the set of all true statements in (t_A, t_B) describing events to which the A-event is causally irrelevant or purely positively causally relevant.[15] Define the set of true statements in that interval which are not cotenable with A as $NC(A, W_{\bar{t}B})$ ('NC' for Not Cotenable). Cotenability is understood here in the sense used throughout this book, i.e, Goodman's sense.[16] The rest of the true statements pertaining to (t_A, t_B) form a third group:[17] the true statements which, though cotenable with A, are such that A bears some negative causal relevance to them (either mixed with some positive causal relevance or else purely negative causal relevance). We shall call this group $CNR(A, W_{\bar{t}B})$ ('CNR' for Cotenable with some Negative causal Relevance; see 2 XII 4). For a member C of $CNR(A, W_{\bar{t}B})$, the counterfactual $A > \sim C$ is not true (since otherwise C would not be cotenable with A). Now the set $CNR (A, W_{\bar{t}B})$ consists of two disjoint sets: One is the set $CCS(A, W_{\bar{t}B})$, the set of consequents in (t_A, t_B) of true con-type semifactuals with antecedent A (cf. 2 XII 1).[18] The other, $CNR(A, W_{\bar{t}B}) - CCS(A, W_{\bar{t}B})$, consists of true statements C such that neither $A > C$ nor $A > \sim C$ is true.

Now, on our approach, $g(A, W_{\bar{t}B})$, that is, $CIP(A, W_{\bar{t}B})$, counts as a part of the implicit premises, but $CNR(A, W_{\bar{t}B})$ does not, even though each of its members is consistent with the set of the implicit premises plus A (otherwise it would not be cotenable with A). However, an approach that aims at maximum similarity to the actual world should aim at including members of $CNR(A, W_{\bar{t}B})$ among the implicit premises. Now insofar as the inclusion of $CCS(A, W_{\bar{t}B})$ among the implicit premises is contemplated, no harm would be done thereby to the extensional adequacy of our analysis; yet the result would be an infinite regress (cf. 2 XII). But things are different when it comes to the question of including members of $CNR(A, W_{\bar{t}B}) - CCS(A, W_{\bar{t}B})$ among the implicit premises. We have argued that if the analysis of counterfactuals is to be adequate this cannot be done — statements to which the antecedent bears some negative causal relevance can spoil the adequacy of our analysis of counterfactuals if taken among the implicit premises (unless they are in their logical closure with A). This was shown by examples 10 and 11 (of 2 VI, VIII), where the antecedent-event bore a mixed causal relevance to the event described by the statement under consideration. This was further supported by the semifactual analysis and the role analysis.

2. As we saw above, with certain qualifications, Lewis's approach amounted to having $A > B$ come out true iff B is true in all the worlds in some A-vicinity of the actual world, i.e., in all the A-worlds in some vicinity of the actual world.[19] I would now like to show that the set of possible-world descriptions associated with a counterfactual $A > B$ in such a way that B must be true in all of its members for $A > B$ to be true, is not, on our analysis, a set of closest A-worlds; i.e., it is not an A-vicinity of the actual-world description. Let me first explain the argument intuitively.

The set $V(A, W_{\bar{t}B})$ is, on my analysis, the set of possible-world descriptions associated with $A > B$ in the above way. This set is the counter-factual span for A and t_B (cf. 2 X). That is, in all its members, A, W_{t_A} and the legitimate premises in (t_A, t_B) are true (and each member is compatible with L). Now when we specified the members of $V(A, W_{\bar{t}B})$, the only constraint that we put on $W'_{\bar{t}B, \infty}$, for any given candidate, was the requirement that $W'_{\bar{t}B, \infty}$ be compatible with A, L, and the legitimate premises that pertain to times prior to $\bar{t}_B$. Obviously, this allows much freedom in the degree to which members of this set resemble the actual-world description, since a large variety of statements pertaining to the interval $(\bar{t}_B, \infty)$ may be included in them. Similarly, since members of the set $\text{CNR}(A, W_{\bar{t}B}) - \text{CCS}(A, W_{\bar{t}B})$ are undetermined by the implicit premises plus A (and L), the option of their being included in members of $V(A, W_{\bar{t}B})$ allowed for a parallel degree of freedom concerning the latter members being closer or farther from the actual-world description.[20] So, take a possible-world description w_1 that belongs to $V(A, W_{\bar{t}B})$, but such that its overlap with members of the set $\text{CNR}(A, W_{\bar{t}B}) - \text{CCS}(A, W_{\bar{t}B})$, as well as with the set of true statements pertaining to (t_B, ∞) (i.e., to times after $\bar{t}_B$), is designed to make it as *dissimilar* as possible to the actual-world description.[21]

Now take some false statement C, such that $\bar{t}_C = \bar{t}_B$ and $A > C$ is true, but the inferability of C from the implicit premises and A can be subverted by eliminating a "minor" set of statements from the legitimate premises pertaining to (t_A, t_C). Take a possible-world description w_2 which includes A as well as all the legitimate premises for $A > C$ *except* such a minor set, which is compatible with L, which includes the true $\sim C$, and which is such that the selection of its other members in (t_A, t_B) and in (t_B, ∞) is designed to make it as *similar* as possible to the actual world. Now a calculated selection of the members of $\text{CNR}(A, W_{\bar{t}B}) - \text{CCS}(A, W_{\bar{t}B})$ in terms of achieving maximal similarity to the actual world in the (t_A, t_B) interval, plus the fact that the true $\sim C$ is in w_2, should be enough to make w_2 more similar to the actual-world description than w_1, for times up to $t_{\bar{B}}$. But be this as it may, since w_2 is constructed so as also to yield maximal similarity to the actual world in the (t_B, ∞) interval, whereas w_1 is designed to yield minimal similarity in that interval, surely the degree of freedom to move further from or closer to the actual world available in the (t_B, ∞) interval is such that a calculated selection of w_2 would make it far more similar to the actual world than w_1.

But although w_1 belongs to $V(A, W_{\bar{t}B})$, since it is compatible with L and includes A and all the legitimate premises , w_2 clearly does not belong to $V(A, W_{\bar{t}B})$, since some members of the legitimate premises pertaining to (t_A, t_B) are not true in it, whereas $\sim C$ is, even though $A > C$ is a true counterfactual. Yet, we saw, w_2 is more similar (presumably much more similar) to the actual-world description than w_1. But for $V(A, W_{\bar{t}B})$ to be a vicinity, or a closest set, of A-possible-world descriptions around the actual-world description, it must be the case that if any A-possible-world description is closer to the actual-world description than some possible-world description in this group, it must also belong to this group. But w_1

and w_2 violate that. Hence $V(A, W_{\bar{t}_B})$ is no vicinity of A-possible-world descriptions around the actual-world description.

3. Let us expand this point a bit further. Choose statements in (t_A, t_B) and in $(\bar{t}_B, \infty)$ that yield, together with the legitimate premises plus A, a possible-world description in $V(A, W_{\bar{t}_B})$ that will be very far from the actual world (relative to the other members of $V(A, W_{\bar{t}_B})$), i.e., pick one of the furthest members of $V(A, W_{\bar{t}_B})$. Call this possible world V_1. Analogously, by an appropriate choice of statements in (t_A, t_B) and $(\bar{t}_B, \infty)$, choose a possible-world description in $V(A, W_{\bar{t}_B})$ that will be one of the closest to the actual world in $V(A, W_{\bar{t}_B})$. Call it V_2. Since V_2 is in $V(A, W_{\bar{t}_B})$, $W_{\bar{t}_A}$ and $g(A, W_{\bar{t}_B})$ are in V_2. Now make very minor changes in $\{W_{t_A} \cup g(A, W_{\bar{t}_B})\}$ — replace some statements in them by their negations, and incorporate whatever minimal repercussions[22] this change has on the rest of V_2 so as to yield a possible-world description differing minimally from V_2. Call this possible-world description U_1. Since these changes decreased similarity to the actual world, U_1 will be less similar to the actual world than V_2.[23] However, these changes are small enough and the distance between V_1 and V_2 wide enough so that U_1 will be more similar to the actual world than V_1. Yet, since some of the legitimate premises for $A > B$ are not true in U_1, U_1 does *not* belong to $V(A, W_{\bar{t}_B})$. It is clear that such a choice of U_1 can be made.

Thus we see that we can have a possible-world description U_1 which does not belong to $V(A, W_{\bar{t}_B})$ but which is more similar to the actual world than some V_1 that belongs to $V(A, W_{\bar{t}_B})$ and yet less similar to the actual world than some V_2 also in $V(A, W_{\bar{t}_B})$. This shows that $V(A, W_{\bar{t}_B})$ is not a compact neighborhood of A-worlds, i.e., a set of A-worlds between two "distances" from the actual world; i.e., not a set of A-worlds more similar to the actual world than a certain degree and less similar than another degree.

Let us continue: V_2 was one of the possible-world descriptions in $V(A, W_{\bar{t}_B})$ closest to the actual world. The changes in V_2 that yielded U_1 were relatively small compared to the "distance" between V_1 and V_2. The members of $V(A, W_{\bar{t}_B})$ varied widely regarding which members of $CNR(A, W_{\bar{t}_B}) - CCS(A, W_{\bar{t}_B})$ and which statements in $(\bar{t}_B, \infty)$, undetermined by the implicit premises and A, belonged to them: fixing the implicit premises (plus A) still left a large degree of freedom as to how to extend them into a possible-world description in $V(A, W_{\bar{t}_B})$. Thus, we can also make some minor changes in V_2 by changing members of $CNR(A, W_{\bar{t}_B}) - CCS(A, W_{\bar{t}_B})$ and of the set of true statements in $(\bar{t}_B, \infty)$ undetermined by the implicit premises plus A, *without* changing the implicit premises plus A, so as to *match* U_1 in its degree of similarity to the actual world. That is, by a careful selection of changes of members of V_2 that are *not* among the implicit premises (plus A) or their consequences, we can obtain a possible-world description U_2 that will be as similar to the actual world as U_1 is.[24] However, because of the way U_2 was formed out of V_2, U_2 belongs to $V(A, W_{\bar{t}_B})$. Thus, U_1 and U_2 are equally similar to the actual world, and both are more similar to it than V_1 but less than V_2; yet, although V_1, V_2, and U_2 are in $V(A, W_{\bar{t}B})$, U_1 is not. This shows that $V(A, W_{\bar{t}B})$ does not include all the A-possible-world descriptions as similar to the actual world as *some* member in $V(A, W_{\bar{t}B})$; that is, being an A-possible-world description and similar to the actual world to a *certain* degree, a degree to which some member in $V(A, W_{\bar{t}B})$ does resemble the actual world, is *not* a sufficient condition for being in $V(A, W_{\bar{t}B})$.

Together, all these conclusions suggest that there is little affinity between our analysis of counterfactuals and their analysis along the lines of closest possible worlds (in the sense of most similar) or minimal changes. Our proposal, resulting in the choice of $V(A, W_{\bar{t}B})$ in the possible-world-descriptions model, is therefore at variance both with the above modification of Stalnaker's position and with Lewis's approach (in *Counterfactuals*; cf. I 3 of this chapter). Thus, apart from methodological differences, their proposals, when compared to my own on the neutral ground of possible-world descriptions, are seen to be considerably different.

III Minimal Changes Again

1. The urge to stay as close as possible to the actual world is but the mirror image, in the possible-world perspective, of the approach favoring minimal changes in the description of the actual world in order to accommodate the antecedent. Both reflect the view that the incompatibility problem is *the* problem confronting the analysis of counterfactuals; i.e., that the crucial problem is how to resolve, in the context of evaluating counterfactuals, the incompatibility of the antecedent and the set of all true statements. This orientation was shared by Goodman and Stalnaker (and by Lewis in *Counterfactuals*). Goodman's starting point was to take the set of all true statements together with the antecedent in evaluating a counterfactual. Stalnaker's starting point was Ramsey's approach to conditionals, that of incorporating the antecedents into the set of one's beliefs. Both faced the immediate difficulty of inconsistency due to the falsehood of the counterfactual antecedent. However, this conception of the centrality of the incompatibility problem is mistaken. The danger of such inconsistency is but one of the difficulties on the way to accommodating the contrary-to-fact antecedent in suitable surroundings of implicit premises. Handling this problem either by making only minimal changes in the actual-world description in order to accommodate the antecedent or by keeping to the worlds most similar to the actual one, leads to severe difficulties. Though it is important not to implant the antecedent in incompatible surroundings, one must also pay close attention to the delicacies concerning the kind of reorientation of the actual-world description that countenancing a contrary-to-fact thesis calls for, in view of the role of counterfactuals as hypothetical predictions, which makes them particularly sensitive to the causal order and to temporal constraints. Overemphasis on, or preoccupation with, the inconsistency problem, may divert one's attention from such matters.

As we have seen (2 X), the set of statements shared by all members of $V(A, W_{\bar{t}B})$, i.e., $Q'(A, W_{\bar{t}B})$, is identical with $\overline{Q(A, W_{\bar{t}B})}^{-L}$, which is generated by $Q(A, W_{\bar{t}B})$, the set of implicit premises plus A.[25] As we observed above (in sec. II 1; cf. also the chart in 2 XII), either a true statement in (t_A, t_B) belongs among the legitimate premises $g(A, W_{\bar{t}B})$, or else the antecedent A bears some negative causal relevance to it. Statements such as the latter are divided into three exclusive sets: $\mathrm{CCS}(A, W_{\bar{t}B})$, the consequents of true con-type semifactuals [with antecedent A and consequent time in (t_A, t_B)]; the set of true statements in (t_A, t_B) not cotenable with A, which we called $\mathrm{NC}(A, W_{\bar{t}B})$; and the remaining set, consisting of true statements C in (t_A, t_B) such that $A > C$ is a false semifactual and $A > \sim C$ is also a false counterfactual, i.e., statements that are cotenable with A and yet are not consequents of true semifactuals with antecedent A: this was the set $\mathrm{CNR}(A, W_{\bar{t}B}) - \mathrm{CCS}(A, W_{\bar{t}B})$. [$\mathrm{CNR}(A, W_{\bar{t}B})$ was the set of true statements in (t_A, t_B), cotenable with A, describing events to which the A-event bore some negative causal relevance; see also the beginning of sec. II above.]

We also saw that the inclusion of $\mathrm{CCS}(A, W_{\bar{t}B})$, or any subset of it, among the implict premises, will make no difference to the constitution of $V(A, W_{\bar{t}B})$, since $\mathrm{CCS}(A, W_{\bar{t}B}) \subset \overline{Q(A, W_{\bar{t}B})}^{-L}$ (see 2 XII 3), although it will make a good deal of difference to the viability of characterizing the implicit premises in the inferential model in a way which does not involve recourse to counterfactuals and which therefore avoids infinite regress. Members of $\mathrm{NC}(A, W_{\bar{t}B})$ cannot be admitted into $Q(A, W_{\bar{t}B})$: they are not cotenable with A, and thus are inconsistent with $Q(A, W_{\bar{t}B})$. They therefore cannot belong to a possible-world description that is compatible with the laws and includes $Q'(A, W_{\bar{t}B})$, a set that belongs to all the members of $V(A, W_{\bar{t}B})$.

2. We are thus left with the set $\mathrm{CNR}(A, W_{\bar{t}B}) - \mathrm{CCS}(A, W_{\bar{t}B})$ when we consider the degree to which we are free to allow further statements from $W_{\bar{t}B}$ into our implicit premises. Members of this set are compatible with $Q(A, W_{\bar{t}B})$ and may be added to the implicit premises without inconsistency, since otherwise $A > \sim C$ would be a true counterfactual. So one can require that members of this set belong to $Q'(A, W_{\bar{t}B})$ and, thus, to all members of $V(A, W_{\bar{t}B})$, without any *logical* difficulty. It is also not redundant to add such statements to the legitimate premises, since they do *not* belong to $\overline{Q(A, W_{\bar{t}B})}^{-L}$: a true statement C [in (t_A, t_B)] which does belong to $\overline{Q(A, W_{\bar{t}B})}^{-L}$ yields $A > C$ as a true semifactual. This set therefore consists of statements C in (t_A, t_B) such that both $A > C$ and $A > \sim C$ are false. The tendency to make minimal changes in the description of the actual world, or to focus on possible worlds closest to the actual world, would tend to preserve members of this set in $Q'(A, W_{\bar{t}B})$ so as to maximize similarity to the actual world. Having extensional adequacy in mind, we argued (e.g., in 2 VI 3 and 2 VII 3) that these statements must *not* be included among our implicit premises and so we have not required that any of them be included in all the members of $V(A, W_{\bar{t}B})$. This

crucial set of true statements pertaining to (t_A, t_B), then, is a manifestation of the nonviability of the minimal-change or closest-possible-worlds approach: members of this set *can* be retained without incompatibility with the rest of the implicit premises, but, if extensional adequacy is to be sustained, they should not be.

The writers discussed in chapters 1 and 3 failed to notice this set. They all held (at least in some form) that $\sim(A > C) \equiv A > \sim C$, a claim against which we have argued repeatedly (especially in 3 I). Failure to realize that this claim is false is possible only if the set $CNR(A, W_{\bar{t}B}) - CCS(A, W_{\bar{t}B})$, the set of all statements that violate this claim in (t_A, t_B), is overlooked. Overlooking it made it easier to adhere to the misguided conception that inconsistency is *the* problem confronting an analysis of counterfactuals. Lewis's analysis is a definite improvement over its predecessors in that it denies that $\sim(A > C) \equiv A > \sim C$ is valid. But, because of the conceptual setup of possible worlds and similarity in which Lewis's analysis has been couched, he too has failed to take notice of this set. In formulating his analysis in terms of the parameter of similarity between possible worlds (whether construed as intuitive over-all similarity or as similarity under respects to be specified), Lewis's approach was at variance with two main features of the approach I have presented in this book: the orientation of retaining particular sets of statements from the actual-world description, and the emphasis on the relations of causal irrelevance and purely positive causal relevance, probabilistically construed.[26]

As is clear from our previous discussion of the semifactual analysis (2 XI), an analysis extensionally equivalent to our own could have been produced by adding the set $CCS(A, W_{\bar{t}B})$ to our legitimate premises for a counterfactual $A > B$. Such a move would yield as legitimate premises the set of all true statements pertaining to (t_A, t_B) less the two sets $NC(A, W_{\bar{t}B})$ and $CNR(A, W_{\bar{t}B}) - CCS(A, W_{\bar{t}B})$. Thus, the legitimate premises in (t_A, t_B) would consist of all true statements C pertaining to times earlier than $\bar{t}_B$, except those which fulfill $A > \sim C$ or those which fulfill neither $A > \sim C$ nor $A > C$. This, with the addition of W_{t_A} and L, is a concise way of specifying an extensionally adequate set of implicit premises for $A > B$ (though it will not do, of course, as an analysis of counterfactuals of the n-d type, since it would plunge us head on into an infinite regress). Recall that Goodman's concern with infinite regress focused on the first of these two excluded groups—the one consisting of statements not cotenable with the antecedent. As our analysis revealed (for counterfactuals of the n-d type), excluding *this* source of infinite regress [i.e, the set $NC(A, W_{\bar{t}B})$] would *still* not suffice for the analysis of counterfactuals: the set $CNR(A, W_{\bar{t}B}) - CCS(A, W_{\bar{t}B})$ has to be excluded too, a point which escaped Goodman's attention, since he was preoccupied with the problem of infinite regress. Yet even the exclusion of the set $NC(A, W_{\bar{t}B})$ obviously cannot be accomplished *directly* without falling into infinite regress. A *positive* characterization of the right implicit premises was required, and not just a method of exclusion such as Goodman's or the one mentioned a few sentences back. This is the strategy I have followed in this book.

3. Notice, too, that a minimal-change theorist does not really have the option of including *all* the members of $CNR(A, W_{\bar{t}B}) - CCS(A, W_{\bar{t}B})$ among his implicit premises in addition to those we have sanctioned. This is because even though each member of this set is compatible *individually* with our implicit premises plus A, the set as a whole need not be. To see this, consider the following example.

Example 1

A well-to-do individual owned three cars, but found himself in a state of economic adversity, necessitating changes in his lifestyle.

Consider antecedent A:

Had he decided to sell one of his cars, . . .

Now consider the three statements B_i:

He still owns car i ($i = 1,2,3$).

Assume that his characteristic determination in carrying out his decisions, coupled with his situation, would make:

(3)   Had he decided to sell one of his cars, he would have done so.

true. Let us also assume that there is nothing in the implicit premises that would entail or rule out the sale of any particular car out of the three. Thus $A > B_i$ are false for each i, but so are $A > \sim B_i$. Now, in fact, he sold none of his cars (he sold his country home instead), which makes each of the B_i true. Thus, the statements B_i belong to $CNR(A, W_{\bar{t}B}) - CCS(A, W_{\bar{t}B})$ (recall that this is the set of true statements C such that $A > C$ and $A > \sim C$ are both false, for an antecedent of the n-d type).[27] Yet, given the above counterfactual (3), the counterfactual:

(4)   Had he decided to sell one of his cars, he would not possess his three cars.

is surely true. Thus, though the statements B_i (for each i) are individually cotenable with A, the conjunction B_1 & B_2 & B_3 is not. This illustrates how $CNR(A, W_{\bar{t}B}) - CCS(A, W_{\bar{t}B})$ need not be compatible with $Q(A, W_{\bar{t}B})$, even though each member of it is. [Which also shows, of course, that $CNR(A, W_{\bar{t}B}) - CCS(A, W_{\bar{t}B})$ is not closed under conjunction.]

4. That our analysis is not a minimal-change analysis can also be seen as follows. So far we have concentrated on the statements in the interval (t_A, t_B), but this is generally a relatively small interval in comparison with $(\bar{t}_B, \infty)$. However, the only constraint we put on a possible-world description's being in $V(A, W_{\bar{t}B})$ concerning the interval $(\bar{t}_B, \infty)$ was that

the consequences of the implicit premises plus A in that interval be true in it (thus preserving the compatibility with L required of all possible-world descriptions). But this is a relatively minor restriction:[28] the set of statements in (t_B, ∞) can vary relatively greatly, thereby yielding more similarity or less similarity to the actual-world description. But we required no further constraints: in particular, we did *not require* that we restrict ourselves to those possible-world descriptions in which this segment is closest to the actual-world description.

In addition, we had a certain degree of freedom within the (t_A, t_B) interval, with respect to the set $\mathrm{CNR}(A, W_{\bar{t}B}) - \mathrm{CCS}(A, W_{\bar{t}B})$. We could have restricted membership in $V(A, W_{\bar{t}B})$ to those possible-world descriptions which satisfy the constraint of compatibility with the implicit premises and A and in which the segment pertaining to (t_A, t_B) is as close to the actual-world description as possible, given this constraint. We have not done that either. (For arguments against doing so, see, again, 2 VI 3 and 2 VIII 3.)

Thus, one who is a minimal-change theorist at heart and who nevertheless has some sympathy for our arguments, might reason as follows: you argued that certain implicit premises are essential on your inferential model. Let us assume that your arguments are valid. This yields as the set $V(A, W_{\bar{t}B})$ of possible-world descriptions to be associated with $A > B$ the set of exactly those possible-world descriptions in which these implicit premises and A are true. What you should do now is take the *subset* of this set consisting of those possible-world descriptions which are closest to the actual-world description, and test the counterfactual in *it*. You will thereby preserve the viability of the implicit premises you have argued for, while also adhering to the directive of keeping as close as possible to the actual-world description.[29]

Would such a proposal correctly reflect the truth conditions we have offered for counterfactuals? Would such a move be extensionally equivalent to our proposal? If so, the extensional force of our theory is invariant under a certain "minimal change" requirement, and the theory can thus accommodate a certain "minimal change" aspect. If not, the proposal will not be extensionally adequate, assuming that our proposal is. We will now turn to this question.

What we can show is that such a move would result in an analysis for counterfactuals which is extensionally *different* from the one we have proposed, and is thus inadequate, if ours is adequate.

The problem is to determine whether the subset of possible-world descriptions in $V(A, W_{\bar{t}B})$ closest to the actual-world description "represents" the set $V(A, W_{\bar{t}B})$ vis-à-vis the role of that set in our analysis of counterfactuals (where 'closest' means most similar in the sense of intuitive over-all similarity). This subset would **represent** $V(A, W_{\bar{t}B})$ in the sense indicated just in case B would be true in all the members of the subset iff it is true in all the members of $V(A, W_{\bar{t}B})$. In this case the above subset of $V(A, W_{\bar{t}B})$ could serve the same role that the set $V(A, W_{\bar{t}B})$ serves — the role of being the set of possible-world descriptions to be associated with $A > B$ for the purpose of testing its truth value.

5. Let us call the set of true statements C in (t_A, ∞) such that neither C nor $\sim C$ is inferable from the implicit premises plus A $\text{UD}(A\bar{t}_B, W_\infty)$ ('UD' for *undetermined*). Surely $\text{CNR}(A, W_{\bar{t}B}) - \text{CCS}(A, W_{\bar{t}B}) \subset \text{UD}(A, \bar{t}_B, W_\infty)$; the latter, of course, also includes statements in $(\bar{t}_B, \infty)$, though in (t_A, t_B) it consists of $\text{CNR}(A, W_{\bar{t}B}) - \text{CCS}(A, W_{\bar{t}B})$.

Suppose for a moment that $\text{UD}(A, W_{\bar{t}B}, W_\infty)$ as a whole (not just each individual member of it) is compatible with the implicit premises plus A.[30] Consider the possible-world description w^* in which the implicit premises, A, and the members of $\text{UD}(A, \bar{t}_B, W_\infty)$ are all true. Then, having fixed the implicit premises that we did, the desire to test the counterfactual in the most similar possible-world description(s) to the actual world should force us to choose from $V(A, W_{\bar{t}B})$ this possible-world description w^* for the purpose of testing the truth value of a counterfactual $A > C$ (with $\bar{t}_C = \bar{t}_B$),[31] since w^* is *the* closest member in $V(A, W_{\bar{t}B})$ to the actual-world description. w^*, however, would *not* represent $V(A, W_{\bar{t}B})$, since its choice would make any such counterfactual $A > C$ in which C belongs to $\text{CNR}(A, W_{\bar{t}B}) - \text{CCS}(A, W_{\bar{t}B})$ come out true; but making such counterfactuals come out true is at variance with our analysis and, we have argued, is mistaken.

Thus, if $\text{UD}(A, \bar{t}_B, W_\infty)$ is consistent with the implicit premises plus A, the resulting possible-world description w^* does not represent $V(A, W_{\bar{t}B})$. In general, of course, we cannot make the above assumption; so we are back to the question of whether the subset of closest possible-world descriptions to the actual-world description in $V(A, W_{\bar{t}B})$ does represent $V(A, W_{\bar{t}B})$, thereby making our approach reconcilable with the desideratum of testing counterfactuals in possible-world descriptions as close to the actual-world description as possible (while preserving the implicit premises that were found to be necessary). The closest possible-world descriptions to the actual-world description in which the implicit premises and A are true will presumably result from making minimal changes in $\text{UD}(A, \bar{t}_B, W_\infty)$. We shall proceed now on the assumption that *some* such minimal changes can be generated by changing a *finite* number of statements in $\text{UD}(A, \bar{t}_B, W_\infty)$, i.e., by replacing them with their negations.

By this I mean the following: a change from the actual-world description of the sort we are dealing with consists in replacing a set of statements in $\text{UD}(A, \bar{t}_B, W_\infty)$ with the set of their negations so that the result of making such a replacement in $\text{UD}(A, \bar{t}_B, W_\infty)$ will yield, together with the implicit premises plus A, a possible-world description. More precisely: If R is a set of statements, define $\tilde{R}$ as the set of the negations of the members of R. A "change" can be conceived as follows: A set of statements S is a **change** iff, for some R, R is a set of true statements in $\text{UD}(A, \bar{t}_B, W_\infty)$ such that $Q'(A, W_{\bar{t}B}) \cup \tilde{R} \cup (\text{UD}(A, \bar{t}_B, W_\infty) - R)$ is compatible with L (and therefore yields, via logical closure, a possible-world description), $S = \tilde{R}$, and such that R is not a proper subset of any other set R' in $\underline{\text{UD}(A, \bar{t}_B, W_\infty)}$ such that $\underline{Q(A, W_{\bar{t}B}) \cup \tilde{R} \cup (\text{UD}(A, \bar{t}_B, W_\infty) - R)} = \underline{Q(A, W_{\bar{t}B}) \cup \tilde{R}' \cup (\text{UD}(A, \bar{t}_B, W_\infty) - R)}$.[32]

What we now assume is that, for *some* such minimal change S', the implicit premises plus A plus S' can be *axiomatized* by the implicit premises plus A plus a *finite* set S in S'; that is, that S' can be generated by a finite subset of it, S, relative to the implicit premises plus A. We shall say in such a case that S' (the "minimal change" in question) can be **finitely axiomatized relative to the implicit premises and A**.[33]

It is quite plausible to assume further that, for an antecedent A of *some* n-d type counterfactual, there will be such a change with a finite axiomatization relative to the implicit premises and A which is itself limited to some interval (t_A, t), for some instantaneous t.[34] Such an assumption will materialize if, for instance, for some antecedent A of a counterfactual of the n-d type, $Q(A, W_t) \cup W_{t, \infty}$ is consistent for some t, $t > \bar{t}_A$. If it is, then $Q'(A, W_t) \cup W_{t, \infty}$ can be extended into a possible-world description that will involve a change finitely axiomatizable in (t_A, t).[35] To see that this particular sort of case is not entirely implausible, notice that A's compatibility with W_{t_A} is assured, since A is an antecedent of an n-d type, and that it is also plausible to assume that *some* such A is compatible with $W_{t, \infty}$, for *some* t, $t > \bar{t}_A$. For the latter, it is required of course that the future actual history from a certain point on does not determine some such past event as $\sim A$. Notice that it is *not* required here that there be some event that does not leave traces; what we do assume is that the traces of some such A-event will be of such a probabilistic character that they do not suffice to logically exclude the occurrence of the $\sim A$-event retrospectively.[36] Given that, the viability of the consistency of $Q(A, W_t) \cup W_{t, \infty}$ for *some* such A and t seems quite plausible.

Now what we need for this assumption is something *weaker*: we do *not* need to assume that, for some such antecedent A, $Q(A, W_t) \cup W_{t, \infty}$ be consistent. Since all we need is that there be such a change and a finite axiomatization of that change which pertains to (t_A, t), the change itself may pertain to times beyond t, since the finite axiomatization is relative to $Q(A, W_t)$. Hence, changes that are finitely axiomatized in (t_A, t) may include logical consequences of this axiomatization [relative to $Q(A, W_t)$] which are false and pertain to (t, ∞). This leads us to assume the following:

Assumption 1

> For some counterfactual antecedent A of the n-d type and for some instantaneous t, $t > t_A$, there is a member of $V(A, W_t)$ which is generated by the actual-world description via a change that is finitely axiomatizable [relative to $Q(A, W_t)$] in (t_A, t).

6. We shall now show that the subset of closest possible-world descriptions in $V(A, W_{\bar{t}_B})$ involving minimal changes in $\mathrm{UD}(A, \bar{t}_B, W_\infty)$ does not represent $V(A, W_{\bar{t}_B})$. This will show that our analysis is *not* in line with the desideratum of testing the counterfactual in the closest possible-world descriptions to the actual-world description.

Now one aspect of a reasonable construal of an assumption to the effect that L is not "too deterministic" would be (given our legitimate premises which pertain only up to $\bar{t}_B$) that the legitimate premises, A, and any *finite* set of statements are not a "complete theory" (relative to L); that is, that they do not determine a unique possible-world description. For our particular purposes we assume that *a certain* finite set of statements of a certain sort pertaining to (t_A,t), for some (instantaneous) $t > t_A$, together with the legitimate premises plus A, does not determine a complete theory up to t; that is, it does not decide (relative to L) the truth value of every statement in the (t_A,t) interval. More specifically, we shall assume that, for *some q* pertaining to (t_A,t) which is the conjunction of axioms for some finitely axiomatizable change [relative to $Q(A,W_t)$] for *some A* and t as assured in assumption 1, $Q(A,W_t)$ and q do not decide the truth value of *every r* in $W_{t_A,t}$. Again, this seems quite plausible as a construal of an assumption to the effect that L is not too deterministic, and it can be formulated as follows:[37]

Assumption 2

For some $r \in W_{t_A,t}$ and for some q such that q is an axiomatization [relative to $Q(A,t)$] pertaining to (t_A,t) of some change (of the sort assured in assumption 1): $\sim r, r \notin Q(A,W_t) \cup \{q\}$.

Finally, given the notion of "change" as defined above, an obvious constraint on the notion of "minimal change" is that a minimal change be a change that does not contain a strictly "smaller" change.[38] Thus:

Assumption 3

If S is a change, then S is a minimal change only if S contains no proper subchange.[39]

Theorem 1

It is not the case that the set of closest[40] possible-world descriptions in $V(A,W_{t_B})$ represents $V(A,W_{t_B})$.

Proof

If for some A, t (A being an n-d type antecedent, $t > t_A$), $UD(A,t,W_\infty)$ is consistent with the implicit premises plus A, then $Q(A,W_t) \cup UD(A,t,W_\infty)^{-L}$ is *the* closest possible-world description to the actual-world description in $V(A,W_t)$. But it does not represent $V(A,W_t)$; since, for any C in $CNR(A,W_t) - CCS(A,W_t)$, $A > C$ would come out true on it, since $CNR(A,W_t) - CCS(A,W_t) \subseteq UD(A,t,W_\infty)$, but would not come out true on $V(A,W_t)$. So let us suppose there is a proper subset $V'(A,W_t)$ of $V(A,W_t)$ whose members are closest to the actual-world description in the sense of resulting via minimal changes from the actual-world description.[41]

Take now some A,t, a possible world description w in $V(A,W_t)$, and a change S as provided for by assumption 1, for which there is an r in $W_{t_A,t}$ as provided by assumption 2. Thus, $Q(A, W_t) \cup S \cup (UD(A, t, W_\infty) - \tilde{S})$ yields the possible-world description w. By assumption 1, S is finitely axiomatizable [relative to $Q(A, W_t)$] in (t_A, t); hence it has a finite axiomatization $\{q_1, \ldots, q_n\}$ such that $t_{q_i} \subseteq (t_A, t)$ $(i = 1, \ldots, n)$ and such that, for some q_i, $\bar{t}_{q_i} = t$.[42] Take $q = q_1 \& \ldots \& q_n$. Hence $\bar{t}_q = t$, $t_q \subseteq (t_A, t)$, $r \in W_{t_A,t}$, and thus $t_r \subseteq (t_A, t)$.

Surely $q \& \sim r$ is false in every member of $V'(A, W_t)$. Otherwise, since q and $\sim r$ are false (the q_i's belong to S, which is a change; $r \in W_{t_A,t}$), some w' in $V'(A, W_t)$ would contain a change including $q \& \sim r$, which would not be a minimal change [since it would strictly contain the subchange S to which $\sim r$ does not belong, since $\sim r \in \overline{Q(A, W_t) \cup \{q\}}$) by assumption 2]. Hence $\sim (q \& \sim r)$ is true in every member of $V'(A, W_t)$. But $q \& \sim r$, by assumption 2, is compatible with $Q(A, W_t)$. Hence $q \& \sim r$ is true in some member of $V(A, W_t)$. Obviously, $t_A \leq t_{\sim(q \& \sim r)}$; $\bar{t}_{\sim(q \& \sim r)} = t$. Hence, $V(A, W_t)$ determines the truth value of $A > \sim (q \& \sim r)$, according to our theory, and determines that it is false. Since $\sim (q \& \sim r)$ is true in all members of $V'(A, W_t)$, $V'(A, W_t)$ does not represent $V(A, W_t)$ vis-à-vis our theory of counterfactuals.   Q.E.D.

7. Thus far we have not defined the notion of a "minimal change," but have only put a necessary constraint on it, in assumption 3. The notion of "closest possible worlds" in the theorem, as well as the set $V'(A, W_t)$, involved this notion of minimal change. The impact of not fully defining this notion beyond imposing one necessary condition on it is thus to make a claim about *any* set of possible-world descriptions fulfilling this necessary condition: any set $V'(A, W_t)$ fulfilling this constraint fails to represent $V(A, W_t)$. This is so since in the proof we have shown that there is a sentence $q \& \sim r$ that is true in some member of $V(A, W_t)$ but false in every member of $V'(A, W_t)$, for *any* choice of $V'(A, W_t)$ which fulfills this constraint on minimal change, and in particular for the set of *all* possible-world descriptions in $V(A, W_t)$ fulfilling this constraint. An intuitive notion of minimal change, embodying assumption 3, would introduce a further constraint; but regardless of what such a constraint would be, the above theorem would hold.

However, assumption 3 reflects a disregard for the possibility of infinite nested series of changes which share no common subchange. With the introduction of the notion of a *metric*, we shall be able to formulate and prove the thesis of theorem 1 without such a limitation, using precise terminology that captures the notion of "closest possible-world descriptions." The thesis of theorem 1, suitably reformulated to reflect this new terminology, can then be proved on the basis of our first two assumptions, also appropriately modified, with the third assumption abandoned.

With this in mind, let us assume that we have some metric on the distances between possible-world descriptions. Suppose first that, for some n-d type counterfactual antecedent A and for some $t > t_A$ for which assumptions 1 and 2 hold, there is in $V(A, W_t)$ a set (of one or more) of *the* possible-world descriptions closest to the actual-world description; that is, suppose that any other member of $V(A, W_t)$ is *further* from the actual world than any of these closest possible-world descriptions, and that none of these closest possible-world descriptions is closer to the actual-world description than any other. In this case, our proof (under its first two assumptions) obviously shows that such a set does not represent $V(A, W_t)$, given another most obvious assumption on the metric (fulfilling the role of the now abandoned assumption 3) as follows: If $w_1, w_2 \in V(A, W_t)$ result from the actual-world description via changes S_1 and S_2, respectively, such that $S_1 \subset S_2$ and $\overline{Q(A, W_t) \cup S_1} \subsetneq \overline{Q(A, W_t) \cup S_2}$ (i.e., if S_1 is a subchange of S_2), then w_2 is further from the actual-world description than w_1.

More generally, whether or not there is such a set for some such A and t, consider the notion of the greatest lower bound ρ of the distances of members in $V(A, W_t)$ from the actual-world description[43]; that is, there is no possible-world description in $V(A, W_t)$ which is at a distance less than ρ from the actual-world description, but for any ϵ, small as you wish, there is a member of $V(A, W_t)$ closer to the actual-world description than $\rho + \epsilon$. Now, with the metric terminology we can reformulate and combine our assumptions 1 and 2 as follows:

Assumption 1'

> For some n-d type counterfactual antecedent A and for some instantaneous t $(t > t_A)$, and for any $\epsilon > 0$, there is a possible-world description in $V(A, W_t)$ whose distance from the actual-world description is less than $\rho + \epsilon$, which is derived from the actual-world description via a change which is finitely axiomatizable (relative to the implicit premises and A) in (t_A, t) by q and for which there is some $r \in W_{t_A, t}$ such that $\sim r, r \notin \overline{Q(A, W_t) \cup \{q\}}$.

Assumption 1' assures us that, for some A and t, there is a series of possible-world descriptions each of which fulfills the requirements of assumptions 1 and 2, whose distances from the actual-world description converge to ρ. (A possible-world description of the sort required whose distance from the actual-world description *is* ρ fulfills the converging-series requirement vacuously.)

As our second assumption, to replace our former assumption 3 above, we shall assume the following:

Assumption 2'

> If a change S includes a proper subchange S', then the possible-world description arrived at via S is further from the actual-world description than the possible-world description arrived at via S'.

Under this new version of the initial assumption, the above proof, appropriately modified, yields the following:

Theorem 2

For $V(A, W_t)$ fulfilling assumptions 1' and 2' and for any $\epsilon > 0$, there is an ϵ', $\epsilon' < \epsilon$, such that the subset of possible-world descriptions in $V(A, W_t)$ which are at least as close to the actual world as $\rho + \epsilon'$, does not represent $V(A, W_t)$.

Proof

Given $\epsilon > 0$, take a possible-world description w in $V(A, W_t)$ involving a "change" S finitely axiomatizable by q at a distance $\rho + \delta_0$ ($\delta_0 < \epsilon$) from the actual-world description and a statement r, as assured by assumption 1'. Take a δ such that the possible-world descriptions containing both S and $\sim r$ are at distances to the actual-world description not closer than $\rho + \delta$ ($\delta_0 < \delta < \epsilon$). (By our assumption 2', such possible-world descriptions must be further from the actual-world description than w, and hence further than $\rho + \delta_0$.)[44] $V'(A, W_t)$, chosen as a subset of $V(A, W_t)$ which contains all the members in $V(A, W_t)$ closer to the actual world than $\rho + \delta$, would not represent $V(A, W_t)$ according to the above proof. (Thus, ρ is the ϵ' required.) This is because $\sim(q \& \sim r)$ as above would be true in all members of $V'(A, W_t)$ so chosen, as shown in the proof of theorem 1, whereas $\sim(q \& \sim r)$ is not true in all the members of $V(A, W_t)$.

Q.E.D.

Now surely if $V'(A, W_t)$ is as described in this proof (where $\rho + \delta$ is the lowest upper bound of the distances of its members from the actual-world description), no *other* subset of $V(A, W_t)$ for which the lowest upper bound of distances of its members from the actual world is *less* than $\rho + \delta$ will represent $V(A, W_t)$ either, since all such subsets would be subsets of $V'(A, W_t)$, and hence $\sim(q \& \sim r)$ would be true in all their members too.

Thus, the above proof assures us of the following:

Corollary

For $V(A, W_t)$ fulfilling assumptions 1' and 2' and for *some* ϵ, there is *no* $\epsilon' < \epsilon$ such that the subset $V'(A, W_t)$ of $V(A, W_t)$ determined by $\rho + \epsilon'$, represents $V(A, W_t)$.

[$V'(A, W_t)$ is the subset of $V(A, W_t)$ *determined by* $\rho + \epsilon$ iff $V'(A, W_t)$ is the set of all members of $V(A, W_t)$ whose distances from the actual world are less than $\rho + \epsilon$.]

Thus, no subset of "closest" possible-world descriptions in $V(A, W_t)$ represents $V(A, W_t)$ for the purpose of analyzing counterfactuals.

Given this result, there is no interest in finding out whether there is *some* subset of $V(A, W_t)$ that represents $V(A, W_t)$. Surely $V(A, W_t)$ does. The point is that there are no "close as you wish" subsets of $V(A, W_t)$ that do so, nor "closer than a certain point" subsets that do so [in the sense that there is no such subset, determined by $\rho + \epsilon$ for ϵ as small as you wish, and there is no ϵ, such that for any $\epsilon' < \epsilon$, the subset of $V(A, W_t)$ determined by $\rho + \epsilon'$, represents $V(A, W_t)$.] This substantiates the point that no set of "closest" (to the actual-world description) members of $V(A, W_t)$ represents $V(A, W_t)$.

Now in proving theorem 1 we relied on assumption 3 (to the effect that no minimal changes included smaller changes), but we did not impose any constraint on how "small" the minimal changes must be. (This is the reason why I used assumption 3 as a constraint upon, rather than as a definition of, the notion of minimal change.) Thus, $V'(A, W_t)$ in theorem 1 could have included members with "massive" changes that included no subchange. On the other hand, in theorem 2 and its corollary, we eliminated this feature by using a notion of a metric on distances between possible-world descriptions, without incorporating assumption 3. Thus, in the sets of "closest possible-world descriptions" in $V(A, W_t)$ acknowledged in this theorem and its corollary (i.e., those which are at least as close to the actual world as $\rho + \epsilon$, for some ϵ, small as you wish), we have *not* provided against there being two possible-world descriptions in such a set that will involve two changes, one strictly included in the other.

IV Difficulties with Lewis's Original Analysis

1. I shall continue to discuss Lewis's analysis as presented in his book and defer to the next chapter consideration of the new version of his theory.

A significant feature of our analysis was that the truth value of a counterfactual $A > B$ did not depend on the *truth value* of its consequent B, except when A was causally irrelevant or purely positively causally relevant to B. Thus, in particular, the truth value of a counterfactual $A > B$ which belongs to the set consisting of con-type semifactuals and their corresponding counterfactuals[45] with antecedent A, did not depend on the truth value of B: it depended exclusively on whether $f(A, W_{\bar{t}B}) \cup \{A\} \to B$. Thus, it depended exclusively on the constitution of the set of legitimate premises $g(A, W_{\bar{t}B})$ and the logical relations among that set, L, A, and B, but *not* on the truth value of B.

Now on Lewis's analysis (limited to n-d type counterfactuals), the truth value of a counterfactual $A > B$ (in the actual world) is determined according to whether B is true in all the A-worlds in some A-permitting sphere (around the actual world). But whether B is true or not partly determines which worlds are more or less similar to the actual world and, hence, which worlds belong to which spheres, which in turn, in general, is relevant to the truth value of $A > B$. Thus, on Lewis's analysis, in contrast to my own, the truth value of $A > B$ *does* depend, in general, on the truth value of B.

Moreover, since distance between worlds is based on over-all intuitive similarity, Lewis's treatment will favor, for inclusion in a given sphere, worlds in which B is true, if B is true in the actual world, or worlds in which B is false, if B is false in the actual world. So Lewis's analysis has a bias, which mine does *not* have, toward having con-type semifactuals, rather than their corresponding counterfactuals, come out true. Accordingly, if we compare a con-type semifactual $A > B$ with its corresponding counterfactual $A > \sim B$, the bias toward B in the truth conditions for counterfactuals will be reflected in the presence of B and $\sim B$ in any given A-permitting sphere, with a bias in favor of B. Thus, suppose we eliminate from the actual-world description W_T[46] some small enough set of statements which includes the true B, thereby producing W_T', such that $L + W_T' \nrightarrow B$ (and, of course, $L + W_T' \nrightarrow \sim B$). Take the set of worlds close to W_T to at least a given degree, call it $W(W_T)$, and the set of worlds close to W_T' to at least the same degree, and call it $W(W_T')$. Now the presence of B in $W(W_T)$ will be *greater* than in $W(W_T')$. This is so since the addition of B to W_T' will drive some worlds in which B is not true out of $W(W_T')$ and bring in from outside $W(W_T')$ some worlds in which B is true. This reflects the way in which Lewis's approach is biased toward con-type semifactuals over their corresponding counterfactuals. By contrast, on my analysis, the determination of the set of possible-world descriptions associated with a counterfactual $A > B$ is independent of whether B is true or false.

Now, except for irrel-semifactuals and pp-semifactuals, whose consequents provide the background against which counterfactual predictions on the basis of A are determined (and, of course, except for their corresponding counterfactuals), it seems that other counterfactual predictions should be *independent* of whether their consequents are *in fact* true or false: what would hypothetically happen in case A were true should not in general depend on whether B is true in the actual world.[47] On Lewis's analysis this is not the case, which I take to be a counterintuitive result.

Furthermore: suppose $B, B_1, \ldots, B_n$ are mutually exclusive statements, given A, such that $A \rightarrow B \lor B_1 \lor \ldots \lor B_n$ and such that A is in some respect negatively causally relevant to each. Suppose B is true, and so is $A > \sim B$. Lewis's system will tend to favor the counterfactual $A > B_i$, for the B_i, if there is one, which is closest to B, whereas my analysis will not. This will be so even if B_i, although closest to the true B, has a conditional probability, given A and the implicit premises, which is no higher, or even considerably lower, than that of other B_is (perhaps even very low). This feature is counterintuitive, as the following example shows:

Example 2
> a's car is painted standard red (call this statement B).
> $b_1, \ldots, b_n$ are different standard colors (blue, green, yellow, etc.), excluding red. a has n sons, and each son has a different favorite color out of the b_is. Let A be: Had one of the sons painted the whole car his favorite color, ... Let B_i be: The whole car is painted b_i. (For each i, A is *neither* causally irrele-

vant to B_i nor purely positively causally relevant; hence it bears *some* negative causal relevance to each of them.) Suppose one of the standard colors b_1 , . . . , b_n is the pink b_j.

Now standard pink resembles standard red more than any of the other standard colors. Thus, it seems that some A-worlds in which B_j is true will be closer to the actual world than any other A-worlds. This will make $A > B_j$ true; but this counterfactual is clearly false.

2. I will not dwell here on counterexamples to Lewis's theory presented in the literature. Such examples typically involve an antecedent that describes an event differing mildly, in itself, from the actual world, and a consequent that describes an event involving a huge difference. The most famous of them perhaps has been the sort of Kit Fine's counterexample, which Lewis called the "future-similarity objection." Lewis discusses it in his article "Counterfactual Dependence and Time's Arrow," and I will come to this example in chapter 8. Here I will mention only a case that, together with example 2 above, brings out an important feature of Lewis's approach which contrasts sharply with the approach I develop in this book.

Example 3

> I flipped a coin in my right hand, and it came out heads.
> Assume that coin flipping is a genuinely stochastic phenomenon.

Now consider the counterfactual:

(5) Had I flipped the coin in my left hand, it would still have come out heads.

I take this counterfactual to be clearly intuitively false. But it seems that this counterfactual should come out true on Lewis's analysis. The reasoning for this is similar to that of the previous example. Apart from which side the coin fell on and whatever is directly related to that, the closest A-worlds in which the coin comes out heads will be as close to the actual world as the closest A-worlds in which the coin comes out tails. But since in the actual world the coin turned out heads, the closest A-worlds in which it turned out heads will be closer to the actual world than the closest A-worlds in which it turned out tails. Hence there should be an A-permitting sphere in whose A-worlds the coin invariably turns out heads. This will make the above counterfactual true.[48]

Notice that on my account the antecedent-event in this counterfactual is causally relevant to the consequent-event, but not purely positively so; and since the outcome of the tossing of the coin is a stochastic event, the consequent does not follow from the antecedent and the implicit premises. Hence the counterfactual will come out false on my analysis (and so will its converse, i.e.: Had I flipped the coin in my left hand, the coin would have come out tails). Counterfactual (5) thus belongs among the con-type semifactuals $A > C$ such that neither $A > C$ nor $A > \sim C$ is true [its consequent C belongs to $\text{CNR}(A, W_{\bar{t}C}) - \text{CCS}(A, W_{\bar{t}C})$], which is the group of counterfactuals that Lewis's analysis tends to make come out true, although, I claim, they are always false — and so indeed they come out under my analysis.[49] Such counterfactuals manifest once again the undue bias of Lewis's analysis in favor of semifactuals over their corresponding counterfactuals, which is rooted in the dependence of his truth conditions for a counterfactual $A > B$ on the truth value of B. Examples 2 and 3 bring out a way in which Lewis's analysis is unduly biased in favor of the features of the actual world.

V   Context-dependence and Interest-relativity

There is another, at least as important, repercussion of Lewis's reliance on the notion of similarity, avoided in our account, which goes beyond the question of extensional adequacy. Similarity, as Lewis would say (see pp. 91/92), is a highly volatile concept that depends on degrees of importance of respects and, thus, can vary from person to person and from context to context. Since for Lewis the truth values of counterfactuals depend on the similarity relation, they turn out to have a *nonobjective* character in Quine's sense: they are interest-relative and context-dependent and so, presumably, of limited philosophical interest, if not altogether empty. In Lewis's analysis this is reflected in the relativization to $\$_i$: it is a strong relativization to the *order* of the possible worlds in the set $U\$_i$. Thus, the distribution of possible worlds into spheres will *vary* with shifts in the similarity relation, thereby effecting changes in the truth values of counterfactuals. Acknowledging this, Lewis still supports the use of this notion of similarity for the analysis of counterfactuals, since their truth conditions are also "a highly volatile matter, varying with every shift of context and interest" (p. 92).

This I deny, at least when it comes to counterfactuals of the n-d type.[50] I deny that the content of these counterfactuals varies with the speaker in the way suggested: that one's notion of similarity determines one's notion of counterfactuals, thereby making one's construal of counterfactuals relative to one's notions of similarity (given that individuals have different interests). I deny that counterfactuals are context-dependent or interest-relative in a way that nonsubjunctive statements are not; in particular, I deny that they are context-dependent in a way that the indicative versions of their antecedents and consequents are not. Parameters of context-dependence such as the times sentences pertain to or the determination of the individuals referred to are common to counterfactuals and syntactically simple sentences alike. Rather, on the analysis I propose, the truth values of counterfactuals depend upon the *pertinent facts* and on the nomological character of the world, that is, upon the history of the world prior to t_B and various *objective* probabilities.

Notice that the *context* in which a counterfactual is couched should be clearly separated from the *world* in which it is evaluated. It is easy not to attend to this distinction when discussing examples. To hold that the truth value of a counterfactual is a function of the world (or possible-world description) in which it is evaluated need not in the least invoke context-dependence, which has to do with the context in which the description of the example (i.e., the partial world in question) is provided. That the same counterfactual can have different truth values when evaluated in different examples, or variations of the same example, need not be an indication of context-dependence: it might only indicate that two different situations are considered on those two occasions; that the counterfactual is evaluated in two different kinds of worlds.[51]

I admit that, when it comes to counterfactuals, there is a feeling that the issue of their truth values is often elusive and agreement on it unattainable, more so than in the case of nonsubjunctive sentences. It may, therefore, be tempting to regard these statements as undetermined in principle, perhaps without truth values, or as not depending solely on fact and on how the world actually is, and to construe them as context-dependent and interest-relative, varying from one speaker to another. This view, however, is not borne out by the analysis offered in this book,[52] according to which the truth values of counterfactuals are a function of facts in the actual world, its lawlike regularities, and various objective probability relations. The air of difficulty in settling disagreements concerning counterfactuals is *not* a result of their being couched in shifting and volatile semantical features; rather, it arises because the objective features of this world that should settle the truth values of counterfactuals are too often *unavailable* to us. Too often we just do not know enough about which events in fact transpired in the actual world up to $\bar{t}_B$. Too often we can only *guess* how the laws of nature will affect the course of a particular situation, since our knowledge of the laws of nature is too fragmentary. Too often we can make only a tentative assessment of probabilistic relations, and are hard pressed to argue for them in detail. Too often we are in a position where we have to *guess*, on the basis of our experience and intuitions, what is causally relevant to what, and how nomological constraints would restrict the development of a given situation. All these shortcomings in our knowledge generate difficulties in settling disputes over the truth values of counterfactuals. But this is *not* because the truth values of counterfactuals are undetermined, or vary with interest and context: it is merely because we do not have access to all the necessary features of this world. To misinterpret the difficulties in settling counterfactual disputes as indicating either that they are not about the actual world and are not empirically determinable, or that they are couched in interest-relative and context-dependent parameters, is, I believe, a distortion of the *objective* character of counterfactuals, which results from an inadequate conception of their analysis, where the unavailability of objective information is misperceived as a dependency on subjective parameters.[53] It is to mistake ignorance for ontological undeterminability.

Furthermore, it is, in part, precisely due to the lack of such information (concerning, e.g., laws of nature) that the counterfactual construction is so useful. It is useful in helping us to arrange our experiences, and

conceptualize the regular aspects of the phenomena around us. It is precisely because we are so often unable to formulate laws of nature in cases
where we feel that regularities prevail, that we resort to *other* forms of expression that *reflect* these regularities in ways that are useful to us.
Likewise, when we do not *need* the high precision of a fully formulated
law of nature, alternative constructions that reflect its relevant respects
without fully specifying it are useful. This is, I believe, the role played by
counterfactual and dispositional statements. Saying that salt is soluble expresses potentially important information, even though it does not provide
the specific functional relation between the rate of solubility and parameters such as features of the liquid, the relative quantities of salt and liquid, temperature, etc. But dispositional terms are *fixed*, thus codifying
highly and prevalently useful ways of describing certain regularities. Inevitably, they comprise a limited vocabulary, whereas the regularities of
the world express themselves in countless new situations and relationships.
To help us express how such regularities are manifested in such particular
cases is one function served by the counterfactual construction. Counterfactuals also help us bring out more specific features of regularities as
operative in particular situations, which dispositional terms cannot do. A
dispositional predicate is very useful for conveying that had the salt been
put in water it would have dissolved, since the salt can be compactly
labeled soluble, thereby *reflecting* regularities in the actual world without
specifying them. In other cases, no such compact dispositional predicate
is available, e.g., when Carter says that he would have preferred to lose
his presidency rather than endanger the lives of the hostages in Iran, that
is, that in the event that he had had to choose between the two, he would
have preferred to give up his presidency. Yet, for such cases, we have the
predicates 'prefer' or 'is committed', which represent a variety of items of
vocabulary that also serve to codify information concerning hypothetical
situations. Such a vocabulary is in abundant supply among our adjectives
and verbs. But, again, it is *fixed*, and too limited to cover the variety of
situations we come upon.[54] Also it is not precise, and leaves ineffable a
variety of specific features. In view of such limitations the counterfactual
construction plays an important role, reflecting either all-pervasive
regularities or local regularities concerning a particular person, institu-
tion, machine, or whatever. It enables us to say that a person would have
been willing to cooperate if he had been politely asked to do so; that the
car would not have endured a cross-country trip; that the building would
have collapsed under an earthquake of a magnitude of 4 on the Richter
scale; that the U.S. would not have gone to war if South Korea had been
invaded. All these modes of expression reveal vital information about the
regularities that underlie the phenomena they describe. But we are not in
a position to formulate these regularities explicitly, and often we do not
even possess the vocabulary necessary for a tentative formulation. Via the
counterfactual construction, however, we can *reflect* these regularities by
specifying the *hypothetical* behavior of the objects or situations involved,
thereby enabling us to convey important information. It is *precisely*
because they serve to reflect such information concerning either the regu-

larities or the facts involved, which we are unable to specify explicitly, that counterfactual statements are often hard to evaluate, and disagreements often hard to settle. This elusive aspect of counterfactuals reflects their usefulness in such epistemic situations. But to conclude from this that their truth conditions depend on shifting parameters of high volatility is a mistake which misrepresents their function and structure. What is reflected is the meagerness of our information about the world and the ingenious ways in which the counterfactual construction enables us to circumvent such limitations. Thus, the counterfactual construction is couched in *objective* parameters, which are determined in specific cases by the way the world actually is, and not by the interests of the speakers.

It is at this level of our discussion that a significant difference between Lewis's approach and my own appears, a difference reflected in the choice of the terminology with which we analyze the counterfactual construction: the difference between basing the counterfactual construction on notions of similarity of possible worlds, thereby introducing context-dependence and interest-relativity, as Lewis does, on the one hand, and basing the counterfactual construction on the facts of the world, its laws and relations of objective probabilities, as my approach would have it, thereby securing the objective character of this construction.

VI Epistemic Accounts of Counterfactuals

1. In this chapter I have concentrated on the closest possible-worlds approach to counterfactuals, and especially on Lewis's book. Lewis's approach, as well as my own, is concerned with the truth conditions of counterfactual statements. Another approach to counterfactuals, however, has considered them from an epistemic perspective. Before closing this chapter, I would like to mention briefly some such epistemic theories which aim at providing assertability conditions for counterfactuals.

J.L. Mackie[55] has developed a supposition theory of if-sentences. According to this theory, conditionals are not to be construed as statements, and do not have truth values. The core of his theory lies in Mackie's condensed-argument theory. Conditionals, according to this theory, are incomplete arguments. To say 'If P,Q' is to assert that Q within the scope of the supposition that P. The antecedent provides one premise out of possibly many premises that the speaker may or may not be able to specify. When it comes to counterfactuals, Mackie's principle for admitting additional premises would rule out those candidates which are such that the adoption of the antecedent as a supposition would undermine the grounds on which they were believed.

Nicholas Rescher's approach to counterfactuals[56] consists in taking one's body of knowledge together with the counterfactual antecedent (and eliminating the negation of the latter) and addressing the conflict that arises as a result. Out of this set one considers the maximally consistent subsets that contain the antecedent, and utilizes a criterion of preference to obtain the preferred subsets among them. The counterfactual is to be accepted in case the consequent is a consequence of all the preferred ones.

The preference criterion consists in assigning degrees of plausibility to different types of statements and in considering the average or the maximum degree of plausibility of the members of each maximally consistent subset. One thereby ranks these sets and obtains the most preferred ones.

According to Ernest Adams,[57] the probabilities of indicative conditionals are the corresponding conditional probabilities (of the consequents on the basis of the antecedents). Adams argues, furthermore, that the probability of an indicative conditional cannot be considered the probability of its being true. When it comes to counterfactuals, Adams entertains the hypothesis that the probability of a counterfactual is the probability that was (or would have been) assigned to the corresponding indicative conditional on an actual prior occasion, or that would have been assigned to it on some hypothetical prior occasion. (Yet Adams takes this hypothesis to be only partially correct.) Brian Skyrms[58] proposes to preserve such a prior-probability account with the following change: the probabilities involved should be the prior propensities rather than the prior epistemic probabilities when the former are known, or the expected prior propensities otherwise.

According to Isaac Levi[59] the counterfactual form of a subjunctive appraisal does not in general have a truth value. Such appraisals are relative to a corpus of knowledge K and to an assessment of informational loss. The appraisal consists in first contracting K to K_1 by removing the negation of the antecedent from K in a manner which minimizes loss of informational value, and then in expanding to K_2, the deductive closure of K_1 and the antecedent, and then determining whether the consequent is included in K_2 or follows via an acceptance.

2. The conception of philosophical analysis as an enterprise with an empirical dimension aimed at modeling the functioning of concepts as we employ them and our competence in mastering them might fit comfortably with attempts to provide mere assertability conditions (rather than truth conditions) for various concepts and constructions. However, those who, like myself, seek to incorporate such concepts into a realist perspective and to answer the question under what conditions such sentences are *true*, i.e., what their truth conditions are, would attempt to go beyond mere epistemic analyses of assertability conditions.

Analyses of truth conditions, however, tend to yield related analyses of assertability conditions. For that purpose, the objective parameters of the analysis would have to be epistemically relativized. Such projected accounts of assertability conditions, with parameters so relativized, often lend themselves to a comparison with *bona fide* theories of assertability conditions. Insights gained from adequate analysis of truth conditions may thus be applied to a critical examination of theories of assertability conditions. I have formulated, in this book, a theory of truth conditions rather than of assertability conditions for counterfactual conditions; and I must leave to another occasion the development of its implications for the theory of assertability conditions and the consequent critical comparisons with the epistemic accounts mentioned above.

Notes: Chapter 7

1. Cambridge, Mass.: Harvard University Press, 1973. Parenthetical page references in this chapter will be to this book, unless otherwise noted.

2. "Counterfactual Dependence and Time's Arrow," *Noûs*, XIII, 4 (November 1979): 455-476. That the position taken in this article is different from that presented in the book is shown below (8 I and fn 2).

3. My concentration on Lewis in these chapters should not be interpreted as a lack of appreciation of the work of other researchers in the field. Another major proponent of the minimal-change theory is John Pollock [in his *Subjunctive Reasoning* (Boston: Reidel, 1976)].

Thus Pollock says: "The basic idea lying behind our analysis of subjunctive conditionals is that they have to do with making minimal changes to accommodate the truth of the counterfactual hypothesis" (p. 91). Pollock adopts Lewis's basic idea that a counterfactual $P > Q$ is true (in the actual world) iff Q is true in all the worlds closest to the actual world, which Pollock takes to be "the worlds that *might* be the actual world if P were true" (p. 20; p. 70). Such worlds Pollock calls P-worlds (and uses the notation αMP, for α being a P-world). Pollock then proceeds to provide an elaborate analysis for this notion. The choice of the P-worlds amounts to choosing a subset of all the worlds in which P is true. (The worlds in which P is true are P-worlds in *Lewis's* jargon, which I adopt in this text; beware of the possibility of confusing the two!). For noncounterlegals, Pollock preserves the laws in his P-worlds. His basic strategy for securing minimal-change worlds [reminiscent of Rescher's, in his *Hypothetical Reasoning* (Amsterdam: North-Holland, 1964)] is to obtain them via maximal subsets (consistent with P) of the set of propositions that constitutes the actual world. But for Pollock not all the propositions in the actual world belong to such maximal P-consistent subsets — only propositions that he calls "stable." Stable propositions can be either certain sets of compounds of certain stable propositions, or stable in their own right. The latter Pollock calls *simple propositions*, which are propositions that cannot be regarded (except artificially) as compounds of simpler propositions (p. 73). But for Pollock the notion of a simple proposition is ultimately an epistemological notion, reducible to "what possible grounds one can have for believing it" (p. 25).

In taking this turn, Pollock seems to rest the analysis of counterfactuals on epistemological foundations, a move quite different from the ontological orientation discussed above. As he says, "P is simple iff it is logically possible for one to know the truth of P non-inductively without first knowing the truth of each proposition in some set Π which entails P. It is unfortunate that the success of this analysis turns upon the truth of certain epistemological theories. Although I had defended those theories elsewhere, a person who does not accept them is not expected to accept the above analysis of a simple proposition either. But I do not think that anything can be done about this. The notion of a simple proposition is basically epistemological, and hence its characterization must turn upon one's epistemological theories" (p. 93).

As Pollock reduces the counterfactual construction to the notion of knowledge, his analysis will be unacceptable to those who believe that the notion of knowledge rests upon a notion of justification and thus presupposes normative elements, though the counterfactual construction does not. Similarly, basing the notion of counterfactual on the notion of knowledge will make it circular to attempt a causal analysis of knowledge (or even a causal-component analysis of knowledge), if one assumes that the notions of causal connection requisite for such an analysis must be unpacked in terms of counterfactuals [as does, e.g., Robert Nozick, in the essay

"Knowledge and Skepticism" in his *Philosophical Explanations* (Cambridge, Mass.: Harvard, 1981)].

4. Thus, suppose a counterfactual $\phi > \psi$ is true in $\$_i^1$ in such a way that sphere S_1 in it fulfills condition (2) of Lewis's analysis. Now suppose S_1 is next in size to S_0 in $\$_i^1$ (the spheres are nested), and S_2 is next in size to S_1 in $\$_i^1$. Suppose also that in S_0 there are no ϕ-worlds, and that in S_2 there are already ϕ-worlds that are not ψ-worlds. Finally, suppose that $\$_i^2$ is just like $\$_i^1$, except that it does not contain S_1. Although ϕ will be true relative to $\$_i^1$, it will not be true relative to $\$_i^2$.

5. That the truth value of a counterfactual is, for Lewis, relative to a system of spheres seems, on the face of it, an undesirable feature. It implies that if you and I disagree about the truth value of any given counterfactual, we may not really have a disagreement at all, since each of us might have in mind a different system of spheres, *even* if we are using the *same* similarity relation. In view of the last remark in the previous subsection, relativization, in the case of such a fixed similarity relation, can thus be taken to be tantamount to relativization to $\cup \$_i$, rather than to the internal constitution of its spheres.

Now it seems that Lewis wanted to allow the relativization to $\cup \$_i$ to serve as an indicator of impossible antecedents: to allow for such antecedents to be those which would not belong to any world in $\cup \$_i$. But such a role for this relativization does not follow from Lewis's characterization of the truth conditions of counterfactuals and his formal definition of a system of spheres, and is thus not really incorporated into his formal analysis of counterfactuals; therefore, the relativization to a system of spheres need *not* reflect it. According to Lewis's analysis, the counterfactual 'If Napoleon had conquered Russia, the world would have been transformed into yellow cheese' comes out true under some systems of spheres (admittedly, very restricted ones) that will have this antecedent unfulfilled in all their worlds, though false relative to other systems of spheres. But making every counterfactual so relativized does not seem to correspond to anything in ordinary discourse about counterfactuals.

6. Cf., for instance, his remarks on p. 51, where he considers the importance of particular respects and takes them to be relative to a world, but in no way peculiar to counterfactuals.

7. See, for example, "Counterfactual and Possible Worlds," *Canadian Journal of Philosophy*, IV, 2 (December 1974): 381-402; and Kit Fine, "Critical Notice" of Lewis's *Counterfactuals*, in *Mind*, LXXXIV, 355 (July 1975): 451-458.

8. Cf. Lewis's rejection of the conditional-excluded-middle principle (pp. 79/80).

9. Cf. "Counterfactuals and Possible Worlds," *op. cit.*, p. 389, for a similar point. Bennett criticizes Lewis's preference for his first formulation of the notion of cotenability,arguing that it does not reflect the notion that metalinguistic theorists had in mind; Bennett does this by producing what intuitively seems to be a statement cotenable with the antecedent of a given counterfactual and then showing that it does not satisfy Lewis's first formulation. Bennett's example exemplifies the general phenomenon that for a statement C which is cotenable according to Goodman's definition with a counterfactual antecedent A, often much less of a change, or difference in similarity, would be involved in making the $C - \sim C$ transition than in making the $\sim A - A$ transition. Consequently, there would be, on Lewis's model, $\sim C$-worlds closer to the actual world than any A-world, thereby violating Lewis's first formulation. Bennett's example demonstrates this phenomenon in particular for a statement that would qualify, by our analysis, as a consequent of a true con-type semifactual. Since such a statement fulfills $A > C$,

surely, on our analysis, it does not fulfill $A > \sim C$, and hence it qualifies as cotenable with A according to Goodman's definition, which we have adopted. Indeed, since factual statements were those which troubled Goodman in the context of the cotenability issue, it is hard to see why Lewis ascribed to metalinguistic theorists the intuition that "a cotenable premise is not only true, but also necessary to some extent" (p. 70). Nevertheless, Bennett's counterexample is effective *only* against Lewis's first formulation of the cotenability relation, but not against the second: a consequent C of a true con-type semifactual $A > C$ is indeed such that C and $A > C$ are true. Bennett's subsequent discussion, as well as the discussion in this section above, show that *both* of the definitions provided by Lewis are incompatible with the notion of cotenability as introduced by Goodman.

10. Though there remains a marked difference even in logical form: Lewis's account (of quote B) is indeed akin to the accounts of various metalinguistic theorists in that it specifies a condition whereby the consequent follows via some auxiliary premises subject to a certain constraint (here it is the cotenability constraint, read in Lewis's way). On the inferential model presented in this book, a set of implicit premises must be *specified*, and inferability has to be checked with respect to a *well specified* set of premises, in contrast to just imposing some constraint and requiring inferability via *some* statements satisfying this constraint. Cf. also 3 II.

11. The inference is valid for Lewis, since if $\phi > \psi$ is not vacuously true, χ is true in all ϕ-worlds in some sphere, in all of which (by the second premise) ψ is also true (cf. p. 35). It is valid on my analysis (for the kind of counterfactuals discussed so far, i.e., counterfactuals of the n-d type) in case $\bar{t}_\chi \leq \bar{t}_\psi$. In this case, and since the implicit premises are a function of the antecedent and the consequent-time only, the implicit premises for $\phi > \chi$ would also be implicit premises for $\phi > \psi$. By the first premise, χ is inferable from them plus ϕ, and, hence, by the second premise, ψ is inferable from them plus ϕ.

12. $[\phi > (\phi \supset \psi)] \equiv (\phi > \psi)$ is true for Lewis, since if one side is vacuously true, so is the other, and ψ is true in all ϕ-worlds in some sphere iff $\phi \supset \psi$ is. On my theory, it would be valid for the kind of counterfactuals discussed so far when $\bar{t}_\phi \leq \bar{t}_\psi$, since then the upper limit of the consequent-time in the counterfactuals on both sides is the same. Since the legitimate premises are a function of the antecedent and the upper limit of the consequent-time, they are the same in both sides. And, of course, ψ is inferable from certain implicit premises and ϕ iff $\phi \supset \psi$ is.

13. The restrictions being that $\bar{t}_\chi \leq \bar{t}_\psi$ and $\bar{t}_\phi \leq \bar{t}_\psi$, concerning, of course, the kind of counterfactuals discussed so far. Cf. the two last footnotes.

14. Bennett (*op.cit.*, p. 390) argues that Lewis's second definition of cotenability will not do for a metalinguistic theory, for which a counterfactual $P > Q$ "is true if and only if Q is law-derivable from P together with true premises which are jointly cotenable with P." His argument is: "In short, if one adopts the consequence theory while defining cotenability by means of (2) [Lewis's second definition of cotenability], the only counterfactuals one can allow as true are ones which don't depend on any particular matter of fact but only on the law-connection of the antecedent with the consequent" (*ibid.*). His reasoning for this argument is that "if R [a conjunctive form of the true premises cotenable with P from which Q is to be derived] must be cotenable with P according to definition (2), then R itself must be law-derivable from Q" (*ibid.*). The plausibility of this reasoning can be seen as follows: plugging Lewis's second definition into his analysis of counterfactuals in terms of cotenability will yield that $P > Q$ is true iff Q is derivable from P and a true statement R_1 such that R_1 is derivable from P and a true statement R_2 such

that . . . etc. That is:

$P > Q$ iff $(\exists R_1)$ $(\exists R_2)(\exists R_3)$ . . . [. . . & R_i is true & $(R_i$ & $P \to R_{i-1})$
& . . . & R_1 is true & R_1 & $P \to Q)$]

But Bennett's reasoning will not do. His reasoning will be subverted if independently specifiable auxiliary premises count as auxiliary premises *for themselves* as well. In this case, they will satisfy the metalinguistic model. Hence, Lewis's account in terms of the second definition of cotenability applies to such cases, but Bennett's argument does not hold. Such cases do not arise on my analysis, since W_{t_A} plays a major role in it, and $A > W_{t_A}$ is not defined in it (since we did not deal with counterfactuals of reverse temporal order). But a variant of my theory in which W_{t_A} *does not* count among the implicit premises will provide this sort of counterexample to Bennett's argument (even though it will not be extensionally adequate as a theory of counterfactuals, but that is beside the point here). Surely, if in the above schema we allow R_i to equal R_{i-1}, the above schema will not sustain Bennett's conclusion. If this were all, the above schema would be fulfilled in case $P > Q$ iff Q is derivable from P and some true R, which would be a gratuitous consequence. But Bennett is rightfully careful enough in his formulation not to rule out some *other* constraint on R that would undercut such trivializability. But given such an extra constraint alone without any prohibition on $R_i = R_{i-1}$, the above schema does not bear out Bennett's argument. Consequently, Lewis's second analysis is not subverted by Bennett's argument.

15. That is, $g(A, W_{\bar{t}B})$ was found to be $\text{CIP}(A, W_{\bar{t}B})$, that is, the set of consequents of irrel-semifactuals and pp-semifactuals with antecedent A and consequents in (t_A, t_B). Cf. 2 IX 1.

16. $\text{NC}(A, W_{\bar{t}B})$ is the set of true statements C such that $A > \sim C$ is a true counterfactual. Thus $C \in \text{NC}(A, W_{\bar{t}B})$ iff $\sim C$ belongs to the counterfactual span of A for t_B, which, as we saw, is $\overline{Q(A, W_{\bar{t}B})}^{(t_A, t_B)}$ (cf. 2 X 5, and 2 XIII 3). Hence the arguments of $\text{NC}(A, W_{\bar{t}B})$ are the correct ones. This use of cotenability must not be confused with that of Lewis: cf. II of this chapter.

17. Cf. the table at the end of 2 XII.

18. Con-type semifactuals are semifactuals that are neither irrel-semifactuals nor pp-semifactuals.

19. Where the "closeness" between worlds is understood in terms of over-all intuitive similarity.

20. Notice that similarity cannot be measured by "overlap" of statements in two possible-world descriptions: slight overlap does not imply nonsimilarity. Thus, if one possible-world description is derived from another by performing a "temporal shift" on the other, that is, by having whatever is true in the first at t be true in the second at $t - \Delta t$, then they may differ significantly if we measure the overlap (or "agreement") of their descriptions. This is because if 'p at t' is true in the first (for "temporally pure" p, see 6 I 1), it may very well be false in the second, in which 'p at $t - \Delta t$' will be true. (This will be especially blatant when you take two worlds in which the scene is changing rapidly, i.e., in which what holds at t tends not to hold at $t + \epsilon$, for some fixed ϵ.) Yet two such possible-world descriptions would intuitively be extremely similar to each other. The same can be said for spatial shifts if one upholds an absolute theory of space. This seems to be an easy mistake to fall into, and prevalent enough to be called the overlap fallacy of similarity. [Cf. Kit Fine, who seems to have committed it (if his 'agreement' is read as overlap) in his "Critical Notice," *op. cit.* p. 455: "For similarity is a matter of agreement in propositions."]

21. For more on this point see below, sec. IV 1.

22. Such minimal repercussions need not, of course, be unique.

23. The point is that we are able to make a relatively small change in V_2 which will involve either W_{t_A} or $g(A, W_{\bar{t}B})$, which will make V_2 similar to the actual world.

24. If you wish, all we need is to make a *simultaneous* choice of such U_1 and U_2 (so we need not make a commitment that for every such U_1 we can choose such an equally-similar-to-the-actual-world U_2).

25. $Q(A, W_{\bar{t}B})$ was the antecedent in the inferential schema for $A > B$, i.e.: $\{A\} \cup W \cup L \cup \text{CIP}(A, W_{\bar{t}B})$. $\text{CIP}(A, W_{t_B})$ was the set of consequents in (t_A, t_B) of irrel-semifactuals and pp-semifactuals with antecedent A, that is, the set of true statements in (t_A, t_B) to which A bore no negative causal relevance whatsoever. Our thesis was that $g(A, W_{\bar{t}B}) = \text{CIP}(A, W_{\bar{t}B})$; that is, $\text{CIP}(A, W_{\bar{t}B})$ comprises the legitimate premises for $A > B$ in (t_A, t_B). Z^{-L} is Z excluding all members of L in Z.

26. In his book, Pollock provides an elaborate analysis of the notion of minimal change which does not rest on an unanalyzed notion of similarity. One feature of Pollock's position which is akin to my approach is its sensitivity to the temporal element in analyzing counterfactuals. The temporal dimension in understanding counterfactuals receives considerable emphasis in the analysis I have developed in this book, hence the introduction of the notion of the time a statement pertains to, the distinction between the history prior to the antecedent-time and the history after it (which are treated differently), and the concentration on the (t_A, t_A) interval. For Pollock, however, the temporal element enters into the analysis of counterfactuals via the problem of how to choose, in performing minimal changes, between two propositions that are collectively, but not individually, incompatible with the antecedent (recall the discussion on Goodman, 1 II). Pollock deals with this problem by requiring that minimal changes be effected "by preserving simple propositions with early dates in preference to those with later dates" (*op. cit.*, p. 80). This is the essence of Pollock's temporal-priority requirement. (In his analysis Pollock uses this requirement rather than his notion of "undercutting," which he introduces but does not attempt to make precise or analyze.)

Now if the antecedent A is compatible with W_{t_A}, Pollock's analysis will agree with ours in preserving W_{t_A}. But when it comes to (t_A, t_B), making minimal changes will require preserving a maximal A-consistent subset of $\text{CNR}(A, W_{\bar{t}B})$ − $\text{CCS}(A, W_{\bar{t}B})$. This, we have argued, is a mistake. Thus, in accordance with minimal-change strategies, Pollock's analysis will result in an undue bias favoring the actual world and thus favoring semifactuals over nonsemifactual counterfactuals, as does the approach criticized above.

27. That is, an antecedent of a counterfactual of the n-d type. Notice that A is surely negatively causally relevant to each of the B_is.

28. That is, relative to the degree of freedom that statements in (t_A, t_B) have in $V(A, W_{\bar{t}B})$. The primary factor that determines the degree of freedom is the degree to which L is restrictive.

$(\bar{t}_B \infty)$ is the interval stretching from the upper end of t_B to infinity.

29. We have argued that no statement in $\text{CNR}(A, W_{\bar{t}B})$ − $\text{CCS}(A, W_{\bar{t}B})$ should be taken as a legitimate premise. Yet, it can be argued that the above proposal may, after all, allow for some statement in $\text{CNR}(A, W_{\bar{t}B})$ − $\text{CCS}(A, W_{\bar{t}B})$ to be taken as a legitimate premise, since it may be the case that some such statement belongs to all members in the proposed set of possible-world descriptions [though not to some other members in $V(A, W_{\bar{t}B})$]. This question will be (negatively) decided below.

30. Cf. above, this section, end of 1, for an argument why the set $CNR(A, W_{\bar{t}B}) - CCS(A, W_{\bar{t}B})$ as a whole need not be compatible with the implicit premises plus A. The same obviously holds for $UD(A, W_{\bar{t}B}, W_\infty)$, which includes this set, as well. (W_∞ is of course the whole world history; '∞' is the infinity sign.)

31. For any n-d counterfactual $A > C$, the set of the possible-world descriptions relevant to the determination of its truth value on our theory is $V(A, W_{\bar{t}C})$. The functional dependence is obviously on $\bar{t}_C$ (the lowest upper bound of t_C), since what needs to be specified is the (t_A, t_C) interval. Thus, according to our theory, for some instantaneous t such that $t > t_A$ (t_A being the greatest lower bound of t_A), $V(A, W_t)$ determines the truth values of all n-d-type counterfactuals $A > C$ such that $t = \bar{t}_C$. That is, $V(A, W_{\bar{t}B}) = V(A, W_{\bar{t}C})$ iff $\bar{t}_B = \bar{t}_C$ (for counterfactuals $A > B$ and $A > C$ of the n-d type).

32. This requirement guarantees that R includes *all* the statements in $UD(A, \bar{t}_B, W_\infty)$ that are to be replaced. We clearly are not interested in distinguishing different *bases* for one change as long as they yield the same total change in $UD(A, \bar{t}_B, W_\infty)$. Only if we require this exhaustive character of R can we talk sensibly about one change being a subchange of another, without including different bases for the same total change [in $UD(A, \bar{t}_B, W_\infty)$].

33. To assure the viability of this assumption of finite axiomatizability certain technical steps have to be taken. It is not possible to outline and justify these steps here. The rest of this discussion should be viewed as proceeding under the assumption noted in the text.

34. That is, t is an instant, rather than a nondegenerate time interval.

35. Of course, if, for *some* t, $Q(A, W_t) \cup W_{t, \infty}$ is consistent, a finite axiomatization of the change may pertain to some interval (t_A, t') *within* (t_A, t). (Its lower limit will most plausibly be t_A, though this point is not crucial either here or in assumption 1 below.) If $t' < t$, then taking t' instead of t might do; or else, take some true statement p, such that $t_p = t$, $t_p \subseteq (t_A, t)$, and add to the change the statement $\sim(p \& \sim q)$, for some q in the change, without modifying the possible-world description obtained via the change [since, of course, $\bar{t}(\sim(p \& \sim q)) = t$].

36. That is, given $W_{t, \infty}$, W_{t_A} and $g(A, W_t)$.

37. An alternative way of putting this assumption is to say that for some A, t, and a member w of $V(A, W_t)$ as assured in assumption 1, if w results from the actual-world description via a change S, S is a subchange of another change S', such that $S^{(t_A, t)} \subsetneq S'^{(t_A, t)}$. [For a set of statements Z, $Z^{(t, t')}$ is its subset consisting of members which pertain to (t, t').] We could combine both assumptions by appending to assumption 1 the phrase 'which is a subchange of another change that does not coincide with it in (t_A, t)'.

38. This constraint on the notion of a minimal change is most plausible as long as we do not anticipate infinite series of nested changes (i.e., where each member in the series is included in its predecessor) which do not include a common subchange. Precluding such cases is the impact of this assumption. Below (7, this section) we prove a theorem that makes the same point using metric distances between worlds; its proof does *not* preclude such series, nor does it resort to this assumption at all.

39. Our assumption 3 above, though highly plausible, does not yet require minimal changes to be minimal in comparison to *other* changes. So we can expect a further restriction to this effect. But such a restriction is not really necessary, given the character of the proof below. The proof shows that a certain appropriate statement is true in the set of all members of $V(A, W_t)$ which result from minimal

changes (in the sense of this assumption 3) in the actual-world description, yet is not true in all the members of $V(A, W_t)$, so that representation fails. But an immediate consequence is that representation will therefore also fail for any *subset* of the above set selected in accordance with assumption 3; and, of course, what a further restriction of the notion of minimal change will do is determine such a subset.

40. In the sense of resulting from minimal changes, subject to our assumptions 1–3.

41. I.e., for each w in $V'(A, W_t)$ there is a minimal change S such that, if w_0 is the actual-world description, modifying w_0 in accordance with the minimal change S yields w.

Recall that Z^{-L}, for some set of statements Z, is Z minus all of its lawlike statements.

42. This is so since, if p is a statement (in S) pertaining to an interval in (t_A, t) such that $\bar{t}_p = t$ and if $\{q_1, \ldots, q_n\}$ is a finite axiomatization for S as above, so would be $\{q_1, \ldots, q_n, q_n \lor p\}$; and, of course, $\bar{t}_{q_n \lor p} = t$.

43. Since all possible-world descriptions in $V(A, W_t)$ include the false A, there obviously is such a lower limit, hence a greatest lower limit, greater than zero. Of course, ρ is a function of A and t.

44. It is *not* required that there be such possible-world descriptions at a distance less than $\rho + \epsilon$ to the actual-world description. Although $\rho + \delta$ is a lower bound of the distances from the actual-world description of possible-world descriptions containing both S and $\sim r$, it need *not* be a greatest lower bound.

45. If $A > B$ is a semifactual, then $A > \sim B$ is its corresponding counterfactual.

46. The subscript 'T' in 'W_T' is a reminder of truth, not of any temporal interval.

47. Given that $t_A \leq t_B$, which we assume all along.

48. The argument here can be expanded into a more rigorous one. Notice that for Lewis the spheres seem to be topologically closed, so that a sphere can be specified by including all the worlds at least as close to the actual world as, or closer than, a given world (if such a world can be specified); cf. Lewis, p. 14. Notice that if for these examples the clarity of their outcomes on Lewis's analysis leaves something to be desired, the situation seems to be even worse regarding numerous counterfactuals whose truth values are intuitively clear: how they fare on Lewis's analysis is often unclear or even totally open (given Lewis's notion of intuitive over-all similarity). See below, sec. VI, for more on this.

49. The counterexamples of example 2 about the painted car and of example 3 concerning the coin tossing would apply to Pollock's analysis as well. His position is: pick up the worlds with minimal changes where the changes are postponed to later times as far as possible. For Pollock, α is not a P-world if for some t, the change in α_t includes the change of some appropriate β_t while P is true in β (where the changes are performed on stable propositions. The null change is included in every change.)

50. More generally, I would argue that counterfactuals are not dependent on such a notion of similarity, nor are their truth conditions context-dependent or interest-relative (apart from the normal context-dependence of the indicative versions of their antecedents and consequents). For further details, see the Epilogue, 9 III 3.

51. Under his "standard resolution of vagueness," Lewis's concern is to reject back-tracking interpretation of counterfactuals. In the Epilogue (chapter 9), I discuss briefly counterfactuals that fall under the so-called "l-p" interpretation. My approach to this kind of counterfactual approves of back-tracking of a very special

sort. It may be argued that in addition to their reading along the lines elaborated in this work (up to chapter 9), n-d type counterfactuals can also have, under certain conditions, a reading along the lines of interpretation typical of the l-p type. But even then it should be emphasized that such alternative readings need not indicate that the truth values of these counterfactuals depend on the *context* — on the beliefs and interests of their evaluators and their relative importance scales. That a construction (or notion) is, under certain circumstances, ambiguous between two readings, does not indicate that the construction (or the notion) *itself* is context-dependent, and in fact it will not be if the two different readings are not. Compare Lewis's claim that two such alternative readings reveal a context-dependence that calls for "different ways of resolving the vagueness in different contexts" (cf. his "Counterfactual Dependence and Time's Arrow," p. 457).

52. Which has so far been limited to counterfactuals of the n-d type. But the same holds as well for counterfactuals in general (apart from context-dependence and interest-relativity *within* the indicative versions of their antecedents and consequents, of course). See fn 50 and the Epilogue.

53. But one should be aware of counterfactual disputes in which the different sides are thinking of different *readings* of the same counterfactual sentence, so there is no real disagreement. Similarly, one will find plenty of cases of context-dependence in counterfactual sentences resulting from context-dependent elements in their antecedents or consequents: but in this respect the counterfactual construction is no different from any other construction. I obviously ignore such context-dependence.

54. Often such terms can be analyzed counterfactually; thus, '*a* prefers *X* to *Y*' arguably amounts to: Had *a* been forced to choose between *X* and *Y*, he would have chosen *X*.

55. *Truth, Probability and Paradox* (New York: Oxford University Press, 1973); "Counterfactuals and Causal Laws," in R. J. Butler, *Analytic Philosophy* (New York: Barnes & Noble, 1962).

56. *The Coherence Theory of Truth* (New York: Oxford University Press, 1973).

57. *The Logic of Conditionals* (Boston: D. Reidel, 1975). See also a review of this book by Ian F. Carlstrom and Christopher S. Hill, in *Philosophy of Science*, XLV (1978): 155-158.

58. *Causal Necessity* (New Haven, Conn.: Yale University Press, 1980).

59. *The Enterprise of Knowledge* (Cambridge, Mass.: MIT Press, 1980); cf also "Subjunctives, Dispositions, and Chance," *Synthese*, XXXIV (1977): 423-455.

8 Lewis Again

I Lewis's New Position

1. Thus far we have considered what was generally taken to be Lewis's position as presented in his book, *Counterfactuals*, where the similarity ordering between worlds was determined by respects (i.e., respects in which worlds can be compared with one another) whose weights are context-dependent and interest-relative; yet the similarity ordering was to fit an intuitive notion of over-all similarity.

In his later article "Counterfactual Dependence and Time's Arrow"[1] (henceforth: **CDTA**), Lewis revises this account. The general framework of his analysis of counterfactuals remains intact and still utilizes a notion of over-all similarity, but this need no longer be our intuitive "familiar notion of comparative over-all similarity" (the notion Lewis used in his *Counterfactuals*, p. 92). As before, over-all similarity is to be determined by respects of similarity which are assigned weights (or priorities). For each such respect separately, the notion of similarity utilized remains the intuitive notion. But the choice of the respects themselves and of their weights (or priorities) need no longer conform to our intuitive notion of over-all similarity: they are to be *specifically tailored* to suit the counterfactual construction. Our intuitions regarding over-all similarity will not count for much any more: our intuitions about similarity under particular respects will still count, but they will have to be weighed (or ranked) in a manner specific to the counterfactual construction.[2] Context-dependence will remain operative in judging intuitive similarity under particular respects, as well as in the selection of weights for various respects. "Overall similarity among worlds is some sort of resultant of similarities and differences of many different kinds, and I have not said what system of weights or priorities should be used to squeeze these down into a single relation of overall similarity" (CDTA, p. 465).

Now since in the revised version the notion of over-all similarity is no longer operative, what notion of similarity are we to use? Lewis tells us to use our intuitions about counterfactuals to find that similarity relation. All he seems to be committed to at this general level is that there is a similarity relation that will make his theory work. Without such a similarity relation, his theory cannot be applied to particular cases. Notice, however, that, given a particular proposal for a similarity relation, what is tested when the theory is applied to a particular case is not Lewis's general theory alone, but Lewis's theory taken *together* with this particular relation. If the combination fails to give the right results, Lewis can put the blame on the particular similarity relation chosen, rather than on his theory.

The onus of providing such an adequate similarity relation should certainly fall on proponents of Lewis's analysis, not on its critics. Without such a relation Lewis's general theory is largely inapplicable to, and thus not testable by, particular cases and not falsifiable by counterexamples. To repudiate Lewis's theory would therefore seem to require an argument to the effect that there is no such similarity relation. To achieve that, no examination of particular similarity relations will suffice. In itself, the general theory is almost empty with respect to predicting the truth values of specific counterfactuals. It has the character, not of a specific analysis counterfactuals, but rather of a framework in which particular analyses of counterfactuals are to be formulated.[3] It constitutes a commitment to the form of such an analysis. By contrast, the analysis I have proposed in this book, though limited so far to one type of counterfactuals, is fairly specific and has a relatively clear predictive capacity.

Thus Lewis's revised account seems to be a disappointing retreat from a theory that predicts the truth values of various counterfactuals to a theory that does not. But surely our long-range goal is the former kind of theory: a theory that leaves a gap so that hardly any predictions can be made is obviously of considerably less force and boldness than a theory that does have predictive capacity. A natural response may be to sit back and wait for Lewis (or someone else) to come up with an account of the similarity relation which is both testable and capable of doing the job. Yet even Lewis's general approach is open to criticism, and various suggestions he made for dealing with Kit Fine's counterexample[4] are substantial enough to make an evaluation possible. Such an evaluation will be undertaken in this chapter.

In the next section I comment on some aspects of the proposal that constitutes Lewis's response to Fine's counterexample, interpreted in the form of a weighted-similarity-respects model. In III I bring a number of counterexamples. In IV I criticize Lewis's priorities version. In V I examine a contrast of major importance between the ordering theory, which is the most general form of Lewis's approach on the one hand, and, on the other, the selection-function theory, which is the most general form of metalinguistic theories, Stalnaker's approach, and my own approach. This contrast will be brought out in what I shall call **the independence characteristic**. In VI I offer an argument to the effect that *no* ordering theory of counterfactuals will do, regardless of whether or not it uses a similarity relation of whatever sort. In the last section I defend the counterexamples of III and IV against attacks related to the issue of context-dependence.

II The Weighted-Similarity-Respects Model

1. In this section I want to take a closer look at Lewis's revised theory. The ordering of worlds is now said to be determined by weighted respects of similarity (for a particular context, relative to a given center world w_0).[5] We look at particular respects, consider intuitive similarities under these

respects, and assign weights to the respects. However, if we wish to make sense of the notion of weights and actually use the model, mere qualitative similarity relations (under respects)[6] will no longer suffice: we must now decide on *quantitative values* for the degrees of similarity between two worlds under given respects, adjust them according to the weights of these respects, and sum them up. The result will constitute a *distance* from the central world. We thus need functions of a *similarity metric* under specific respects. Surely, instead of talking about similarity functions for specific respects we can talk of dissimilarity functions for these respects; these are two sides of the same coin.

Let us then talk of a function $DS^i_{w_0}(w_1)$, a *dis*similarity function which yields a measure of the dissimilarity under respect i of the world w_1 to the world w_0. Let us also suppose that r_i is a distribution of weights to the respects i (for any i in J, the set of respects). Then one can define the distance of w_1 from w_0 $d_{w_0}(w_1)$ on Lewis's revised model, as follows:

$$(1) \quad d_{w_0}(w_1) = \sum_{i \in J}^{E} r_i DS^i_{w_0}(w_1)$$

Notice that certain items have to be specified before this can serve as a workable model: we must know the set of respects J, the distribution of weights r_i, and the dissimilarity function $DS^i_{w_0}(w_j)$. The model will be fully testable once these parameters are fully specified.

Lewis's first model suffered from a certain failure of applicability due to the vagueness of the intuitive similarity notion. But, however vague the notion of over-all similarity, we do have enough intuition about it to use Lewis's first model for various predictive purposes — for deciding the truth values of various counterfactuals. In various specific cases our intuitions about a certain kind of world's being more similar to a given world than another kind of world were sufficiently decided, and the cases sufficiently clear, for a judgment to be made. But there is no way we can use his second model unless we know the respects of similarity and possess sufficient information about the weights and the similarity function. If, for instance, we are given only a couple of respects of similarity to be weighed, without any commitment to an exhaustive list, the model is insufficiently specified to be applicable in practice: the decisive factor may be a respect that has not been given, and the truth values of particular counterfactuals cannot then be predicted. Recall that Lewis stresses that the respects he has in mind are *not* the intuitive respects used for intuitive over-all similarity judgments: so intuitions are no help in determining the relevant respects here. Nor is the model fully applicable without quantitative specification of weights, even when we possess specific similarity functions (for given respects). Notice that, in general, on this model it will not do simply to make rough judgments to the effect that one weight is greater, or much greater, than another. The weights are not just to be ordered: they are to be used to weigh numerical values yielded by the similarity function. Only in extreme cases will rough estimates of the values of the similarity functions for specific respects allow a reasonable guess by rough qualitative judgments as to the weights; this will not generally be the case. And indeed, Lewis acknowledges that this revised model "does little to predict the truth values of particular counterfactuals in particular contexts" (p. 465).

2. In his discussion of Fine, however, Lewis attempts to find a similarity relation that will be capable of handling Fine's counterexample. Lewis suggests respects of similarity and certain constraints on their weights. To what extent does Lewis succeed in handling Fine's example? If the proposed similarity respects and the constraints on their weights are to handle more than this counterexample — if they are also to cope with certain particular variations on it, then, I am afraid, they will not do.

Let us elaborate on this point. (It will also help familiarize us with the workings of this model, which will be useful in the ensuing sections.) **Fine's example** (concerning the nuclear warfare button) was as follows:

(2)   If Nixon had pressed the button, there would have been a nuclear holocaust.

This true counterfactual comes out false on Lewis's first version, which utilized intuitive over-all similarity. On the revised version, Lewis wants the analysis of counterfactuals to conform to what he dubs "Analysis 2," with over-all similarity taken as determined by respects and weights which need not be intuitive and need not yield an intuitive over-all similarity relation:

Analysis 2

A counterfactual "If it were that A, then it would be that C" is (non-vacuously) true if and only if some (accessible) world where both A and C are true is more similar to our actual world, over-all, than is any world where A is true but C is false (p. 465).

(We will see below what further concrete proposals Lewis considers necessary for dealing with Fine's counterexample.)

In order to evaluate Fine's example (under the assumption of determinism), Lewis considers five worlds that typify the worlds relevant to this example. We suppose the antecedent in Fine's counterfactual (2) pertains to time t. In w_0 (which may or may not be actual) Nixon does not press the button at t and no nuclear holocaust ever occurs, although the American nuclear machinery is in perfect condition. Counterfactual (2) is expected to be true in w_0. w_1 is a world that matches w_0 perfectly until shortly before t, when a minor miracle occurs to allow the antecedent to be true in w_1. After that, w_1 proceeds according to laws that are the same as those of w_0 (except for allowing for that small miracle). In w_1 the future after t thus differs considerably from that of w_0. w_2 is a world with exactly the same laws as w_0 (and thus no miracle), in which the antecedent is true. w_2 is thus always quite different from w_0. Next, consider w_3, which is ex-

actly like w_1 until just after t, when the antecedent occurs. Then there is
another small miracle preventing the explosion of the American nuclear
arsenal, and then this world proceeds on its lawful course (i.e., according
to the laws of w_0). Finally, w_4 is a world exactly like w_1 until just after
t, when the antecedent occurs. Then there is a major miracle, which is
what it takes to have the course of w_4 after the occurrence of the
antecedent-event match that of w_0 *perfectly*. Graphically, we can present
these worlds in Figure 1. In this graphical picture, local deviations from
the laws of w_0 are represented by small dents when small miracles are involved, and by large dents when major miracles are involved. Angular
shifts from the vertical represent major deviations from the factual history
of w_0 when they are sharp, minor deviations when they are mild. The vertical direction represents perfect match with the history of w_0.

For Fine's counterfactual to come out true in w_0, as it should, w_1 must
be closer to w_0 than w_2, w_3, and w_4, as Lewis points out.[7] But in terms
of intuitive over-all similarity, w_3 seems more similar to w_0 than w_1 does.

In his book Lewis mentions two respects of similarity: laws and facts
(pp. 75-77). (He toys with the possibility of distinguishing earlier from
later similarities of facts, but in the end does not endorse it.) For these two
respects (call them 'L' and 'F'), the distance function $d_{w_0}(w_i)$ will be:

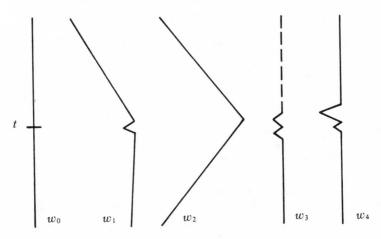

Figure 1

(3) $d_{w_0}(w_i) = r_L \mathrm{DS}_{w_0}^L(w_i) + r_F \mathrm{DS}_{w_0}^F(w_i)$

Now, on his revised approach, given these as the relevant respects of similarity, Lewis would, in order to have w_1 closer than w_2 to w_0, need to arrange his weights so as to have considerable factual similarity add enough closeness to w_0 to offset a small miracle. But merely doing that will not suffice to render w_3 further than w_1 from w_0, since the considerable gain in factual similarity in w_3 (over w_1) would outweigh its small additional miracle. Thus, not only does Fine's example constitute a counterexample to Lewis's original theory, understood as having an intuitively determined notion of over-all similarity, it also constitutes a counterexample to the more refined model of weighted respects of similarity when restricted to the two respects, laws and facts, which Lewis mentioned in his book (and even when not necessarily intuitive weights are used for these two respects). To rule this out, Lewis believes he needs a respect of *perfect match*. This, I am willing to argue, cannot qualify as a similarity respect. But I will not address myself to this issue here, and will ignore this point in the discussion below.[8]

3. To cope with this counterexample, Lewis suggests certain respects and constraints on their weights. He says:

> That means that a similarity relation that combines with
> Analysis 2 to give the correct truth conditions for counterfactuals
> such as the one we have considered, taken under the standard
> resolution of vagueness, must be governed by the following
> system of weights or priorities.
> (I) It is of the first importance to avoid big, widespread, diverse
> violations of law.
> (II) It is of the second importance to maximize the spatiotem-
> poral region throughout which perfect match of particular fact
> prevails.
> (III) It is of the third importance to avoid even small, localized,
> simple violations of law.
> (IV) It is of little or no importance to secure approximate similar-
> ity of particular facts, even in matters that concern us greatly.[9]

(I shall refer to these constraints as **conditions I - IV**.)
Lewis thus does not commit himself on whether similarity (short of a perfect match) of particular facts should have any weight at all. Since he does not use it as a similarity respect in his discussion of Fine's example, neither will we. Conditions I - III now (using '**PM**' for the "perfect match" respect) yield 'L' and 'PM' as the relevant similarity respects. The corresponding dissimilarity function will therefore be:

(4) $d_{w_0}(w_i) = r_L \mathrm{DS}_{w_0}^L(w_i) + r_{PM} \mathrm{DS}_{w_0}^{PM}(w_i)$

Notice that these conditions should be interpreted as constraints on the coefficients r_L and r_{PM}. Thus, making the avoidance of small miracles count as of less importance than securing a lot of perfect match reflects Lewis's dictum that "a lot of perfect match of particular fact is worth a little miracle" (p. 469), which yields the result that, in the ranking of weights, condition II comes before III, and should be translatable into a constraint on r_L and r_{PM}. But which constraint? It must mean that the contribution to distance of a small miracle is smaller than the contribution to distance of considerable lack of "perfect-match." That is, that the value of $r_L DS^L_{w_0}(w_i)$ for a small value of $DS^L_{w_0}(w_i)$ is less than that of $r_{PM}DS^{PM}_{w_0}(w_i)$ for a medium value of $DS^{PM}_{w_0}(w_i)$. [Thus, it would be "worth" trading the distance contribution of the latter for the distance contribution of the former. Notice that w_1 is closer to w_0 than w_2 owing to the perfect match of w_1 (with w_0) prior to t (which w_2 does not have), which outweighs the small miracle of w_1 (which w_2 doesn't have). Since the difference in perfect match between w_1 and w_2 applies to "half" a history only, rather than to the whole history, it should yield a "medium" value on the perfect-match dissimilarity scale.]

4. In the next section I will discuss Lewis's revised analysis as expressed in conditions I - IV. But first I want to concentrate upon his choice of laws and perfect match as the salient respects, coupled with his desideratum that Fine's example come out true, as indeed it should. Now for his analysis of Fine's example to come out right it is necessary that w_1 be closer to w_0 than w_4; that is: $d_{w_0}(w_1) < d_{w_0}(w_4)$. This yields [via (4), omitting the constant relativization for w_0 for simplicity]:

(5) $r_L DS^L(w_1) + r_{PM}DS^{PM}(w_1) < r_L DS^L(w_4) + r_{PM}DS^{PM}(w_4)$

i.e.[10]:

(6) $$\dfrac{DS^{PM}(w_1)}{DS^L(w_4)} - \dfrac{DS^{PM}(w_4)}{DS^L(w_1)} < \dfrac{r_L}{r_{PM}}$$

Let us call the expression on the left $DS(w_1, w_4)$. (6) can then be expressed as:

(7) $DS(w_1, w_4) < \dfrac{r_L}{r_{PM}}$

But suppose we modify Fine's example. Keeping w_0 as described by Lewis, i.e., with a faultless nuclear-attack system,[11] the following counterfactual will be true in it if Fine's is:

Example 1

(8)   Had Bjorn Borg pushed the nuclear button while the nuclear attack system remained faultless and fully automatic, there would have been a nuclear holocaust.

But to incorporate the truth of the antecedent here will take a major miracle. Let us call the analogues of $w_1 - w_4$ here $w_1' - w_4'$. They will differ from $w_1 - w_4$ in that, instead of a small miracle at t, they will have a major miracle at t. Still, for this counterfactual to come out true, the analogues $w_2' - w_4'$ must be more distant from w_0 than the analogue w_1' of w_1', as was the case in Fine's example.

Hence, for counterfactual (8) to come out true, one necessary condition is that w_1' be closer to w_0 than w_2' is.[12] Hence it must be the case that

$$r_L DS^L(w_1') + r_{PM} DS^{PM}(w_1') < r_L DS^L(w_2') + r_{PM} DS^{PM}(w_2')$$

i.e.,

(9) $\quad \dfrac{r_L}{r_{PM}} < \dfrac{DS^{PM}(w_2') - DS^{PM}(w_1')}{DS^L(w_1') - DS^L(w_2')}$

In accordance with our previous notation, the expression on the right-hand side in (9) is $DS(w_2', w_1')$. What we have then is:

(10) $\quad \dfrac{r_L}{r_{PM}} < DS(w_2', w_1')$

Hence, conditions (8) and (9) (which are *necessary* for these two counterfactuals to come out right) together yield:

(11) $\quad \dfrac{DS^{PM}(w_1) - DS^{PM}(w_4)}{DS^L(w_4) - DS^L(w_1)} < \dfrac{r_L}{r_{PM}} < \dfrac{DS^{PM}(w_2') - DS^{PM}(w_1')}{DS^L(w_1') - DS^L(w_2')}$

or [see (7) and (10)]:

(12) $\quad DS(w_1, w_4) < DS(w_2', w_1')$

Now $DS^{PM}(w_2') - DS^{PM}(w_1')$ and $DS^{PM}(w_1) - DS^{PM}(w_4)$ are of about the same value: in both the difference in perfect match involves an infinite stretch running to $+\infty$ with one end around t. Now in view of the kind of neutralizing miracle it takes to cancel out the effects of Nixon pushing the button in Fine's example, I chose example 1 so as to have the miracle it takes to allow for its antecedent to be a *larger* miracle. [Recall that what it takes (in w_4) to neutralize the pushing of the button by Nixon is the interruption of the signal and the elimination of all traces of the button-pushing, a smaller miracle than what it would take to allow Bjorn Borg access to the button.[13] Also notice that Lewis is still committed to *intuitive similarity under respects*, so that the intuition that the major miracle at t in example 1 is greater than the canceling miracle in w_4 at $t + \Delta t$ in Fine's example will have to be honored.]

The denominator in $DS(w_1, w_4)$ measures the distance contribution of the major neutralizing miracle of w_4 (the miracle at t cancels out). The denominator in $DS(w_2', w_1')$ measures the distance contribution of the *very major* miracle it takes to allow for the antecedent of the new counterfactual (8), which is *greater* than that of the major neutralizing miracle of w_4. Hence the denominator of $DS(w_2',w_1')$ is now *greater* than that of $DS(w_1,w_4)$. Hence surely DS (w_2',w_1') is *smaller* than $DS(w_1,w_4)$. But for each counterfactual to pass as true, as we saw in (7) and (10), under these respects, it must be the case that $\frac{r_L}{r_{PM}} < DS(w_2',w_1')$, and also the case that $DS(w_1,w_4) < \frac{r_L}{r_{PM}}$, which entail (12); i.e., $DS(w_1,w_4) < DS(w_2',w_1')$. But, as we have just seen, $DS(w_2',w_1') < DS(w_1,w_4)$, and this is a clear contradiction.

So what we have shown (before getting into the details of conditions I - IV, which constitute constraints on the coefficients r_L and r_{PM}), is that the choice of L and PM as the respects to be used in the weighted-similarity-respects model is incompatible with the desideratum of not having either Fine's example or example 1 clearly come out wrong.

III Counterexamples

1. I now turn to Lewis's weighted-similarity-respects model as expressed in conditions I - IV above. This model faces still other difficulties over and above those discussed in the preceding section: the choice of respects and the general constraints Lewis puts on the weights via these conditions will not do, as the following examples seem to show.

Example 2.   Consider a counterfactual of the following sort:

(13)   Had Nixon had more hair at t than he actually had, he would have had one more hair at t.

This counterfactual is obviously false. Like Fine's counterfactual, counterfactual (13) constitutes a counterexample to Lewis's original theory of intuitive over-all similarity, discussed in chapter 7. The false counterfactual (13) comes out true according to that theory, since in the respect of number of hairs on Nixon's head, antecedent-worlds in which he had just one more hair than he actually did have will be closer to the actual world than worlds in which he had more than one hair, and there will be nothing else that will systematically differentiate worlds of the first sort from worlds of the second sort. Hence the greatest lower bound of distances from the actual world of worlds of the first sort will be smaller than the greatest lower bound of distances from the actual world of worlds of the second sort. There will be a sphere around the actual world with worlds of the first sort, but with no worlds of the second sort, which will make counterfactual (13) come out true.

However, although Lewis's revised model avoids Fine's counterexample, it does not avoid this one. In order to evaluate it according to Lewis's model, compare to the actual world w_0 a world w_1 in which Nixon, via a small miracle, had at t one more hair than he actually had, and which from t on developed according to the laws it shares with w_0 (except for that small miracle), and which up to t is perfectly matched with the history of the actual world.

Now consider a world w_n, which also has the same history up to t, but which has a different minor miracle at t (though less minor than that of w_1), whereby Nixon at t has n more hairs on his head.[14] After t, w_n continues according to the laws of w_0. Recall that, as explained in section II, the distance function (from w_0) to be associated with Lewis's account was:

$$d(w_n) = r_L DS^L(w_n) + r_{PM} DS^{PM}(w_n)$$

Now surely $DS^L(w_n)$ is greater the higher n is—it takes more of a miracle (though perhaps only a tiny bit more) for Nixon to have n more hairs the higher n is. Yet $DS^{PM}(w_n)$ is exactly the same for every $n > 0$: there is a perfect match with w_0 in all these worlds right up to t, and only then. Hence $d(w_n)$ is greater, the greater n is. Hence the closest antecedent worlds to the actual world will be those with Nixon having just one more hair $(n=1)$, thus making the false counterfactual (13) come out true. (Notice that, given Lewis's considerations concerning Fine's example, it would take more than a small miracle to restore perfect match after t, and so such worlds, with the antecedent of (13) true, will be further from w_0 than our w_n.)

Notice that if (in addition to perfect match) we also take factual similarity into account as another respect of similarity, giving it positive weight, the situation will not change: w_1 is more similar in particular facts to w_0 than any w_n, for $n > 1$. Thus Lewis's model fails, given the respects it involves (laws and perfect match), and would still fail even with a factual-similarity respect, in view of constraints I - IV regardless of what the similarity function under the respects is (as long as it is intuitive enough).[15]

2. Consider the following counterfactual antecedent:

Had the law of gravitation changed greatly at t, . . .

Compare w_1 in which the law of gravitation as it actually is (in w_0) is retained up to t along with the other laws and the factual history, but in which there is a very different gravitational constant from t on; and w_2, which is identical with w_1 until shortly *after* t, when the gravitational law reverts to what it actually is.

Note that, for Lewis, "It is of first importance to avoid big, widespread, diverse violation of law" (p. 472). In this respect w_2 does better than w_1: in both we have a miracle at t, but in w_1 we have a continuing, thus "widespread," violation (compared with the actual world w_0) which goes on after w_2 has returned to the actual law of gravitation; in w_2, on the other hand, the violation of law (compared, of course, with the actual world) occurs only around t. In both worlds there will be no perfect match of facts after t. But with respects to the *laws*, the law of gravitation in w_2 is much more similar to that of the actual world than the law in w_1 is. (Notice that, for Lewis, *relative* to a given respect, the similarity relation must be intuitive — otherwise his use of 'similarity' rather than 'some ordering relation' is wholly empty.) The avoidance of major, widespread changes in the laws is the most important respect for Lewis. Since in neither world are we going to have a perfect match after t,[16] these two worlds are going to fare equally in the respect of perfect match. The following counterfactual would therefore be true for Lewis:

Example 3

(14)   Had the law of gravitation changed greatly at t, at some later time it would have changed back to what it actually was.

This, however, I take to be a false counterfactual.
    The same point can also be made by considering the following variation of the above example:

Example 3'

(15)   Had the law of gravitation been very different at t from what it actually is, it would still have been what it actually is at times sufficiently later than t.

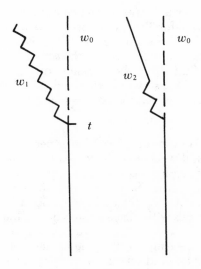

Figure 2

This counterfactual is also false. But imagine a world w_1 where the law of gravitation is very different from that of the actual world at t, and then undergoes a major change, becoming what it actually is. Compare it with w_2 where the law of gravitation is very different at t and remains so at all later times. Now intuitively it seems clear that a law of gravitation which is the same as the actual law at all times after $t + \Delta t$ is more similar to the actual law than a law of gravity very different from the actual law at all times after t. In view of Lewis's highest priority of avoiding widespread diverse, major difference in laws (and his third priority of avoiding even small and simple violations of laws), this counterfactual (15) should come out true for Lewis.[17]

3. According to Lewis, more perfect match yields smaller distance from the actual world. So when a counterfactual antecedent involves an existential quantification over time, the worlds that count are those which maximize perfect match as much as the antecedent allows. This, however, will yield a distorted construal of the counterfactual antecedent. To see this, consider the following:

Example 4

(16)   Had Harry Truman become a devout Catholic at some point in his adult life, he would have died shortly afterward.

This is false, but for Lewis it is true, since presumably it would take as much of a minor miracle for Truman to become a devout Catholic at one point in his (adult) life as at any other. But then worlds in which he becomes a Catholic later would be closer to the actual world than worlds in which he becomes a Catholic earlier, because of the gain of a stretch of perfect match, and the closest worlds will be those in which he converted shortly before he died, in which the perfect-match stretch would be maximal.[18]

4. Now as we noted, Lewis considers a lot of perfect match to be worth a small miracle. Thus, if we were to have a case in which, in some world, a small miracle after the antecedent's occurrence would restore perfect match with the actual world, the resulting sort of world would be closer to the actual world than the original which has no such miracle. This will make true counterfactuals with such an antecedent if their consequents are tailored to reflect such a small miracle. Now Lewis would apparently expect that restoring perfect match with the actual world after the occurrence of the antecedent would take a major miracle, even if all that was required to allow for the antecedent was a minor miracle. I shall now try to construct a case in which a minor miracle will be sufficient to restore perfect match.

Consider the following example. Suppose we have, in a world w_0 in which we evaluate our counterfactual, an isolated system — a tiny hollow black box with an electromagnetic field and an electron traveling in it in a vacuum.[19] Imagine a world w_1 which is identical with w_0 up to time t, but in which the position of the electron at t is changed in comparison with what it is in w_0, and other aspects of this isolated system are also adjusted so that when (via a small miracle relative to the laws of w_0) a minor shove of the electron occurs in w_1 at $t + \Delta t$ putting it back at the position where it is then in fact in w_0 (in which the counterfactual is evaluated) with the same momentum, and the system from $t, + \Delta t$ on continues on exactly the same course as it does in w_0, w_1 after $t + \Delta t$ enjoys a perfect match with w_0. Consider the hypothesis that includes the change in position of the electron at t plus the adjustment mentioned, but *not* the minor shove of the electron back to its w_0 state. Then consider a world w_2, which enjoys perfect match with w_1 up to (including) t, in which this hypothesis is true but in which the adjusting shove of the electron back to its w_0 state at $t + \Delta t$ does *not* occur. (In w_1, *in addition* to the truth of this hypothesis, at $t + \Delta t$ the electron is shoved back to its position in w_0.) Now consider the following counterfactual:

Example 5

(17) Had the above hypothesis been true, the world after $t + \Delta t$ would have been exactly as it actually is.

Evaluated in w_0, I take this to be false. (Recall that the minor shove bringing the electron back to its original position is *not* part of this hypothesis.) But take w_2, in which the hypothesis is true, and in which after t (and before t, yet not at t) the world proceeds by the lawful nature of w_0: w_2 will be different from w_0 from t onward. Now consider w_1, which is exactly like w_2 up to and including t, but where the tiny shove occurs at $t + \Delta t$, switching the state of the electron back to where it is then in w_0. Surely this little shove of an electron would count as a minor miracle. Now w_1 has a lot more perfect match with the actual world than w_2 (that is, at all times after $t + \Delta t$, whereas w_2 has no perfect match after t) at the price of a little miracle — the "balancing shove" it takes to bring the electron back to its w_0 state at $t + \Delta t$. So w_1 should be closer to w_0 than w_2 is, according to Lewis, since "a small miracle is worth a lot of perfect match." Thus the above counterfactual would come out true, but it should not.

5. Another type of counterfactual for which Lewis's conditions will not work is one which the antecedent A requires a major miracle to fit the prior history of a deterministic world. Here the choice is between a world like w_1 in Lewis's discussion of Fine's example (cf. II above), where the history up to around t_A is identical with that of the actual world, followed by a major (rather than a minor) miracle which allows for the antecedent; or between a world like w_2 (cf. II) where the laws are identical with those of the actual world, but the prior history must be radically different all the way to the infinite past. In the discussion of Fine's example in section II, a world like w_1 there (with a *minor* miracle) could be kept

closer than w_2 to the world in which the counterfactual was evaluated since a minor miracle is worth a lot of perfect match. But here it would take a major miracle to secure a perfect match, which Lewis cannot allow, since he would then have to prefer w_4 to w_1 in his discussion of Fine's example (cf. II again), which would make Fine's counterfactual false. Hence, in a case of the sort discussed here, in which a major miracle would be required to reconcile the antecedent with its prior history, w_2 must be closer to w_0 than w_1, since a lot of perfect match isn't worth a major miracle.

But in worlds like w_2 we don't have any handle over the past: we no longer retain any past history. Consider an example:

Example 6

(18)   Had 6 million European Jews immigrated to Palestine during the 1920s, a massacre of millions of Jews would not have occurred in Europe in the course of the Second World War.

I take this counterfactual to be true.[20]

But for this antecedent to be true in a deterministic world with the actual prior history intact, it would take a very major miracle. (Recall: for Lewis, erasure of the traces of Nixon's futile pushing of the button would count as a major miracle; here we are dealing with a miracle more major in orders of magnitude.) Hence the kind of world in which no miracles occur but the past history is very different would be closer to the actual world than worlds with perfect match (up to the antecedent time) and a major miracle. But with such worlds in mind there is no reason to expect this counterfactual to come out true: the histories that would yield the antecedent under the laws we have may vary wildly. In some, for example, there would have been 10 (rather than 6) million Jews in Europe, 6 million of which would have immigrated to Palestine and the rest would have been massacred. Thus, true counterfactuals such as the above need not come out true on Lewis's model.[21] This would be typical of the class of counterfactuals with antecedents which it would take a major miracle to bring about.[22]

IV   *The Priorities Model*

1. Now Lewis may claim that he is not exclusively committed to the weighted-similarity-respects model; that what he committed himself to was "weights or priorities" (pp. 465, 472). We have seen what a weighted-similarity-respects model would look like. How would a priorities model look?

Construing his conditions I - IV as determining priorities, the ordering of possible worlds would seem to work as follows: If you compare two worlds for their distances from the center world, check to see how they fare under the respect of the highest priority (the avoidance of major miracles). If one world avoids major miracles but the other does not, the first is closer than the second. If they both do — or both do not — but to different degrees, the closer world is the one that fares better under this respect (i.e., the one that has less major miracles than the other). If they avoid major miracles to the same degree, move down one priority and repeat the process. Let us call this version I. Another version of the ordering under conditions I - IV could be: if both worlds under comparison have major miracles or if both don't, move to the second priority *without* comparing how well they fare under this highest priority. Call this version II.

This way of ordering worlds thus involves comparing two worlds under a given priority-respect and, in the case of a tie, moving to a comparison under a lower priority. When there is no tie under a given priority, lower priorities are irrelevant. This model frees us from weights and heavy reliance on quantitative measures, and is thus more fully specified than the weighted-similarity-respects interpretation of conditions I - IV.

But this model, with priorities I - IV, still will not do. Recall the false counterfactual (13): Had Nixon had more hair at t than he actually had, he would have had one more hair. To accommodate the antecedent of such a counterfactual, only a minor miracle is needed, which allows for perfect match until about the antecedent time. As before, it would take a major miracle to restore perfect match afterwards; but such a perfect match would not be worth a major miracle. So we are down to considering worlds with lawful regularity as in the actual world after and before the necessary minor miracle, with perfect match before it, and no perfect match after it, worlds in which Nixon has one extra hair, two extra hairs, etc. These worlds would all fit the first two priorities: avoiding major miracles and maximizing perfect match (short of introducing major miracles). Now on version I, it would take a smaller miracle to provide Nixon with one extra hair than with two or more. Hence, on this version counterfactual (13) would come out true; therefore this version will not do. (On version II, worlds with various small miracles that would provide Nixon with several extra hairs would be on a par.)

Version I of the priorities model is also in trouble regarding other kinds of examples (and, as in the above example, regardless of whether similarity of particular facts is regarded as of lower priority than I - III or whether it is not taken into account at all). Recall example 3′ of the previous section, and its false counterfactual (15); all worlds in which the antecedent is true would have to involve, at the very least, a major difference (from the actual world) with respect to their laws (in comparison with the actual world). But on version I of the priorities model this counterfactual would come out true, since there is less of a major miracle (or major difference) in a law that breaks with ours at t but coincides with it later than there is in a law that continues to differ from ours from t onward (the former difference is less "widespread"). For similar reasons example 4 in III above would also be a counterexample to version I.[23]

2. Let us move on to version II. If Lewis opts for granting no priority to similarity of particular facts, then our counterfactual 2(5) concerning the

stock market (2 III, example 3) will serve as a counterexample. Counterfactual 2(5) was: If Jones had not sold his stock, he would have become rich a few weeks later. Taking our world (the one in which the counterfactual is evaluated) to be nondeterministic, the closest antecedent worlds under priorities I - III will require no miracle, major or minor, for incorporating the antecedent and preserving the prior history, and will allow the subsequent history (after the antecedent-time) to run its lawful course. In the example under consideration, the subsequent actual rise in the stock market was in fact undetermined by the history prior to the antecedent-time. Therefore, if we do not grant priority to similarity of particular facts, counterfactual 2(5), which is true, will turn out false, since worlds in which no rise in the stock market occurs would be equally close to the world in which the counterfactual is evaluated as worlds in which there is a rise.

But if we do take into account the similarity respect of particular facts (condition IV), we run into trouble with example 3 of 7 IV concerning the flipping of the coin. There the counterfactual was 7(5): Had I flipped the coin with my left hand, it would still have come out heads. Two worlds in which the coin was flipped with the left hand, in one coming down heads and in the other tails (both with no miracles and with perfect match up to the antecedent time), would fit the first three priorities equally well. But giving priority to the respect of similarity of particular facts would make counterfactual 7(5) come out true, though it should not.

Notice also that example 6 of the previous section (the one involving 6 million Jews in Palestine) is also a counterexample to the (two versions of the) priorities model.[24] The antecedent of counterfactual (18) there can be true in a world like w_2 (in Lewis's discussion of Fine's example), without any major miracle, but with no perfect match of the prior history either. Such a world will fare better on the priorities model than a world that preserves some prior history at the price of a major miracle. This true counterfactual will not, then, come out true on the priorities model in either version (thus reflecting a typical syndrome of back-tracking).[25]

Hence I conclude that the two versions of Lewis's priorities analysis will do no better than the weighted-similarity-respects version. Both options share certain features: first, use of perfect match as a similarity respect, and second, the ordering of worlds according to context, but independently of this or that counterfactual. The second feature is also shared by the intuitive over-all-similarity approach of Lewis's book. The first feature is central to the particular suggestions Lewis makes in his article and to the way he responds to Fine's example. Both features, I believe, lead his analysis into trouble and must be given up. However, in this critical analysis I will not dwell on the use of perfect match as a similarity respect,[26] and will concentrate in the rest of this chapter on the more fundamental second feature. (For convenience I shall often refer below only to the option of weighted-similarity-respects, but all that will be said applies *mutatis mutandis* to the priorities model as well.)

V   *The Ordering Theory versus*
    the Selection-Function Theory

1. I now want to discuss a fundamental difference between Lewis's theory and my own. To facilitate this discussion I will first outline the skeletal forms of a couple of major theories of counterfactuals.

One general theory of counterfactuals can be called the **ordering theory (OT)**. According to OT, there is an ordering relation (perhaps context-dependent) such that, for any three worlds i, j, k, either j and k are equally close to i, or one of them is closer to i than the other, thus allowing for a system of spheres around world i (in Lewis's sense). A counterfactual $A > B$ is true at i (in case A is true in some world under consideration, relative to i) iff B is true in all the A-worlds in some sphere of worlds (containing an A-world) around i (under that ordering). This is the general framework of Lewis's account. One particular respect in which his theory is more specific is that the ordering is taken as a relation of weighted similarities under certain respects, yielding the **weighted-similarity-respects theory (WSRT)**.[27] WSRT is thus a special case of OT.

The general theory of counterfactuals to be contrasted with OT is the **selection-function theory (SFT)**. According to this theory, there is a selection function f, whose arguments are worlds (from among those under consideration), and which selects sets of worlds as values. A counterfactual $A > B$ is true (in world i) in case B is true in all the A-worlds selected by f (for i).[28]

Stalnaker's theory is a special case of SFT, in that his selection function f is supposed to pick out a single world.

Now an important feature that a particular SFT f may or may not have is that of taking as an argument the counterfactual being evaluated. f may select different sets of worlds for i depending on the counterfactual being evaluated, or it may select a set of worlds for i regardless of which counterfactual is being evaluated, and thus be *independent* of any particular counterfactual (or any feature of it). We will call the characteristic of a selection function f, that it is independent of the counterfactual being evaluated, the **independence characteristic (IC)**. Thus, an SFT may or may not possess IC. (Of course, Stalnaker's theory does not possess IC, since according to it the counterfactual being evaluated is an argument of the selection function.[29])

An important feature of OT, and thus of WSRT, is that the ordering of worlds is independent of any particular counterfactual. This feature is crucial for Lewis's account, since it is essential in guaranteeing the picture of spheres which characterizes his theory. This system of spheres is fixed (for a given context) independently of particular counterfactuals. This is because the similarity relation that governs the ordering relation is independent of any particular counterfactual (though it may be dependent on context). If the ordering relation were a function of the counterfactual being evaluated, the spheres would change with each counterfactual. That the ordering is independent of particular counterfactuals constitutes the independence characteristic for OT. IC is thus a feature of OT, of Lewis's WSRT, and of Lewis's particular suggestions concerning the respects and the weights or priorities of conditions I - IV discussed above.

2. According to the *metalinguistic theory*, $A > B$ is true iff B is inferable from some set of true statements Z (fulfilling a certain constraint) together with A. My own account of counterfactuals of the n-d type is a special case of the metalinguistic theory. For Goodman, this constraint included the requirement of cotenability with A.

Let the **generalized metalinguistic theory** be the metalinguistic theory without the requirement that the requisite "extra premises" be true. The **multiply generalized metalinguistic theory (MGMT)** will require several such sets Z_i. Thus, on MGMT a counterfactual $A > B$ is true iff, for certain sets Z_i (specified in a certain way), $\{A\} \cup Z_i \rightarrow B$ for each such Z_i. (As I shall indicate in the Epilogue, my general position concerning counterfactuals is a case of MGMT.)

Instead of talking about possible worlds we can talk about possible-world descriptions, as we did above: we can thus talk of OT and SFT involving possible-world descriptions. The metalinguistic theory, the generalized metalinguistic theory, and MGMT are more naturally couched within a framework of possible-world descriptions than within a possible-worlds framework. Viewed this way, they are special cases of SFT. Thus, for the metalinguistic theory, the selection function will select possible-world descriptions in which the set of (true) implicit premises and A are true, and similarly for the generalized metalinguistic theory. For MGMT, the selection function will choose possible-world descriptions in each of which one such set Z_i and A are true. Of course, every model of the metalinguistic theory is a generalized-metalinguistic-theory model, and every generalized-metalinguistic-theory-model is an MGMT model, and all are SFT models. In what follows all that will be said concerning OT and SFT will hold regardless of whether we adopt the possible-world descriptions approach or the possible-worlds approach.

OT and SFT are general frameworks: they do not determine the truth value of any particular counterfactual. Models of these theories will be specific theories that fall under them. Two models will be equivalent just in case they give the same counterfactuals the same truth values. Two general theories will be equivalent iff every model of the one is equivalent to some model of the other.

3. It is quite clear that every model of SFT *with* IC is equivalent to some model of OT. To see this, if f is a selection function of a model of SFT with IC, choose the following ordering: all the worlds in the scope of f will be equally close to the central world, and closer than all other worlds, which themselves will also be equally close to the central world. This will give us just two spheres, or neighborhoods, in addition to the central world.[30]

It is also clear that every model of OT is equivalent to a model of SFT *without* IC. This is so since one can choose a selection function that will select an $A\&B$-world if there is an A-fulfilling neighborhood whose A-worlds are B-worlds or, otherwise, will select an $A\&\sim B$-world. Such an SFT model will be *parasitic* on OT in the sense that the values of the selection function will be computed via a certain ordering on the possible worlds involved.

Notice that, for any selection function f belonging to an SFT model with sets of worlds as its values, there is a selection function f' belonging to an equivalent SFT model *without* IC with single worlds as its values.[31] Thus, if for a given counterfactual $A > B$, B is true in all the A-worlds in the scope[32] of f (provided it includes A-worlds, or in all A-worlds otherwise), let f' pick out some $A\&B$-world; otherwise, let it pick out an $A\&\sim B$-world.[33] Of course, the set of SFT models without IC with selection functions that pick out single worlds as values is a subset of the set of SFT models without IC. Thus, the set of SFT models is *represented* by SFT models without IC with selection functions that pick out one world only (in the sense that, for every model of the former set, there is an equivalent model of the latter sort and vice versa).

Now in the standard conception of the metalinguistic theory, the restriction placed on the implicit premises is typically a function of A. This is especially so on my own theory, where the set $\mathrm{CIP}(A, W_{\bar{t}B})$, which depends on A (and $\bar{t}_B$), must be preserved.[34] Hence, various metalinguistic theories are cases of SFT *without* IC. It seems therefore that many metalinguistic theories cannot be accommodated under OT; i.e., that there are no OT models euqivalent to them, since OT possesses IC. Recall: every SFT model *with* IC has an equivalent OT model, and every OT model has an equivalent SFT model *without* IC. But it is on the question of whether every SFT model *without* IC has an equivalent OT model that the viability of my claim that metalinguistic theories cannot be accommodated under OT depends. I want to answer this question *negatively*, and so suggest that my own model, along with various metalinguistic theories, does not have an equivalent OT model. If so — and if I am right in insisting on the retention of a set of statements such as $\mathrm{CIP}(A, W_{\bar{t}B})$, with a strong dependence on A in an SFT-model of counterfactuals — it is plausible that OT is false. (In particular, then, Lewis's weighted-similarity-respects theory, as a special case of OT, will be false.)

4. *Theorem*

Some SFT models without IC (in particular, some generalized metalinguistic theory models) do not have equivalent OT models.

Proof

Assume we have an implicit premises function f of a generalized metalinguistic model (i.e., a function whose values are the implicit premises for a given counterfactual). If A_1, A_2 are false (though possible) in the actual world and if $A_1 > B_1$ and $A_2 > B_2$

are counterfactuals which are made true by f (in the actual world),[35] then, for some statements C_1 and C_2,[36]

(19) $f(A_1 > B_1) = C_1$
      $f(A_2 > B_2) = C_2$

and so:

(20) A_1 & $C_1 \rightarrow B_1$
      A_2 & $C_2 \rightarrow B_2$

(The values of f are the sets of implicit premises; let us assume for simplicity that they are finite, so that we can take C_1 and C_2 to be their conjunctions.[37]) Assume that C_1 and C_2 are not logically equivalent, thus depriving this SFT model of IC. Assume, too, that the implicit-premises function chooses, for some such $A_1 > B_1$ and $A_2 > B_2$, C_1 and C_2 which fulfill the following (recall that C_i may include law statements as well):

(21) C_1 & $C_2 \rightarrow \sim A_1$ & $\sim A_2$

(22) $\sim C_1$ & $\sim C_2 \rightarrow A \sim A_1$ & $\sim A_2$

We will try to ascertain whether there are orderings that will yield OT models equivalent to an SFT model such as the above, thus making both counterfactuals true. This being our goal, our investigation can be limited to A_1-worlds and A_2-worlds. (21) and (22) are thus facilitating assumptions allowing us to limit our investigation to worlds in which either C_1 & $\sim C_2$ or C_2 & $\sim C_1$ are true, and to try and find out whether there is an ordering on *them* that makes the counterfactuals $A_i > B_i$ true. (If there is, it can then be extended to an ordering on the rest of the worlds, which will also make these counterfactuals true.) Let us also assume for C_1 and C_2 that:[38]

(23) $C_1 \rightarrow A_2$ & $\sim B_2$

(24) $C_2 \rightarrow A_1$ & $\sim B_1$

Clearly requirements (21) - (24) are consistent, and so there are SFT models that fulfill them all.

Now if there were an ordering that would make $A_1 > B_1$ and $A_2 > B_2$ true, there would have to be a sphere substantiating $A_1 > B_1$, i.e., a sphere β_1 containing A_1-world w_1, all of whose A_1-worlds are B_1-worlds; and there would have to be a sphere substantiating $A_2 > B_2$, that is, a sphere β_2 containing an A_2-world w_2, all of whose A_2-worlds are B_2-worlds. By assumption (22), in both w_1 and w_2 either C_1 or C_2 must be true. By assumption (24), C_2 cannot be true in w_1, and hence C_1 must be true in it. Hence a sphere β_1 making $A_1 > B_1$ true must have a world w_1 in which $A_1 \& B_1 \& C_1$ is true. Similarly, by assumption (23), C_1 cannot be true in w_2; hence [by (22)] C_2 must be true in it. Hence a sphere β_2 which makes $A_2 > B_2$ true must contain a world w_2 in which $A_2 \& B_2 \& C_2$ is true.

Now because of the way worlds in OT models are ordered, either $\beta_1 \subseteq \beta_2$ or $\beta_2 \subseteq \beta_1$. Hence one of them contains both w_1 and w_2. But [by assumption (23)] w_1 is an $A_2 \& \sim B_2$-world, and [by assumption (24)] w_2 is an $A_1 \& \sim B_1$-world. Hence this sphere substantiates *neither* one of the counterfactuals $A_i > B_i$; but we assumed that it substantiated one of them. Contradiction.

Q.E.D.

What we have shown is that there are SFT models [without IC, since different C_i's are chosen for different counterfactuals, in view of (21) and (22)[39], which are not OT models. In particular, we have shown that some generalized metalinguistic models and, hence, some multiply generalized metalinguistic models, are not OT models.

5. Much of our discussion in previous chapters concerned counterfactuals of the n-d type (in a nondeterministic world, of course). I would like to point out that such counterfactuals fare badly under Lewis's weighted-similarity-respects model with the weights determined in accordance with conditions I - IV (see section II above), in a way which reflects the importance of a major component of the analysis I have proposed in this book. According to Lewis's model, the closest antecedent-worlds (for such counterfactuals) involve no major miracles (for Lewis "it is of the first importance" to avoid major miracles). Perfect match with the past history prior to the antecedent-time, and with it only, is also ensured for such counterfactuals in the closest antecedent-worlds, since perfect match is for Lewis "of the second importance," and since, on his reasoning (as in his discussion of Fine's example), no small miracle would suffice to yield perfect match after that time. So far we are in agreement with Lewis. Now if priorities I - III are the only constraints on the ordering of worlds, that is, if, in particular, similarity of particular facts is ignored, then our emphasis on the importance of the set $CIP(A, W_{\bar{t}_B})$ goes unheeded here, and true counterfactuals such as 2(5), concerning the stock market ('If Jones had not sold his stock, he would have become rich a few weeks later'; see 2 III, example 3) become false. This is so since retention of, say, the rise in the stock market, would have no weight here, and would not affect distance, and thus there would be as-close-as-you-can-get antecedent worlds with no rise in the stock market.[40] This example then becomes a counterexample to Lewis's analysis. If, on the other hand, Lewis decides to give weight to over-all similarity of particular facts, then, in handling the (t_A, t_B) interval he will be faced with the problem of the bias toward semifactuals discussed above (7 IV) which manifested itself in the car and coin-tossing examples (examples 2 and 3), which would then, in turn,

become counterexamples to his analysis. The respect of over-all similarity of facts cannot, by itself, take into account the discriminative role of $CIP(A, W_{\bar{t}B})$. This is accordingly a serious defect in Lewis's ordering model with the respects and constraints on weights prescribed by conditions I - IV.

In accordance with our discussion in 3 above, these examples, in addition to undermining Lewis's analysis as expressed in conditions I–IV, can be seen to indicate a much more basic flaw in Lewis's general ordering model, apart from these respects or priorities and apart from any particular constraint on the way in which such an ordering is to be determined. This is because fundamental to the general ordering theory, as held by Lewis, is the independence characteristic (i.e., the characteristic that the ordering of worlds is independent of particular counterfactuals). We saw that when it comes to counterfactuals of the n-d type (in a nondeterministic world, of course), it is crucial to let the set $CIP(A, W_{\bar{t}B})$ play a significant role in their analysis. But $CIP(A, W_{\bar{t}B})$ varies with the counterfactual $A > B$. Thus, it does not seem plausible that an ordering of possible worlds possessing the independence characteristic can adequately take this set into account. But not taking $CIP(A, W_{\bar{t}B})$ into account, as we showed, is a serious defect that cannot be compensated for by over-all factual similarity considerations which are not relativized to features depending on the counterfactual in question.

What transpires, if our argument to the effect that $CIP(A, W_{\bar{t}B})$ must be preserved is correct, is that it is unrealistic to expect a satisfactory ordering of worlds that is independent of the counterfactual being evaluated. Thus, the above considerations show that the fundamental flaw in the ordering theory is that the orderings reflected in the original intuitive-over-all-similarity analysis and in the new conditions I-IV manifest the independence characteristic, which reflects Lewis's general conception of counterfactuals (as presented in his book and in CDTA). To give up the independence characteristic is to give up the picture of a system of spheres around a world via which counterfactuals are evaluated in that world, which is one and the same for all counterfactuals (at a given context, say), a picture which is at the heart of Lewis's approach.

Similar considerations also bear, of course, against SFT with IC. They do not, however, cast a shadow over SFT *without* IC.

As noted above, metalinguistic models that incorporate a cotenability requirement would not possess the independence characteristic. Such a requirement imposes a dependence on the counterfactual in question, when cotenability is taken in its classical sense (*not* in Lewis's sense; cf. section I, chapter 7). As noted above, the model proposed in this book for counterfactuals of the n-d type, although devoid of a cotenability requirement, fits into the framework of SFT *without* IC.

VI   *The Case of the Siamese Twins*

1. Siamese twins S_1 and S_2 were once in a critical state — their condition was touch-and-go — because of a serious illness Q. The

twins were of a special sort; they were connected to each other in such a way that, as a matter of a lawful regularity L, if one were to die from illness Q, the other would inevitably die from it too within a short time. Let us call Siamese twins that fulfill L **H-Siamese** twins. (Of course, if someone is an H-Siamese twin of someone else, the latter is also an H-Siamese twin of the former.) In fact, however, both S_1 and S_2 survived the illness, never caught it again, and lived to a ripe old age. We shall assume here that the world is nondeterministic and that it was undetermined whether or not either of these two would die from illness Q. Now, given the illness Q of both twins and their critical state, it is clear that the following counterfactual is true: Had twin S_1 died from illness Q, his twin S_2 would have died from it shortly thereafter. Analogously, the following counterfactual is true too: Had twin S_2 died from illness Q, his twin S_1 would have died shortly thereafter.

The antecedents of these two counterfactuals are, respectively,

A_1' : S_1 (an H-Siamese twin of S_2) died from illness Q.
A_2' : S_2 (an H-Siamese twin of S_1) died from illness Q.

The consequents of these two counterfactuals are, respectively,

B_1: S_2 died shortly after his H-Siamese twin S_1.
B_2: S_1 died shortly after his H-Siamese twin S_2.

The counterfactuals

$A_1' > B_1$
$A_2' > B_2$

are therefore true.[41]
Now surely if we were to replace A_1' and A_2' by their conjunctions with the true lawful statement L and the factually true statement w:

w: In the period involved, it is false that S_1 or S_2 died of any non-Q cause.

these two counterfactuals will remain true. Thus, taking A_1 and A_2 to be:

$A_1 = A_1' \ \& \ L \ \& \ w$
$A_2 = A_2' \ \& \ L \ \& \ w$

clearly the two counterfactuals

$A_1 > B_1$
$A_2 > B_2$

are equally true.

Now by our assumptions:

(25) $A_1 \to A_2$

(26) $A_2 \to A_1$

It is also clear that B_1 and B_2 are contradictory. Thus:

(27) $B_1 \to \sim B_2$

(28) $B_2 \to \sim B_1$

From (25) — (28) we conclude:

(29) $A_1 \& B_1 \to A_2 \& \sim B_2$

(30) $A_2 \& B_2 \to A_1 \& \sim B_1$

We thus have two counterfactuals, $A_1 > B_1$ and $A_2 > B_2$, which are intuitively true, and which fulfill (29) and (30). However, no model of the ordering theory [42] OT can make two counterfactuals that fulfill conditions (29) and (30) true in the same world. This is so regardless of what ordering relation we use, so long as, for any given world w_0, two other worlds w_1 and w_2 from the collection of worlds under consideration are such that one is closer to w_0 than the other or else they are equally close to w_0 (so that Lewis's spheres would be available).

The argument for this result is as follows:[43] Suppose $A_1 > B_1$ and $A_2 > B_2$ are true in w_0. Then there is an A_1-fulfilling sphere β_1 around w_0 including some $A_1\&B_1$-world w_1 but no $A_1\& \sim B_1$-world, and there is also an A_2-fulfilling sphere β_2 around w_0 including some $A_2\&B_2$-world w_2 but no $A_2\& \sim B_2$-world. Now any two spheres around w_0 must either coincide or else be such that one includes the other. Let β be the bigger sphere in the second case, or either of the spheres in the first case. β then includes both w_1 and w_2. However, by (29) and (30), w_1 is an $A_2\& \sim B_2$-world, and w_2 is an $A_1\& \sim B_1$ world. Hence β can be neither β_1 nor β_2. Contradiction.

2. The upshot of the above example and argument is the following. If (25) - (28) and the two counterfactuals in the above example are acknowledged to be true, given the setup of the example, then it follows that no model of OT can make these two true counterfactuals come out true. This is so regardless of what ordering relation is being used, so long as it is such that, for every three worlds w, w', and w_0, one of w and w' is closer to w_0 than the other, or else they are equally close to w_0. (This is necessary to generate spheres as Lewis conceived them.) This relation in particular need have nothing whatever to do with similarity (although, of course, it may be some sort of similarity relation). Now Lewis's theory of weighted similar-

ity respects and his priorities theory are special cases of OT. Hence, regardless of which respects, or weights, or priorities, or similarity-under-respects relation, are chosen, the two counterfactuals from the above example *cannot* be made true by models of such theories. These counterfactuals therefore provide a counterexample to *all* models of OT, in particular to *all* models of Lewis's weighted-similarity-respects theory and his priorities theory. If (25) - (28) and the truth of these counterfactuals are acknowledged in the above example, there is no choice of respects and weights or priorities and no similarity relation that will make Lewis's theory true, thereby making these true counterfactuals come out true. This sort of example therefore provides a most general argument against Lewis's most general claim (as reflected, for instance, in his analysis 2, quoted above in section II).

Notice, moreover, that the reasoning behind this example is not limited to this single counterexample, but holds the promise of allowing for a host of kindred examples. Thus, any two true counterfactuals $A_i > B_i$ $(i = 1,2)$ that fulfill (29) and (30) will analogously constitute a counterexample to Lewis's general theory, since no OT model can accommodate them. Notice that the particular example given above falls short of exploiting the degrees of freedom provided by (29) and (30). In our example, we used $A_i \rightarrow A_j$, whereas the more general $A_i \& B_i \rightarrow A_j$ (for $i \neq j$) would also do. We also used $B_i \rightarrow \sim B_j$, whereas the more general $A_i \& B_i \rightarrow \sim B_j$ (for $i \neq j$) would do too. Moreover, in the Siamese-twins example the A_is and B_is were syntactically simple sentences. We can, however, expect that examples of this sort can also be generated with A_is and B_is that are compounds (e.g., truth-functional) of other simple sentences, which would make it possible to exploit (29) and (30) more fully.

In section V we employed similar reasoning to show that not every SFT model without IC is equivalent to an OT model. The argument we used did not lend itself easily to intuitive instantiation: to finding two intuitively true counterfactuals that could be made true by an SFT model (without IC) but not by an OT model. Here we have provided a concrete counterexample to OT along similar lines. It is obvious that, since IC is characteristic of OT, this kind of example (which utilizes a pair of counterfactuals) does not pose a fundamental problem for SFT without IC, as it does for OT.

Now of course the force of this example hinges on the recognition that the two counterfactuals $A_1 > B_1$ and $A_2 > B_2$ are intuitively true. But, as has been shown above, an OT is committed to the claim that any two such counterfactuals which fulfill (29) and (30) are false. This claim seems fallacious even if the specific example brought above is challenged. From the above discussion, it is clear that this *type* of example covers a host of different cases, and one must be willing to argue that *none* of them involves such a pair of true counterfactuals if one wishes to consider OT immune from this criticism. Such a claim, however, would be highly implausible.[44]

VII Counterfactuals and Contexts Again

Having introduced (in V 1) the notion of the independence characteristic IC, which is characteristic of OT in general and of Lewis's theory in particular, I would like to add another point which is related to Lewis's emphasis on the context-dependence of the similarity relation that is suitable for his analysis of counterfactuals, and particularly relevant to the force of the counterexamples proposed in sections III and IV above.

Lewis's conditions I-IV are designed to apply to various contexts in which Fine's example comes out true (and for which the standard resolution of vagueness has been adopted with the effect of ruling out backtracking). As far as I can see, however, such contexts will also generally tend to make the above counterexamples come out as we claimed. Therefore, since conditions I-IV are designed to apply to these contexts, these examples do constitute counterexamples.

Now one may respond that, in such contexts which make Fine's example come out right, the very introduction of the counterfactuals brought in the above counterexamples changes the context (in such a way that conditions I-IV are no longer appropriate to them). Such a response would obviously make the resolution of Fine's example via conditions I-IV rather limited in applicability, and thus Fine's example would remain problematic in cases in which I-IV are no longer operative. However, to argue that, in such contexts in which Fine's example and some of my examples come out as they intuitively should, the mere consideration of some of these examples changes the context not merely in some such cases but *as a rule* (since otherwise we would still have some contexts in which conditions I-IV apply and some of my examples come out right), would seem an unmotivated and quite suspicious move. In making such a claim one comes close to saying that the mere consideration of a new counterfactual in a certain context changes that context. I have no reason to believe that Lewis would make such a claim. But if such a claim were to be made, it would, I believe, be unreasonable, and I would argue that it will not do.

This is so since the claim that the addition of another counterfactual *ipso facto* changes a context would impoverish Lewis's analysis. First, his picture of context-relative concentric spheres will now change with every new counterfactual. If contexts must depend on which counterfactual statements are being assessed, then the ordering of worlds, which is itself context-dependent, will also become dependent on the particular counterfactual being evaluated. This will violate IC, which, we showed, is central to OT, and thus to Lewis's analysis as well.

Furthermore, the analysis will become trivial insofar as semifactuals are concerned.[45] Lewis takes his program (under the weighted-similarity-respects option, say) to be successful iff for every context there is a set of respects and weights such that the resulting ordering relation will make true those counterfactuals which are true in this context. It is tautologically true that, for any semifactual, there is a similarity relation that will make it true: just take the content of the consequent to determine a respect of similarity to which you assign overriding weight.[46] In this manner a trivial account can also be provided for the falsehood of false nonsemifac-tual counterfactuals.[47] Further still: if a criticism I make elsewhere of the choice of perfect match as a similarity respect is valid, then under this conception the analysis becomes trivial in its full generality (at least for counterfactuals with entertainable antecedents, evaluated in the actual world).[48]

I therefore conclude that the above objection to my counterexamples is not a viable option for Lewis.

Notes: Chapter 8

1. *Noûs*, XIII, 4 (November 1979): 455-476.

2. I believe that pronouncements by Lewis in *Counterfactuals* and its general spirit indeed substantiate the way he has been standardly understood and, there-fore, that the position in CDTA does count as a new version. Thus, in his book he says: "Somehow, we *do* have a familiar notion of comparative overall similar-ity, even of comparative similarity of big, complicated, variegated things like whole people, whole cities, or even — I think — whole possible worlds" (p. 92). His reference to a "familiar notion of comparative overall similarity" can scarcely be understood as anything but the *intuitive* notion of over-all similarity. A notion of similarity can hardly be "familiar" if we have no intuitions concerning it, but rather have to tailor it to fit a particular construction, e.g., the counterfactual con-struction. In his book, this "familiar" notion of comparative over-all similarity which is utilized in the analysis of counterfactuals is taken to be like that of over-all similarity between cities, construed intuitively; it is to this notion that his analysis of counterfactuals is reduced, thereby making it true that "[h]owever mysterious that notion may be, if we can analyze counterfactuals by means of it we will be left with one mystery in place of two" (*ibid.*). His revised version surely requires a relation different from the intuitive "mysterious" one, which we need in any event, e.g., when comparing cities. Thus, the analysis of counterfactuals in the new version saddles us with *two* mysteries rather than one: that of the intuitive notion of similarity and that of the similarity relation suitable for the counterfac-tual construction. In his book, Lewis maintains that no similarity metric is needed for his analysis (pp. 50-52). This is indeed true if the intuitive notion of similarity is used in the analysis of counterfactuals, but false if his new nonintuitive notion, understood as a weighted-similarity-respects notion, is used, since the weights can-not be put to work except when applied to *measures* of similarity (for more on this point, see below, section II).

3. Yet Lewis advances a partial account of such a relation in response to Fine's example; it will be discussed in the following two sections.

4. See Fine's Critical Notice of Lewis, *Counterfactuals*, in *Mind*, LXXIV, 335 (July 1975): 451-458, p. 452.

5. Lewis may be held to allow both a weighted-similarity-respects model and a priorities model. I shall discuss the priorities model in IV below.

6. That is, relations of the form: under a given respect, world *i* is at least as similar to w_0 as a world *j* is.

7. CDTA, p 469. Lewis wants w_2 to be further from w_0 than w_1 is in order to avoid back-tracking. Yet he should also want it in order to assure that Fine's counterfactual come out right, since w_2-type worlds may involve no holocaust (w_2 shares no prior history with w_0).

8. In my forthcoming "Priorities Models and Perfect Match" I argue that taking perfect match as a similarity respect not only runs contrary to the normal structure of similarity respects, but would deprive Lewis's theory of any genuine similarity aspect.

9. *Ibid.*, p. 472. I have changed the numbering of Lewis's conditions from arabic to roman numerals, in order to avoid confusion with the sequence of numbered formulas and sentences of this chapter.

Again, I shall address myself here only to the weighted-similarity-respects version of Lewis's account.

10. That $r_{PM} \neq 0$ follows from the choice of perfect match as a salient respect [otherwise no dissimilarity in the respect of perfect match will contribute anything to $d_{w_0}(w_i)$]. Because of the nature of w_4 and w_1, $DS^L(w_4) - DS^L(w_1) \neq 0$. I also assume that, in the weighted-similarity-respects model, the coefficients r_L and r_{PM} are constant, rather than functions of $DS^L(w_i)$ and $DS^{PM}(w_i)$, respectively, which would be a different story altogether.

11. Recall how Lewis describes the system in w_0: "Consider w_0, a world that may or not be ours. In w_0, Nixon does not press the button at t and no nuclear holocaust ever occurs. Let w_0 also be a world with deterministic laws, since we have confined our attention here to counterfactual dependence under determinism. Let w_0 also be a world that fits our worst fantasies about the button: there is such a button, it is connected to a fully automatic command and control system, the wired-in war plan consists of one big salvo, everything is in faultless working order, there is no way for anyone to stop the attack, and so on. Then I agree that Fine's counterfactual is true at w_0: if Nixon had pressed the button, there would have been a nuclear holocaust" (pp. 467/468).

12. Lewis wants $d(w_1) < d(w_2)$ in order to avoid back-tracking. Yet surely Borg's pushing the button coupled with a faultless nuclear attack mechanism seems compatible with the laws and there not being a nuclear holocaust (e.g., if all bombs are dummies). Hence in some such worlds the consequent will be false. For an analysis to yield the correct truth value for this counterfactual, therefore, worlds like w_2' must be further from w_0 than w_1' is, in complete analogy to Fine's example. (All bombs are not dummies in w_1' since they are not so in w_0, and w_1', unlike w_2', is perfectly matched with w_0 until t).

13. Notice that we can pick an example similar to the above in which the miracle it takes to allow for the antecedent will have to be really big. We can have as antecedents 'Had Brezhnev pushed the American nuclear button when the American mechanism was faultless' or even 'Had Stalin (or even Lenin) pushed the nuclear button in 1975 when the mechanism was faultless'. So it seems clear that we can get a counterfactual for which the miracle it would take to allow for the antecedent will be greater than the one it takes to cancel out Nixon's pushing of the button. (But see below, III, fn 21, for further discussion of this point and for arguments against the availability of the option of having a minor miracle some time earlier.)

It does not seem that giving positive weight to similarity of particular facts (short of perfect match) will be of much help to Lewis in examples such as these. (This is what got him into trouble in the first place, since the relevant worlds in which there is no holocaust are more similar with respect to particular facts than worlds in which there is a holocaust in cases of the sort discussed here. And notice that here we did not rely on w_3, in which there is factual similarity short of perfect match.)

14. If you wish, take n to be 2; surely if having one more hair takes a tiny miracle, so does having two more.

15. I have used this sort of example against Lewis's original theory in a postscript to my Ph.D dissertation, University of Pittsburgh, November 1974: microfilm, Ann Arbor, 1975. (Cf. also a related example there at the end of chapter 1, directed against Stalnaker's theory.) John Pollock (in *Subjunctive Reasoning, op. cit.*) and Hans Herzberger [in "Counterfactuals and Consistency," *Journal of Philosophy*, LXXVI, 2 (February 1979): 83-88] have used similar examples as well; they take off from Lewis's example against Stalnaker.

16. Such a perfect match would cost a major miracle, which according to Lewis, isn't worth it.

17. In the previous example the notion of a "change in a law" was used. This implies sameness with the actual law up to that time. But this variation of the example shows that resorting to such a locution is not central to the point being made. Thus in this example, unlike example 3, no explicit assumptions concerning the gravitational law prior to t are being made.

18. I take it to be true that such a conversion would not have affected Truman's longevity. If this is disputed, change the consequent to: 'he would have done so in the late 1960s'.

19. The notion of an isolated system involves a lack of effect on the external world of goings-on within it, and vice versa.

20. Regardless of whether these Jews would have been killed during the war, they would not have been killed in Europe.

21. Now Lewis might want to say that the above evaluation was not performed properly. He might suggest that if only a major miracle will allow us to preserve the whole prior history, then sacrificing perfect match of a certain small interval prior to the antecedent-time by a *minor* miracle at the beginning of that interval will do better in accommodating the antecedent. But the thesis that such a minor miracle could be found, seems, in general, wrong. What minor miracle a short time before the 1920s would have yielded the antecedent in the example under consideration? How can the firing of millions of neurons in the heads of millions be considered a small miracle? It certainly cannot be considered minor when Lewis counts the neutralizing miracle in w_4 in his discussion of Fine's example as a major miracle, as he indeed must in order for his analysis to handle Fine's example correctly. Similarity under respects is intuitive for Lewis, and by any reasonable standard the firing of millions of neurons in the heads of millions would count as more of a major miracle than the neutralization of the traces of Nixon's pushing the button.

Furthermore: remember that Lewis wants his analysis to apply to deterministic worlds. If we were dealing with a sufficiently nondeterministic world, it would be plausible that often a minor miracle at an earlier time could make the antecedent *compatible* with the history prior to that miracle. But this is not enough in a deterministic world: the laws, modified to accommodate a minor miracle, must, given the state of the world at that earlier time, *determine* that the antecedent-event will occur. On what grounds can one believe that in general such a minor miracle — i.e., one that would so determine the occurrence of the antecedent-event — could be found prior to the antecedent-time? Thus, the thesis that every antecedent that it would take a major miracle to accommodate so as to preserve the prior history, could instead be accommodated via a minor change during some short interval before its occurrence, amounts to the following claim: For any such antecedent, there is a counterfactual in which that antecedent is a consequent, a counterfactual which is in standard temporal order (i.e., in which the antecedent-time is weakly later than the consequent-time; cf. below, 9 III, 2) and true via Lewis's analysis, and whose antecedent can be accommodated with its own prior history via a small miracle (or whose antecedent-event specifies a small miracle). But, in view of what has been said above, there seems little reason to believe that this is the case.

Moreover: Lewis was concerned about back-tracking since it yielded a loss of control over counterfactual consequents. An attempt to have an earlier minor miracle yield the antecedent-event in a deterministic world represents a similar loss of control: we are hardly in a position to tell which, if any, minor miracles would do the job. Consequently, we are hardly in a position to say much about the history of the world during that interval (or later on), and thus in a poor position to make counterfactual predictions along the lines of the above analysis in such cases.

The same points apply to the modification of Fine's example in section II (example 1) which yielded an antecedent requiring a major miracle. What reason can we give for believing that a minor miracle at an earlier time would suffice to determine Borg's or Brezhnev's pushing of the American nuclear button? (cf. fn 13 above). Perhaps it would take a *continuous* miracle throughout this stretch, or a series of miracles at various different places and times. But those would both be major miracles by Lewis's standards. Yet if it is a major miracle that is involved, a w_2-type world would then be *closer* to w_0 than a w_1-type world with such a major miracle, regardless of whether there is a transitional period or not. And if this is the case, our argument from section II above applies here as well.

22. It will not help to say that I - IV were designed to fit contexts like that of Fine's example, but need not suit contexts which make the above examples true, and that these examples call for different weights and respects. The reason is that these examples do not manifest any overt context-dependence or ambiguity. Respecting Lewis's direction, the above examples would seem to remain true even if we adopt his standard resolution of vagueness and resist back-tracking arguments. We can take the kind of contexts in which Lewis agrees that Fine's example is to be evaluated as true, and consider the above examples *in such contexts*: in many of them they still intuitively come out true. If I - IV are suitable for the context of Fine's example, they should be suitable for handling our examples in that kind of context as well. (Recall that contexts must be distinguished from stories accompanying the examples, which determine the kind of worlds in which the counterfactual is evaluated.) Recall that the concerns that Lewis mentions as relevant to his endorsement of context-dependence include: varying interests and importance attributions, the avoidance of back-tracking, and handling cases such as the Caesar-and-the-catapults example — all of which are very different from the features exhibited by the examples used here. (See 8 VII, 7 IV, and 9 IV 4 for further discussion of context-dependence.)

23. This is so since the two relevant kinds of worlds to compare concerning counterfactual (16) would differ in the timing of the minor miracle that is needed to turn Truman into a devout Catholic (but would involve perfect match up to that miracle). The kind of world in which the small miracle is delayed (and is thus close to Truman's death) would be closer to the actual world according to version I than a kind of world in which this miracle occurred earlier. This is so since the two kinds of worlds would fare equally by way of avoiding major miracles, but the first would enjoy more perfect match.

24. The counterfactual there was (18): Had 6 million European Jews im-

migrated to Palestine during the 1920s, a massacre of millions of Jews would not have occurred in Europe in the course of the Second World War.

25. Cf. the discussion of this example at the end of section III. Notice also that on the priorities model, w_2-type worlds will be closer to the center world than w_1-type worlds (with a major rather than minor antecedent-adjusting miracle), since the w_2-type worlds involve no miracle. This is therefore a counterexample to both versions of the priorities model, at least when priority IV (similarity of particular facts) is given no weight.

26. But cf. my forthcoming "Priorities Models and Perfect Match."

27. Or it may be construed via similarities under certain respects ordered by priorities. Again, I shall ignore this version below, but what I say about *WSRT* applies to it as well, *mutatis mutandis.*

28. I limit myself to counterfactuals with possible antecedents; so there will always be A-worlds in the realm of worlds under consideration. Cf. also the following fn.

29. A natural expectation concerning the selection function of an SFT model without IC is that, for a given world and a counterfactual $A > B$, there will be A-worlds among the worlds f selects (if there are A-worlds at all among the worlds considered). However, this cannot be expected in general of SFT models with IC. It is only natural to take a counterfactual $A > B$ to be true under such a selection function that selects no A-worlds when all A-worlds (which are thus outside the scope of f for the world under discussion) are B-worlds.

30. We are ignoring counterfactuals with true antecedents here. The proof of this claim is straightforward: Suppose f is the selection function of an SFT model with IC. Let $\mathcal{a}$ be the OT-model specified via f as described. Suppose $A > B$ is true in f's SFT model. If there are A-worlds in f's range, then B is true in all of them. Otherwise, B is true in all A-worlds. In the first case, B is true in all the A-worlds of the smaller sphere in $\mathcal{a}$; in the second case, in all the A-worlds in the larger sphere. Hence in both cases $A > B$ is true in $\mathcal{a}$. The reverse direction is completely analogous. (Cf. also the previous fn for the complementation of the definition of an SFT model with IC in case the selection function has no A-worlds in its range.)

31. Assuming a choice function.

32. For a given world and context. For simplicity, I shall omit these relativizations in what follows.

33. There are A-worlds, since we assume throughout that A is possible; see fn 28.

34. $\text{CIP}(A, W_{\bar{t}B})$ is the set of consequents in (t_A, t_B) of irrel-semifactuals and pp-semifactuals with antecedent A.

35. This proof will work, *mutatis mutandis,* for a choice of a world other than the actual world.

36. For simplicity I shall omit the relativization to the actual world even as an argument of f.

37. The same proof will work, *mutatis mutandis,* without assuming that the set of implicit premises is finite.

38. This rules out f as a metalinguistic-model function, since a true C_i cannot entail a false A_j.

39. (21) and (22) rule out that C_1 is equivalent to C_2. This is so even when one allows a tautology to be a logical consequence of any statement, since $\sim A_1 \& \sim A_2$ cannot be a tautology, given our assumption that A_1 and A_2 are possible.

40. We are assuming, of course, that this event was not determined by W_{t_A}.

41. Notice that we evaluate these two counterfactuals in the same context. For further defense of their truth, see below, fn 44.

42. For the definition of the ordering theory, see above, section V.

43. We used a similar line of argument in section V above.

44. The intuitive truth of $A_1 > B_1$ (and, analogously, of $A_2 > B_2$) should become clear once we bear in mind the circumstances described: the actual sickness of both twins and their being in critical condition, yet alive. Notice that this provides for the compatibility of the antecedent with the prior history, which includes, of course, both twins being alive. If this information is borne in mind, it should be intuitively clear that had S_1 died from illness Q, his twin S_2 would have died from it shortly thereafter. Hence counterfactuals $A_1 > B_1$ and $A_2 > B_2$ are intuitively true as well.

To deny the truth of $A_1 > B_1$ is to entertain, when considering the counterfactual hypothesis A_1, the possibility that A_2 occurred before it. But this possibility should be disregarded, just as the possibility that S_2 died long before that from cancer, or was murdered as an infant, or any number of kindred possibilities that could forestall the truth of this counterfactual, should be disregarded. At the very least, one must concede that a reading that makes $A_i > B_i$ true is sustained in *certain* contexts. But this is enough for the argument that no OT can make these two counterfactuals (which are therefore both true in *some* context) simultaneously true in that context, since there is then no appropriate ordering of worlds for that context.

Notice that to raise the objection considered is to resort to a back-tracking argument. Lewis should thus be inclined to reject such an interpretation here, since on his "standard resolution of vagueness" back-tracking arguments should be excluded here, at least in some context, which is sufficient for my purpose. Cf. Lewis's CDTA, pp. 455-457; in particular: "We ordinarily resolve the vagueness of the counterfactuals in such a way that counterfactual dependence is asymmetric (except perhaps in cases of time travel or the like). Under this standard resolution, back-tracking arguments are mistaken: if the present were different the past would be the same" (p. 457). Lewis specifically characterizes the task of finding the appropriate similarity relation as one that excludes such back-tracking: "Our present task is to see what sort of similarity relation can be combined with Analysis 2 to yield what I have called the standard resolution of vagueness: one that invalidates back-tracking arguments" (p. 465).

And yet, these two counterfactuals must come out false under Lewis's theory — if indeed there is nothing wrong in the above proof or in the characterization of the example: after all, the point of the above argument is that no (consistent) OT can make two such counterfactuals come out true.

And indeed, on Lewis's analysis of conditions I-IV, two worlds will be among the closest to w_0, the world in which we evaluate $A_1 > B_1$ and $A_2 > B_2$: w_1, in which there is perfect match with w_0 up to a certain point t at which A_1' becomes true, and in which A_2' becomes true at $t + \Delta t$; and w_2, in which it is A_2' which becomes true at t while A_1'' becomes true at $t + \Delta t$. In both worlds the antecedents A_1 and A_2 are true, there is no miracle, and there are equal stretches of perfect match. Hence $A_1 > B_1$ will come out false, and so will $A_2 > B_2$.

If one were to raise the objection that the simultaneous occurrence of A_1 and A_2 is not ruled out, despite its being counterintuitive in normal contexts with A_1 as a counterfactual hypothesis, we can change the example as follows: Assume that there is some sort of machine to which the twins are attached which rules out the possibility of the twins' dying from Q simultaneously: if they are both just seconds from death (as indicated by their life signals), it artificially sustains one of them long enough for him to survive the other. Assume the operation of the machine to be deterministic. Adding an assumption to this effect to our story (and in the A_is) would, I believe, rule out such an objection to the truth of the two counterfactuals.

45. More specifically, for semifactuals with entertainable antecedents that are consistent with their consequents. This qualification applies to fn 47 below as well.

46. Thus, a family of properties, suitably chosen, one of which is a property specifying the content of the consequent, chosen as a respect of similarity with an overriding weight, will yield as possible worlds closest to the actual world (in which the antecedent is true) those possible worlds in which the consequent is true too.

47. That is, take the content of the negation of the consequent to determine a similarity respect with overriding weight.

48. In a forthcoming article "Priorities Models and Perfect Match" I argue that if perfect match is allowed as a similarity respect, then every property shared by the actual world determines a similarity respect. For a counterfactual $A > B$ (when $A\&B$ is consistent), take the only similarity respect to be determined via the feature $A\&B \vee R$, and give it a positive weight (where R uniquely specifies the actual world, in which, say, we shall evaluate the counterfactual). There will then be two spheres: in the worlds of the closer sphere $A\&B$ is true (except in the actual world), and of course, this sphere includes A-worlds. This will make the counterfactual true regardless of whether it is a semifactual or not. (Counterfactuals $A > B$ such that $A\&B$ is inconsistent are false anyway.)

In this article I argue that if perfect match is allowed as a similarity respect, the use of the notion of similarity becomes redundant. Here I argue that, coupled with this radical view of context-dependence, it trivializes the analysis.

9 Toward a Comprehensive Theory of Counterfactuals

The bulk of this book has been devoted to counterfactuals of the natural-divergence type, i.e., counterfactuals whose antecedents A are compatible with the prior history of the world W_{t_A}.[1] In this epilogue I would like to present a proposal (which will, however, be sketchy at some places[2]) for extending this treatment of the n-d type into a general theory of counterfactuals.

I The Leading-Process Interpretation

1. I shall comment below (in III) on how counterfactuals with impossible or counterlegal antecedents are to be treated. But the kind of counterfactuals that is by far the most prevalent and useful kind not discussed so far consists of those counterfactuals with contrary-to-fact antecedents which, though logically and metaphysically possible and compatible with the laws (*colegals*), are nonetheless *incompatible* with the prior history. For these counterfactuals, a natural extension of the n-d interpretation is available, which will be called the **l-p interpretation** (for *leading processes*). A natural extension of our analysis for counterfactuals of the n-d type into the l-p interpretation will in turn reassure us that the analysis of the n-d type was on the right track.

As already stated, counterfactuals amenable to the leading-process interpretation are those with an antecedent A which, though logically, metaphysically, and law-wise possible, is incompatible with the prior history W_{t_A}. Such an antecedent A would not typically involve human decisions or spontaneous actions, but rather states of affairs that could not, without a violation of laws of nature, succeed W_{t_A}. But these states of affairs could have occurred if certain processes that did not in fact occur, processes that could have "led" to their occurrence, had actually taken place. An example would be the following:

Example 1: Suppose John sees a beautiful car for sale and loves it, and (correctly) says:

(1)   If I had had an extra $5,000, I would have bought this car.

Another would be Example 2:

(2)   Had Gerald Ford been president in 1978, he would have urged the Shah of Iran to use his army to the fullest extent in order to remain in power.

233

For the antecedent of (1) in example 1 to hold, some process should have led to John's having an extra $5,000, rather than his just having it "out of the blue," as the result of a *deus ex machina* act (or a miracle). For the antecedent of (2) to hold, some process should have led to Ford's still (or again) being president in 1978. Thus, the natural background against which to consider such a contrary-to-fact assumption A comprises various processes which diverge[3] from the actual world at some point prior to t_A and which "lead" to the antecedent. Each such process is a series of events or states, and the counterfactual should be assessed separately against the background of each such different process. A natural extension of our treatment of counterfactuals of the n-d type would yield the manner in which such an assessment is to be made. Thus, the consequent B would have to follow (via the laws), for a given process,[4] from premises which would include the history of the world prior to the process, the process description, the antecedent A, and an augmentation of true, factual information from the actual-world description concerning the time to which the process pertains and the (t_A, t_B) interval. This augmentation would be conducted along lines similar to those followed in the n-d interpretation: at each stage of the process, statements from the actual-world description would be retained which describe events to which the portion of the process not later than this stage is causally irrelevant or purely positively causally relevant. The augmentation extracted from the history of the world pertaining to (t_A, t_B) interval will consist of true factual statements to which the process itself and the antecedent-event are causally irrelevant or purely positively causally relevant. For each such process, B would have to follow from the premises assembled around this process in the way described for the counterfactual to be true.

Thus, consider the case of Example 3:

(3)   Had Rudolf Carnap been teaching philosophy in Princeton during the 1940s, Princeton would have turned out more logical positivist graduates.

Now there are obviously various hypothetical processes that could have resulted in Carnap's teaching at Princeton in the 1940s. But if the above counterfactual is true, then the consequent should follow according to the above procedure when applied to every such process that should be considered, e.g., processes in which a vacancy would have occurred through faculty death, processes in which the department would have expanded, or whatever. A failure of the consequent to follow under any one such process would reflect the falsehood of the counterfactual.

For another case, take as Example 4 a Gettier-type example. Suppose John has two men in his office, Mr. Nogot and Mr. Havit. The latter has a Ford, the former does not; but John believes that neither of them has a Ford. Consider this counterfactual:

(4)   Had John believed that someone in his office had a Ford, he would have known it.

This counterfactual is false. Although John might have come to such a belief via a process in which he noticed Mr. Havit driving his own Ford, he might have also come to this belief via a process in which all he saw was Mr. Nogot driving a rented Ford. For one of these processes, therefore, the consequent would not come out true, and the counterfactual would accordingly come out false, as it should.

But of course not *every* process leading to A should count in the evaluation of $A > B$. Among such processes there would be highly *esoteric* processes we would want to ignore. Thus, consider, as Example 5, the counterfactual:

(5)   Had Reagan been president on 1/21/77, a massive process of strengthening the military power of the U.S. would have started in the late 1970s.

Now one type of process leading to the antecedent would diverge from the actual-world description at the time of the G.O.P. convention in 1976, when the Mississippi delegation wavered between Ford and Reagan. Such a process would have the delegation decide to support Reagan fully, thereby giving him the nomination, and then proceed to have Reagan win the general elections. But another process leading to the antecedent would have the Soviet Union occupy the U.S., turning it into a Soviet satellite, and appointing Reagan as puppet president. Under such a process the consequent need not of course come out true. But the possibility of such a process should not upset the truth of the above counterfactual: it should not be counted among the processes according to which the counterfactual should be evaluated.

As another example, Example 6, suppose John sits in room 1 in New York at time t, while no one is in the adjacent room 2, where there is only a match and a matchbox. Now consider Goodman's famous counterfactual:

(6)   Had this match been struck, it would have lighted.

One type of process leading to the antecedent would have John get up, go from room 1 to room 2, lift the match and the matchbox, and strike the match. But another type of process would have a huge wave from the ocean flood the area and throw the match so as to strike it (say, against the matchbox). Surely the match would not light under this second process. But, again, this type of process need not upset the truth of counterfactual (6), since it is too esoteric to count.

Accordingly, only *certain* processes should be selected for the evaluation of a counterfactual of the kind under discussion. Only for certain processes should the above procedure be applied, with the counterfactual coming out true iff its consequent is inferable under each of them. Which should these selected processes be? Primarily, they should be *those most likely to have led to the antecedent*. This way esoteric processes will be counted out. Thus, in example 5, the process in which the Soviet Union occupied the U.S. would not be selected, since it is considerably less likely to have led to the antecedent of (5) than the first kind of process described there. Yet the two processes described in example 4, the Gettier-type example, would be comparably likely to have led to the antecedent of (4) under the setup imagined for this example, and indeed both of these processes should be selected for the evaluation of counterfactual (4), which, as we have seen, would then turn out to be false, as it should.

2. Let us now be more specific regarding the above outline. We can take a process to be represented as a series of events or states in temporal succession. For our purposes, we shall concentrate on process descriptions rather than on processes. That a process may be described in more than one way need not concern us: we shall apply the probabilistic test to the various descriptions, and select those which pass this test. In view of this, the question of process individuation will also be of no concern to us here. So let P^i be a process description, i.e., a set of statements $\{P_1^i, \ldots, P_h^i\}$, each describing an event or a state of affairs, fulfilling the temporal requirement that $\bar{t}_{P_{j-1}^i} < \underline{t}_{P_j^i}$.[5] We shall require that a process description count as describing a process leading to the A-event only in case $P_h^i = A$. For our purposes we shall consider process descriptions P^i describing processes that "diverge" from the actual-world description (at $\underline{t}_{P_1^i}$, i.e., for which P_1^i is compatible with $W_{\underline{t}_{P_1^i}}$).[6] Now for a counterfactual $A > B$ to pass the test for such a selected process P^i, its consequent B would have to follow (via the laws) from the prior history $W_{\underline{t}_{P_1^i}}$, the process description $\{P_1^i, \ldots, P_n^i\}$, A, and an augmentation of (factual) statements from the actual-world description pertaining to times within the interval $(\underline{t}_{P_1^i}, t_B)$, all taken together [the latter would be analogous to CIP$(A, W_{\bar{t}_B})$ in the analysis of the n-d interpretation; cf. 2 IX 1]. Thus, for each stage j of the process, we should retain the set of statements pertaining to $(\underline{t}_{P_j^i}, \underline{t}_{P_{j+1}^i})$ to which the process stages described as $P_1^i, \ldots, P_j^i$ are causally irrelevant or purely positively causally relevant.[7] Let us call this latter set of statements CIP$(\underset{k=1}{\overset{j}{\&}} P_k^i, W_{\underline{t}_{P_{j+1}^i}})$. When taken together for all stages of the process (except for the last one, A), we get $\underset{j=1}{\overset{n}{\text{U}}}{}^1$ CIP$(\underset{k=1}{\overset{j}{\&}} P_k^i, W_{\underline{t}_{P_{j+1}^i}})$. For the augmentation of statements pertaining to the (t_A, t_B) interval we take of course the usual supplementation as on the n-d interpretation, adjusted to our present process analysis. That is, we add the set of statements pertaining to (t_A, t_B) describing events to which $\underset{k=1}{\overset{n}{\&}} P_k^i$ is causally irrelevant or purely positively causally relevant (recall that $P_n^i = A$); call this set of statements CIP$(P^i, A, W_{\bar{t}_B})$. The supplementation from the actual-world description for the process P^i would thus consist of:

(7) $\underset{j=1}{\overset{n}{\text{U}}}{}^1CIP(\underset{k=1}{\overset{j}{\&}} P_k^i, W_{\underline{t}_{P_{j+1}^i}})$ + CIP$(P^i, A, W_{\bar{t}_B})$

Let us call expression (7) Sup$(P^i, A, W_{\bar{t}_B})$ ('Sup' for supplementation). The inferential schema for a counterfactual $A > B$ of the sort under consideration, for each such process P^i, will thus be as follows (where $P^i = \{P_1^i, \ldots, P_n^i\}$ and $P_n^i = A$):

(8) $W_{tP_1^i} \cup P^i \cup \{A\} \cup Sup(P^i,A,W_{\bar{t}B}) \overset{L}{\to} B$

3. As we have already pointed out, we should not consider, in evaluating a counterfactual, just any process that diverges from the actual-world description and terminates in A, since we do not want to consider relatively esoteric processes. Let us further illustrate this point for counterfactual (1) in example 1. The various processes under consideration should indeed yield the consequent 'John buys this car'[8] via schema (8). But we do not want to require, for the counterfactual to be true, that this be the case also for a process such as one in which the whole economy collapsed and the dollar devalued 100 times, so that even though John would then have the extra $5,000, he would nevertheless be unable to buy a car (he might barely be able to buy a tire. This is, of course, so long as we take it that in this example no such collapse of the economy has in fact been a "real" possibility). Such a process, if taken into account via schema (8), would make the above counterfactual false, and we would want to rule it out. What makes such processes so esoteric is that, relative to other processes, they are highly unlikely to have led to A. Thus, we want to consider the set of processes that could have led to our antecedent A, given the actual prior history W_{tA}, to select those *most likely to have led to A* (again, relative to the prior history W_{tA}), and to screen out of these those which are relatively unlikely to have led to A.

Consider now another famous example[9] (Example 7):

(9)   If Bizet and Verdi had been compatriots, Bizet would have been Italian.

as opposed to:

(9′)   If Bizet and Verdi had been compatriots, Verdi would have been French.

Now the processes that could have led to the antecedent of (9) and (9′) would include one kind in which Bizet had moved to Italy and become Italian and another kind in which Verdi had moved to France and become French. Some processes of *both* kinds would seem to be among the most likely to have led to the antecedent. But the consequent of (9) would be false under processes of one such kind, and the consequent of (9′) false under processes of the other kind. Hence neither consequent would have followed under schema (8) for all selected processes, and both counterfactuals would come out false. And indeed, intuitively, this is as it should be.

4. Our account has relied on two intuitive notions: that of a process leading to the antecedent-event, and that of the processes most likely to have led to A. Obviously, a full-fledged theory would have to offer a more precise account of these notions. I would like to try to sketch one way of doing so,[10] and I shall start with the first notion. The reader who wishes

to skip the details can move directly to 6 (of this section) for a more general discussion of the viability and plausibility of these notions.

Surely not every temporally ascending series of possible events or states terminating in A and diverging from the actual world should be considered for our purposes as "leading" to A. Thus, processes whose stages (prior to the last, A) do not enhance the occurrence of A cannot count as processes that could have led to A. The key to the notion of a process that could have led to A lies in the probabilistic status of the various links in the process-description chain. The probabilistic status of each link P_j^i in the process description P^i must be measured by its probability assessed on the basis of $W_{tp_1^i}$ (the actual history prior to that process) and the information accumulated via the previous stages of the process. That is, the probabilistic status, or **strength**, of link P_j^i ($1 \leq j \leq n$) should be measured by the following:

$$(10) \qquad P(P_j^i / W_{tp_1^i} \cup \underset{k=1}{\overset{j-1}{\cup}} P_k^i \cup \underset{k=1}{\overset{j-1}{\cup}} \text{CIP} \, (\underset{m=1}{\overset{k}{\&}} P_m^i, W_{tp_{k+1}^i}))$$

that is, the probability of P_j^i on the basis of $W_{tp_1^i}$ (the history prior to the process P^i), the subprocess $\{P_1^i, \ldots , P_{j-1}^i\}$, and the statements retained from the actual-world description up to $t_{p_j^i}$. Let us call the strength of a link P_j^i in the process P^i as specified in (10) $S(P_j^i, P^i)$. A link is "weak" or "strong" in accordance with how low or high this probability is. A chain is as weak as its weakest link. The relative strength of a process should be an important component in the determination of whether it should count as leading to A. When we compare various processes diverging from the actual-world description and terminating in A, we want only the relatively strong processes to play a role in evaluating a counterfactual $A > B$.

There are lower limits on how weak a process could be and still qualify as leading to A. A process all of whose stages but the last describe goings-on in the lives of giraffes in Africa, with the last stages being 'Reagan is president of the U.S. on 1/22/77', should not qualify as leading to its last stage. Thus, not every process P, diverging at t_p[11] and terminating at A, leads to A. A nonempty process P should be contrasted with its corresponding *empty* process diverging at t_p and including $(P_1 \vee \sim P_1)$ & A as its sole link. For a process P to lead to A, it must strengthen A better than its corresponding empty process, in the sense that the strength of its last link A must be higher than the strength of the last (and only) link of its corresponding empty process, which is $P(A/W_{tp})$.[12] Similarly, the notion of a process $\{P_1^i, \ldots ,P_h^i\}$ leading to A should also involve the requirement that every stage in the process (prior to A) should help lead to a later stage; that is, it should enhance the probabilistic status of some later stage. In other words, each member P_j^i ($j < n$) must belong to some subprocess $\{P_{j_1}^i, \ldots ,P_{j_k}^i\}$ ($j_u < j_h$ if $u < h$; $j_k < n$), which enhances (with a non-vacuous contribution by P_j^i) the status of some later stage which in turn belongs to some subprocess . . . which enhances the status of A. Thus, for every stage P_j^i (prior to A) there ought to be a later stage P_k^i that is led to by a subprocess $\{P_1^i, \ldots ,P_j^i, \ldots ,P_{j_m}^i\}$ preceding it and such that P_j^i contributes to this subprocess leading to P_k^i. We thus want to require that, for each stage P_j^i $(j<n)$, there be a later stage P_{j+k}^i $(j+k\leq n)$ such that the strength of P_{j+k}^i in the initial subprocess $\{P_1^i, \ldots ,P_{j+k}^i\}$ is greater than the strength of P_{j+k}^i in $\{P_1^i, \ldots ,P_{j-1}^i, P_{j+1}^i, \ldots ,P_{j+k}^i\}$ and greater than the strength of P_{j+k}^i in its corresponding empty process $(P_1^i \vee \sim P_1^i)$ & P_{j+k}^i.

One may also want to frown upon processes that are "too fat"; i.e., processes with links that contain information that does not contribute to the strength of later links (and thus to the process leading to A). Since the contribution of each stage (prior to A) to a process leading to A is to increase the strength of subsequent stages, extra "fat" in a stage would be information that does not add to the strength of the subsequent stages. Since the last stage is A, the optimal "lean" figure of a process is dictated from the top by A. Given a process leading to A, the specifications given so far unduly allow us to add unnecessary and immaterial information to its links without affecting the viability of the process as leading to A (or even its strength as a whole, in cases in which the links added to are not the weakest). We may well want to weed out such immaterial information.

Accordingly, let us consider conjunctive decompositions $(P_j^i)'$ and $(P_j^i)''$ of each stage P_j^i such that $(P_j^i)'$ and $(P_j^i)''$ together contain the same factual information as P_j^i relative to the information accumulated via the previous stages of the process and the world history prior to the process (and, of course, the laws), and such that $(P_j^i)'$ and $(P_j^i)''$ are not equivalent in terms of factual information (relative to the same accumulated information). What we may require now for a process description to be "lean" is that, if one component of any such decomposition of a stage is eliminated from the process description, the strength (i.e., the probabilistic status) of some later stage will be adversely affected. Of course, freeing a stage of a process from extra "fat" that does not increase the strength of later links also increases the strength of this stage itself.

5. Now the notion of the strength of a process is significant for the notion of the processes most likely to have led to A. The higher the strength of respective stages of the process, the more "naturally" would the process lead to A. The stronger a process is, the more probable its weakest stage would be,[13] and the more "naturally" it would therefore lead to A. The weaker the stages of a process are, the less qualified it would be to count among the most likely processes[14] to have led to A. What one wants from the processes most likely to have led to A is that the ascending route of the process should proceed through stages that are optimally probable (A being the final destination) in comparison with possible alternatives (given the previous stages, the history prior to the processes, and the supplementary accumulated information); that is, one wants to maximize the strengths of the stages. Yet there is a trade-off in the strengthening of earlier and later stages: excessive accumulation of information at stages just before the last need not make the process more likely to have led to A (if that would make the strength of the very last stage high at the price of lowering the strengths of these very stages below the range of strengths

of the other stages in the process). Thus, the first step in selecting the processes most likely to have led to A is to select the processes leading to A with the greatest relative strength. To do that, take a process out of this lot with the greatest strength,[15] and select the set of processes leading to A whose strength is close enough (relative to the spectrum of strengths of this lot) to the strength of this one. Selecting this set will be the first step toward selecting the processes most likely to have led to A.[16]

Having performed the above selection, we perform a second selection on this set in order to get the set of process descriptions most likely to have led to A: From the above set, we select the most probable processes. Now in assessing here the probability of a process P (of course, under a description), one would want to make use of those features of the actual-world description in the interval t_p to which the process is causally irrelevant or purely positively causally relevant as it progresses through its stages. This is so since our perspective in finding the processes most likely *to have led* to A is that of W_{tA} rather than that of W_{tp} (for some process P; contrast this with the notion of the most probable process to *lead* to A given W_{tP}, for some t_P). Given the actual history W_{tA}, which was succeeded by the occurrence of the $\sim A$-event, we are asking which processes would be those most likely to have led to A. Thus, we should not assess the probability of a process P for our purposes here by simply taking $P(\underset{i=1}{\overset{k}{\&}}P_i/W_{tP})$. Rather, we should add to the evidence the pertinent information from the actual-world description, that is, information specifying features of the actual-world description in the interval t_P to which the process is causally irrelevant or purely positively causally relevant as it progresses through its stages. This information is (see 2 above):

(1) $\quad \underset{k=1}{\overset{n}{\overline{U}}}{}^{1}\mathrm{CIP}(\underset{m=1}{\overset{k}{\&}}P_m, W_{tP_{k+1}}) \qquad$ for $P = \{P_1, \ldots, P_n\}$

If we were to ignore this pertinent information, the probability of a process $\{P_1^i, \ldots, P_h^i\}$ would be the product of the "modified" strengths of its stages, where the modified strength of a stage P_j^i consists of its strength [as in (10)] with the last item omitted, i.e.: $P(P_j^i/W_{tP^i} \cup \underset{k=1}{\overset{j-1}{\&}} P_k^i)$. But since we want this pertinent information taken into account in calculating the probability of a process that is suitable for our concerns here, we should rather take the probability of the process P^i to be the product of the strengths of its stages, i.e.:

(12) $\quad \underset{i=1}{\overset{n}{\Pi}}S(P_j^i,P^i)$

Thus, the second step in the selection amounts to picking the most probable of the processes selected in the first step, in this sense of the probability of a process. So take the lowest upper bound of the probabilities of the processes selected in the previous selection, and select all the processes (from this group) with probabilities that fall within a small neighborhood of this lowest upper bound (relative to the spectrum of probabilities of processes selected in the first selection).[17] Thus, the processes to be considered for the analysis of a counterfactual under the l-p interpretation are the most probable (given W_{t_A}) of all the processes with the highest strength from among those processes which could have led to A: these are the processes that are the most likely to have led to A. Thus, considering again the Goodman-type example 6 concerning the match and the matchbox, some processes in which John got up and went to the next room, picked up the match and a matchbox, and struck the match against the matchbox, will be selected in the second selection over processes in which a flood from the ocean threw the match and struck it against the matchbox (in which case the match would not have lit), by virtue of being more probable (given W_{t_A}).

(Notice that the preference for "leaner" processes would be reflected in both selections. If to a stage, which is not the weakest in a process, extra "fat" is added, it may thereby become the weakest, thus making the resulting process description lower in strength in comparison with the original process description. Moreover, adding information to a process description will lower its probability. Thus, even if the addition of some "fat" to a process description does not affect its strength, it will nonetheless lower its probability.)

We have taken here a strategy of double selection which would yield the most likely processes to have led to A: first, a highest-strength selection and then a highest-probability selection. One may wonder, of course: why not immediately take a highest-probability selection of all the processes leading to A? The reason is that, to a considerable extent, the probability of a process description is determined by how detailed it is. The more informative a process description is, the less probable it is. A hasty highest-probability selection from the start would have yielded the most meager processes — which is not what we seek. This factor of how informatively rich a process description is must therefore be neutralized first. This is done in the first selection. Surely the stronger the stages of a process are, the more probable it is. So in performing the strength selection we stay in line with our main objective. But maximizing the strength would also yield processes with increasing number of stages with additional information conducive to the strength of later stages. By first selecting the strongest processes, we attempt to neutralize the factor of how detailed a process description is and are then free to exercise a straight probability selection.[18]

Notice also that the n-d interpretation on which I have concentrated up to this chapter is a special case of the l-p interpretation. For the n-d interpretation, the antecedent A is compatible with W_{t_A}, and so the only relevant process is the empty process consisting of A alone and diverging at W_{t_A}. For this process, schema (8), the inferential schema for a given process on the l-p interpretation, yields just the schema of the n-d interpretation. Recall that schema (8) was

(8) $W_{t_{P^i}} \cup P^i \cup \{A\} \cup \mathrm{Sup}(P^i, A, W_{\bar{t}_B}) \overset{L}{\rightarrow} B$

This is so since, in $\mathrm{Sup}(P^i, A, W_{\bar{t}_B})$, defined in (7) as

(7) $\overset{n}{\underset{j}{\,\bar{\underset{=}{U}}\,}}^1_1 \text{CIP} \, (\overset{i}{\underset{k=1}{\&}} P^i_k, W_{tP^i_j+1}) + \text{CIP}(P^i, A, W_{\bar{t}B})$

the first component will be vacuous (since $n=1$), and $\text{CIP}(P^i, A, W_{\bar{t}B})$, when $P^i = \{A\}$, is just $\text{CIP}(A, W_{\bar{t}B})$, the last component of the schema of the inferential model on the n-d interpretation [schema 2(18″) of 2 IX], or

$$W_{tA} \cup \{A\} \cup \text{CIP}(A, W_{\bar{t}B}) \overset{\text{L}}{\to} B$$

Thus, on the n-d interpretation, instead of considering various processes that could have led to A, we simply took the actual history that *in fact* led to A. Since on the l-p interpretation the augmentation of information from the portion of the actual-world description pertaining to the time interval t_p to which a selected process P pertains is conducted along the same lines as those governing the preservation of information from the portion of the actual-world description pertaining to the (t_A, t_B) interval under the n-d interpretation, the l-p interpretation is clearly a *natural extension* of the n-d interpretation, the latter being a *special case* of the former.[19]

6. The account presented in 4 and 5 is somewhat tentative, and it would be premature at this point to endorse it as it stands. But it should give an idea of how the notion of "the processes most likely to have led to A" could be made more precise in a plausible way. And apart from the question of whether or not the specific account in 5 is right for the purpose of interpreting counterfactuals along l-p lines, I would like to argue that the central notion of the analysis which is at issue here — the notion of the processes most likely to have led to A — is not a contrived or artificial one and that, regardless of how adequate the account presented above is, it is a basic and important notion worth clarifying.

Consider the following situation (Example 8). Suppose you are in charge of Israel's emergency civil defense system. You are told now to prepare for the possibility of a war breaking out a year from now.

There are various ways you can organize the available resources. It would be foolish to attempt to prepare for *every* conceivable scenario of war breaking out one year from now — this would be spreading the fixed and limited resources allotted to you too thin to ensure adequate preparation for any of the eventualities. Thus, it would be imprudent to waste resources preparing for an invasion by extraterrestrial creatures, or for a war with Argentina, or for a war that would erupt in circumstances in which Israel is allied with the Soviet Union, or for a war in which Israel in alliance with neighboring Arab countries is fighting Western Europe. Also to be ignored are processes under which most of Israel's population would die from some disease within half a year, or under which 20 million people would immigrate to Israel over the next year, or under which within a year a kangaroo would be Israel's prime minister. The problem, then, is to prepare for the most probable eventualities or scenarios that could lead to war in a year. Now intuitively this notion of the most probable scenarios for war one year hence is far from an empty notion. The challenge is to make this notion precise.[20]

Now I suggest that there is a close affinity between the situation described here and the problem of how to make precise the notion of the processes most likely to have led to A. Suppose no war with Israel will erupt over the next year and a half (starting from the time you read this book). A year and a half from now someone may entertain the counterfactual antecedent 'Had a war involving Israel erupted half a year ago, . . . '. Suppose he decided to consider processes leading to this antecedent and diverging from the actual world at the time at which you read this book. Now if he were to pursue our course here and look for the processes most likely to have led to the antecedent, he would be in a problem situation with strong affinity to the situation just described,[21] in which we want to specify the most probable scenarios that could lead to war a year from now.[22]

II   De Dicto *and* De Re *Counterfactuals*

1. When applying the l-p interpretation to counterfactual antecedents of the form 'Had *a* been *F*' or 'Had *a* been $\imath x G x$' (where '*a*' is a proper name and '$\imath x G x$' is a definite description) such as the antecedent discussed in (5) of the previous section ('Had Reagan been president of the U.S. on 1/21/77, . . . '), we consider a variety of processes leading to situations in which the antecedent is literally true, that is, situations in which the very "same" character as the actual *a* is *F* or is $\imath x G x$ (in our example, situations in which Reagan himself was president). Such counterfactuals thereby receive a *de re* interpretation (with respect to that occurrence of the proper name '*a*'[23]). But in some cases such a literal *de re* reading under the l-p interpretation seems highly implausible. For instance, consider a metaphorical counterfactual such as:

(13)   Had Carter been a dog, he would have barked but not bitten.

It would be gratuitous to endorse a literal, *de re* l-p interpretation for such a counterfactual, and consider processes under which Carter could have turned into a dog.[24] What, then, does counterfactual (13) convey? Its message is rather of the following sort:

(13')   Carter has a certain character feature which, when present in dogs, is manifested in barking-but-not-biting behavior.

Such a counterfactual serves therefore to draw attention to a certain alleged *feature* that Carter is taken to have, without specifying it directly, by pointing out its manifestations in other creatures. Often our vocabulary is too lean to allow for a direct characterization of certain features. The counterfactual construction enables us to complement this limited vocabulary by drawing attention to the consequences of having such features in hypothetical situations. The above counterfactual, so interpreted, serves to draw attention to a certain feature that the bearer of the proper name in it is taken to have.

Another case in point would be a counterfactual such as[25]:

(14)   Had Ben Gurion been a Palestinian, he would have joined the
PLO.

It would likewise be highly implausible to impose a literal *de re* interpretation here. It would be inappropriate to consider processes leading to situations in which Ben Gurion himself was a Palestinian. If we are to have a
counterfactual with a metaphysically possible antecedent, we observe that
Ben Gurion could have hardly been born a Palestinian.[26] And it would also
be misguided to consider here such processes of his becoming a Palestinian
as his being abducted and adopted by a Palestinian family as a child,
which a literal *de re* l-p interpretation would call for — and notice that
under such processes this counterfactual need not come out true (his
character might have developed differently, etc.). Rather, this counterfactual conveys the following sort of message:

(14′)   Ben Gurion had certain features of character and a conception
of nationalism that would lead Palestinians who have such
features and conceptions to join the PLO.

Again, the counterfactual serves to draw attention to certain alleged
features of Ben Gurion, and does not lend itself to a plausible literal *de re*
l-p interpretation.[27]

2. Notice now a certain vagueness which appears in certain counterfactuals. For instance, consider:

(15)   Had I been in your situation, . . .

(16)   Had X been in Y's shoes, . . .

In (15) your particular situation-token is alluded to. Now, of course, it is
never possible for me to have been in *exactly* the very same situation that
you have been in, since that situation involved you, not me. Nor is it often
feasible just to relax a bit and allow for the very same situation *except* that
I replace you. Thus, in the counterfactual:

Had General McArthur been in Napoleon's situation in
Waterloo, he would . . .

such a "relaxed" interpretation would yield a metaphysically impossible
antecedent.[28] Rather, the allusion is to a *type* of situation manifested by
a situation token of that type. Thus, the natural reading of (15) would be:

(15′)   Had I been in *the sort* of situation you are in, . . .

But the specification of the situation-type is not made explicit here: it is
made only via a token, which leaves considerable vagueness, since any

particular is a token of many types. Thus, such a counterfactual involves a *type-specification vagueness*. But once a situation type is selected, the counterfactual can be interpreted along l-p lines in a natural way (by considering processes that could have led to my being in this situation-type).

Notice incidentally that counterfactuals of the sort:

(17)   If I were you, I would have acted thus.

cannot plausibly receive a literal interpretation, since, as I take it, it is metaphysically impossible for me to be you. Rather, they are really elliptic for other forms: often their antecedents are elliptic for (15). Normally, they have the import of advice, such as:

(17′)   You would be better off if you acted thus.

[This is normally also a viable reading of the corresponding counterfactual with antecedent (15), i.e., 'Had I been in your situation I would have acted thus'.]

We have just seen cases in which a literal *de re* l-p interpretation would be inappropriate. As another example, consider:

(18)   Had Kissinger been the prime minister of China, he would have worked toward detente with the Soviet Union.

Now it would be gratuitous to interpret this counterfactual along literal *de re* l-p lines, and consider processes leading to situations in which Kissinger himself is China's prime minister. Rather, the message of this counterfactual is that Kissinger has certain general principles of political strategy which, were they to be applied in Chinese foreign policy, would lead to aiming at detente with the Soviet Union. Thus, again, a typical feature of Kissinger is alluded to by the use of the proper name. But although it singles out a feature of Kissinger, the counterfactual should not be construed under a literal *de re* reading, for it does not call for consideration of situations in which the antecedent is literally true. This comes out clearly in the following way of rendering the antecedent of this counterfactual, which lends itself smoothly to an l-p interpretation:

(18′)   Had *a* Kissinger been the prime minister of China, . . .

Like the counterfactual antecedent (15) considered above ('Had I been in your situation, . . . '), this construction alludes to some *type* of which Kissinger is a token, without explicitly specifying the type. A similar use is made of this construction in such sentences as:

(19)   Had Hitler become an anonymous art teacher, someone else might have become a Hitler.

meaning: someone else might have become of the same type that Hitler represents. Use of this construction is also being made in noncounterfactual sentences such as:

(19′)   This dictator is a real Hitler.

which means that he is of the type that Hitler represents. Thus, the English construction 'an *a*', when '*a*' is a proper name, serves the role of alluding to a feature typical of *a*. The counterfactual 'Had a Kissinger been a prime minister of China, . . . ' however, is not to be read as a *de re* counterfactual (with respect to the occurrence of 'Kissinger'), but rather as *de dicto*. Interpreted along l-p lines, it calls for consideration of processes that would lead to there being someone who is both a Kissinger and a prime minister of China. If, as I argue, the formulation with 'a Kissinger' is the right rendering of the original counterfactual (18), then the original counterfactual should be construed along *de dicto* rather than *de re* lines.

Of course, here we face the same vagueness in specifying a type when a token is given which we faced in the counterfactual 'Had I been in your situation, . . . '. This vagueness in both counterfactuals would be resolved differently in different contexts. Notice though that this vagueness infects the antecedents (15′) and (18′) (i.e., their indicative versions) but does not inhere in the counterfactual construction *per se*. The proper name in the counterfactual (18) above, concerning Kissinger, the way we read it, serves as a *feature indicator*, reflecting the fact that this counterfactual is not to be read *de re* with respect to this proper name. Thus, this counterfactual yields a natural interpretation along l-p lines when read *de dicto*; its antecedent is understood as (18′), in which 'a Kissinger' replaces 'Kissinger'.

Such a *de dicto* reading also applies naturally to counterfactuals that might seem to suggest a sort of time-transplant. Consider a counterfactual of the sort:

(20)   Had Abraham Lincoln been the U.S. president in the 1960s, he would have handled the civil rights problems thus.

Here again a literal *de re* l-p interpretation would seem to be out of place. To consider it is to entertain processes that could have led to Lincoln's being alive in the 1960s, which would seem to require the invention of life-elongation methods, or a time machine, or the like.[29] Rather, what is called for is an interpretation that would make a counterfactual of this sort read as:

(20′)   Had *a* Lincoln been president in the 1960s, . . .

which is now readily interpreted along l-p lines (calling for the consideration of processes leading to a president in the 1960s who is a Lincoln). So interpreted, the occurrence of 'Lincoln' in this counterfactual does not function in the normal capacity of proper names in *de re* counterfactual contexts, and the reading of the counterfactual is *de dicto* rather than *de re* with respect to the locution 'a Lincoln'.

Another example of this kind would be Quine's[30] famous counterfactual:

(21)   Had Caesar been the U.S. commander in Korea, . . .

Again, a literal *de re* interpretation (with respect to 'Caesar') seems unacceptable here: it would be off base to consider, under the l-p interpretation, processes that would keep Caesar alive up to 1953. Rather, the *de dicto* reading of this counterfactual would amount to:

(21')   Had *a* Caesar been the U.S. commander in Korea, . . .

It remains vague which typical features of Caesar are alluded to here. If the allusion is to his military aggressiveness, then perhaps the consequent 'he would have used the atomic bomb' would make for a plausible counterfactual. If the allusion is to his commitment to a specific military doctrine, then perhaps the consequent 'he would have used catapults' would become a candidate for making it a true counterfactual. Which typical features are alluded to will depend on the context in question.[31]

We have seen cases in which the literal *de re* reading is inappropriate, and in which the counterfactual should rather be read along *de dicto* lines. There are, however, intermediate cases were both readings are viable. Thus, consider the counterfactual:

(22)   Had Harry Truman been president in 1980, he would have
        handled the Iranian hostage crisis differently.

It is not so inappropriate to consider here a literal *de re* interpretation with processes leading to Truman himself being president in 1980 as it is to consier Lincoln instead. Yet, even here we would have to consider Truman as president in his nineties, possibly senile. But of course, it is open to us to consider the *de dicto* reading, on which *a* Truman is president in 1980. In such a case, where a *de re* reading is not gratuitous and yet is quite far-fetched, it seems that both readings are viable. Yet, when a *de re* reading is clearly appropriate, it is dominant, and the *de dicto* reading gives way: the normal functioning of proper names is *de re*, and when such a reading is viable, the sentence is to be read accordingly. Also notice that in the *de re* reading we need not resort to type-token context-dependence, which allows the counterfactual to be objective in character.

3. In 1, above, we discussed counterfactuals (13) and (14). It is not, however, necessary to resort to noncounterfactual constructions such as (13') and (14') in order to express the *de dicto* reading of counterfactuals (13) and (14), as we did there. On the basis of our discussion there, we can attempt to express them as: Carter has a certain quality such that, had

some dogs had it, they would have barked (tended to bark) but not bitten (tended to bite); and: Ben Gurion had certain qualities such that, had some Palestinians had them, they would have joined (tended to join) the PLO. But it would not be quite right to interpret these counterfactuals in this way, as involving claims to the effect that so-and-so merely had certain sorts of properties, characterized counterfactually. The false counterfactual 'Had Ben Gurion been a Palestinian, he would have spoken Hebrew' would come out true under such a construal, since speaking Hebrew is a feature that Ben Gurion had (and, of course, had some Palestinians had this feature, they would have spoken Hebrew). Rather, what is involved here is that attention is drawn to some *salient* quality of Carter or Ben Gurion. Above we considered cases in the *de dicto* reading of which the proper name served as a feature indicator, a role explicitly manifest in forms such as 'a Kissinger', 'a Lincoln', etc. It seems plausible that a similar mechanism is at work in counterfactuals (13) and (14) as well. Thus, we should render (13) as:

(13″)   Had some dogs been of a Carter type, they would have barked (tended to bark) but not bitten (tended to bite).

and render (14) as:

(14″)   Had some Palestinians been of a Ben Gurion type, they would have joined (tended to join) the PLO.[32]

Again, as in counterfactual (18), these forms involve a basic vagueness as to which types (manifested by Carter and Ben Gurion) are alluded to here by the type indicators 'a Carter', 'a Ben Gurion', 'a Kissinger', etc. Such vagueness would involve context-dependence as well: one type would be alluded to in some contexts, a different type in others. It is inherent in the role of proper names in the *de dicto* reading of such counterfactuals that they allude to a feature or a type that is not specified uniquely or explicitly (indeed, the counterfactual construction involving proper names in such cases often helps to further characterize such features, which might be hard to specify otherwise). But such context-dependence, again, now resides in the surface form of particular locutions that occur *within* the antecedent (or the consequent) when the counterfactual is rendered into a transparently *de dicto* form [as in (15′), (18′), (13″) and (14″)], just as this context-dependence is manifested in noncounterfactual constructions (e.g.: we need a Roosevelt for president); but this context-dependence does not reside in the counterfactual construction itself.[33]

III   An L-P/N-D Ambiguity

1. In section I we discussed the l-p interpretation, which involves a selection of a set of processes leading to A, such that the determination of the truth value of the counterfactual requires its evaluation via all these processes. These processes were primarily selected in virtue of their prob-

abilistic characteristics as the processes most likely to have led to A (as elaborated there). Thus, the selection involved the most probable of the set of processes of the highest strength leading to the antecedent A. For a given counterfactual antecedent A, let us call the lowest upper bound of probabilities represented in the final selection of processes the **plausibility characteristic of** A, or for short: **PC(A)**. Of course, the plausibility characteristic of A would vary with the counterfactual antecedent A: for some counterfactuals, relatively probable processes would be selected, for others, relatively improbable ones.

Throughout most of this book (up to this chapter), we have concentrated on the n-d interpretation, spelled out in schema 2(18) of 2 IX. In presenting the l-p interpretation, of which the n-d interpretation is a special case, in section I 5 above, we took the l-p interpretation to apply to counterfactuals whose antecedents are *incompatible* with their prior history (but are still logically, metaphysically, and law-wise possible). We may now observe that, for various counterfactuals whose antecedents are *compatible* with the prior history of the world, the l-p interpretation can nevertheless be applicable too. It is quite obvious that the procedure for determining whether a counterfactual does or does not come out true on the l-p interpretation is also well determined for counterfactuals whose antecedents are compatible with the prior history. Thus, actual as well as hypothetical processes can lead to antecedents that are compatible with their prior history. A selection on the basis of strength and probability is no different here from such selection in the case of antecedents incompatible with their prior history, and schema (8) is equally applicable for both kinds of antecedents. The point to notice, however, is that on occasion we intuitively want to allow an l-p interpretation for a counterfactual with an antecedent compatible with the prior history. Some counterfactuals manifest an ambiguity which reflects the application of the n-d interpretation on the one hand, and of the l-p interpretation on the other (as we shall see in an example below). That is, the n-d interpretation is not always the exclusive interpretation for counterfactuals of this sort, though normally it is. The question thus arises as to when a counterfactual with an antecedent A compatible with W_{t_A} should be read on the n-d interpretation and when it should be read according to the l-p interpretation.[34]

What is crucial, I propose, in deciding when a counterfactual with an antecedent A compatible with W_{t_A} has a viable l-p reading, is the comparison between the following features of the counterfactual antecedent under the two interpretations: For the n-d interpretation, the important feature is the probability $P(A/W_{t_A})$. For the l-p interpretation, in which processes leading to A are contemplated (even though A is compatible with W_{t_A}), the important feature is PC(A), the plausibility characteristic of A. When $P(A/W_{t_A})$ is at least as high as PC(A), the n-d interpretation is the dominant one: this case is the exclusive province of the n-d interpretation. In this case, the l-p interpretation does not offer us significantly more probable alternatives to the actual course for consideration; and when alternatives are not more appealing, the actual course is naturally in a privileged position. (Remember also that the analysis under the n-d interpretation is clearly simpler than under the l-p interpretation.) When, however, $P(A/W_{tA})$ is lower than $PC(A)$ to a significant degree, we get cases of ambiguity, in which both interpretations are viable and which therefore allows for two readings of the counterfactual with possibly two different truth values. This is natural, since when $P(A/W_{tA})$ is too low, it is only reasonable to consider alternatives that provide for higher probability than is offered by the actual course of events.

In cases where there is ambiguity, the principle of charity will be operative: we shall prefer a reading that maximizes the chances of the sentence being true. Regarding a counterfactual $A > B$, the truth values of both $A > B$ and its opposing counterfactual $A > \sim B$ are relevant here. If under one reading either $A > B$ or $A > \sim B$ seems true, whereas on the other reading both are false, the first reading will be preferred. If, however, on one reading $A > B$ is true but on the other $A > \sim B$ is also true, we get a case of ambiguity in which both readings are viable but yield different truth values. When the two readings agree, the n-d interpretation has an edge in virtue of its simplicity.

Thus, to conclude, when the antecedent A is incompatible with the prior history W_{tA}, the counterfactual is amenable only to the l-p interpretation. When the antecedent A is compatible with the prior history and $P(A/W_{tA})$ is higher than or equal to $PC(A)$, only the n-d interpretation is viable. Otherwise, if A is compatible with W_{tA} and $P(A/W_{tA})$ is significantly less than $PC(A)$, the counterfactual is amenable to both interpretations. Which interpretation will dominate will be decided by the principle of charity (with respect to $A > B$ and $A > \sim B$).

We are now in a position to explain Downing's counterfactual,[35] cited by Lewis:

> Jim and Jack quarreled yesterday, and Jack is still hopping mad. We conclude that if Jim asked Jack for help today, Jack would not help him. But wait: Jim is a prideful fellow. He never would ask for help after such a quarrel; if Jim were to ask Jack for help today, there would have to have been no quarrel yesterday. In this case Jack would be his usually generous self. So if Jim asked Jack for help today, Jack would help him after all.

The counterfactual antecedent A here is 'Had Jim asked Jack for help today', with the consequent B being 'Jack would not help him'. Now, according to the story told, it seems that $P(A/W_{tA})$, i.e., the probability of Jim's asking Jack for help after what has actually transpired between them, is very small, and processes leading to A in which the two have not quarreled are of a higher probability (and thus more viable). Thus, the plausibility characteristic here seems higher than $P(A/W_{tA})$, which opens the way for an ambiguity. The n-d interpretation would made $A > B$ true. On the other hand, since under the processes most likely to have led to A, Jim and Jack would not have quarreled, the l-p interpretation would make $A > \sim B$ true. Thus, the n-d interpretation and the l-p interpretation would make the opposing counterfactuals $A > B$ and $A > \sim B$ true respectively, and would thus yield an ambiguity,[36] in accordance with the foregoing account.[37]

IV   Odd Counterfactuals: World De Re versus World De Dicto

1. Reverse Temporal Order. So far we have considered only counterfactuals $A > B$ of **standard temporal order**, in which $t_A \leq t_B$. Counterfactuals that do not fulfill this condition are of **reverse temporal order**. Among counterfactuals of reverse temporal order we must distinguish, however, counterfactuals in which $\bar{t}_B < t_A$, which can be called counterfactuals with **purely reverse temporal order**. Both the n-d interpretation and the l-p interpretation can be applied to counterfactuals with reverse temporal order, and our normal analysis remains intact regarding them. Notice though that, in the case of purely-reverse-temporal-order counterfactuals, there will not be any legitimate premises pertaining to times weakly later than t_A: on the n-d interpretation for this sort of counterfactuals, there will not be any members of $\text{CIP}(A, W_{\bar{t}_B})$ among the implicit premises [since there is no interval (t_A, t_B) when $\bar{t}_B < t_A$], and similarly, in schema (8) above of the l-p interpretation, $\text{CIP}(P^i, A, W_{\bar{t}_B})$ [in $\text{Sup}(P^i, A, W_{\bar{t}_B})$; cf. (7)] will be empty. Of course, on the n-d interpretation, a counterfactual $A > B$ with purely reverse temporal order is true iff B is true (i.e., iff B belongs to W_{t_A}). Normally, counterfactuals of this sort seem awkward (e.g.: 'Had Carter decided in 1979 not to run for reelection, he would still have been elected president in 1976'). This awkwardness is adequately explained in terms of conversational efficacy: since such counterfactuals are equivalent to their consequents, one may just as well assert the consequent alone; thus, resorting to the much more complex counterfactual construction is awkward. On the other hand, a counterfactual $A > B$ with purely reverse temporal order under the l-p interpretation will be true iff B follows by law from the complex antecedent in schema (8) [with $\text{CIP}(P^i, A, W_{\bar{t}_B})$ being empty] for every selected process P^i leading to A. Thus, for counterfactuals with purely reverse temporal order, the counterfactual will not, of course, be equivalent to its consequent. Thus, counterfactuals with purely reverse temporal order are degenerate under the n-d interpretation, but not under the l-p interpretation.[38]

In section III we have discussed the question of when a counterfactual antecedent is amenable to the n-d interpretation alone, to the l-p interpretation alone, or to both. Notice that these considerations hinged on the antecedent alone, and not on the consequent. Whether a counterfactual is amenable to one interpretation or the other (or to both) is therefore independent of whether it is of standard or reverse temporal order.[39]

2. Counterlegals and World De Dicto vs. World De Re. Counterlegals are counterfactuals whose antecedents, alone, are incompatible with the laws of nature (i.e., apart from any description of factual circumstances). Now

sometimes they assume a relatively innocuous form: this is so when the antecedent is interpreted to mean that a certain change occurred in the laws at a certain time without implying that some laws have *always* been different. An example of a counterlegal of this simpler kind, which we can call a **weak counterlegal**, would be:

(22) If the gravity constant dropped by a third yesterday, various satellites would escape to outer space.

The interpretation of this sort of counterlegal is akin to that of counterfactuals of the n-d type, in that the world history and the laws prior to the time of change specified in the antecedent are preserved. Such counterlegals would then be *of* the actual world (when assessed there): this is manifested by their truth value's being a function of facts in the actual world,[40] and is reflected in their being interpreted along lines of divergence from the actual world, via the preservation of W_t for some t. Thus, in analogy to the n-d interpretion, weak counterlegals of the above sort have a literal interpretation, in that they can be read as drawing attention to courses of events in which the antecedent is literally true, which diverge from the actual course.[41]

But if a counterlegal antecedent is understood to imply that some laws have been different from time immemorial (in which case it can be called a **strong counterlegal**), the situation is radically different. Then, no natural divergence interpretation is possible, and the counterlegal is no longer *about* the actual world. A counterfactual is **world *de re*** if it is *about* the particular possible-world description (or world) in which it is evaluated, in which case its truth value is a function of, and its interpretation therefore relies on, factual features specific to that possible-world description (or world) which are neither explicitly formulated in the antecedent nor semantically presupposed. Thus, counterfactuals falling under the n-d or the l-p interpretations are of course world *de re*: the use made of W_{tA} and of $\mathrm{CIP}(A, W_{\bar{t}B})$ in the n-d interpretation indicates the world *de re* character of counterfactuals under the n-d interpretation, and analogously for counterfactuals under the l-p interpretation. But a counterfactual is **world *de dicto*** when its truth value is not dependent upon facts not explicitly specified or semantically presupposed and when no use of such facts is made in its interpretation.[42] Fundamental to my conception here is that being world *de re* requires an interpretation that incorporates a divergence from the actual world at some point in time. Counterfactuals that are world *de dicto* must be interpreted *without* recourse to information that is not specified in the indicative versions of their components, either explicitly or in a presupposed manner (of a standard sort, i.e., *not* unique to the counterfactual construction). Strong counterlegals are thus true iff their antecedents (via their noncounterfactual presuppositions) yield their consequents. Their interpretation does not allow, therefore, for a dependence on factual features of the world in which they are assessed, and of course for no divergence from it either. Strong counterlegals are, therefore, world *de dicto*. Strong counterlegals thus come out as a fairly impoverished sort of relatively uninteresting sentences in that the counterfactual construction collapses in these cases to the relation of logical consequence (plus accommodation for noncounterfactual presuppositions).[43] Their interpretation is accordingly quite formal, and not literal like that of weak counterlegals. Yet, counterfactuals that do not allow for a natural divergence from the actual world in their interpretation *must* be, according to my view, world *de dicto*.[44]

One must distinguish between the world *de re*/world *de dicto* distinction, on the one hand, and, on the other hand, the object *de re*/object *de dicto* distinction, which is the standard *de re*/*de dicto* distinction. A counterfactual that is object *de re* is necessarily world *de re*. A counterfactual that is world *de dicto* is necessarily object *de dicto*. But a counterfactual can be object *de dicto* but world *de re*: this would be the case with (object) *de dicto* counterfactuals falling under the n-d and l-p interpretations. Strong counterlegals can be sensibly interpreted in a world *de dicto* way (as indicated above), but not in a world *de re* way.

3. Metaphysically Impossible Antecedents. A word on metaphysically impossible antecedents is now in order. If a denoting singular term occurs *de re* in a counterfactual, it must pick up the "same"[45] character in all possible-world descriptions used for the evaluation of that counterfactual. On my view, identification across possible-world descriptions hinges on there being a common root, traceable via genidentity.[46] Thus, two characters in two different possible-world descriptions are "the same" provided they share a common root. This requires that those two possible-world descriptions diverge from each other at some point late enough to allow both characters to belong in the history that these two possible-world descriptions share. Characters that are the "same" as a certain actual individual can therefore be found only in possible-world descriptions that diverge from the actual course at points in time later than the beginning of the interval that covers the actual existence of that actual individual.[47] Such a view would see various aspects of the circumstances of its coming into existence as common to all the possible-world descriptions in which the individual is to be found and, thus, as essential to that individual. On such a view of essentialism of origins, then, it would not be true that Carter could have lived in the seventeenth century (since in all possible-world description diverging from the actual world before the end of the seventeenth century there is no Jimmy Carter), nor would it be true that Napoleon might have been identical with Caesar (both read *de re*, of course). Thus, for (object) *de re* counterfactuals, the divergence times contemplated (under the n-d or the l-p interpretation) must not be prior to the actual existence of the individuals denoted by the singular terms that occur *de re* within them.[48] If the divergence times required (for the n-d or l-p interpretations) are too early to allow for a *de re* reading, then the counterfactual does not have a viable literal *de re* reading, as indeed is the case in, e.g,:

Had Carter lived in the seventeenth century, . . .

since counterfactuals with impossible antecedents do not get a literal interpretation,[49] and, on the view of essentialism of origins presented here, it
is impossible for Carter to have lived in the seventeenth century.[50]

However (recalling our discussion in section II), it is clear that such a
counterfactual can nevertheless receive a literal counterfactual interpretation provided it is read *de dicto* with respect to the proper name in it.
Thus, an l-p interpretation would apply in a straightforward way to the
counterfactual:

Had *a* Carter lived in the seventeenth century, . . .

and would require the consideration of processes leading to a Carter-type
(determined via the context in question) living in the seventeenth century.

In section II 1 we considered counterfactual (13) ('Had Carter been a
dog, he would have barked but not bitten'), which had an impossible
antecedent. This counterfactual was shown to be elliptic for a counterfactual *de dicto* in character. However, in other cases, the resort to other
counterfactual forms for which a counterfactual with an impossible antecedent is elliptic seems pointless: sometimes when a speaker wants to convey a message that is not hypothetical in character, a ride is taken on the
counterfactual construction based on the entrenched relation between
laws and counterfactuals parasitic on them which are automatically true
(when the antecedent is possible).[51] Thus, instead of *asserting* a generalization, the speaker uses the counterfactual construction in a way that *suggests* the generalization, which constitutes the real import of the assertion
made via the counterfactual sentence. Thus, if someone claims:

If I had been a home cat, I would have had no worries in life.

the message conveyed is that home cats have no worries.[52] In terms of its
form, the counterfactual is parasitic on this generalization. The antecedent is metaphysically impossible, however, and the use of the counterfactual construction is not literal. There is no point here in resorting to a *de
dicto* reading, since, because of the character of the generalization, nothing specific to the speaker plays any role here. This counterfactual sentence
is a mere pseudo counterfactual: it has no literal counterfactual interpretation; it is merely elliptic for the corresponding generalization.[53]

Notice, however, that, when there is a viable literal *de re* interpretation, the *de re* reading is the primary reading for a counterfactual involving a proper name. The *de dicto* reading seems to be viable only when a
literal *de re* interpretation is not. The *de re* reading, unlike the *de dicto*
one, yields a context-independent interpretation that is objective in
character, which is a very important feature not to be given up lightly.

4. Context-Dependence Again. I would like to conclude by emphasizing
a difference between Lewis's latest approach (discussed in chapter 8) and

my own. On Lewis's view, context-dependence is a central feature of the counterfactual construction. According to such a view an adequate theory would have the central parameters of the analysis vary heavily with context. In accordance with this conception, Lewis called for the development of a theory that would determine the general parameters of his approach — respects, weights, priorities — as functions of the context, thereby sacrificing considerable predictive capacity (CDTA, p. 465).

By contrast, context plays a peripheral role in my analysis of counterfactuals, that is, apart from the role it plays in the context-dependence of the *non*counterfactual components in the counterfactual construction (which are on a par with the context-dependence of 'I' in 'Had I acted thus . . . ') and apart from the role it plays in the general phenomenon that sometimes two alternative readings are viable, where the dominance of one versus the other may depend on context. We have thus observed certain ambiguities and vagueness in counterfactuals: there was the ambiguity between the l-p and n-d interpretations in certain cases; there was the *de dicto/de re* ambiguity; and there was type/token vagueness in certain counterfactuals (on a *de dicto* reading). But in various examples we have shown that what was taken by various authors to be vagueness inherent in the counterfactual construction itself, calling for a highly context-dependent analysis, was merely a matter of ambiguity in the l-p/n-d interpretations, or type/token vagueness [e.g., the Caesar-Korea counterfactual (21), Downing's Jim-Jack counterfactual (in section III), the 'Had Lincoln been president in the 1960s, . . .'' type counterfactual (20), the 'If I were you, . . . ' type counterfactual (17), and the 'Had Carter lived in the seventeenth century, . . . ' type counterfactual of this section, 3], or *de re/de dicto* ambiguity, or else was not a matter of ambiguity or vagueness at all. In the theory I have developed in this book, context does not enter the analysis of counterfactuals under any of the various readings to any extent beyond the way it affects their noncounterfactual components.[54] For Lewis, context-dependence is a central and omnipresent feature in the similarity relation, which lies at the heart of his analysis of counterfactuals. This is therefore a major difference between his analysis and mine. It is the difference between upholding a crucial context-dependence in the determination of the basic parameters of the analysis (e.g., respects, weights, priorities) on the one hand, and, on the other, resorting to specific alternative readings for a couple of specific ambiguities (*de dicto/de re*, n-d/l-p), and recognizing that context-dependence which affects the *components* of the counterfactual construction rather than the construction itself (e.g., the type token vagueness).

I therefore conclude that Lewis assigns exaggerated importance to the role that context-dependence plays in understanding counterfactuals, and that the heavy emphasis placed on context-dependence in his recent analysis (CDTA) is ill-advised. Thus, to expect an analysis in terms of respects and weights or priorities that are heavily context-dependent, as Lewis does, seems misguided. The right interpretation of counterfactuals, I believe, does not reside primarily in figuring out the alleged heavy dependence on context of central parameters such as these. There is much less context-dependence in counterfactuals than has been appreciated. Whatever context-dependence there is in counterfactuals either is of the familiar kinds manifested in indicative noncounterfactual sentences[55] or else is playing a role in deciding between alternative readings in cases of two limited and well-specified ambiguities, such as those I have noted (of which only one—the n-d/l-p type—is specific to the counterfactual construction). Since on my account the counterfactual construction is not context-dependent and interest-relative, it does not come out nonobjective and empty on Quine's perspective; yet under Lewis's conception, it would become just that.[56]

V Counterfactuals and Determinism

1. The analysis of counterfactuals provided in this book was couched in probabilistic terms, and the notion of probability used was the notion of objective (nonepistemic) probability of degree of determination (cf. 4 I 1 and 4 X). But such objective probabilities other than 1 and 0 can be found only in a nondeterministic world. Similarly, the notion of divergence on which both the n-d interpretation and the l-p interpretation relied was formulated in terms of compatibility of a false sentence (the antecedent)[57] with a prior history. In a deterministic world a probabilistic conception of causal relevance is inapplicable, and so is consideration of diverging processes as relatively more probable or less probable. Accordingly, this analysis would not fit a deterministic world: in such a world, no counterfactual would qualify for either an n-d or an l-p interpretation. What, then, is the status of counterfactuals in a deterministic world?

Consider again a nondeterministic world, and suppose I ask you what would have happened had Reagan decided last May 1 not to spend last summer at his ranch in California. As I see it, you would consider the actual history prior to the decision together with the decision, and take it from there. If I asked you what would have happened had Kissinger been the Secretary of State yesterday, you would go back in time to a recent point where relatively probable processes leading to such a state of affairs would diverge from the actual world (while being, of course, compatible with their prior history),[58] and take it from there. But what could you say if I asked you what would have happened had Jimmy Carter both invaded Iran and had not invaded Iran? Or what would have happened had Carter turned during the Iranian crisis into the number π? It seems to me that the natural response to such counterfactuals, if taken literally, would be to shrug: one cannot seriously consider such counterfactual questions, nor can one seriously entertain counterfactuals with such antecedents. Obviously, counterfactual questions with logically and metaphysically impossible antecedents don't have literal answers;[59] such counterfactuals, if taken literally, involve a misuse of the counterfactual construction. To ask whether in such a case the number π would be a democratic president is ludicrous: the answer should be that the hypothesis in question is just impossible, and that counterfactuals with such antecedents, if taken literally, should just be dismissed.[60] Such counterfactuals simply don't have a literal interpretation.

Thus, counterfactuals can appear on the two extreme sides of the spectrum. Various counterfactuals, e.g., concerning what would have happened had I decided to stop writing now (in a nondeterministic world), possess a literal interpretation and a truth value. On the other extreme, counterfactuals with logically or metaphysically impossible antecedents have no literal interpretation. Counterfactuals in a deterministic world constitute an intermediate group: their antecedents are impossible, unlike those of the first kind, yet not logically or metaphysically so, but rather *historiophysically* (that is, given the history of the world up to any time and the laws). The question thus arises: Which of the above two kinds should they be assimilated to? I want to argue that they belong with the second class: that they are devoid of a literal *de re* interpretation.

Suppose now we move to consider a deterministic world. Let us consider the heavy burden of this assumption. In a deterministic world things have been determined to be the way they are since time immemorial. Whatever happens now or does not happen now has been fully determined, to the smallest detail. Whatever has happened now *must* have happened now, and whatever has not happened now necessarily did not happen now. Whatever did or did not transpire did so as a matter of sheer and total necessity. So consider such a world. The consideration in such a world of what would have happened had Ford been president on 2/2/81, should encounter the response that this is just impossible: the world the way it is has been determined to be that way from time immemorial. So it has been determined that Reagan, rather than Ford, be president on 2/2/81, and it is just impossible for Ford to have been president on that date, as a matter of historiophysical necessity. Since the hypothesis is just impossible, because Ford couldn't possibly have been president on 2/2/81, the question, taken literally, is pointless.

The same holds, given that the world is deterministic, regarding the counterfactual question: What would have happened had Reagan, the very person, turned suddenly on Christmas Eve of 1978 into a communist sympathizer? In such a world it has been determined as a matter of necessity that Reagan retain his anti-communist convictions throughout 1980. It was clearly historiophysically *impossible* for the counterfactual antecedent to have materialized (that is, given some prior history and the laws). Thus, the proper answer to this question should be: But Reagan *couldn't possibly* have turned into a communist sympathizer on Christmas Eve, and a counterfactual with such an antecedent is simply devoid of a *de re* literal interpretation.

Similarly, if we impress upon ourselves the implications of this world's being deterministic, we realize that it was a matter of *necessity* that the lamp on my desk (which is there now, and has been there for a while) be there now; it was entirely impossible for it not to have been there now and for the last while. To ask what would have happened had this very lamp fallen to the floor a couple of minutes ago is just to ignore this very impossibility: this very lamp simply *couldn't* have fallen to the floor a couple of minutes ago, as a matter of sheer and complete necessity; and it is futile to attempt to answer literally such hypothetically impossible questions.

Of course, this may be hard to grasp, since, if we regard the world as *non*deterministic, surely, we would say, this lamp *could* have fallen to the floor, e.g., if I had pushed it. And indeed it seems that we do intuitively tend to regard the world as nondeterministic, that this outlook is natural for us, and that as a result we are willing to view the counterfactual question as worthy of consideration. In a nondeterministic world it might clearly be possible for the lamp to have fallen. But this is *not* so in a deterministic world. The difficulty lies in *fully* realizing that we are no longer dealing with a nondeterministic world, as we normally and habitually do. The difficulty lies in *seriously integrating* the perspective according to which this is a deterministic world and it is a *sheer impossibility* for this lamp to have fallen: it was *determined* not to have fallen; it is just impossible, as of time immemorial, that it should have fallen. Our natural perspective seems so grounded in a nondeterministic outlook that it calls for a genuine *gestalt switch* to contemplate seriously the world's being deterministic. In testing one's intuitions, one must not therefore simply approach the same counterfactual hypothesis once under the assumption of nondeterminism and then, casually, assuming determinism instead. If one does that, one is likely to treat the two worlds alike, that is, to assimilate the deterministic case to the nondeterministic case in which one's natural perspective and intuitions are comfortably couched. One must seriously perform the gestalt switch of outlook in order to allow oneself to be genuinely impressed with things' being the way they are as a matter of *necessity* and with the literal and strict impossibility of things' having turned out otherwise. It seems to me that, once the attempt to take fully into account the implications of the world's being deterministic is carried out, the affinity of a counterfactual such as the one about the lamp to the one about Carter's turning into the number π, becomes appreciable. Both hypotheses are impossible (though in different ways), and with regard to both it is pointless to ask what would have happened in case what *couldn't* have happened happened. Such counterfactuals just don't have a literal *de re* interpretation.

As I indicated above, it seems to me that, often enough, when counterfactuals are assessed under the assumption of determinism, the determinism is not taken seriously enough, and the judgment passed on the counterfactual under an assumption of *non*determinism is simply projected without scrutiny to the deterministic case. To overcome this temptation, the deterministic assumption must genuinely be forced on one: the gestalt switch here really has to take hold. Let me illustrate. Suppose the world is deterministic, and there is a regular glass in front of you. It is determined that you never touch this glass (hence, of course, you don't). Now ask yourself: Had you smashed this glass, would it have been broken? My response would be: you couldn't possibly have smashed this glass; the counterfactual is devoid of literal *de re* interpretation. Yet the champion of counterfactuals in a deterministic world would say: The counterfactual is true; I couldn't have smashed the glass, but if I had, it would have broken.

Now let us try to make the deterministic character more vivid. Suppose a deterministic machine has been invented and supplied with glass material. The machine is designed to construct a glass and display it. But it is so built that any attempt to touch the glass leads to destruction, by electronic death rays, before the attempt is successful, of the arm or tool used. Furthermore, the machine is so programmed that any attempt to tinker with its operation immediately activates a self-destruction mechanism that destroys the machine and the glass. This deterministic machine should make it vivid that it is *determined* that the glass could not be smashed: it is determined that no attempting hand could reach it. Now try the counterfactual again: Had you smashed this glass, would it have been broken? Now it seems that the reluctance to affirm or deny the counterfactual would be more vigorous, and that the response, accompanying a reluctance to address this question, would seem more naturally to be: But this glass just can't be smashed!

2. It seems that our common-sense conception of the world involves a conception of an *open future*. That is, the world, as we common-sensically take it, can unfold in many different ways in and of itself, not just insofar as what we know is concerned. There seem to be, according to the common-sense conception, various contingencies that might or might not materialize. The past history and the laws of nature allow for more than one such contingency to materialize, though in fact only one will. And it seems that, according to our common-sense conception, many of our actions, as agents, belong to this realm of the undetermined, thus participating in pinning down the possible course that will turn into the actual course.

Such a view of what may be inherent in the common-sense perspective need not in the least imply that the world is in fact that way. Whether it is or not, it is up to science to tell. So far, if quantum mechanics is our last guide, then, though controversial and ill understood, it seems to lend support to a nondeterministic view of the world. But be that as it may, it has no implication as to what the common-sense conceptual framework has taken the world to be. And there are grounds for arguing that the common-sense conceptual frame incorporates a nondeterministic outlook. According to R.G. Collingwood's conception of causal terminology, the function of a wide and central range of verbs such as 'to break', 'to move', 'to throw', etc., etc., reflects a *manipulative* conception of our causal capacity to interfere with the way things are and to mold things to come, a conception that fits most comfortably in a nondeterministic world view.

The view that the common-sense conceptual frame reflects a nondeterministic orientation is not uncontroversial, and determinists may wish to offer another account of the manipulative function of verbs such as the above. I do not claim to have given conclusive reasons for the above position. Yet, *if* indeed the common-sense conceptual frame incorporates a nondeterministic outlook, as I believe it does, it would seem not at all surprising that the counterfactual construction appears to fit ill with a deterministic universe. Let us recall that we are dealing with an ordinary-language construction which has developed within a common-sense framework. The impetus for the development of the counterfactual mode into an entrenched syntactic form in natural language, as well as the function of this construction, must be understood *within* the context of the common-sense frame within which it has developed. It is wholly irrelevant to argue that there are good reasons to have a counterfactual construction in a deterministic world, or even that a useful interpretation can be invented for a counterfactual construction in a deterministic world. As long as *in fact* the common-sense perspective incorporates a nondeterministic outlook, it could have served no purpose *within* this framework to have the counterfactual construction fit a deterministic universe. The particular semantic features that a construction such as the counterfactual construction might assume are numerous: it *might*, e.g., have taken on numerous features of the various available competing theories of counterfactuals. *In fact*, however, in our conceptual frame, certain specific semantic features have been selected, and it is sensible to ask the question, Why have these specific features been selected rather than others? primarily against the background of the conceptual frame within which this construction developed and in view of the roles it was designed to fulfill. Within a nondeterministic outlook a conceptual construction *need not* fit a deterministic universe. If in fact the common-sense conceptual framework is grounded in a nondeterministic outlook, then it should not be surprising that such a construction, developed within it, would be tailored to fit a nondeterministic world *only*. And in this case, it should not be surprising if our intuitions do not acknowledge literally construed nondegenerate counterfactuals within a deterministic world. Whether this nondeterministic conception, if indeed ingrained in the common-sense framework, will prove in fact to be right or wrong is beside the point: if the world proves deterministic, the counterfactual construction might turn out to be useless. If various other ontological assumptions grounded in the common-sense frame prove wrong, the usefulness of this very conceptual frame itself and its survival value may be questioned. By arguing that the counterfactual construction is degenerate (i.e., devoid of a literal *de re* interpretation) in a deterministic world, one argues neither that the world is *in fact* nondeterministic nor that *no* counterfactual construction can be *devised* to fit a deterministic world (though what useful role it could fulfill there remains to be seen). What the position advocated comes down to is that we engage here in an enterprise with an empirical dimension in trying to provide an analysis for a construction which in fact is operative within our conceptual framework, and that in doing so we are *not* engaged in revisionary metaphysics or in the production of concepts that are to be useful for certain specialized interests or for particular philosophical perspectives. Thus, if the common-sense frame is indeed grounded in a nondeterministic outlook, we should expect that such an outlook will be reflected in the conceptual constructions that have developed within that framework, and we need not be surprised if they do not fit alternative outlooks, regardless of whether this is useful for us now, fits our metaphysical convictions, fits our scientific outlook, or whatever. Yet, of course, it will remain open to one to say: this construction is rooted in a scientific or metaphysical conception that is alien to me. It may be couched in the common-sense frame, but as such it is of no use for me, given my own scientific or metaphysical outlook; so much the worse then for this construction, or even for the common-sense framework as a whole. Taking such an attitude is a distinct option, and I am not here arguing against it. As long as it is the *actual* construction in our language that we are concerned with and as long as it is our common-sense intuitions that we are testing our theory against, we must respect the common-sense framework as governing general features of this construction whether we like them or not. Accordingly, those who desire a nondegenerate counterfactual construction in a deterministic world, may well come and produce one, and then argue for its usefulness. But they should not expect that the construction available to us in the ordinary-language conceptual scheme should fulfill their special desiderata if indeed this conceptual frame incorporates a nondeterministic orientation.

3. As indicated above (9 IV 3), for a counterfactual statement to be world *de re*, its interpretation must involve divergences (from the actual world, when assessed in it) in which the antecedent is true. Surely a deterministic universe does not allow for such divergences (when the antecedent is false[61]): no future courses other than the actual course are compatible with any given history and the laws. A *fortiori*, no object *de re* interpretation of counterfactuals is possible in a deterministic world. In an object *de re* interpretation of a counterfactual, I argued,[62] divergences from the actual world (in which it is evaluated) during the lifetimes of the individuals mentioned must be considered (in which the antecedent is true), so as to allow for the sameness of individuals across possible-world descriptions to consist in the sharing of a *common root*. A *de re* interpretation of counterfactual (and modal) statements requires consideration of the same individual in diverging possible-world descriptions, which in turn requires traceability via genidentity to a common root.[63] Thus, no object *de re* counterfactuals (with false antecedents) can be literally interpreted in a deterministic universe, since divergences in which the antecedent is true are excluded.[64]

However, we do want to be able to make sense of dispositional concepts in a deterministic world. Even if this piece of sugar has never been (nor ever will be) put in water, it is still soluble. But in a deterministic world no analysis of this concept in terms of counterfactuals *de re* is feasible, nor are any *de re* counterfactual conclusions.[65] Rather, what such a statement conveys is that there is an appropriate true nomological statement to the effect that certain materials (which in fact are of the sort of this sugar) dissolve when put in water in certain conditions (which cover so-called "normal" conditions). Thus, such a dispositional statement should be construed in a deterministic world as *parasitic* upon certain laws of nature which are not readily specifiable, rather than in terms of *de re* counterfactuals (cf. 7 V).

However, various counterfactuals in a deterministic world need not be rendered unintelligible. Some of them, though devoid of literal *de re* interpretations, can be construed as world *de dicto* or as elliptic for noncounterfactual statements (a phenomenon we find elsewhere, too; see 9 IV 3). Thus, the statement that if this piece of sugar had been immersed in a large volume of water in normal circumstances, it would have dissolved, when considered in a deterministic world, though devoid of a literal *de re* interpretation, can be construed as world *de dicto*, i.e., as stating that if a substance of the same sort as this piece of sugar had been immersed in a large volume of water in so-called "normal" circumstances, it would have dissolved. Alternatively, it can be construed as elliptic for the claim that there is a true nomological statement to the effect that certain substances (of the same sort as this piece of sugar), when immersed in a large volume of water under certain circumstances (which cover normal ones), dissolve. Of course, such a place-holder for a nomological statement, as well as the world *de dicto* formulation, lean heavily on contextual parameters. The world *de dicto* formulation has the force of stating that the sort of information determined by the antecedent in the context in question (even when not specified explicitly), together with the laws, yields the consequent. The noncounterfactual formulation has the force of stating that an adequate introduction of contextual information of the right sort would result in a true nomological statement. (Yet, again, in both cases the context-dependence here is *not* of any sort specific to the counterfactual constructions: it is a context-dependence that can be extracted from the antecedent and the consequent *separately*, e.g., as in 'large', 'normal', or in the type/token sort). Thus, when so read, the making of such a counterfactual statement is elliptic for alluding to certain nomological regularities, specifiable via characteristics of the object at hand (e.g., the kind of substance this piece of sugar is made of). Such a counterfactual claim then, in a deterministic world, though not literally interpretable along *de re* counterfactual lines, can be read as world *de dicto*, or as elliptic for a claim to the effect that there are true nomological statements of a certain sort.

Of course, one should resist the temptation to attempt such sweeping wholesale world *de dicto* or elliptic interpretations in the case of a nondeterministic world as well. The elliptic and world *de dicto* readings always land us with additional type/token ambiguities and context dependence and with the absence of a literal *de re* interpretation. It would be a mistake unnecessarily to embrace such a reading uniformly in a nondeterministic world. In a deterministic world, however, where a literal *de re* interpretation is not feasible, such world *de dicto* readings or elliptic formulations are often the only reasonable course available. Notice also that counterfactuals that are elliptic for noncounterfactual constructions even under indeterminism function in the same fashion under determinism as well (e.g., 'Had I been a dog, I would have had a life span of about 15 years', is elliptic in both cases for: Dogs have a life span of about 15 years).

A sort of counterfactual examples naturally couched in deterministic surroundings are mechanistic examples (and related examples in physics). On a frictionless inclined plane there is a perfect ball constrained by a barrier. Now you ask what would happen if the barrier were to be removed. This kind of example seems to call for a special sort of a world *de dicto* reading. It allows for a full specification of a world-state type by reference to an already fully specified one (whether actual or not)[66] via a complete specification of a certain modification (the removal of the barrier). Such a completely specified state-type allows for the truth value of the counterfactual to be well determined via the application of the laws: the counterfactual (read *de dicto*) is true just in case a world-state of the type specified yields the consequent via the laws.[67] In such a case no allusion to unspecified features of the world history is needed:[68] we are dealing with a variant of a world *de dicto* counterfactual involving an antecedent that completely specifies a world state.[69]

Notes: Chapter 9

1. And subject to the restrictions we have been operating under, i.e., factual antecedent and consequent, false antecedent, and standard temporal order (i.e., $t_A < t_B$).

2. I have in mind here I 4 and I 5, where the account is tentative, and certain aspects of III. I hope the account presented here will give enough of a picture of my general approach to counterfactuals to put the present work in perspective. (Cf. also fn. 19 below.)

3. The requirement of divergence is designed to ensure a world *de re* character. See below, section IV.

4. I take the process to be specified via a process description. Thus, when I talk below of a process, it is always under a description. Cf. also chapter 2, fn 33.

5. $\bar{t}_P$ and $\underline{t}_P$ are the temporally higher and lower ends of the interval to which the statement P pertains.

6. For further discussion, see below, section IV, 2.

7. In accordance with our practice in most of this book, we shall allow ourselves to refer by 'P^i_j' both to the statement and to the process stage described by it (under this description), and by 'P^i' both to the process description and to the process described by it (so described), in order to avoid cumbersome formulations.

8. Adjusting the first-person form in which (1) was put; (1) was 'If I had had an extra $5000, I would have bought this car'.

9. The example is Quine's, from his *Methods of Logic* (New York: Holt, 1950), p. 15; (Cambridge, Mass.: Harvard, 1983), p.23.

10. Although only tentatively. Cf. footnotes 18 and 19 below.

11. I shall take t_P to be the smallest interval covering all the t_{P_j}s ($1 \leq j \leq n$, when $P = \{P_1, \ldots, P_n\}$). $\underline{t}_P$ is, as usual, the greatest lower bound of t_P.

12. $P(A/W_{tp})$ must be greater than 0, or else tp would just not qualify as a divergence time (for a process leading to A). Cf. also fn 18. [Of course, $P(A/W_{tp})$ $\geq P(\underset{j=1}{\overset{k}{\&}} P_j/W_{tp})$, and $P(A/W_{tp}) = P((P_1 \vee \sim P)\&A/W_{tp})$.] The empty process leading to A and diverging at t_P was taken to be $(P_1 \vee \sim P_1)$ & A rather than A, in order to assure a divergence point at t_P. Surely if $P(A/W_t) > P(A/W_{t'}) = 0$, then some processes with divergence time t terminating at A will be stronger than any process with divergence time t' terminating at A. For A to qualify as a possible antecedent (of some world *de re* counterfactual; cf. below, IV 2), A must be compatible with W_t, for some $t \leq t_A$.

13. That is, on the basis of the history prior to the process, of what preceded this stage in the process, and of the supplementary information accumulated via prior stages. (This is so for every stage, including the last, which is A.)

14. Notice that if we take the "modified" strength of a stage by excluding in (10) the last component, then the probability of a process (given the prior history) is the product of the modified strengths of its stages. And surely the notion of the processes most likely to have led to A must be closely related to the probability of the processes that lead to A. Cf. the discussion below leading to (12).

15. If there are no such processes, take instead the lowest upper bound of the strengths of the processes leading to A.

16. One may wonder whether the strength of a process is not a function of how finely the information it contains is carved into stages, in a way that can trivialize this notion. But this does not appear to be as serious a problem as it might seem at first. Suppose we have a process description $P^1 (= \{P_1^1, \ldots, P_n^1\})$. Now suppose we were able to take a finer temporal carving of this process description, so that, for some P_j^1 pertaining to $(t_{P_j^1}, \bar{t}_{P_j^1})$, we would be able to decompose P_j^1 into $P_j^1{}'$ and $P_j^1{}''$ such that for some t, $t_{P_j^1} < t < \bar{t}_{P_j^1}$, $t_{P_j^1}{}' = (t_{P_j^1}, t)$ and $t_{P_j^1}{}'' = (t, \bar{t}_{P_j^1})$, and such that $P_j^1{}'$ & $P_j^1{}''$ is equivalent to P_j^1 (relative to W_{tp} and the laws). In such a case, a switch to a description in which the pair: $P_i^1{}'$, $P_i^1{}''$ replaces P_i^1 will tend to result in a higher strength for the new two links $p_j^1{}'$ and $p_j^1{}''$ in the new process as compared with the single original link p_j^1 in the old process, and thus will tend to increase the strength of the process (if P_j^1 was the weakest link). Thus, moving to finer carvings along these lines would tend to increase the strengths of the resulting processes. But there are natural limits to the extent to which this can be done without *adding* information to the process description. Take the process description used in Goodman's match example above. How would you decompose in this way 'John moved from room 1 to room 2 at (t_1, t_2)'? (Recall: every stage description must determine the time it pertains to.) True, with further information this can be done. But adding further information will now work *against* increasing the strength of the process. So it need not be the case that highly detailed finely temporally carved processes will have higher strength than others. [Thus, it need not be that the strength of 'John moved from room 1 to point Z_2 in (t_1, t^{Z_2}) $(t_1 < t^{Z_2} < t_2)$ has a higher strength (relative to the previous stages $P_1, \ldots, P_m$) than the event description mentioned above.]

Notice also that if one wishes to neutralize further whatever impact mere finer carvings (without added information) may have on strength, one may move from the notion of the strength of a stage to a notion of a *temporally modified strength*. Thus, suppose $P^i = \{P_1^i, \ldots, P_n^i\}$, where each P_j^i pertains to $t_{P_j^i}$ and $S(P_j^i, P^i)$ is the strength of stage j in P^i. Now consider some measure α (with values between 0 and 1) of temporal intervals. One can then consider the *temporally modified strength* of stage P_j^i as $S(P_j^i, P^i) \cdot \alpha (t_{P_j^i})$. Thus, the strength gained by finer carvings would be counteracted by the temporal factor in the temporally modified strength.

This notion opens some possibilities for further formal elaboration. I shall not, however, pursue the discussion of this possibility here.

17. We take such a small neighborhood, since the lowest upper bound of the set of probabilities of the processes selected in the first selection need not be the probability of any such process.

18. I have said little about the determination of the divergence points of the processes most likely to have led to A, that is, about whether any divergence point is a reasonable one. A plausible hypothesis I would like to put forward, but not discuss in detail, is the following. Take $P(A/W_t)$ to be a function of t (for $t < t_A$). Now the temporal points to be selected as divergence points for the processes most likely to have led to A seem to be the points at which the values of $P(A/W_t)$ are maximal, and the latest such points. Of course, for the typical cases in which the l-p interpretation is applicable, $P(A/W_{t_A}) = 0$. But the value of $P(A/W_t)$ will not be 0 for all $t < t_A$, unless A is an impossible antecedent. Thus, for the counterfactual antecedent 'Had Reagan been President on January 21, 1977', such selected divergence points could be at t_1, right before the Republican convention, or at t_2, the fall of 1975 before the primaries [depending on $P(A/W_{t_1})$ and $P(A/W_{t_2})$]. The choice of selected divergence points according to this principle can be motivated by noticing that our final selection of processes yields the most probable processes so far selected (whose last stage is A). Processes diverging at points at which $P(A/W_t)$ is maximal will in that respect have a clear edge over other processes. (There is also a related effect on strength.)

19. In the account presented in 5, this section, of the notion of the processes most likely to have led to A, considerable use is made of the notion of the strength of a process. This account, however, can, I believe, be improved. In particular, it is clear that the probability of a process and the strength of its stages are closely connected (and coincide for a one-stage process description). Perhaps the notion of strength can give way to another informationally normalized notion of "the processes that could have led to A" out of which a selection of the most probable processes could do the job. This would allow us to present the result as a selection of the most probable processes that could have led to A, and save us the need to resort to a separate strength selection. I hope, though, that the option developed above has made it at least plausible that these notions can be made precise in a satisfactory way along some lines of this sort.

Another direction for developing the notion of the most probable processes to have led to A is the following: assume time is discreet. Then one may assume that the transitional probabilities of moving from world-state S to world-state S' (when these are "complete states") depend solely on S and S'. Then, for a fixed divergence point at time i and a world-state S_i at i which is actual, assimilate a process leading to an A-state at time j ($j > i$) to a series of states $S_{i+1}, \ldots, S_{j-1}, S_j$ (where S_j is an A-state). The probability of such a process, given S_i, can be formulated in terms of the transitional probabilities:

$$P(S_j/S_{j-1}) \cdot P(S_{j-1}/S_{j-2}) \cdot \ldots \cdot P(S_{i+1}/S_i)$$

Now take the variety Z of such series of states leading from S_i to some A-state at j. The sum r of the probabilities of members of Z would be less than 1 (since, in cases relevant to our concerns, one could move from S_i to $\sim A$-states at j). Inflate the probabilities of each process in Z by $1/r$. The members of Z thus form a set whose collective probability is now 1. If the former probability of each member h in Z was q, then q/r would now yield the probability of h relative to the process-like series that could lead from S_i to A at j; that is, the likelihood to have arrived at an A-state at j from S_i via h; that is, the likelihood of h to have led from S_i to A at j. The top layer of those probabilities would yield (via their respective processes) a natural concept of the processes most likely to have led to A at j from S_i.

A key idea for extending this concept to a case of continuous time is that what is objectively given, instead of the *consecutive* transitional probabilities of the discreet-time case which are no longer applicable, are the general transitional probabilities of moving from a state S (at a certain time t) to a state S' at a later time $t + T$, which depend solely on S, S', and T. (Cf. also 4 VI.)

Another direction I would propose for pursuing the elaboration of the notion of the processes most likely to have led to A is the following. If, in accordance with the spirit of my approach here, the basic probability notion is taken as that of the probability of a sentence at time t (when t is some temporal interval or the like), and since obviously one way of viewing a process is as a series of states of affairs, one natural way of representing a series of states of affairs is by indicating the temporal segments (or some more complex temporal sets) at which sentences are true. Thus, if the probability of a sentence being true at an interval (or the like) is defined, so is then the probability of a process, as the probability of the intersection of all its sentences being true at the intervals (or the like) at which they are (in this process). If the probability of a process is defined, then the notion of the most probable processes (of a given set) can also be easily defined.

I hope to explore these lines of thinking in detail and perhaps combine them with the direction taken in the text, in an article in the near future. I will not, however, pursue them any further here.

20. Of course, your decisions as to how to allocate resources will not only be a function of what the most probable scenarios that could lead to war are, but also of other factors, such as the expected damage to the civilian population in each of them. I ignore such factors here.

21. With one important difference: in retrospective assessments the actual history of the world that has transpired up to half a year before the time of assessment must be taken into account; but not so in the future-planning case.

22. Note that, with counterfactual antecedents such as the one discussed (i.e., 'Had a war involving Israel erupted half a year ago, . . . '), we are again at odds with the similarity approach to counterfactuals. If one thinks in terms of magnitude of *miracles* rather than in terms of *probabilities*, it seems that it might take just as much of a *miracle* to get a war to have started (say, in 1975) between Israel and Jordan as it will to get a war to have started between Israel and Brazil, and it seems that in a nondeterministic world one would need the same "transitional period" to allow for either. Yet the vulnerability of Brazil to Israel and vice versa is small relative to that of Israel and Jordan. Hence dissimilarities from the actual world in a course involving a war with Brazil will be far less than those in a course involving a war with Jordan. If some weight is given to similarities of particular facts, then a world with a war between Israel and Brazil should have an edge over a world with a war between Israel and Jordan. If no positive weight is given to similarity of particular facts, such two worlds will be on a par. Both outcomes are unwelcome. However, a process leading to 'Israel was engaged in a war in which Jordan was involved' would clearly be much more *probable* than a process leading to a war with Brazil, and the latter would then be ruled out on my probabilistic approach, as it should be.

23. I shall often omit such relativizations below.

24. And, according to my view, it is metaphysically impossible for Carter to

have been a dog from the very beginning; cf. my "Quine and Modalities *De Re*: A Way Out?", *Journal of Philosophy*, LXXIX, 6 (June 1982): 295-328, section X.

25. Ben Gurion is said to have in fact asserted a statement to this effect in the first person, though he used the term 'Fatah'.

26. Again, cf. my "Quine and Modalities *De Re*: A Way Out?", section X.

27. We shall analyze these two counterfactuals more fully at the end of this section.

Pollock also notices that some uses of demonstratives (his examples are formulated with 'I', 'that'; e.g., 'If that were gold, . . . ') in counterfactual antecedents should mean something like "If some gold were like that (i.e., had the properties that has), . . . " (*op. cit.*, p. 97). Pollock expects such a construal *not* to be context-dependent, but rather to be subject to constraints on minimal changes typical to his approach. Thus he takes 'the properties that has' to apply to *all* those properties, subject to the above constraint (p. 99). In this we part ways, and I take the type-token context-dependence route. Furthermore, Pollock takes this phenomenon to be a matter of ambiguity of emphasis; but I fail to notice any crucial dependence on emphasis here, and see this reading as part of a general phenomenon of proper names (and demonstratives) serving as feature-indicators, which is not limited to the counterfactual construction, and the occurrence of this phenomenon in the counterfactual construction as an instance of the *de re/de dicto* distinction. See below, this section, for further details.

28. I am assuming here that one's date of coming into being is an essential property, as Kripke holds. Again, cf. my "Quine and Modalities *De Re:* A Way Out?", section X.

29. But inventions of this sort are likely to have so massive an impact that entertaining them would render false (true) many counterfactuals with such antecedents that we would consider true (false), e.g.: Had Roosevelt been President in 1980, he might have appointed Dean Achison as Secretary of State. Notice, of course, that it would be gratuitous to entertain, for such a counterfactual, mere life-elongation devices, since in such a case Roosevelt would have been so old and senile by 1980 that he himself would have handled no crisis whatsoever.

30. This is a variation on Quine's counterfactual; see W.V. Quine, *Word and Object* (Cambridge, Mass.: MIT Press, 1960), p. 222.

31. Donald Nute's *Topics in Conditional Logic* (Boston: Reidel, 1980) introduces the distinction between reasonable and unreasonable hypothetical situations. Nute emphasizes the importance of looking for counterexamples when assessing a counterfactual. Which hypothetical situations should be considered in such an assessment? Only the reasonable ones. Surely most of the weight of analyzing counterfactuals lies on this term. But Nute does not proceed to specify when a hypothetical situation should be considered reasonable, beyond using this term intuitively, since this is not the goal he sets for himself. Rather, his goal seems to be, primarily, the investigation of counterfactual logic. Other theories have attempted to give more specific answers. Lewis would consider unreasonable those hypothetical situations which are not among those most similar to the actual world in which the antecedent is true. Pollock would consider reasonable possible worlds resulting from performing minimal changes on the actual world in a way that satisfies his requirement of temporal priority (cf. 7 III, fn 26). I have suggested that, when a counterfactual falls under the n-d type, the class $V(A > B)$ specifies what Nute might call "reasonable" hypothetical situations and that, when the l-p interpretation is applied, what Nute might call a "reasonable" hypothetical situation would be one in which a process most likely to have led to the antecedent-event occurs (and which satisfies the retention of certain elements from the actual

history; cf. section I above). Surely, to say, as Nute does, that a counterfactual is true provided there is no reasonable situation in which the antecedent is true but the consequent is false, is on the right track, but the heavy work in analyzing counterfactuals and providing their truth conditions lies in spelling out just what those reasonable situations are.

In considering an example such as the Caesar counterfactual (21), Nute (*ibid.*, p. 11) suggests that two different criteria of reasonableness are operative here in different contexts. I disagree. Rather, on their *de dicto* reading these counterfactuals involve a context-dependent type-token vagueness inherent in the role of the proper name as a feature-indicator. In different contexts the *antecedent* would be interpreted differently. Yet in all the reasonable hypothetical situations for this counterfactual the antecedent is true (as Nute would agree). Thus, different contexts would determine different interpretations of the antecedent, but the rules determining the reasonable situations *as a function* of the antecedent and the consequent (or of features thereof) would be just the same. Here Nute makes a move in the direction of Lewis, regarding context-dependence of counterfactuals, which I consider wrong (cf. below, IV 4, and also 7 V).

32. It should be noticed that (13) and (14) may involve true antecedents. I shall not dwell on such counterfactuals here. Lewis has convincingly argued that they should be given truth values (cf. his *Counterfactuals, op. cit.*, pp. 26-31). But though I agree with him on what he is more confident about — that such counterfactuals with false consequents should be false — I disagree with him on what he is less confident about: that such counterfactuals with true consequents should all be true. I would be inclined to suggest that such counterfactuals fall under the l-p interpretation, somewhat modified so as to include in the final selection also the most probable *actual* process descriptions leading to A. This will pretty much assure that such counterfactuals with false consequents come out false, but will allow for a richer interpretation when the consequent is true.

33. In this respect the context-dependence of counterfactuals recognized here is very different in nature from that envisaged by Lewis (cf. above, 8 I and VII, and this chapter, IV 4). Whereas for Lewis context-dependence affects the fundamental parameters inherent in the interpretation of counterfactuals, the context-dependence I have recognized above involves a standard kind of a type-token context-dependence of noncounterfactual locutions which may occur *within* the indicative versions of the antecedent or the consequent of the counterfactual (under the proper *de dicto* reading), the character and resolution of which is independent of counterfactuals altogether.

34. Of course, when it comes to an antecedent A *in*compatible with W_{t_A}, *only* the l-p interpretation is available.

35. P.B. Downing, "Subjunctive Conditionals, Time Order, and Causation," *Proceedings of the Aristotelian Society*, LIX (1958/9): 125-140; Lewis, "Counterfactual Dependence and Time's Arrow," *op. cit.*, p. 457.

36. I have argued above that the case in which A is compatible with W_{t_A}, though $P(A/W_{t_A})$ is very low and lower than $PC(A)$, opens the way for ambiguity between the n-d and the l-p interpretations. For Pollock, because of his requirement of temporal priority, according to which changes should be postponed as much as possible, one should retain W_{t_A} in such cases since one can retain W_{t_A} consistently with A. This would prevent Pollock from recognizing the sense in which the above counterfactual is true (on one reading). To avoid that, he would have to offer still another interpretation and extend his account so as to recognize such an ambiguity.

37. Features of the account presented in this section depend on the tentative ac-

count of the most probable processes presented in I 4 above. Since the notion of PC(A) was introduced via that account, improvements and changes in the latter might have repercussions on the account presented in this section, which is thus tentative as well.

38. This distinct feature, within the group of counterfactuals of purely reverse temporal order, of counterfactuals that fall under the n-d interpretation, provides another indication of the independent status of counterfactuals of the n-d type.

39. Pollock's theory is incompatible with my l-p interpretation. For him, a later divergence point in which there is a process leading to A would always *rule out* processes with earlier divergence points, *even if* the former process is very improbable compared with the latter. (Provided the process naturally diverges, as I require, so no antecedent histories have to be modified.)

So the false counterfactual 'Even if Carter had been president on January 23, 1981, Reagan would still have won the 1980 election' would come out true for Pollock, since it is possible that on January 21, 1981, Bush resigned, Reagan appointed Carter in his place, the Senate confirmed him the next day, and Reagan immediately resigned. This, I presume, was possible, and—by the requirement of temporal priority—would therefore make the above counterfactual come out true. But this counterfactual is false—such a process is surely much less probable than that in which Carter won the 1980 election. For Lewis, of course, this counterfactual is true too—under his standard resolution of vagueness—since the consequent is true. Thus Pollock would be in substantial agreement with Lewis on reverse-temporal-order counterfactuals except for the very close temporal vicinity of the antecedent.

40. Over and beyond those which are presuppositions for the indicative form of the antecedent.

41. Yet with weak counterlegals there is a problem of whether genidentity, which is necessary for a *de re* interpretation of the consequent, is applicable after the nomic change. I will not pursue this question here.

42. I take the relation of semantic or pragmatic presupposition to depend on linguistic conventions or beliefs of a speaker, but not on what the actual state of the world is in other respects.

43. World *de dicto* counterfactuals are impoverished relative to world *de re* ones in that their antecedents would typically have (informationally) narrower counterfactual spans (cf. 2 X 5), since they do not take true factual information into account in their inferential schemata.

44. One may attempt to enrich the counterlegal type by imposing conditions that will allow for the retention of various laws, so that the counterlegal will be true in case the consequent follows from the antecedent via those selected or modified laws. I will not discuss this option here, but my point is that, even then, there will still be no dependence on the factual history of the world, and thus no change in the world-*de dicto* character of counterlegals.

45. There is no identity in the strict sense across possible-world descriptions. But, unlike identity, sameness is a way of grouping distinct characters under some classification.

46. Cf. my "Quine and Modalities *De Re*: A Way Out?", section X, for further discussion.

47. Unless the antecedent (in the case of an n-d interpretation) or the antecedent and each of the selected processes (in the case of an l-p interpretation) of the counterfactual that determines the contemplated divergence are causally irrelevant (or purely positively causally relevant) to the circumstances of his coming into

existence, and unless his existence is necessitated by earlier circumstances. (In cases of composite objects whose identity is determined by the identity of the parts they are made of and the manner of their being put together, one may consider liberalizing here by tracing the genidentity of the parts.)

48. But cf. previous fn. Notice also that Kripke's view of the essentialism of origins has been left quite unmotivated by him. But such a view emerges as a consequence of my view that transworld identification requires a common root, to be traced via genidentity, and thus requires divergences from a common past after the beginning of the lifetime of the individual involved.

49. Though they may get a nonliteral interpretation, e.g., as elliptic for some noncounterfactual statements, or some different counterfactual statements, or via a metaphorical interpretation. Cf. also fn 53 and fn. 54 below.

50. The l-p interpretation brings out a feature of *de re* modal contexts which is almost dormant in counterfactuals of the n-d type. Thus, in the most perspicuous version of this problem, a *de re* antecedent may have the form 'If $\imath xFx$ had not been $\imath xFx$, . . .'. Surely we would not, in interpreting the counterfactual, just take the indicative version of the antecedent together with some implicit premises and expect consistency. Now the obvious way to handle this situation. is to pay closer attention to the quantificational character of the counterfactual sentence, and adjust our analysis in the case of counterfactuals with outside quantification (like this counterfactual). However, since we have avoided getting into this aspect of logical form, and have talked as if we deal with antecedents and consequents that do not involve variables bound together by an outside quantifier, I shall address the problem on the level of independent antecedent and consequent as discussed so far.

The point to be used is that a *de re* occurrence of a singular term is substitutable *salva veritate* for a coreferential term. The problem with various definite descriptions in particular counterfactuals (though much less so with proper names) is that they may not be helpful in picking out the individual they in fact denote if only times prior to the proper divergence time associated with the counterfactual are considered (and thus in possible-world descriptions diverging at such times). Counterfactuals of this sort should be evaluated on the inferential schema via counterfactuals in which the definite description in question is replaced by an appropriate singular term that already applies to the individual in question when times prior to the divergence time are considered. In addition to proper names, which will almost always do the job, terms that can serve in most cases as standard designators for our purposes would be definite descriptions such as 'the nth son (daughter) of so-and-so' (where 'so-and-so' is replaced by the proper name of the mother of the person in question).

51. Cf. 2 V 1. A counterfactual is parasitic on a law that asserts that certain conditions Q hold whenever conditions P hold, in case it constitutes an instantiation of it in a counterfactual form. Cf. also 7 V.

52. Context may combine with such a pseudo counterfactual to convey a yearning to have no worries. But such pragmatic conversational implicatures are not part and parcel of the content of the counterfactual, and they need not play a role in its analysis.

53. Notice, though, that the schema of the l-p interpretation may, without further ado, be applied to counterfactuals with impossible antecedents. Thus, under the l-p interpretation, the only processes leading to impossible antecedents will be processes with 0 probability. The general schema of the l-p interpretation is of the following form: $A > B$ is true iff

(S) S is a process description of a certain sort $\supset$ $(S \cup X(S,A,t_B) \; \stackrel{L}{\rightarrow} \; B)$

where $X(S,A,t_B)$ is a certain set of true factual statements, and the last stage of any such S is A. If A is impossible, $S \cup X$ would have to count as impossible as well. Similarly, a world *de dicto* reading for $A > B$ with an impossible antecedent would make it true just in case $A \rightarrow B$ (presuppositions aside). Such counterfactuals may then be assigned world *de re* and world *de dicto* readings that will yield the same pattern for all counterfactuals of this type. Thus, whether and when counterfactuals with impossible antecedents would come out true will depend, on this construal, primarily on how the relation of logical consequence with an impossible antecedent is construed. Under a narrow interpretation of logical consequence, a contradiction need not entail everything. (Thus, even though I agree with Lewis that "it seems that a counterfactual in which the antecedent logically implies the consequent ought always to be true," I disagree with him that this is a good argument for taking counterfactuals with logically contradictory antecedents as always true, as he does.)

Thus, one may take the above line and let counterfactuals with impossible antecedents fall under our analysis of the world *de re* and world *de dicto* readings in whichever way one's favored concept of entailment would yield. But at this stage a commitment to this construal would be premature. It is always open for one to offer an independent account for such counterfactuals, which seem to form an odd group. (Thus, Lewis's position that they are all true is a stipulative adjunct to his theory, not a natural consequence of it.) But even though such a construal will allow us to assign a truth value to such counterfactuals, it will trivialize them, since $A > B$ and $A > \sim B$ will have the same truth value. So even if we can save a truth value for a *de re* reading under the l-p interpretation, such a reading will be a *degenerate* one, and may therefore be ignored when a *de dicto* reading (which is world *de re*) is viable or when an ellipsis to a noncounterfactual construction is available, as indicated above.

54. Thus, e.g., if you read counterfactual (20) *de dicto*, the indicative version of the antecedent would read as 'A Lincoln was president in the 1960s', and any vagueness involved in interpreting the counterfactual would be limited to the construal of this indicative version of the antecedent.

55. Notice that the feature-indicator role of proper names, responsible for the type-token vagueness, occurs in indicative sentences as well, e.g., 'He is the Kissinger of China'; 'Begin is an intelligent person, but he is not Sadat'; 'We need a Roosevelt to put the economy back on its feet'.

56. Notice also that the notion of similarity is clearly a characteristic of the particular structure of our cognitive system: intelligent creatures with a different cognitive system might have a different working conception of similarity. The wholesale reduction of counterfactuals (or, for that matter, of transworld identity) to a similarity notion would make them mind-dependent, and would not therefore be available to those who, like myself, want to construe counterfactuals as objective and mind-independent (at least when it comes to, in a nondeterministic world, the n-d type and the l-p type).

57. And, in the case of the l-p interpretation, of non-actual descriptions of processes as well.

58. For the more specific formulation, cf. chapter 9, section I. Cf. in particular fn 18 there for the determination of the divergence time.

59. I.e., answers which call for the consideration of (descriptions of) states of affairs in which the antecedent is literally true.

60. Of course, one may decide by decree to give them all a truth value; this would seem, however, in general to be a matter of an arbitrary decision.

61. As elsewhere, I shall assume false antecedents for the counterfactuals under discussion.

62. Cf. my "Quine and Modalities *De Re*: A Way Out?", sec. X. Cf. also 9 IV 3 above.

63. This condition is somewhat too strong. Consider the following way of liberalizing it (although no substantial part of the ensuing discussion hinges on this liberalization): allow for sameness across possible-world descriptions to be established also when the antecedent (in the case of an n-d type counterfactual) or the antecedent and the selected processes (in the case of an l-p type counterfactual) are causally irrelevant (or purely positively causally relevant) to the parameters and circumstances of the coming-into-existence of the individual in question. (Sameness across possible-world descriptions is also to be established when these circumstances and parameters happen to be determined by a history prior to the antecedent (in case of a counterfactual of the n-d type; or prior to the selected processes, in case of an l-p type) in a generally nondeterministic world. A (partial) corresponding liberalization in the case of modal statements (of the sort: it was necessary as of time *t* that *p*) should be considered so as to allow for a true *de re* reading (and for sameness of individuals across possible-world descriptions) in the case of a nondeterministic world if the parameters and circumstances of the coming-into-existence of the individual mentioned have been determined by the history prior to *t*. I will not pursue these points here.

64. Of course, the actual course of events from any point in time onwards qualifies as a divergence. In the case of a deterministic world, such are the only divergences. In the case of counterfactuals, the only divergences to play a role in their interpretation are the ones in which the antecedent is true.

65. This is not, however, to exclude world *de dicto* consequences or reformulations. In a non-deterministic world, of course, *de re* counterfactual consequences would also be forthcoming.

66. That is, the world-state type specified in the example. Obviously, in outlining this example, I chose merely to sketch the sort of world state involved.

67. Another device that can be used for completely specifying a world-state by reference to an already completely specified one is that of specifying spatial permutations of congruent regions of space.

68. A completely specified world state may, thus, pertain to a small time-interval.

69. I have argued that, in a deterministic world, no literal (world) *de re* interpretation of counterfactuals is feasible. A literal interpretation of counter*factuals* requires the consideration of the factually false antecedent as true, and a *de re* interpretation requires the preservation of the world history up to some point. There is thus, in a deterministic world, no way to reconcile the two, unless, of course, we are willing to tinker with the laws, that is, to contemplate some change in the laws that would make possible the compatibility of the antecedent and some prior history. There is, I believe, a widespread intuitive resistance, which I share, to tinker with the laws when the antecedent is not *explicitly* counterlegal. An interpretation that calls for such a modification in the laws in fact treats counterfactuals in a deterministic world as *implicit counterlegals*, that is, as contrasted with explicit counterlegals whose antecedents alone are incompatible with the laws (even without any history). It is the treatment of seemingly *bona fide* counter*factuals* as implicit counter*legals* that seems counterintuitive. There is a gulf between counterfactuals and counterlegals, and there is considerable reluctance to cross over from counterfactuals to counterlegals, and interpret seeming counterfactuals as counterlegals. Such a course would make the counterfactual 'Had I smashed the

glass, it would have broken' in a deterministic world equivalent to something like 'Had I smashed the glass and had the laws been (minimally?) different so as to allow for that, the glass would have broken'. But many would want to object to considering the first counterfactual equivalent to the second sort of formulation as an instance of such a general schema.

Appendix

In this appendix the validity of a few inferences regarding counterfactuals will be examined. The discussion will be informal and limited to counterfactuals of the n-d type. The purpose of this appendix is to give a flavor of how the theory of n-d counterfactuals presented in this work bears upon the validity of various counterfactual inferences, and to classify as valid or not some of the notorious counterfactual inferences (concerning n-d counterfactuals). Although a more rigorous and comprehensive account is called for, it will not, however, be undertaken here.

Inference I: $A > B$
          $B > C$
          _____
          $A > C$

This inference is *invalid*. To see that, take a case where $t_A < t_B < t_C$, C is true, and is undetermined by its prior history (thus, $W_{t_C} \xnrightarrow{L} C$); A is false and is negatively causally relevant to C (so as to make $A > C$ false); B is false; B is causally irrelevant to C (hence $B > C$ is true); and A is positively causally relevant (or even purely positively causally relevant) to B so as to allow for $A > B$ to be true. Consider an example:

   A - Reagan won the Republican nomination and was elected President in 1976.
   B - Brockton Adams was not nominated Secretary of Transportation in 1977.
   C - There was a vocal, public emphasis on civil rights in the U.S. foreign policy in 1978.

C, of course, is true. It is also quite clear that the conduct of U.S. foreign policy would not have been affected by who happened to be nominated as Secretary of Transportation in 1977. So B is causally irrelevant to C, and $B > C$ is an irrel-semifactual, and thus true: Had Brockton Adams not been nominated as Secretary of Transportation in 1977, there would still have been a vocal public emphasis on civil rights in U.S. foreign policy in 1978.

Suppose, however (as indeed seems to be the case), that Reagan (unlike Carter) strongly believed that vocal public pursuit of civil rights issues in foreign countries is counterproductive. Then the counterfactual $A > C$ is false: It is false that had Reagan been nominated and elected President in 1976, there would still have been a vocal, public emphasis on civil rights in U.S. foreign policy (in 1978). However, it is quite clear that A is (over all) positively causally relevant to B: Reagan would not have the reasons

275

Carter had for appointing Brockton Adams as Secretary of Transportation. Indeed, $A > B$ seems quite true: Reagan, if nominated and elected President in 1976, would not have nominated Brockton Adams as Secretary of Transportation (in 1977). This example is thus an instance of the type indicated above, with true premises but false conclusion.

Inference II: $A > B$
$$\overline{\sim B > \sim A}$$

This inference is *invalid*. To see that, take any false semifactual $\sim B > \sim A$ with $\sim B$ false, A false, $t_B < t_A$ (and $\sim B$ and A being n-d type antecedents). Then $A > B$ is true. As an example, consider the following:

B - Johnson offered Humphrey the Vice Presidency in 1964.

A - Humphrey did not defend Johnson's Vietnam record in 1968.

B is true, A is false. The counterfactual $A > B$ is true: Had Humphrey not defended Johnson's Vietnam record in 1968, Johnson would still have offered him the Vice Presidency in 1964. (This latter counterfactual comes out true of course on the n-d model.) The counterfactual $\sim B > \sim A$, however, is false: It is not the case that had Johnson not offered Humphrey the Vice Presidency in 1964, Humphrey would still have defended Johnson's Vietnam record (in 1968).

Inference III: $A > B$
$$\overline{A \& C > B}$$

The inference is *invalid*.[1] Suppose that $A > B$ is true ($t_A < t_B$). Hence:

$\{A\} \cup W_{t_A} \cup \text{CIP}(A, W_{\bar{t}B}) \overset{L}{\nrightarrow} B$. Now take a case in which some q in W_{t_A} is crucial for the above inferential schema; that is, take a $q \in W_{t,t_A}$ for some $t < t_A$, so that

$\{A\} \cup W_t \cup \text{CIP}(A, W_{\bar{t}B}) \overset{L}{\nrightarrow} B$ (and where

$\{A\} \cup W_t \cup \text{CIP}(A, W_{\bar{t}B}) \overset{L}{\nrightarrow} q$).

Now take C such that $t_C < t$, and such that C is appropriately negatively causally relevant to B (and to q), so that $\{A \& C\} \cup W_{t_{A \& C}} \cup \text{CIP}(A \& C, W_{\bar{t}B}) \overset{L}{\nrightarrow} B$. Since $t_{A \& C} = \min(t_A, t_C)$, $W_{\bar{t}_{A \& C}} \subseteq W_{tC} \subset W_t$ ($\subset W_{tA}$). $W_{t_{A \& C}} \cup \text{CIP}(A \& C, W_{\bar{t}B}) \subseteq W_{t_A} \cup \text{CIP}(A, W_{\bar{t}B})$, since for any $r \in W_{t_A, t_B}$, both A and C must be causally irrelevant to it for $A \& C$ to be causally irrelevant to it. For $A \& C$ to be purely positively causally relevant to r, it must be the case that either both A and C are, or at least one is and the other is causally irrelevant to r. Thus, $A \& C > B$ is false.

Thus, the invalidity of the inference in question would be established by cases in which some statement q in W_{t,t_A} ($t < t_A$) is crucial (in the above sense) for the truth of some (true) counterfactual $A > B$, and in which some C ($t_C < t$) is negatively causally relevant to B (and q). As a case in point consider the following example.

Consider the counterfactual $A > B$: Had Nixon chosen Rockefeller to replace Agnew as Vice President in 1973, Ford would have been a congressman throughout the rest of the 1970s. $A > B$ seems quite true. But for the above inference to be valid, the counterfactual would have to remain true even when the antecedent is conjoined with a true statement C such as: Ford chose a career other than politics. Thus, we can expect a possible-world description (with the same laws as ours) which coincides with ours entirely until 1948 (when Ford entered politics) and from 1948 until 1973 in respects to which C is not negatively causally relevant; in which Ford did not run for Congress and did not enter politics at all (thus making C true); and in which A is true too, though B is false. Thus, although in fact the above counterfactual is true, the following counterfactual is false: Had Nixon chosen Rockefeller to replace Agnew as Vice President in 1973, and had Ford chosen a career other than politics, Ford would have been a congressman throughout the rest of the 1970s. Therefore, the inference is invalid.

Thus, the truth of $A > B$ hinges partially on the true statement D: Ford was a Congressman by 1973. Yet C is negatively causally relevant to D (C, of course, is also negatively causally relevant to B). $D \in W_{t_A}$, but $D \notin W_{t_{A\&C}}$ ($\underline{t}_D > \underline{t}_{A\&C}$), and $D \notin \mathrm{CIP}(A\&C, W_{\bar{t}B})$, since C is negatively causally relevant to D.

As Stalnaker noticed,[2] however, Inference III follows from Inference I. The invalidity of Inference I therefore follows from that of Inference III.

Inference IV: $\quad A > B$
$$D \to A$$
$$\overline{D > B}$$

This inference is *invalid* because of the invalidity of Inference III. Every case that inference III sanctions is sanctioned also by Inference IV. For A, B and C, take D as $A\&C$; hence $D \to A$. Inference IV will thus sanction $D > B$, i.e., $A\&C > B$ on the basis of $A > B$, and so will sanction Inference III for these A, B, C. Inference IV is thus a stronger inference. Since inference III is invalid, so is Inference IV.

Inference V: $\quad A > B$
$$A$$
$$\overline{B}$$

Counterfactual Modus Ponens is *valid*. Suppose $A > B$ is true and A is true. Then (on the n-d interpretation), $\{A\} \cup W_{t_A} \cup \mathrm{CIP}(A, W_{\bar{t}B}) \overset{\mathrm{L}}{\to} B$, and hence B is true (since all the components in the antecedent of this schema are true).

Formula VI: $\quad \Diamond A \supset [(A > \sim B) \equiv \sim (A > B)]$

This formula was endorsed by Stalnaker, but is not a logical truth on my theory. Take a case in which A is compatible with W_{t_A} (hence possible), and bears a mixed causal relevance on B, which in turn is not only undetermined by W_{t_B} (i.e., $W_{t_B} \overset{\mathrm{L}}{\nrightarrow} B$ and $W_{t_B} \overset{\mathrm{L}}{\nrightarrow} \sim B$), but is also undetermined by the implicit premises plus A, that is:

(1) $\quad \{A\} \cup W_{t_A} \cup \mathrm{CIP}(A, W_{\bar{t}B}) \overset{\mathrm{L}}{\nrightarrow} B$

(2) $\quad \{A\} \cup W_{t_A} \cup \mathrm{CIP}(A, W_{\bar{t}B}) \overset{\mathrm{L}}{\nrightarrow} B$

Both $A > B$ and $A > {\sim}B$ are then false.

Counterfactuals with true antecedents would offer a simpler case. If a true B is undetermined by W_{t_B}, then one can in general expect a true A $(t_A < t_B)$ with some mixed causal relevance to B to make (1) and (2) hold, and thus to make both $A > B$ and $A > {\sim}B$ false.

Formula VII: $A \supset (A > B \equiv B)$

This formula is a logical truth for Stalnaker and for Lewis (since for Lewis the actual world is a sphere).[3] [It was adopted (though not endorsed) by Allen Gibbard and William Harper (cf. their Consequence 1)[4]]. It is *not* a logical truth on my account, since the following case can be constructed. Take a case in which $\bar{t}_A < t_B$, A is true, B is true, and B is undetermined by the implicit premises plus A; thus: $\{A\} \cup W_{t_A} \cup \mathrm{CIP}(A, W_{\bar{t}B}) \overset{L}{\not\rightarrow} B$. $A > B$ is thus false (on the n-d model), and hence Formula VII is false. (An attempt to provide an intuitive example will probably not help much here since we do not seem to have much by way of intuition concerning counterfactuals with true antecedents.)

Formula VIII: $A > (B \lor C) \supset (A > B) \lor (A > C)$.

This formula, like formula VI, is *not* a logical truth on my account. Suppose that $t_A < t_C$, $t_C = t_B$, and that $B \lor C$ is determined (to be true) by A and W_{t_A} and $\mathrm{CIP}(A, W_{\bar{t}C})$, but that neither B nor C is. Then:

(3) $\{A\} \cup W_{t_A} \cup \mathrm{CIP}(A, W_{\bar{t}B \lor C}) \overset{L}{\not\rightarrow} B \lor C$

(4) $\{A\} \cup W_{t_A} \cup \mathrm{CIP}(A, W_{\bar{t}B}) \overset{L}{\not\rightarrow} B$

(5) $\{A\} \cup W_{t_A} \cup \mathrm{CIP}(A, W_{\bar{t}C} \overset{L}{\not\rightarrow} C$.

Hence $A > (B \lor C)$ is true, though $A > B$ and $A > C$ are false.

As an example, suppose a match between two contestants a and b was about to begin, subject to approval (or dismissal) by the Commissioner. The rules of the match guaranteed exactly one winner of the two contestants. The two contestants were roughly equal in their skill and their chances of winning. But the Commissioner did not approve the match. It is true in this case that had the Commissioner approved the match, contestant a would have won or contestant b would have won. But if, as invisaged in the example, it was entirely open (undetermined as of the time of the decision of the Commissioner) who the winner would be, it is not the case that had the Commissioner approved the match contestant a would have won, and equally not the case that had the Commissioner approved the match contestant b would have won. Thus, though $A > (B \lor C)$ is true, $A > B$ and $A > C$ are both false.

Inference IX: $A > B$
                   $A > C$
                   ———————
                   $A > (B \& C)$

This inference is *valid.* Assume the premises true; then:

$$\{A\} \cup W_{t_A} \cup \text{CIP}(A, W_{\bar{t}B}) \overset{\text{L}}{\not\to} B$$
$$\{A\} \cup W_{t_A} \cup \text{CIP}(A, W_{\bar{t}B}) \overset{\text{L}}{\not\to} C.$$

But $t_{B\&C} = \max(\underline{t}_B, \underline{t}_C)$, and thus $\text{CIP}(A, W_{\bar{t}B}) \subseteq \text{CIP}(A, W_{\bar{t}B\&C})$, and $\text{CIP}(A, W_{\bar{t}C}) \subseteq \text{CIP}(A, W_{\bar{t}B\&C})$. Hence:

$$\{A\} \cup W_{t_A} \cup \text{CIP}(A, W_{\bar{t}B\&C}) \overset{\text{L}}{\not\to}$$

and $A > (B\&C)$ is true too.

Footnotes: Appendix

1. This Inference is discussed by Stalnaker (in his "A Theory of Conditionals"; cf. *Ifs*, p. 48), Lewis (*Counterfactuals*, p. 31), and others.
2. In his "A Theory of Conditionals," reprinted in *Ifs*; cf. there, p. 48.
3. Cf., e.g., his *Counterfactuals*, p. 26.
4. Cf. their "Counterfactuals and Two Kinds of Expected Utility," in *Ifs*, p. 156.

Word Index

A-event, 38; 43, 44; 46, 48; 73

~A-A transition, 38, 39; 43, 45; 47–50; 59; 73; 104–105; 108; 112; 115; 120; 127–129; 130–132

A-vicinity, 169

A fortiori, 48

Antecedent, 20; 26–27, 29; 31–32; 39–40; 42; 45–46; 50; 59; 70, 72; 91–95; 127; 172–173; 202–203, 206; 210–212; 244; 249–250; 251–252; 253–254; 256–257

Antecedent-event, 28; 39–40; 41; 44; 46–48; 185; 203

Antecedent-time, 20; 27, 28; 219

Atomic propositional wff, 152–153

Atomic quasi formula, 154

Atomic temporal wff, 152

Between, 20

Canonical representation of p, 148, 150; 151, 153

Causal chain, 48, 50; 108–110; 111–113; 114; 120–121; 127, 129; 130, 131

Change, 177–179

Change from ~A to A. See ~A-A transition

Cip world-range of A. See World-range of A

Conditions I–IV, 204–205, 207; 212–213; 216, 219–220; 224

Consecutive transitional probabilities, 122–123

Consequent, 20; 33; 44–46; 48–50; 59, 60–62; 64–65; 92, 94–95; 127; 173; 210

Consequent-event, 28; 44, 46; 48–50; 61; 85; 185

Consequent-time, 20; 28; 57; 173

Con-type semifactuals. See Counterfactual-type semifactuals

Cotenable. See Cotenability

Cotenability, 12; 40; 70–71; 92–95; 98, 99, 100; 166–168; 169; 220

Counterfactuals of the natural-divergence (n-d) type, 29–32; 43–44; 156; 219–220

Counterfactual span of A for t_B, 57–58; 67; 170

Counterfactual-type semifactuals, 60–63; 69–72; 86–87; 95, 96; 183–184

Determinism, 31; 70; 178–179; 202; 211–212; 256–263

Deterministic. See Determinism

Dispositional terms, 188

Diverge, 27, 29; 37; 59; 234, 236, 238; 252–253; 256, 261

Divergence. See Diverge

Divergence time, 27; 37; 59; 253